The Politics of Military Unification

The Politics of

Military Unification

A STUDY OF CONFLICT
AND THE POLICY PROCESS

By Demetrios Caraley

COLUMBIA UNIVERSITY PRESS

New York and London 1966

INSTITUTE OF WAR AND PEACE STUDIES

The Politics of Military Unification is one of a series of studies sponsored by the Institute of War and Peace Studies of Columbia University. *Defense and Diplomacy* by Alfred Vagts; *Man, the State, and War* by Kenneth N. Waltz; *The Common Defense* by Samuel P. Huntington; *Strategy, Politics, and Defense Budgets* by Warner R. Schilling, Paul Y. Hammond, and Glenn H. Snyder; *Political Unification* by Amitai Etzioni; and *The Stockpiling of Strategic Materials* by Glenn H. Snyder are other volumes in the series. *Theoretical Aspects of International Relations*, edited by William T. R. Fox; *Inspection for Disarmament*, edited by Seymour Melman; and *Changing Patterns of Military Politics*, edited by Samuel P. Huntington are all volumes of essays planned and edited by Institute members. The Institute of War and Peace Studies and the Research Institute on Communist Affairs jointly sponsored the publication of *Political Power: USA/USSR* by Zbigniew Brzezinski and Samuel P. Huntington.

FOR JEANNE, CHRISTOPHER,

DAVID, AND ANNE

Foreword

The vocabulary of everyday political life is filled with words that demean the political process. We speak of "politicians" as if "politics" were a not quite honorable calling. We speak of "interest groups" as if they were necessarily conspiracies against the public good. When we say glibly that "politics ends at the water's edge," we imply that there is no room for honest men to differ in making foreign policy and national security policy. National defense, in particular, is thought not to be a fit subject for "playing politics." True enough, Congress, by its control over the purse-strings, and the President, by virtue of his being Commander-in-Chief, are expected to maintain civilian supremacy (though without "political meddling"); but within the limits set by Congress and the Chief Executive, making national security policy is, according to the prevailing mythology, a technical determination by the men who know best of "what is best for the country."

Another feature of the prevailing mythology is that the place for "politics" in Washington, if there is any place at all, is within Congress or in relations between the White House and Congress. Thus, the "politics of military unification" would seem to be disreputable on two counts, for the civil and military servants of the government are supposed to be above, or at least apart from, politics. Any politics in the executive branch is, according to a common view, wrong; any politics in the defense activities of the executive branch is doubly wrong. Any public evidence of controversy among the armed services or the departments of government concerned with national security leads to denunciation as "interdepartmental squabbling."

Political scientists take a more clinical view of the political process; they know that only in heaven, hell, and other perfect dictatorships, as it has been said, can there be an end to politics. Their discipline presupposes them to be slower to attribute base motives to men who first differ, then discover they cannot convince each other, and end up by "playing politics."

The process of conflict adjustment and consensus-building is central to the study of both domestic and international politics. Several books in the series editorially sponsored by the Institute of War and Peace Studies have dealt with the politics of policy-making at the point where domestic and international politics intersect. They include Samuel P. Huntington's *The Common Defense,* Glenn H. Snyder's *The Stockpiling of Strategic Materials,* and the series of case studies, *Strategy, Politics, and Defense Budgets,* by Warner R. Schilling, Paul Y. Hammond, and Glenn H. Snyder, already published. Forthcoming are books by Roger Hilsman, *Politics of Policy-Making,* and Kenneth N. Waltz, *The Politics of Democratic Foreign Policy.* Professor Caraley carries the analysis one step further. As his study demonstrates, there is not only politics in policy-making but politics in the struggle to modify the process by which policy is to be made.

WILLIAM T. R. FOX
DIRECTOR, INSTITUTE OF
WAR AND PEACE STUDIES

Preface

This is a study of the intense political conflict that took place between 1943 and 1947 over the unification of the military services. Its purpose is twofold: to describe and analyze that particular conflict in terms of the different actors involved, their goals and perceptions, and their strategies and tactics of influence and to contribute to the understanding of how conflict develops and becomes resolved more generally as part of the policy process in executive branch and congressional politics.

In November, 1943, General George C. Marshall, the Chief of Staff of the Army, proposed during a meeting of the World War II Joint Chiefs of Staff that in the postwar period the existing Departments of War and the Navy be unified into a single military department. Marshall's War Department colleague on the Joint Chiefs, General Henry H. Arnold, the Commanding General of the Army Air Forces, supported his proposal, but the two other Joint Chiefs, Admiral Ernest J. King, the Chief of Naval Operations–Commander-in-Chief U.S. Fleet, and Admiral William D. Leahy, the Chief of Staff to President Franklin D. Roosevelt, immediately opposed it. It was not until some four years, three Congresses, five sets of lengthy congressional hearings, and numerous White House conferences later, after what was one of the most intense political conflicts of the whole post-World War II era, and one that involved the fullest mobilization of lobbying, public relations, and propaganda campaigns by the military services, that a degree of "unification" was achieved with the passage by Congress of the National Security Act of 1947 and the establishment of a Secretary of Defense.

Why should such an intense political conflict have developed over proposals to unify the military services? The major participants in the conflict—the President, the Secretaries of War and the Navy, various leading senators and representatives, and high Army, Army Air Forces, Navy, and Marine officers—all steadily proclaimed identical ultimate goals: combat effectiveness, economy, and civilian control of the military. Such being the case, why should the determination of the form of the military structure not have been simply a matter of applying technical administrative expertise—a completely uncontroversial process of designing optimum organizational means to reach common ends? Was the conflict the result of anything more than pure negativism—blind resistance to change on the part of a few selfish individuals who placed their own interests above the "public interest"?

The "devil theory" type of explanation implicit in these questions has had wide currency ever since the unification conflict first broke out. It continues to color interpretations of the more recent (and apparently never-ending) controversies over increased "unification" within the Department of Defense. I do not think the theory is correct. One aim of this study of the unification conflict is to present a more complex, and hopefully more accurate, explanation of why it occurred and of the strategies and tactics used by its different civilian and military participants in trying to resolve it in their favor. The subject is not merely one of historical or academic interest: The general organizational framework established as a result of the unification conflict to a considerable extent still exists. Of the objectives that were to be furthered, combat effectiveness has now come to involve even the question of national survival itself, economy has to do with military expenditures of some $50 to $60 billion a year, or over half of the federal budget, and civilian control of the military continues to be an American value of the highest priority that more that a few observers see increasingly threatened by our enormously powerful defense establishment.

It should be recognized at the very beginning, however, that since this is primarily a study of certain aspects of the process of politics, it will neither explicitly judge the merits of the issues concerning unification nor offer organizational blueprints of its own. Still, the study does provide a sufficiently detailed reconstruction of the conflict, including the various proposals and the supporting arguments of the different participants, to enable any reader to come to a considered judgment on the original issues and, indeed, to alert him to the kinds of considerations that he must take into account in understanding or evaluating other proposals for defense reorganization, now or in the future. In this respect, the study is also one in the politics of administrative reorganization.

Any description and explanation of the unification conflict must obviously reflect some general conception of the nature of political conflict in the policy process. Although most existing case studies of the policy process in the executive branch or in Congress are, in fact, analyses of situations of conflict, there is still no clear-cut and generally accepted set of assumptions, or "conceptual scheme," in political science to guide such research. This is unfortunate, since a common framework could increase the value of individual case studies by facilitating the consolidation of their findings into an organized body of knowledge about an important part of the political process. Furthermore, the development of such a conceptual scheme could provide a corrective to the popular notion that conflict in the policy process represents some kind of serious abnormality. The conception of political conflict on which this study is based is simply that of a kind of human interactivity in which one actor exerts influence to promote and another actor exerts influence to obstruct or interfere with the adoption of some proposed course of governmental action. It is assumed consequently that any satisfactory explanation of a political conflict must provide answers to at least the following questions: What was the exact nature of the controverted proposals? Who were the individual or group actors involved in the conflict? How did differences in the actors' goals and perceptions account for their disagreement over the proposals? What were the different actors' resources, strategies, and tactics of influence? What accounted for the conflict's particular outcome?

The second aim of this study is, in trying to answer the preceding questions specifically for the unification conflict, to explain something about the operation and functions of political conflict in the policy process generally.

The study is organized in five parts. Part I provides the background for the unification conflict, briefly describing early interservice relations, the abortive post-World War I unification movements, and the evolution of the World War II Joint Chiefs of Staff organization. Part II describes the development of the unification conflict between the fall of 1943 and the winter of 1945–46, explains the nature of the various proposals presented, and attempts to account for the dispute between what will be called the "War Department coalition" and the "Navy Department coalition" at the point of their maximum disagreement. Part III describes the gradual resolution of the conflict between the spring of 1946 and the summer of 1947, first primarily by means of bargaining within the executive branch and then through the activation of voting majorities in Congress. Part IV analyzes the kinds of intra-legislative and extra-legislative influences that affected congressional behavior over the course of the unification conflict. Part V attempts to account for the outcome of the unification conflict, traces some of the more recent organizational trends in the Department of Defense, and presents some tentative generalizations about the role of political conflict in the policy process.

The data for this reconstruction of the unification conflict have been drawn principally from some ten thousand pages of congressional hearings, reports, and debates; from newspapers; from memoirs and biographies; from unpublished materials, including the diary and other papers of former Secretary of War Henry L. Stimson (on deposit at Yale University Library), the personal papers of former Secretary of the Navy James Forrestal (on deposit at Princeton University Library), and two extensive files of personal papers, documents, and other materials bearing on the unification conflict that were generously made available to me without restriction by General Lauris Norstad (who was actively in charge of the War Department's unification campaign from December, 1945, to July, 1947) and by Clark Clifford (who as President Truman's naval aide and then Special Counsel had the White House staff responsibility on the unification question for most of the same period); and from personal interviews and correspondence with actual participants in the conflict from Congress and the executive branch, including the military services. Although some of my informants prefer to remain unnamed, I see no reason not to acknowledge my thanks at least to the following: former Representative Sterling Cole, Clark Clifford, General J. Lawton Collins, U.S. Army (retired), Ferdinand Eberstadt, Representative F. Edward Hébert, Senator Lister Hill, General James D. Hittle, U.S. Marine Corps (retired), former Representative Clare E. Hoffman, former Assistant Secretary of the Navy W. John Kenney, former Assistant Secretary of War John J. McCloy, General Lauris Norstad, U.S. Air Force (retired), Senator Leverett Saltonstall, and General Maxwell D. Taylor, U.S. Army (retired).

Special thanks are due also to Forrest Pogue, General Marshall's official biographer, for providing valuable insights into Marshall's thinking on unification, to B. Vincent Davis, Jr., of the University of Denver for generously sharing certain materials collected in connection with his own study of Navy strategy and policy, and to Paul Y. Hammond of the RAND Corporation for making available to me while still in manuscript, his study *Organizing for Defense*.

It is, finally, a distinct pleasure to have this opportunity to record publicly the following more general obligations: to the Samuel S. Fels Fund of Philadelphia, to Columbia University's Institute of War and Peace Studies and Council for Research in the Social Sciences, and to Barnard College's own separate Faculty Research Fund for various grants and releases from teaching obligations that made this study possible; to David B. Truman, Samuel P. Huntington, and Wallace S. Sayre for, among other things over the years too numerous to mention, reading and commenting upon various versions and parts of the manuscript and providing me with my general conceptions of congressional, military, and executive branch politics; to William T. R. Fox, the Director of the Institute on War and Peace Studies, for bringing his own extensive knowledge of national security affairs to bear on the complete final manuscript; to Bernard Barber and H. Douglas Price for providing useful suggestions on the manuscript's more theoretical portions; and to Jeanne Caraley, a political scientist in her own right, for competently bringing up our children while this study was being written without all the help from her husband that she had a right to expect.

One last word of appreciation is owing to my wife and to Katherine Purcell, Audrey Slesinger, and Sheila Berkman for such tasks as improving the manuscript's style and helping with the proof and index. While obviously none of the persons I have named are responsible for any of the study's remaining flaws, they all have my sincerest and deeply felt thanks for contributing to whatever may be regarded as its merits.

DEMETRIOS CARALEY

New York, N.Y.
February, 1966

Contents

Part I

The Background of
the Conflict

1

The Origins of Unification

The intense conflict that took place between 1943 and 1947 over proposals to unify the Departments of War and the Navy had its roots in the earliest history of the United States. Actually, during the first few years of the Republic, all military affairs had been the responsibility of only one department of government. When the First Congress met in 1789, it had established a Department of War, whose Secretary was given authority over both land and naval forces.[1] The grant of authority over a navy did not mean much, however, since the new government did not own a single combatant ship. All the vessels of the Revolutionary Navy had been sold or given away by the end of 1785.[2]

Congress began to create a new navy in 1794, when it voted the construction of six frigates to protect American commerce in the Mediterranean against the Algerian pirates.[3] This building program, cut in half when an accommodation was reached with the Algerians in 1796, went very slowly. By the spring of 1798 there were various complaints in Congress about the "unaccountable delays" and the "enormous expenses" that had developed over the building of the ships.[4]

Secretary of War James McHenry met the criticism directed against him by explaining that he was overworked and recommending that the naval business be separated from his department. After considerable debate, and a close vote of 47 to 41 in the House of Representatives, Congress passed an act in April, 1798, "to establish an Executive Department to be denominated the Department of the Navy" with authority over "the procurement of naval stores, the construction, equipment, and employment of vessels of war, and other naval matters." [5] The debate over the new department had been couched largely in terms of "efficiency" and "economy," but the overriding goal of its Federalist proponents appears to have been to provide an organizational home that could better protect the Navy against possible future attempts by the Republicans to emasculate it after the cessation of the undeclared naval war then being waged with France.[6]

Early Interservice Relations

In the almost 150 years from 1798 to 1947, there was no common superior to the War and Navy Departments and their respective military services except for the President of the United States as Chief Executive and Constitutional Commander in Chief of the Army and Navy. For most of that period, when coordination of the services' activities was necessary (and this was seldom, since the Army was busy chiefly fighting Indians, while the Navy was showing the flag overseas and protecting commerce), it was conducted on an *ad hoc* basis. The effectiveness of this coordination varied greatly, depending to a large extent on the attitudes toward cooperation of the Secretaries of War and the Navy and, during joint combat operations, on those of the respective combat commanders.[7]

Before World War I, the most typical outlook on the part of the Secretaries was probably best expressed by President Woodrow Wilson's Secretary of War, Lindley Garrison. When, for example, Secretary of the Navy Josephus Daniels once approached him about giving more attention to better coordination of their departments' operations, the Secretary of War reportedly responded,

Joe, I don't care a damn about the Navy, and [don't you] care a damn about the Army. You run your machine and I will run mine. I am glad if anyone can convince me I am wrong, but I am damn sure nobody lives who can do it. I am an individualist and am not cut out for cooperative effort. I will let you go your way, and I will go my way.[8]

Not all the Secretaries of War were as indifferent as Garrison. Lincoln's Secretary of War, Edwin M. Stanton, actively sought to improve interservice coordination during the Civil War simply by placing the Navy under Army control. Navy Secretary Gideon Welles writes in his diary that he never recognized "these pretensions" and insisted "that we were equal and would be ready at all times to cooperate with the armies in any demonstration, but . . . not under orders." [9] Lincoln supported Welles' view.

Joint Army-Navy combat operations in the field were conducted up to World War II under the principle of "mutual cooperation," which held that the wartime commanders of the two services could be expected to reach friendly agreement on how best to coordinate their forces in battle. At times, such as at the Battle of Mobile Bay and the second attack on Fort Fisher in the Civil War and during various operations in the Mexican War, "mutual cooperation" proved effective,[10] particularly when, because of differences in prestige or reputation, the commander of one of the two services informally deferred to the wishes of the other. Just as often, "mutual cooperation" was not effective, with the classic example of its failure being the Army-Navy campaign to capture Santiago, Cuba, in 1898 during the Spanish-American War. The Army commander at the scene, Major General William R. Shafter, had Santiago virtually surrounded by land. Before Shafter would advance further, he wanted the Navy to force its way into Santiago harbor and bombard the Spanish troops from the rear. The Navy commander, Rear Admiral William T. Sampson, refused to force the harbor unless the entrance were first cleared of mines and urged the Army to advance and capture the Spanish forts overlooking the harbor entrance, so that the Navy could proceed to remove the mines without being subjected to bombardment from the shore. After ineffectual attempts by each of the commanders to get the other to make the next move, Shafter complained by cable to Secretary of War R. A. Alger, who took the matter up with President McKinley. The result was the following message cabled to Shafter from the War Department:

Secretary of War instructs me to say that the President directs that you confer with Admiral Sampson at once for cooperation in taking Santiago. After the fullest exchange of views you will agree upon the time and manner of attack.[11]

A similar message was sent to Sampson by the Secretary of the Navy. The Secretaries themselves, incidentally, were communicating at this time by formal letter. Eventually the Navy bombarded Santiago from outside the harbor, and soon thereafter the Spanish forces surrendered without either the harbor having been forced or the Army occupying any of the forts in question. Shafter then had the final satisfaction of having the articles of capitulation with the Spanish signed at his headquarters before anyone could be present to represent the Navy.[12]

Great dissatisfaction arose over the failure of Army-Navy cooperation at Santiago and in the fighting elsewhere in Cuba and in Puerto Rico during the Spanish-American War and later over the various jurisdictional disputes that developed between the services with regard to the administration of the newly acquired overseas possessions. This led to an attempt in 1903 to improve matters by institutionalizing certain lines of coordination between the services through the creation of a Joint Army and Navy Board. This "Joint Board," as it was usually called, was set up by agreement of the Secretary of War Elihu Root and the Secretary of the Navy John D. Long. Its charter directed it "to hold stated sessions and such extraordinary sessions as . . . appear advisable for the purpose of conferring upon, discussing, and reaching common conclusions regarding all matters calling for the cooperation of the two services." [13] Either department could submit proposals to the Board for consideration.

The Joint Board consisted of four Army and four Navy officers of high rank, who retained their primary duties within their own departments and thus could not give much attention to matters of joint concern. Furthermore, the Joint Board had neither a full-time nor a part-time subordinate group to do detailed staff work.[14] For these and other reasons, such as President Woodrow Wilson's hostility toward it,* the Joint Board fell into almost complete disuse during World War I.[15] In its early years, the Board is reported to have considered primarily problems of "personnel, rank, honors, salutes, and other matters of like import [that] . . . could have been solved by other means or placed in the waste basket without seriously affecting either service." [16] Nevertheless, occasionally it did also consider important questions of military policy and strategy [17] and even drew up rough joint plans for the eventuality of war between the United States and Colombia and the United States and Japan.[18]

The Joint Board was reconstituted in 1919 on a much more satisfactory basis by Secretary of War Newton D. Baker and Secretary of the Navy Josephus Daniels. The Board was not responsible, however, for

---

* Wilson had first become irritated with the Joint Board in 1913. The Board had protested the rejection of one of its recommendations concerning certain fleet maneuvers to counter possible hostile Japanese action against the Philippines and had asked that the recommendations be reconsidered. The President reportedly became furious and warned "that if this should occur again, there will be no General or Joint Boards. They will be abolished." Quoted in Ernest R. May, "Wilson," in E. R. May, ed., *The Ultimate Decision: The President as Commander in Chief* (New York, Braziller, 1960), p. 113.

the proposals that arose after World War I to place all the military services in a single Department of Defense. The agitation for "unification" was rather a consequence of two different but related movements —that for comprehensive administrative reorganization within the executive branch and that for increased autonomy for the Army's Air Service.

Movement for Comprehensive Administrative Reform

To a large extent the movement after World War I for comprehensive administrative reorganization was initiated by W. F. Willoughby, who was at the time director of the Institute for Governmental Research (later The Brookings Institution) and who had been in 1910 a member of President Taft's Commission on Economy and Efficiency. Willoughby generated sufficient congressional interest in administrative reform so that in April, 1920, Senator Reed Smoot introduced a joint resolution setting up a six-man joint committee of Congress to consider the reorganization of the executive branch of the government so as to further "efficiency and economy in the conduct of Government business." The resolution, which was passed in December, 1920, directed the Joint Committee on the Reorganization of Government Departments specifically

to determine what redistribution of activities should be made among the several services, . . . and what departmental regrouping of services should be made, so that each executive department shall embrace only services having close working relations with each other and ministering directly to the primary purpose for which the same are maintained and operated.[19]

Congress authorized President Harding to name a representative "to cooperate with the Joint Committee," [20] and Harding's appointee, Walter F. Brown, became chairman of the group. The Joint Committee undertook very limited investigations under Brown's direction, and it was only after prodding by one of its congressional members that the Chairman finally reported to the President in January, 1922, a plan for the general reorganization of all departments and agencies of the executive branch on the "single-purpose" principle. Since Brown conceived of the waging of war by both the Army and the Navy as one purpose, he proposed that the two existing military departments be unified into a Department of Defense under a single cabinet secretary, who would be assisted by undersecretaries for the Army, the Navy, and National Resources.

Brown also recommended that the War and Navy Departments be divested of all components not directly related to national defense, such as the Army's Corps of Engineers and the Navy's Hydrographic Office and Naval Observatory.

It was over a year later when the President, in February, 1923, reacted to Brown's proposals by sending to the Joint Committee an organizational chart purporting to show his own views. Harding appeared to favor the single Department of Defense, but he indicated that his Cabinet had not been in agreement on this point.[21] About a year still later, in January, 1924, the Joint Committee proceeded to hold hearings.

The first three witnesses before the Committee were Secretary of War John W. Weeks, Secretary of the Navy Edwin Denby, and W. F. Willoughby. The two secretaries opposed unification of their departments, relying chiefly on arguments prepared by their military subordinates when Brown's proposals had first been aired, to show that unification would hurt military effectiveness. Willoughby, of course, favored the merger, but when it soon became apparent that almost no one but he and Chairman Brown did, the attention of the Committee turned exclusively to the possible transfer of nonmilitary activities out of the military departments.[22] When the Joint Committee finally made its recommendations to Congress in June, 1924, the main report did not even mention the unification of the War and Navy Departments.[23]

Movement for Air Force Autonomy

The second post-World War I movement that led eventually to recommendations for the establishment of a single overall military department was the agitation in favor of independent Cabinet status or increased autonomy for the Army Air Service. An aviation unit had first been established within the Army in 1907 as the Aeronautical Division of the Signal Corps. Airplanes at this time were likened to balloons, and the Signal Corps had been using balloons for observation and communication purposes for some years. In 1914, the Aeronautical Division was redesignated the Aviation Section, and four years later, in the middle of World War I, the Aviation Section was taken out of the Signal Corps and given separate organizational status within the Army as the Air Service.[24] Even before the end of the war, a few bills to take the Air Service completely out of the War Department and to establish it as an independent Department of Aeronautics were introduced in Congress, and in 1917 short hearings had been held on them by a sub-committee of the Senate Committee on Military Affairs.[25]

The campaign for a separate air force got seriously under way after the Armistice, when the Army aviators who had served in France came home convinced of the very great, if not decisive, importance of military air power in all future wars. The aviators were also convinced, however, that air power would never be allowed to develop adequately unless it were given an organizational home separate from the purportedly land-minded War Department. Testimony along these lines was first developed by Brigadier General William ("Billy") Mitchell and others during hearings held between August and December, 1919, by a subcommittee of the Senate Military Affairs Committee under Senator James W. Wadsworth on a bill that eventually became the National Defence Act of 1920.[26]

In December, 1919, hearings were begun in the House dealing entirely with the question of a separate air force. These were held by a subcommittee of the House Military Affairs Committee and were chaired in the beginning by Representative Fiorello LaGuardia, himself a major in the Army Air Service in the war. During these hearings the official heads of the War and Navy Departments, all the nonflying Army officers, and all the Navy officers opposed the establishment of a separate cabinet department for military aviation, while the Army aviators and former Army aviators almost all favored it. This line-up of forces was to continue for over twenty years.

The position of the War and Navy Departments was that they needed control of their own aviation to fulfill their missions on the ground and at sea and that increasing the number of military departments to three would greatly aggravate the problems of coordination. Mitchell, who was leading the Army flyers, dismissed the first part of this claim by arguing that aviation which pertained "strictly to the Army or Navy is only for observation purposes," and constituted "only a twentieth part of the whole." [27] Mitchell had no answer during these hearings to the coordination objection, referring simply to the existing powers of the President to coordinate the services as Commander in Chief. In any event, no action was taken by the subcommittee, and the Air Service remained, as it saw it, chained to the Army General Staff's archaic "long-bow men."

The airmen were not easily discouraged, and in 1924 they stated their case once again. Rumors had arisen the year before about possible scandals in the awarding of contracts for airplanes, and in October, 1924, a select committee was created in the House of Representatives under the chairmanship of Representative Florian Lampert to investigate.[28] The Select Committee sat for over fourteen months and took over 3,500 pages of testimony. After it became apparent early in the hearings that the rumors of irregularities in procurement had been unfounded, the Lampert Committee turned its attention to other aspects of military aviation and especially to the question of a separate air force.[29]

Mitchell was, as usual, the most spectacular witness the Committee heard. He attacked the services for their alleged extreme conservatism and obstruction of the maximum possible development of aviation. He urged the establishment of a Department of Aeronautics to provide a sympathetic home for the airmen. When questioned about the problems of coordination that a third military service might create, Mitchell now thought that the problems could be solved by putting all three services into a single department of national defense. Other airmen, including the Chief of the Army Air Service, Major General Mason M. Patrick, were ready to settle for an autonomous Air Corps within the War Department similar in status to the Navy's Marine Corps. When the Lampert Committee finally reported its findings in December, 1925, it did not recommend a separate Department of Aeronautics, but it did recommend the establishment of a Department of National Defense headed by a single civilian cabinet secretary in order to promote economy and efficiency in the defense effort.[30]

In the fall of 1925, while Congress was adjourned, Mitchell found another forum for his advocacy of a seperate air force and unification. Mitchell, who had not been reappointed that year as Assistant Chief of the Air Service—a post he had held since 1919—and so had reverted to the grade of colonel, was stationed at Fort Sam Houston near San Antonio when, in early September, 1925, two serious air accidents occurred. These involved the Navy seaplane PN-9, which was attempting a flight between California and Hawaii, and the Navy dirigible *Shenandoah,* which fell apart in a storm over Ohio. Forty-eight hours after the *Shenandoah* crash, Mitchell gave out a 6,000-word statement to the press, in which he charged that the accidents were "the direct results of incompetency, criminal negligence and almost treasonable administration of the national defense by the war and navy departments." [31] Mitchell then proceeded to make a general attack on the way the two departments were developing air power, contending that it had been "so disgusting in the last few years as to make any self-respecting person ashamed of the cloth he wears." [32]

The press statement was eventually to lead to Mitchell's court-martial and conviction for "conduct prejudicial to military discipline" and to his resignation from the Army. It also led to President Coolidge's appointment of a nine-man panel from among the general public, Congress, and retired Army and Navy officers to look into Mitchell's charges and to make an impartial study of the best means of applying air power to national defense. Dwight W. Morrow, senior partner in the J. P. Morgan bank, was appointed chairman of the panel, and the group became known as the Morrow Board. Representative Carl Vinson, then ranking minority member of the House Naval Affairs Committee, was one of the members.

The Morrow Board held hearings in September and October, 1925. As could be expected, the most prominent issues to develop were over the establishment of a separate department for military aviation and the establishment of a department of defense. The official representatives of the War and Navy Departments continued to oppose any change in the existing organization. Their main line of argument against a separate air force was to stress the great problems that would develop in coordinating three military services instead of two, while their argument against a single department of defense was that the problems of coordinating the Army and Navy were being handled perfectly satisfactorily.[33] The majority of the fliers who appeared before the Board had obviously concluded that their best response to arguments over the increased difficulties of three-service coordination lay in the advocacy of such a single department, and they testified accordingly. General Patrick continued to advocate a semiautonomous air corps responsible only to the Secretary of War and consequently free from General Staff domination.

When the Morrow Board reported to the President on November 30, 1925, it recommended unanimously against either the creation of a separate air department or the establishment of a department of national defense. The first, the Board felt, would overemphasize the military role of the airplane, and the second would result in too much complexity for the advantages to be gained. The Board did recommend the creation of Assistant Secretaries for Air in the two existing military departments, increased influence and representation of airmen in the formulation of department policies, and a change of name for the Army Air Service to the Army Air Corps.[34] The Board's unanimous report appears to have carried considerable weight and to have counterbalanced to some extent the "separation" and "unification" opinion that had been developing in the years after World War I.[35]

Notwithstanding the Morrow Board report, when the Sixty-ninth Congress convened in December, 1925, there was still strong sentiment for some kind of legislation on overall military organization. A number of separate-air-force and unification bills were introduced, and hearings were held by the House Committee on Military Affairs.[36] On March 9, 1926, one of the members of the Committee indicated [37] that it probably would not report any bill calling for a separate air force or for a department of defense.* It was later revealed that the crucial committee vote against the unification bill had been 11 to 10.[38] A bill was reported later that month, and this eventually became the "Air Corps Act of 1926." The Act changed the name of the Army Air Service to the Army Air Corps, it authorized higher rank for its officers, it directed that more airmen be appointed to the War Department General Staff, it required that thereafter flying units be commanded by flying officers, and it authorized the appointment of an additional Assistant Secretary of War "to aid the Secretary of War in fostering military aeronautics." [39]

1932 Economy Movement

Between 1926 and 1944 there was but a single congressional attempt to deal with unification serious enough to warrant the holding of hear-

* President Coolidge may have influenced this Committee decision. He is reported to have sent for the Chairman of the Military Affairs Committee, John M. Morin, to discuss the separate air force bills with the conversation having gone like this:
" 'Mr. Representative, what can I do for you?' . . . 'Nothing, Mr. President. You sent for me,' replied Morin. . . . 'Ah, yes,' Coolidge resumed. 'Will that unified [separate] air service bill get by your committee?' 'Yes, Mr. President,' Morin answered. 'Will it get by the House?' 'Yes.' 'Will it get by the Senate Committee?' 'I am quite sure, Mr. President.' 'Will it get by the Senate?' 'Yes.' 'Well,' drawled Coolidge, 'it won't get by me.' And he got up and extended his hand: 'Good morning. I'm glad you called.' " Isaac Don Levine, *Mitchell: Pioneer of Air Power* (New York, Duell, Sloan and Pearce, 1943), pp. 320–21.

ings. The great stress on governmental economy during the depression of the 1930s inspired proposals to unify the War and Navy Departments. It was argued by its proponents that unification would save money, chiefly by eliminating duplication of facilities by the two departments such as the adjacent Bolling (Army Air Corps) and Anacostia (Navy) airfields in Washington. Three bills to create a Department of National Defense were introduced when the Seventy-second Congress convened in December, 1931, and a month later hearings were started in the House by the Committee on Expenditures in the Executive Departments.

Secretary of War Patrick Hurley and Secretary of the Navy Charles Francis Adams both testified against the unification measures, stressing that hopes for significant savings without loss of combat effectiveness were unfounded. General Douglas A. MacArthur, the Army Chief of Staff, put this argument into its most colorful language when he wrote to a member of the Committee,

The history of Government demonstrates that the parasitical development of bureaucracy springs from the setting up of superfluous echelons of control such as the one proposed. . . . Although I recognize the possibility of effecting relatively unimportant economies in isolated activities, the ultimate cost of this superimposed structure would . . . exceed by millions any economies that could be safely effected. . . . Rather than economy, this amalgamation would, in my opinion, represent one of the greatest debauches of extravagance that any nation has ever known.[40]

MacArthur also gave it as his "fixed opinion" that unification "would endanger victory for the United States in case of war" and predicted that if the bill were passed, "every potential enemy of the United States will rejoice." [41]

Although the Expenditures Committee did not report any of the bills it considered, one of them (H.R.4742) found its way into the so-called Economy Bill of 1932, which was reported in late April by a special House Economy Committee. The Special Committee was trying to find ways of cutting government spending, and its bill was an omnibus measure. One of the bill's titles cut the pay of government employees and another gave President Hoover authority to transfer and consolidate agencies within the executive branch (subject to congressional veto). Its Title VI was the unification bill, establishing a Department of National Defense and giving the new Secretary the right to consolidate the aviation activities of the Army, Navy, and Marine Corps.[42] The Economy Bill was passed as an amendment to the Legislative Appropriations Act of 1932,[43] but not before Title VI was struck on the floor of the House by a teller vote of 153 to 135,[44] thus foiling the unifiers once again.

The year 1932 was the last time that any great congressional interest was shown in unification until the end of World War II. Depression, rearmament, and finally war left little time and energy to deal with the niceties of overall military organization. A more important reason probably was that one of the most vitally interested parties had ceased its active proselytizing. Beginning in 1933, most Army Air Corps officers had given up temporarily the campaign to secure a separate air force and its perceived necessary concomitant, a department of national defense.[45] They concentrated instead on more limited objectives, such as the creation within the War Department of an air striking force independent of the control of the various ground corps area commanders and the establishment of a separate budget, promotion list, and policy staff for the Air Corps.[46] These tactics were largely successful. In 1935 the air combat units then distributed among the corps areas were brought together into a General Headquarters Air Force under a commanding general directly responsible to the Chief of Staff of the Army.[47] In 1940 the Chief of the Air Corps, Lieutenant General Henry H. Arnold, was designated Deputy Chief of Staff of the Army for Air. In 1941 Arnold was appointed to the Joint Board and made Chief of a newly created Army Air Forces with a separate air staff and almost complete control over Army aviation.[48] By the middle of World War II, the Army aviators were well on their way to having achieved a *de facto* independence from the ground Army which was to satisfy most of them until the grand opportunity for the attainment of their ultimate objective appeared after the war was won.

The World War II Command Structure

ORIGINS OF THE JOINT CHIEFS OF STAFF

The Joint Army and Navy Board reconstituted in 1919 differed in two important respects from its predecessor: first, membership on the Board was now designated by position rather than by name, thus making the filling of vacancies automatic and insuring continuity of operations; and, second, the Board was now provided with a subordinate staff group, the Joint Planning Committee, consisting of three or more officers from the General Staff's War Plans Division and from the Office of Naval Operation's Plans Division who were to consider service on the Committee their primary duty. After 1923, the members of the Joint Board included the Army Chief of Staff, the Deputy Chief of Staff, and the Chief of the General Staff's War Plans Division, and the Navy Chief of Naval Operations, the Assistant Chief of Naval Operations, and the Director of the Office of Naval Operation's Plans Division.[49] In July, 1941, the Deputy Chief of Staff for Air (who was also the Chief of the Army Air Forces) and the Chief of the Navy's Bureau of Aeronautics were added to the Board, apparently as a result of the increased appreciation of the capabilities of military air power after Hitler's spectacular air-supported victories in Europe.[50]

The Joint Board had never been organized as a command body prepared to provide strategic direction of military operations in the field. It met once a month (the Joint Planning Committee met weekly) and devoted much of its attention until the late 1930s to peacetime problems involving actual or potential Army-Navy disputes in such activities as harbor and coastal area defense and in the maintenance of airdrome facilities in overseas possessions. Its most important combat-oriented activities in the interwar period were the preparation of Joint Basic War Plans. The war plans indicated the actions to be taken by each of the armed services in the event of specific emergency situations such as attacks on the United States, on its possessions, or on areas in which the United States had an interest.* The series of so-called "color" plans dealt with possible enemies operating singly, while the later "rainbow" plans dealt with enemies acting in combination. The Joint Board's last rainbow plan, Rainbow Number 5, incorporated the strategic concept that was actually followed by the United States in World War II.[51] The Joint Board also prepared and issued various editions of the command guide, *Joint Action of the Army and Navy,* which indicated generally the military tasks for which each service was responsible and outlined methods of cooperation during combat operations.[52]

Until 1939 any decisions of the Joint Board required the approval of the Secretaries of War and the Navy before they could be effected within

---

* Providing that the forces were available, which for the execution of the most important plan (ORANGE), for war against Japan, they were not. War Plan ORANGE has been called "really more a statement of hopes than a realistic analysis of what could be done." Louis Morton, "Interservice Co-operation and Political-Military Collaboration," in Harry L. Coles, ed., *Total War and Cold War: Problems in Civilian Control of the Military* (Columbus, Ohio State University Press, 1962), p. 141.

the services. On July 5 of that year, when the Danzig crisis was raging and general war was expected to break out imminently in Europe, President Roosevelt directed that thereafter the Joint Board should report directly to him rather than through the Secretaries of War and the Navy on such matters as strategy, tactics, and military operations. The Board was to exercise its functions "under the direction and supervision of the President as Commander in Chief of the Army and Navy of the United States." [53] In May, 1941, the Joint Board established a Joint Strategical Committee under the Joint Planning Committee to relieve the latter of the increasing burden of working out the details of the joint war and operating plans that were now being prepared in expectation of active U.S. military participation. In July, 1941, the Joint Board began to meet weekly.[54] It was this Joint Board system that was in effect when the Japanese attacked Pearl Harbor.

The Joint Board evolved into the Joint Chiefs of Staff (JCS) when Churchill and his military advisers came to Washington in late December, 1941, to confer with Roosevelt and his advisers about collaboration in the war against the Axis powers. One of the most pressing problems to develop during this so-called ARCADIA conference concerned the command structure in the Southwest Pacific. The Japanese offensive into the Netherlands East Indies, the Singapore area, and the Philippines was being resisted by the land, sea, and air forces of four nations: the United States, Great Britain, Australia, and the Netherlands. The American military advisers thought that for the allied military effort to have any hope of success, the traditional principle of "mutual cooperation" had to be discarded and all these military forces put under a single field commander. After some original opposition by Churchill, the principle of "unified command" in the field was agreed to and British General Sir Archibald Wavell was designated as Supreme Commander ABDA (American-British-Dutch-Australian) area. It was later decided that Wavell should report to an Anglo-American military group designated as the "Combined Chiefs of Staff" (CCS), a term defined simply as the "United States Chiefs of Staff and the British Chiefs of Staff." [55]

The "British Chiefs of Staff" was the designation of an existing body, namely, the British Chiefs of Staff Committee. This group was formed in 1924 as a subcommittee of the Committee of Imperial Defense—Britain's top-level foreign policy–military policy advisory council—and charged with providing advice on overall military policy. Its members included the military heads of the three services—the Army's Chief of the Imperial General Staff, the Navy's First Sea Lord, and the separate British Royal Air Force's Chief of the Air Staff—and it was to constitute "as it were, a super-chief of a War Staff in Commission." [56]

The "United States Chiefs of Staff" did not exist as such, the Joint Board being its nearest equivalent. When it was decided early in 1942 that the CCS would provide strategic direction not only for the ABDA area but for all operations under Anglo-American responsibility, the Chief of Staff of the Army, General George C. Marshall; the Chief of Naval Operations, Admiral Harold R. Stark; the Commander in Chief of the United States Fleet, Admiral Ernest J. King; and the Chief of the Army Air Forces, General Arnold, constituted themselves, with the President's tacit approval, as the United States, or "Joint," Chiefs of Staff, and for all practical purposes, the Joint Board, which had largely overlapping membership, ceased to operate.[57] The JCS, incidentally, continued to operate throughout the war without being authorized in writing by so much as a chit or memorandum from the President.

The only changes in the wartime membership of the JCS occurred in 1942. In March of that year, Admiral Stark left for a new post in England after being replaced as Chief of Naval Operations by Admiral King, who still retained his other position as Commander in Chief of the Fleet; in July, Admiral William D. Leahy joined the group after being recalled to active service by President Roosevelt and appointed "Chief of Staff to the Commander in Chief of the Army and Navy of the United States." [58]

FUNCTIONS AND OPERATION OF THE JCS

The JCS had two sets of responsibilities in World War II. They were the American representatives on the Combined Chiefs of Staff and, subject to President Roosevelt and Prime Minister Churchill's authority, engaged in negotiating with their British opposite numbers the grand strategy of the war and the overall allocation of men, munitions, and shipping among the various commands and theaters of operations. Subject only to the President, the Joint Chiefs were also the supreme command and planning body for all the American armed forces and in charge of developing operational strategy for the combat theaters within the American area of responsibility. In the spring of 1942 Roosevelt and Churchill had divided the parts of the world in which British or

American forces were operating into three areas of responsibility: the Pacific Area, which included the American continents, Australia, New Zealand, and Japan; the Indian Ocean and Middle East Area, which extended from Singapore to Libya and included India, the Indian Ocean, the Persian Gulf, the Red Sea, and the eastern Mediterranean; and the Atlantic and European Area. Within the limits of the grand strategy decided upon by Roosevelt, Churchill, and the CCS, operational responsibility for the Pacific Area was given to the United States, operational responsibility for the Indian Ocean and Middle East Area was given to Great Britain, with operational responsibility for Europe and the Atlantic being retained by the two countries jointly. The United States proceeded further to divide the Pacific Area into a Southwest Pacific Area (SWPA), which included Australia, New Guinea, and the Philippines, and a Pacific Ocean Areas (POA), which included the rest of the Pacific. It designated General Douglas A. MacArthur Supreme Commander of the SWPA and Admiral Chester W. Nimitz Supreme Commander of the POA and, under the principle of "unified command," gave each of them general control over all the allied armed forces within his area.[59]

The Joint Chiefs met weekly to consider various proposals raised either by the Chiefs themselves or by the elaborate subordinate committee structure that they developed by the middle of the war. They also met whenever other circumstances required. When action to be taken was decided upon, the JCS issued directives to that one of their members who was the senior military executive of the service responsible for the command or theater of operations being affected.[60] Thus, directives for MacArthur's SWPA or, later, for General Dwight D. Eisenhower's European command were issued to General Marshall, who, as "executive agent" for the JCS, used the War Department General Staff to carry them out. Similarly, directives for Nimitz' POA were issued to Admiral King, who implemented them through his staff at the Navy Department. When the heavy bomber forces operating in Europe and the Pacific were constituted as separate operational commands independent of the theater commanders toward the latter part of the war, directives for these forces were handled by General Arnold and his Air Staff.

The JCS did not reach their decisions by majority vote. In the summer of 1942, the Joint Chiefs were considering a proposal to reduce the Navy's battleship and cruiser construction programs in order to divert steel to the construction of other types such as landing craft and convoy escort vessels. Admiral King was the only one opposed to the change. "When Leahy remarked that it looked to him as though 'the vote is three to one,' King replied coldly that so far as he was concerned, the Joint Chiefs were not a voting organization on any matter in which the interests of the Navy were involved." [61] The principle was accepted and throughout the war decisions had to be reached unanimously with irreconcilable differences being brought to the President for resolution. According to Admiral King, "matters of major import that required presentation to the President could be counted on the fingers of one hand. We usually found a solution. Sometimes it was a compromise." [62]

The President's Chief of Staff, Admiral Leahy, had no more authority than any of the other Joint Chiefs. Leahy presided over the meetings, prepared the agenda, and signed official papers on behalf of the JCS, but he did this by virtue of being the senior military officer in the group and not because of his position as Roosevelt's adviser.[63]

In making operational decisions, the JCS gave a great deal of leeway to the theater commanders. The Chiefs generally reserved to themselves only the choice of who the theater commander was to be, the designation of the objectives to be assaulted, and the time of the assault. The detailed operational plans, especially after the very early part of the war, were prepared by the theater commander in informal liaison with the planners in the War and Navy Departments and the subordinate committee structure of the JCS, and these were not generally questioned by the Chiefs.[64] The JCS were also responsible for deciding jurisdictional disputes among the theater commanders—these were most often between MacArthur and Nimitz—and for allocating limited forces and equipment among the different theaters.[65]

The relations between the JCS and the President were as follows: In routine matters where policy was clearly established, the JCS took action and issued directives without reference to the President. In matters of importance where policy was already established, the JCS took action without the prior approval of the President, but referred the matter to him for any action that he might care to take. In matters involving new questions of major policy, and this involved primarily questions regarding relations with America's allies, the JCS referred their decisions to the President for approval before putting them into effect.[66]

The evidence suggests that President Roosevelt did not overrule his Chiefs on more than one or two occasions during the entire war.[67] One occasion certainly was his cancellation in 1943, against their opposition, of the plan to mount an extensive campaign to recapture Burma from the Japanese and reopen land communications with China; the other occasion may be considered to have been when he directed his Chiefs to reach agreement with the British on an invasion of French North Africa in the fall of 1942 so as to get American ground troops in action against the Germans as soon as possible. Of course, Admiral Leahy, who saw the President daily, carried over Roosevelt's thinking into the JCS discussions and thus made it unlikely that the JCS would formally recommend anything that they were fairly sure the President would reject. As an official historian of the JCS has pointed out,

It may be true that the President formally overruled [the Chiefs] on very few occasions but this was only because informal discussions of the President with Leahy, Marshall, King and Arnold usually led them to know in advance the President's views. They, no doubt, frequently recognized the advantages of accepting the President's suggestions with their own interpretations, rather than risking an overruling by presenting formally proposals they knew would not be accepted.[68]

The Secretaries of War and the Navy were obviously bypassed by the JCS system. Even though they were still the legal superiors of three of the four Joint Chiefs, Roosevelt almost never had the Secretaries attend the periodic conferences that he held with Churchill and with other allied leaders to map out grand strategy and at which the Joint Chiefs always advised him. The Secretary of War and the Secretary of the Navy were not even included on the regular distribution list for routine JCS papers, fifty-five copies of which were circulated within the Army and the Navy toward the end of the war.[69] It was certainly no exaggeration when Admiral Leahy explained in the fall of 1945 to the Senate Military Affairs Committee that during World War II, except for the President, "the Joint Chiefs of Staff . . . [had been] under no civilian control whatever." [70]

Part II

The Conflict Develops

2

The Proposals Are Presented

Marshall's 1943 JCS Proposal

The conflict over military unification that eventually led to the passage of the National Security Act of 1947 can be said to have begun November 3, 1943. On that date General Marshall broke officially with long-standing War Department anti-unification policy and submitted to the JCS for consideration a proposal favoring a "Single Department of War in the Post-War Period." [1] Admiral Stark had proposed a Joint General Staff, under a single Chief responsible directly to the President, at a Joint Board meeting in January, 1942. No agreement could be reached on Stark's proposal after a split recommendation from the Board's Joint Planning Committee, and the proposal had consequently been "held open for further study." [2] Marshall's proposal was not to die such a painless death.

Marshall's position was that although only Congress could ultimately create a new government department, a tentative decision by the JCS was necessary to provide a basis for effective planning within the services on postwar problems. Marshall recommended that agreement be reached on the broad principle of a single Department of War comprised of ground, naval, and air components, and a separate service of supply. Each of the four subunits would be under its own civilian under secretary and military chief of staff. There would also be a Chief of Staff to the President, who, with the other four chiefs, would constitute a "United States General Staff (joint)." [3] The appendix to Marshall's proposal covered the desirability of avoiding duplication and overlap among the services and argued that "coordinating committees" caused "delays and compromises" and so were "a cumbersome and inefficient method of directing the efforts of the Armed Forces." [4] The JCS agreed to send Marshall's proposal to the Joint Strategic Survey Committee, one of their subordinate staff groups, for study and recommendation. In agreeing to the referral, Admiral King made it clear that he was not convinced of the desirability of a single department and that the staff study did not have to come up with a recommendation in its favor.[5]

The Joint Strategic Survey Committee reported back to the JCS in March, 1944, that it had found it impracticable to study comprehensively such a "far reaching, extremely complicated . . . problem" as "the most effective practicable organization of that part of the executive branch . . . which is primarily concerned with national defense." [6] Since the Strategic Survey Committee also saw no prospects of being able to conduct such a study in the future, it recommended that the JCS appoint a special committee of two officers from the Army (one to be from the Army Air Forces) and two officers from the Navy to consider the problem at length and to make recommendations. The Committee also recommended that the JCS first approve of "the idea of a single military organization" in order to guide the study of the special committee.[7]

Action in the JCS on the Strategic Survey Committee's report was deferred for a number of meetings. Although all the Chiefs were in favor of the study by a special committee, Admiral Leahy and Admiral King were unwilling to agree to a single department even in principle, purportedly because that would restrict the Committee's possible findings. King insisted that instead the committee should be given instructions to investigate the advantages, the disadvantages, and the practicability of one department (War or Defense), two departments (War and Navy), or three departments (War, Navy, and Air). Marshall reluctantly agreed to King's conditions, even though he believed that on that basis, the special committee would not come up with unanimous recommendations. On May 22, 1944, the JCS approved the final reworked version of their directive to the "Special Joint Chiefs of Staff Committee on Reorganization of National Defense," and by the end of the month all its members had been named. The senior member was Admiral James O. Richardson (Retired), a former Commander in Chief of the Pacific Fleet, and the group became known as the "Richardson Committee." [8]

1944 Woodrum Committee Hearings

Even while the JCS were considering the report of their Joint Strategic Survey Committee, another participant had become active in the conflict developing over unification and managed to divert it into a more public arena. On March 9, 1944, Representative James W. Wadsworth, a long-term War Department congressional ally,[9] introduced a resolution in the House creating a "Select Committee on Post-war Military Policy," authorized "to investigate all matters relating to the post-war military requirements of the United States; . . . and to report to the House . . . from time to time . . . the results of findings made and conclusions reached." [10]

Wadsworth's resolution was referred to the Rules Committee, whose chairman, Adolph J. Sabath, kept it bottled up until he received assurances from President Roosevelt and from the Secretaries of War and the Navy that they did not object to the investigation being made.[11] The resolution was reported favorably on March 24 and passed the House four days later after being endorsed by Speaker Sam Rayburn, House Minority Leader Joseph Martin, and the chairmen of the Military Affairs and Naval Affairs Committees, Andrew J. May and Carl Vinson.[12] Representative Clifton A. Woodrum was appointed chairman of the Select Committee; its membership included seven representatives each from the Military Affairs and Naval Affairs Committees and nine representatives from the House at large.

The Select Committee on Post-war Military Policy, which became generally known as the Woodrum Committee, began its hearings on April 24. The first matter to which it turned was "Item No. 3" on its tentative agenda: "A study of the development of unity of command as practiced during the present war, with a view to determining to what extent that unity of command and administration may be developed and applied as a part of future military policy." [13] Before calling the first witness, Chairman Woodrum emphasized that his committee was not concerned with considering or reporting specific legislation but that its sole function was to study and to make broad recommendations to the House. Woodrum also stressed that the Committee had "no purpose or intention whatsoever to suggest any organizational change in the military establishment that would affect its operation during the present war. Our concern is purely for the post-war period." [14]

The first witnesses called by the Woodrum Committee were representatives of the War Department. All of them, including the Secretary of War, Henry L. Stimson, spoke of the desirability of a single military department. They also recommended, despite Chairman Woodrum's opening remarks, congressional approval of the "principle" of unification immediately, with the organizational details to be worked out at a "proper time" (not necessarily after the end of the war) within the executive branch.

The War Department witnesses admitted that cooperation between the services had never been better in the history of the country but attributed this harmony, in Secretary Stimson's words, "not to the form of the present organization, but to the personalities of the military leaders, their good will, and their intelligent and devoted efforts, assisted by the pressure of circumstances which furthered their action." [15] The War Department representatives also argued that in any case, despite the good cooperation existing, failure to have a single department during the war was causing "many duplications of time, material, and manpower, with the loss of effectiveness, resources, and power which such duplications inevitably produce." [16]

It should be pointed out that Secretary of War Stimson, knowing, as he put it, "that his friends * the 'well-known Admirals' were strongly opposed to unification" and envisaging a "terrific and acrimonious row over the subject on the Hill and in the press," had not at first been favorably inclined toward letting his department raise the issue before the Woodrum Committee.[17] Stimson "dreaded" the effects on the "unity of our nation" at that stage of the war, and only after he talked to Navy Secretary Frank Knox and discovered "rather to [his] surprise" that Knox was not personally opposed to a single military department did

---

* About his "friends," the admirals, Stimson has written,

"Some of the Army-Navy troubles, in Stimson's view, grew mainly from the peculiar psychology of the Navy Department, which frequently seems to retire from the realm of logic into a dim religious world in which Neptune was God, Mahan his prophet, and the United States Navy was the only true Church. The high priests of this Church were a group of men to whom Stimson always referred as 'the admirals.' These gentlemen were to him both anonymous and continuous; he had met them in 1930 in discussions of the London Naval Treaty; in 1940 and afterwards he found them still active and still uncontrolled by either their Secretary or the President. This was not Knox's fault, or the President's, as Stimson saw it. It was simply that the Navy Department had never had its Elihu Root. 'The admirals' had never been given their comeuppance." Henry L. Stimson and McGeorge Bundy, *On Active Service in Peace and War* (New York, Harper, 1947), p. 507.

Stimson allow the War Department plans for proposing such a development to proceed.[18]

The specific War Department plan for a single military department was presented to the Woodrum Committee on April 25 by the Army Deputy Chief of Staff, Lieutenant General Joseph T. McNarney. It was very similar to the plan Marshall had submitted to the JCS the previous November. It had a Secretary of the Armed Forces presiding over a department consisting of an Army, Navy, and Air Force component and of a separate Common Supply Service. Each of the military services had its own civilian under secretary, while the supply service was under a military "Director." The plan continued a "United States Joint Chiefs of Staff," consisting of a Chief of Staff to the President, a Chief of Staff of the Army, a "Chief of Staff" of the Navy, a Chief of Staff of the Air Force, and the Director of Common Supplies (who was to be in a status subordinate to the other Chiefs). The Chief of Staff to the President would in some unspecified way "head" the Chiefs, who jointly were to have the duty of

submitting recommendations [directly] to the President concerning . . . military strategy and the general determination of budgetary needs. . . . They would also, after final approval of the military budget, recommend to the President the general breakdown or allocation of funds to the several armed services and for common supply.[19] [See Chart 1.]

Although, according to McNarney, "naturally, the appropriated funds will be expended under the direction of the Secretary of the Armed Forces," [20] the civilian Secretary was given no actual means of control over any aspect of the budgetary process. The Secretary was to be the "principal adviser to the President and the Congress on political and administrative matters relating to national defense," and within the department he would be restricted to supervising such activities as procurement, recruitment, public relations, and congressional relations.[21] McNarney concluded his prepared statement by reiterating for the Committee

the importance of securing early congressional action which will prescribe in broad terms the organization and status of the United States Chiefs of Staff, and which will establish the principle of three services within one single Department of the Armed Forces. An essential part of the proposed legislation is that broad authority be granted to make the change in an evolutionary manner. . . . It is likewise essential that this broad question of overall organization be determined as a matter of principle, and that unnecessary involvement in unimportant details be avoided so that they will not confuse or delay a settlement on the overriding issue.[22]

McNarney gave some indication of what he considered "unimportant" during the questioning a few minutes later. When asked what the place of the Navy's Marine Corps would be in the new organization, the General replied, "That is [a] detail of organization which I don't believe I care to comment on at the moment." [23] When another member of the Committee asked whether the new Air Force would include "just the Army Air Forces or if you had in mind the over-all Air Forces [including the Navy's]," McNarney answered,

Personally, I have in mind a considerable consolidation of the existing Air Forces.
Mr. MILLER.   One command of all Air, instead of three as you have now?
General McNARNEY.   That is another detail, and I hesitate to discuss it.[24]

Assistant Secretary of War for Air Robert A. Lovett was the most candid and outspoken of the War Department witnesses. When he came before the Committee on April 26, Lovett made it clear that the Army aviators looked to a separate Air Force that would take over all land-based airplanes in operation, including those then owned and operated by the Navy for long-range reconnaissance, antisubmarine warfare, and the protection of shipping. Lovett also explained that in order to effect "economies," the new Air Force should serve both as the research, procurement, and recruitment agency and as the elementary, primary, and basic flight-training establishment even for the Navy's carrier-based air force.[25] When Lovett was asked whether he thought the Navy should continue to have "a landing force, a fighting army of marines as it has at the present," his answer was, "Well, I haven't given much thought to it, but it seems to me to be a clear duplication of function, unless it can be proven to be so highly specialized as to require segregation." [26]

The Navy Department witnesses began to appear before the Woodrum Committee on April 28. With Secretary Knox critically ill, they were led by their Under Secretary, James V. Forrestal, who told the Congressmen that he was "not prepared to say that the Navy believes that the con-solidation into one department is desirable." [27] The Navy witnesses did not, however, directly oppose unification for the postwar period. Their main line of argument was that the desirability of any particular type of organizational structure—such as a single military department or a sepa-

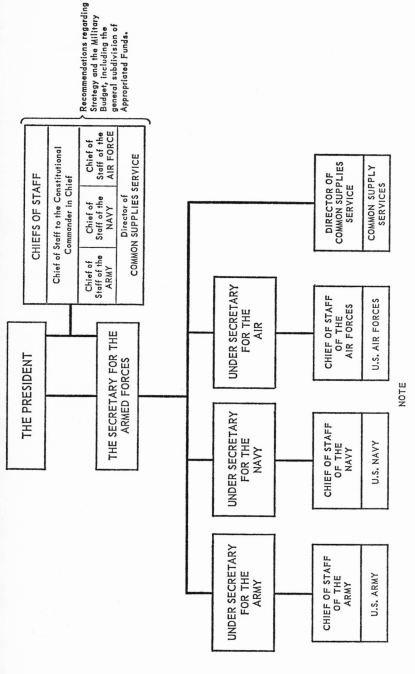

NOTE

Under the proposed reorganization the Chiefs of Staff would have the statutory duty to make recommendations direct to the President in his capacity as Commander-In-Chief regarding matters pertaining to strategy* and the budgetary requirements involved, as indicated on the chart. The Chiefs of Staff would obtain the information regarding budgetary requirements by request to the Secretary of the Armed Forces and they would be required to furnish him with copies of their recommendations to the President in order that he may be prepared to exercise his duty as adviser to the President. Communications in all other matters would be channeled through and would be subject to the direction of the Secretary of the Armed Forces.

*By "strategy" is meant the military posture and preparations of the United States in times of peace.

CHART 1. THE MCNARNEY PLAN.

rate air force—could not simply be assumed. They believed, in Forrestal's words,

that the whole question of military organization deserves, and should receive an objective and thorough study. [The Navy] believes that the question should be approached by detailed examination with the conclusion to be reached at the end of such an examination rather than acting upon the assumption that the case is already established. Personally, I do not believe it is.[28]

The only thing that Forrestal and the other Navy witnesses definitely opposed during the hearings was any organizational change being made before the end of the war. They stressed the complicated nature of impending military operations that might be disrupted by any change.[29] Forrestal also warned the Committee that any attempt to pass legislation at that time "would inevitably be attended by extensive debate" and expressed doubt whether Congress would want to take any action without hearing the views of the various high-ranking field commanders who obviously could not be called away from fighting the war in order to testify.[30]

For the rest of their testimony, the Navy witnesses simply staked out claims for the Navy, raised questions about (but without opposing) the Army plan, and denied certain allegations of fact made by the War Department witnesses. When, for example, Assistant Secretary of the Navy Artemus L. Gates testified on May 15, without referring to Lovett's statements, Gates claimed for the Navy the right to use whatever aircraft, including land-based types, it deemed necessary to carry out its assigned tasks.[31] When the various bureau-chief admirals testified, they denied that any facilities or weapons development programs maintained by the Navy were wasteful or were unnecessarily duplicating any other service. They also denied that, if such duplications actually existed, they could be cured by overall organizational change.[32]

Some of the most pointed Navy queries were directed against the McNarney plan's placing budgetary control in the hands of the Joint Chiefs. Secretary Forrestal just "wondered," for example, "whether the Congress would want the preparation of the Budget to flow solely from a military authority? I do not know. I just raise that question. It runs somewhat counter to our concept, I think, of government." [33] Similarly, Assistant Secretary Gates reminded the Committee that Congress had seen fit to lodge control over funds "in civilian hands for over 150 years." Gates could, therefore, "not favor such a radical change" as that proposed by McNarney.[34]

The Navy's final objections were over the consolidation of the Military Affairs and Naval Affairs Committees that was likely to take place in Congress in the event of unification. In response to a direct question, Secretary Forrestal expressed

some misgivings . . . on the question of whether you get, in a single committee, the advocacy you might need. Take the Navy, the very point you raised. It would depend upon how that committee was weighted and at the conclusions reached if it were in the direction of cutting down of the Navy. It seems to me that we would be deprived of very valuable assistance which we have had from the Naval Affairs Committee in presenting our case [before Congress].[35]

It should be noted that two witnesses with Navy affiliations did testify in favor of a postwar single military department during these hearings. Josephus Daniels, Woodrow Wilson's Secretary of the Navy, and retired Admiral H. E. Yarnell, Commander in Chief of the Asiatic Station from 1926 until 1939, both endorsed unification generally,[36] with the Admiral presenting his own unification plan, previously published in the *U.S. Naval Institute Proceedings*,[37] which kept the Marines and naval aviation within the Navy. Budget Director Harold D. Smith also submitted a long statement to the Committee in which he favored generally a single department but not a separate air force,[38] pointing out, however, that "the degree of civilian influence in and control over the military establishment" would be greatly affected by whether the overall department resembled the War or the Navy Department in its internal structure.[39]

Throughout the Woodrum Committee hearings (and indeed until his death ten months later), the person formally most concerned with military organization, the Commander in Chief, President Franklin D. Roosevelt, did not take any public position on the unification issue. The day after Budget Director Smith's statement favoring unification was inserted into the record of the hearings, the Washington *Post* speculated that Smith's position might have enjoyed Presidential support, since Smith had in the past broken ground for Roosevelt on controversial matters.[40] The New York *Times,* on the other hand, had reported a few days earlier that some Washingtonians thought it was the President who had inspired the Navy's opposition, which started just after Roosevelt returned to Washington from a southern vacation.[41] The President's wartime Chief of Staff, Admiral Leahy, has since given his opinion that Roosevelt was never privately "in favor either of a unification of the armed forces, or of an independent air force separate from the Army and Navy." [42] There is also a brief note in Secretary of War Stimson's diary dated about a week before the end of the hearings,[43] which reports Marshall telling Stimson that it appeared "the President was siding against us on this consolidation of departments" and that the Navy was consequently "running wild." *

Most of the members of the Woodrum Committee also remained noncommittal during the hearings. Only Representative Wadsworth, who had introduced the resolution setting up the Committee, was clearly in favor of unification.[44] Chairman Woodrum intimated that the wisdom of a single department had been proven by the war but allowed that there could be questions about its detailed form and about when it should be established.[45] Vinson, another member of the Committee and the Chairman of the House Naval Affairs Committee, announced that he too was in favor of unification "in principle" but that he could not understand how the Army's plan promoted unification when it further split the armed forces by creating a separate air force as a third military service.[46] Vinson questioned many of the War Department witnesses on

---

* It would, of course, have been completely out of character with Roosevelt's more general method of "competitive administration" to approve any setting up of a single officer such as a Secretary of Defense or a single Chief of Staff to coordinate an important area of policy at a level below the President and thus possibly preclude him from having access to all the relevant information and alternative lines of action. As Schlesinger has explained,

"The first task of an executive, as [Roosevelt] evidently saw it, was to guarantee himself an effective flow of information and ideas. . . . An executive relying on a single information system became inevitably the prisoner of that system. . . . Given this conception of the Presidency, he deliberately organized—or disorganized—his system of command to insure that important decisions were passed on to the top. His favorite technique was to keep grants of authority incomplete, jurisdictions uncertain, charters overlapping. The result of this competitive theory of administration was often confusion and exasperation on the operating level; but no other method could so reliably insure that in a large bureaucracy filled with ambitious men eager for power the decisions, and the power to make them, would remain with the President."

Schlesinger reports Roosevelt observing that there was "something to be said . . . for having a little conflict between agencies. A little rivalry is stimulating, you know. It keeps everybody going to prove that he is a better fellow than the next man." Arthur M. Schlesinger, Jr., *The Age of Roosevelt.* Vol. II: *The Coming of the New Deal* (Boston, Houghton, Mifflin, 1958), pp. 522–23, 527–28, 535.

Actually, Roosevelt had to be pressed even into appointing Admiral Leahy as his personal Chief of Staff to act as a liaison man with the JCS in the early part of the war. When asked during the news conference announcing Leahy's appointment whether the Admiral was to become the overall commander or chief of staff of the armed forces that was being demanded at the time in some quarters, Roosevelt pointedly reminded the questioner that he was still the only Commander in Chief and that Leahy would be only a sort of "leg-man" to help him digest, analyze, and summarize the mass of material on military matters that he had been trying to handle all by himself. William D. Leahy, *I Was There: The Personal Story of the Chief of Staff to Presidents Roosevelt and Truman* (New York, McGraw-Hill, 1950), pp. 119–20.

this point, and the following exchange with Brigadier General H. S. Hansell, the Deputy Chief of the Air Staff and the highest Army Air Forces officer to testify, illustrates the Congressman's purported perplexity:

Mr. VINSON. [Do] you think that unity can be brought about by a merging together of the two armed services in their entirety, the Army and the Navy?

General HANSELL. No, sir; I do not.

Mr. VINSON. You think the unity can only be brought about by further division?

General HANSELL. Yes, sir; I do.

Mr. VINSON. Then, the only way you can attain unity is by further cutting up one of the armed services? [47]

The Woodrum Committee closed its hearings on the single department question on May 19. Earlier, on April 28, a few days after Knox's death, Forrestal had gotten in touch with Stimson and tried to get him to use his influence with the Committee to have the hearings stopped then. Forrestal's line of argument appears to have been that pressing for any kind of immediate decision on unification before the Committee was creating acrimony and great bitterness between the services and could injure interservice coordination and military effectiveness at a time when major joint operations, such as the invasion of northern Europe, were imminent.[48] Since it had become "at once apparent" even to Stimson that "the hearings might become a free-for-all in which nothing but bitterness would be produced," the Secretary of War agreed to talk to Chairman Woodrum.[49] Woodrum refused to cut off the hearings, reportedly because he felt that "the public and the press wouldn't possibly understand any cessation of the meetings." [50]

Some kind of agreement was reached, however, in a conference on May 5 among Stimson, Forrestal, Woodrum, and Representatives May and Vinson, the chairmen of the House Military and Naval Affairs Committees and two of the Woodrum Committee's leading members, whereby the hearings were to continue, but the War Department would cease to argue for an immediate decision in favor of the principle of a single department, and the Navy, in exchange, would restrict itself chiefly to urging the need for further study and not attack the Army plan in detail. Woodrum, on his part, agreed to request his Committee not to ask any more controversial questions but to confine themselves to listening to the prepared statements presented, a request that was not completely followed.[51]

When the Woodrum Committee submitted its formal report to the

House the following month, it was in accord with the May 5 agreement. The short report, which was unanimous, simply summarized the hearings and concluded on this note:

The committee does not believe that the time is opportune to consider detailed legislation which would undertake to write the pattern of any proposed consolidation, if indeed such consolidation is ultimately decided to be a wise course of action. The committee feels that many lessons are being learned in this war, and that many more lessons will be learned before the shooting stops, and that before any final pattern for a reorganization of the services should be acted upon, Congress should have the benefit of the wise judgment and experience of many of the commanders in the field.[52]

The Woodrum Committee's report also noted the establishment of the Richardson Committee and indicated that Congress would expect to receive its findings.[53]

After the Navy's tactical victory in the Woodrum Committee hearings, many high naval officers in Washington apparently were ready to dismiss once and for all any further possibility of unification being adopted. Forrestal was not so optimistic: writing to Vinson on August 30, 1944, the Secretary indicated that he did "not think for a moment we can take this [question of a single Department of Defense] lightly, and I have so told Admiral King." [54]

The Richardson Committee Report[55]

The Richardson Committee, whose members had been appointed in May, wasted little time. It began meeting in June and continued to meet regularly throughout the summer. By October it had gathered the opinions of most of the high military officers in Washington. In November and December it visited the European, Mediterranean, and Pacific theaters of operations to obtain the views of the principal field commanders, their subordinates, and their staffs. During these travels, the Committee interviewed, among others, Generals MacArthur, Eisenhower, Clark, Bradley, Kenny, and Spaatz and Admirals Nimitz, Halsey, Stark, Spruance, and Kinkaid.

On April 11, 1945, the Richardson Committee reported to the JCS that "excepting its senior naval member [Admiral Richardson]," it was "unanimously in favor of a single department system of organization of the armed forces of the United States." It claimed that its view was shared by MacArthur, Eisenhower, Nimitz, and Halsey, by "the great majority of Army officers and almost exactly half of the Navy officers" interviewed in the field, and by "many" officers in Washington. The Committee did admit, however, that "strong differences of opinion" existed with respect to the details of the organization.

The plan recommended by the Richardson Committee, while obviously meant to be a compromise between the views of the War and Navy Departments, was quite radical. It provided a Secretary of the Armed Forces to head the overall department but no civilian secretaries, under secretaries, or assistant secretaries for the Army, the Navy, or the separate Air Force component that it also recommended. The Air Force, incidentally, was specifically to include only

that aviation which is not an integral part of the land forces or of the sea forces, . . . at the present stage of development of naval warfare and within the foreseeable future, . . . naval aviation as presently constituted, should be an integral and essential part of the sea forces.

With respect to the departmental chain of command, the Committee called for a single Commander of the Armed Forces and an Armed Forces Staff to be in charge of strategic planning and to direct military operations in the field. The Commander was also to be Chief of Staff to the President and, on strategic and operational matters, responsible only to him. The Secretary, on the other hand, would advise the President "on the political, economic, and industrial aspects of military problems" and would be responsible for "administration" and for the preparation and justification of the departmental budget. The civilian Secretary, the Commander, and the chiefs of the three military services were to constitute a "United States Chiefs of Staff," who would advise the President only "on broad matters of military strategy and on the overall estimated expenditures showing the amounts required by each major component of the armed forces." The plan's Chiefs, as opposed to the Joint Chiefs to which the Richardson Committee was reporting, were to have no operational authority at all, since this was reserved for the Armed Forces Commander.

To help the Secretary of the Armed Forces, the Richardson Committee recommended one civilian under secretary to run the "business side" of the department with duties mainly in the fields of procurement and industrial mobilization. It also recommended an unspecified number of assistant secretaries for such matters as personnel, public relations, and congressional relations. Finally, the Committee thought that a council ought to be created within the executive branch, consisting of the Secretary and Under Secretary of State and the Secretary of the Armed Forces and the Armed Forces Commander, "to realistically equate, unify and correlate national policy with military preparedness as well as to recommend to the President the national strategy to attain national objectives." (See Chart 2.)

It should be pointed out that the Committee considered as an essential part of its plan that certain "basic agreements" be incorporated into the enacting legislation, guaranteeing that the existing status of naval aviation and of the Fleet Marine Force could not be changed within the ten years subsequent to the enactment of the legislation without the unanimous agreement of the U.S. Chiefs of Staff and the approval of the President. Thereafter, changes could be made by the Armed Forces Commander with the approval of the Secretary of the Armed Forces.

Richardson wrote a short minority report. The Admiral thought that the existing two-department system with the JCS established by statute to insure their continuity after the war and with the possible addition of a "Joint Secretaryship" was the most satisfactory organizational solution for the foreseeable future. Richardson did not think that the lessons of the war were yet sufficiently clear to justify changing an organization that was the result "of over 150 years' experience." Richardson also indicated that many of the key officers interviewed had told the Committee that they had been unable to give sufficient study to the subject of unification, because they were too busy fighting the war, thus implying that their views may not have been considered ones.

Among Admiral Richardson's specific objections to the plan advanced by the majority were that it was unwise to concentrate such great powers in the hands of the Secretary of the Armed Forces and the Armed Forces Commander, that the full development of both the Army and the Navy would be hampered by being placed in the single department, and that the creation of a separate air force would inevitably "draw the naval aeronautical organization out of the fabric of the Navy into which it is now intimately woven" and "be prejudicial to the effectiveness of the armed forces as a whole." Richardson did admit that "if those in authority" decided to establish a single department system, he could think of no better plan than that proposed by the Special Committee's majority.

The JCS could not agree on the report of their special committee,

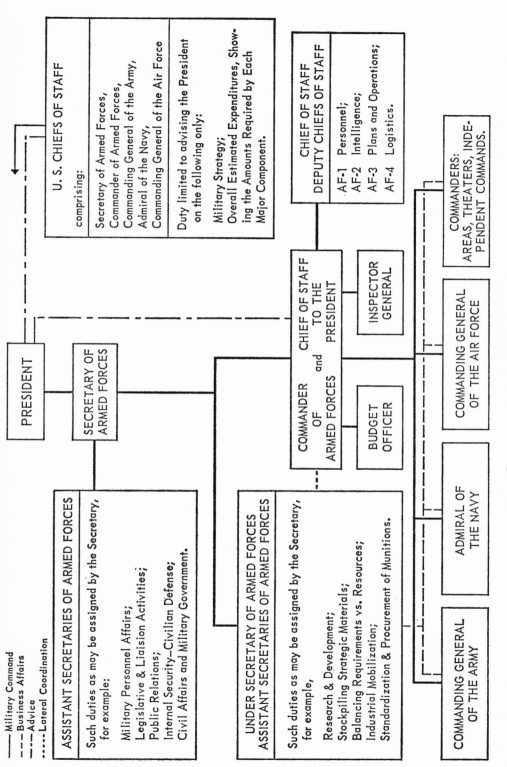

CHART 2. THE RICHARDSON COMMITTEE PLAN.

and consequently no action was taken on it until September, when the war was over. Marshall and Arnold continued to press for agreement on the principle of a single department before the report was sent to President Truman. Leahy and King would not agree to this, so on October 16, 1945, the JCS forwarded the Richardson Committee report to the President with their four sets of individual views.[56] This final disagreement prevented the JCS as a body from having determinative or even major influence on the form of the organizational structure that was eventually adopted. The following day, October 17, the Senate Military Affairs Committee began hearings on bills proposing a single Department of the Armed Forces.

Forrestal and the Eberstadt Report

As early as September, 1944, when the Richardson Committee was still interviewing people in Washington, Secretary of the Navy James Forrestal had become convinced that Congress and the public had already become converted to the idea of a single military department.[57] "I have been telling King, Nimitz and Company," he wrote to a friend, "that as of today the Navy has lost its case, and that either in Congress or in a public poll the Army's point of view would prevail." [58] But with a kind of tacit truce in effect while the Richardson Committee was conducting its investigations, Forrestal largely marked time for the rest of the year.

By the spring of 1945 it must have become clear to Forrestal that vigorous action would again have to be taken to defend the Navy's position. The Richardson Committee had made its long-awaited report, which was found unacceptable by the Navy. On April 12, President Roosevelt died, shattering the conviction no doubt held by most Navy leaders that as long as that former Assistant Secretary of the Navy was in the White House, no military reorganization seriously damaging to the Navy's fortunes would be approved. Just six days after Roosevelt's death, Forrestal and Admiral King went to the White House to discuss various matters with President Truman. Truman not only did not have Roosevelt's Navy background, but as the vice-presidential nominee the previous summer, he had published a magazine article strongly in favor of unification.[59] Forrestal began to try to "educate" the new President, suggesting that "he reread the [anti-unification] Morrow Board Report with the thought that this form might be followed in the study of consolidating the two Services." [60]

About three weeks later, on May 9, Forrestal arranged a lunch at his house for Admiral King, General Marshall, and Harry Hopkins "to explore with King and Marshall the possibility of the Army and Navy reaching an agreement as to the form of our postwar national defense." Forrestal thought that it was not "a very wise use of our time to be conducting a debate between the Army and Navy on this question." Marshall agreed with Forrestal on that point, but since the General remained "unshakably committed to the thesis of a single civilian Secretary with a single military Chief of Staff," no meeting of the minds took place.[61]

On May 15, 1945, Senator David I. Walsh, the Chairman of the Senate Naval Affairs Committee and a long-time friend and protector of the Navy Department, wrote to Forrestal to suggest a new tack for the Navy to take in the unification conflict. Walsh doubted very much, he explained, whether under the circumstances "any useful purpose would be served by merely objecting to plans which propose the consolidation of the War and Navy Departments." It seemed to him that those who thought that such a consolidation would not be effective should formulate a better alternative plan. "If," Walsh continued, "we discard an 'either/or' logic, we may find it is not necessary or desirable to either consolidate the War and Navy Departments into a Department of National Defense, or let them remain entirely separated as they were before the war." Walsh suggested that Forrestal have the Navy Department make a "thorough study" of the reorganization problem to determine, for example, whether the establishment of a "Council on National Defense" along the lines of Great Britain's Committee of Imperial Defense might not provide a suitable alternative to the single-department proposal.[62]

Forrestal agreed completely. He replied to Walsh the following week that Walsh's point of view corresponded substantially to what was in his own mind, "namely, that the Navy Department cannot be in the position of merely taking the negative in this discussion, but on the contrary must come up with positive and constructive recommendations." [63] To get these recommendations, Forrestal commissioned Ferdinand Eberstadt, former chairman of the Army-Navy Munitions Board and a former vice-chairman of the War Production Board. Although it was Forrestal who had been instrumental in originally bringing Eberstadt to Washington and the two men had been close friends since college days and business associates for a time, Eberstadt was not considered an extreme Navy partisan by the War Department, and he enjoyed the respect of many of its top officials.* In a letter to Eberstadt on June 19, 1945, Forrestal asked him to make a study and prepare a report with recommendations on the following questions:

1. Would unification of the War and Navy Departments under a single head improve our national security?
2. If not, what changes in the present relationships of the military services and departments has our war experience indicated as desirable to improve our national security?
3. What form of postwar organization should be established and maintained to enable the military services and other Government departments and agencies most effectively to provide for and protect our national security? [64]

Eberstadt was provided with a staff of about thirty, most of whom were naval reserve officers on active duty.[65] By September 25, he turned out a three-volume report of some 250 pages. Two of the volumes were background studies of such subjects as the military conduct of the war, industrial mobilization, procurement and logistics, science and the armed services, past unification proposals, the history of military air power, and organizational trends within the War and Navy Departments. The first volume was the report proper and stated Eberstadt's conclusions and recommendations.

Eberstadt's answers to Forrestal's three questions could be summarized as follows:

1. There is no evidence that unification would improve our national security. The unification plans recently advanced fail to meet the "presently urgent military need" for reforms within each of the War and Navy Departments and

---

* Eberstadt has related that when approached about making the report, he asked Forrestal, "Do you want an advocacy of the Navy's position or do you want a study of this question, letting the chips fall where they may?" When Forrestal said, "Let them fall where they may," Eberstadt answered, "All right, I will do it." 1946 Hearings, p. 181.

Eberstadt has also recalled that before agreeing finally to make the study, he paid courtesy calls on Chairmen Walsh and Vinson of the Senate and House Naval Affairs Committees. Vinson reportedly asked Eberstadt, "What do you know about the subject?" to which Eberstadt replied, "Nothing." Vinson then asked, "Why did Forrestal pick you?" Eberstadt answered, "That's what I've been asking myself," at which point Vinson commented, "You'll be all right. You don't know all the answers already." (Interview with Eberstadt.)

also fail to provide "stronger organizational ties" between the military services and the other parts of the government concerned with national security.

2. Our war experience has revealed serious defects of coordination, especially between the State Department and the military departments and between the Joint Chiefs of Staff and the military and civilian agencies responsible for industrial mobilization. These weaknesses call for institutionalizing desirable lines of coordination within the existing system and not for "dangerous experiments" like unification.

3. The following form of postwar organization should be established to protect our national security: the existing Departments of War and the Navy should be continued with a cabinet Department of Air added to absorb that aviation presently under control of the Army Air Forces; the JCS should be continued, have their responsibilities defined by statute to include primarily strategic planning and direction of military forces, and be provided with a full-time subordinate Joint Staff; to coordinate all these elements and to integrate them with other relevant governmental agencies, two new major bodies should be constituted—a National Security Council (NSC) and a National Security Resources Board (NSRB). The NSC, consisting of the President as chairman, the Secretaries of State, War, the Navy, and Air, and the chairman of the NSRB (with the JCS "in attendance" and with its own permanent secretariat), would formulate and coordinate overall policies in foreign and military affairs and advise on the combined military budget; the NSRB would formulate and be prepared to implement plans and programs for industrial mobilization; a Central Intelligence Agency should also be constituted to coordinate national security intelligence; finally, certain other bodies should be constituted to coordinate military procurement and logistics, scientific research and development, and military education and training.[66] [See Chart 3.]

Eberstadt also recommended that the President or Congress or both acting jointly establish a commission to make a still more comprehensive study of all problems of national security including military organization.[67]

The Eberstadt Report thus reflected what had come to be Forrestal's and Walsh's central views: that apart from coordinating strictly military matters there be some institutionalized manner of consciously integrating military policy with all aspects of high-level foreign policy. Although rejecting the concept of a single Secretary of Defense in favor of superdepartmental coordinating committees and denying the JCS control over the budget, the Report did go beyond the authoritative Navy Department position of the time by recommending a separate Department of Air. The Eberstadt Report was well received. According to Arthur Hays Sulzberger, publisher of the New York *Times,* which was strongly backing the Army plan for unification, the Report made "definite prog-

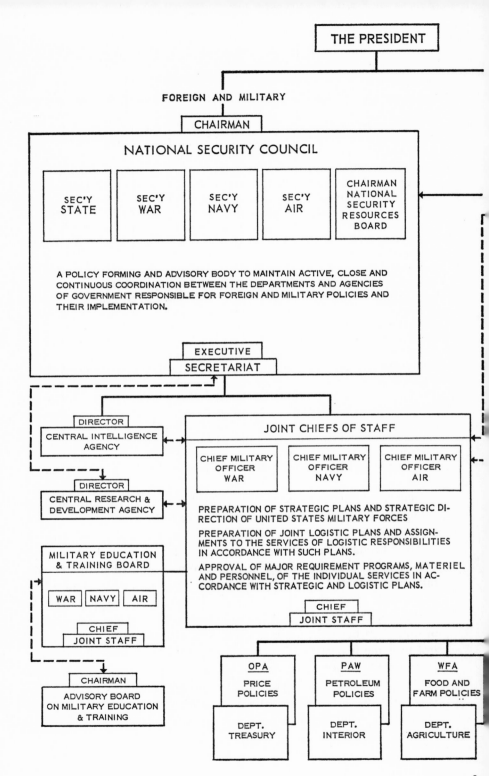

THE PRESIDENT

FOREIGN AND MILITARY

CHAIRMAN

NATIONAL SECURITY COUNCIL

| SEC'Y STATE | SEC'Y WAR | SEC'Y NAVY | SEC'Y AIR | CHAIRMAN NATIONAL SECURITY RESOURCES BOARD |

A POLICY FORMING AND ADVISORY BODY TO MAINTAIN ACTIVE, CLOSE AND CONTINUOUS COORDINATION BETWEEN THE DEPARTMENTS AND AGENCIES OF GOVERNMENT RESPONSIBLE FOR FOREIGN AND MILITARY POLICIES AND THEIR IMPLEMENTATION.

EXECUTIVE SECRETARIAT

DIRECTOR CENTRAL INTELLIGENCE AGENCY

DIRECTOR CENTRAL RESEARCH & DEVELOPMENT AGENCY

MILITARY EDUCATION & TRAINING BOARD

WAR | NAVY | AIR

CHIEF JOINT STAFF

CHAIRMAN
ADVISORY BOARD ON MILITARY EDUCATION & TRAINING

JOINT CHIEFS OF STAFF

| CHIEF MILITARY OFFICER WAR | CHIEF MILITARY OFFICER NAVY | CHIEF MILITARY OFFICER AIR |

PREPARATION OF STRATEGIC PLANS AND STRATEGIC DIRECTION OF UNITED STATES MILITARY FORCES

PREPARATION OF JOINT LOGISTIC PLANS AND ASSIGNMENTS TO THE SERVICES OF LOGISTIC RESPONSIBILITIES IN ACCORDANCE WITH SUCH PLANS.

APPROVAL OF MAJOR REQUIREMENT PROGRAMS, MATERIEL AND PERSONNEL, OF THE INDIVIDUAL SERVICES IN ACCORDANCE WITH STRATEGIC AND LOGISTIC PLANS.

CHIEF JOINT STAFF

| OPA PRICE POLICIES | PAW PETROLEUM POLICIES | WFA FOOD AND FARM POLICIES |
| DEPT. TREASURY | DEPT. INTERIOR | DEPT. AGRICULTURE |

CHART 3.

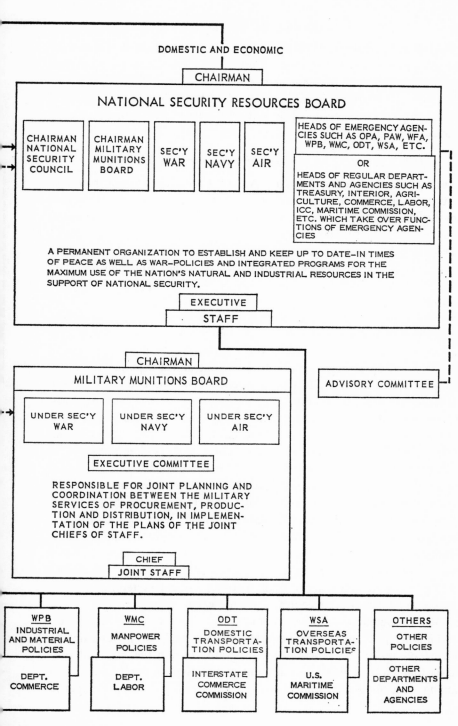

DOMESTIC AND ECONOMIC

CHAIRMAN

NATIONAL SECURITY RESOURCES BOARD

CHAIRMAN NATIONAL SECURITY COUNCIL

CHAIRMAN MILITARY MUNITIONS BOARD

SEC'Y WAR

SEC'Y NAVY

SEC'Y AIR

HEADS OF EMERGENCY AGENCIES SUCH AS OPA, PAW, WFA, WPB, WMC, ODT, WSA, ETC.

OR

HEADS OF REGULAR DEPARTMENTS AND AGENCIES SUCH AS TREASURY, INTERIOR, AGRICULTURE, COMMERCE, LABOR, ICC, MARITIME COMMISSION, ETC. WHICH TAKE OVER FUNCTIONS OF EMERGENCY AGENCIES

A PERMANENT ORGANIZATION TO ESTABLISH AND KEEP UP TO DATE–IN TIMES OF PEACE AS WELL AS WAR–POLICIES AND INTEGRATED PROGRAMS FOR THE MAXIMUM USE OF THE NATION'S NATURAL AND INDUSTRIAL RESOURCES IN THE SUPPORT OF NATIONAL SECURITY.

EXECUTIVE STAFF

CHAIRMAN

MILITARY MUNITIONS BOARD

UNDER SEC'Y WAR

UNDER SEC'Y NAVY

UNDER SEC'Y AIR

EXECUTIVE COMMITTEE

RESPONSIBLE FOR JOINT PLANNING AND COORDINATION BETWEEN THE MILITARY SERVICES OF PROCUREMENT, PRODUCTION AND DISTRIBUTION, IN IMPLEMENTATION OF THE PLANS OF THE JOINT CHIEFS OF STAFF.

CHIEF JOINT STAFF

ADVISORY COMMITTEE

WPB INDUSTRIAL AND MATERIAL POLICIES	WMC MANPOWER POLICIES	ODT DOMESTIC TRANSPORTATION POLICIES	WSA OVERSEAS TRANSPORTATION POLICIES	OTHERS OTHER POLICIES
DEPT. COMMERCE	DEPT. LABOR	INTERSTATE COMMERCE COMMISSION	U.S. MARITIME COMMISSION	OTHER DEPARTMENTS AND AGENCIES

HE EBERSTADT PLAN.

ress with the public in . . . dissipating the idea of [the Navy's] merely stubborn opposition to the merger and . . . succeeded in showing that it was a much deeper problem than simply the merger of the two Cabinet offices." [68] In fact, a great many of Eberstadt's recommendations were to appear in the National Security Act when unification was finally enacted in 1947.

1945 Senate Military Affairs Committee Hearings

As noted, the Senate Military Affairs Committee began hearings on two unification bills on October 17, 1945. It was then only a few months after the end of the war in the Pacific, and the wartime members of the JCS, the famous field commanders, and the other high-ranking combat commanders and staff officers were still at the height of their popularity and prestige. Almost all of them—Marshall, Arnold, King, Leahy, Eisenhower, Nimitz, Halsey, Bradley, Spaatz—were sent by their departments to testify during these hearings. The bills purportedly under consideration were S.84, introduced by Senator Lister Hill the previous January, and S.1482, introduced by Senators Edwin C. Johnson and Harley M. Kilgore two days before the hearings began.[69] Both bills set up a single military department and a separate air force and gave broad authority to the President and to the overall Secretary to determine detailed structure; they differed slightly on the internal organization of the overall department. As it turned out, these bills were ignored during the hearings and were hardly mentioned even by their sponsors, who were all members of the Military Affairs Committee.

The first two witnesses to appear before the Committee were Secretary of War Patterson, who had recently succeeded Stimson as head of the War Department, and General Marshall.[70] Their approach—followed by the other War Department witnesses—was to refer to allegedly unsatisfactory aspects of the wartime organization, to predict that even its satisfactory aspects could not continue during peacetime, and to assert that reorganization into a single military department would cure all the existing and potential defects of the two-department system.

Secretary Patterson concentrated on the economy argument when he testified on October 17. He spoke of "waste" and of "cases of conflict, overlapping, and duplication between the War and Navy Departments in vital phases of the procurement program" during the war and predicted that "with a single Department of the Armed Forces, the overlapping . . . should be eliminated." [71] Patterson guessed, in response to a question, that "billions of dollars" would have been saved had a single department been in existence in World War II but admitted that he "would have a hard time proving any particular figure. It is always . . . an educated guess." [72]

Marshall came before the Committee the following day and devoted much of his testimony to the operation of the JCS. He mentioned that "numerous compromises" and "long delays" were involved at times in reaching unanimous agreement within the JCS and concluded that the Chiefs did not provide "an effective substitute for . . . necessary unified direction." Marshall went on to explain that

Committees at best are cumbersome agencies, especially when the membership owes loyalty and advancement to chiefs installed in completely separate governmental departments. Local service enthusiasms become a source of weakness instead of a source of strength. Resulting diversity of opinions, common to Americans on almost all subjects, present increasing difficulties.[73]

Marshall admitted that the level of voluntary cooperation reached between the Army and Navy in operational matters near the end of the war equaled anything that could be expected under unification. He simply did not believe that under the existing system that degree of cooperation could continue in peacetime, when the stress of war no longer compelled the reaching of agreement on at least major problems and the key decisions would become the allocations of limited funds. General Marshall would not completely eliminate the JCS but would restrict them to the role of periodic advisers to the President on the budget and other major matters.[74] When Marshall was asked whether he thought victory would have come sooner if a single department had been set up and operating by 1939, he replied,

That is quite a difficult question to answer, Senator. I think that I would have had fewer gray hairs, and that in our early build-up we would have been able to proceed with less confusion and more celerity than we did. It is possible, I think it is probable that we might have achieved victory at a little earlier date, but the main benefit would have come in the balanced development of the armed forces during the period that we were all struggling so desperately to create power.[75]

Both Patterson and Marshall directed their most bitter criticisms against what was, in Marshall's words, "the present system, or lack of system," under which "two separate executive departments compete for annual appropriations," and each asserts its independent viewpoint before separate committees and subcommittees of the Congress. And each tends to seek the maximum appropriations for itself. Such a procedure offers no assurance that each dollar appropriated buys the largest measure of protection for the Nation.

The National Security is a single problem, and it cannot be provided for on a piecemeal basis. The Congress should have the opportunity of passing on a balanced program that makes provision at one and the same time for all the needs of the armed forces.[76]

Patterson and Marshall also urged the Committee to take rapid action in favor of the principle of a single department and not to let "the great objectives of unification . . . be obscured by a cloud of details." [77]

Lieutenant General J. Lawton Collins presented the War Department's specific proposals to the Military Affairs Committee on October 30. Collins was the spokesman for a group of senior Army officers who had attempted to prepare a plan incorporating both the views of Marshall and those of the Richardson Committee majority. Collins brought along an organizational chart but did not dwell at any length on its details. The "Collins Plan," as it became known, provided a cabinet-level Secretary to head a Department of the Armed Forces and a Chief of Staff of the Armed Forces to be the Secretary's "principal military adviser and executive." The Chief of Staff was shown on the chart in the chain of command between the Secretary, on the one hand, and the military chiefs of the Army, Navy, and separate Air Force, the theater field commanders, and the military "Director of Common Supply and Hospitalization" (who was to have charge of the procurement of common supply items like food and blankets and to supervise military hospitals), on the other. As in the Richardson Committee's proposal, there were no civilian under secretaries or assistant secretaries provided for the three military services, since, according to General Collins, it was "believed that the military staffs can administer the military components." [78] The Secretary of the Armed Forces was, however, given one overall under secretary and three "functional" assistant secretaries to coordinate the activities of the three components in the fields of scientific research and development, procurement and industrial mobilization, and legislative affairs and public relations. (See Chart 4.)

The Collins Plan retained the membership of the wartime JCS with the addition of the new Chief of Staff of the Armed Forces. These Chiefs were to have the right by law to formulate "recommendations only as to military policy, strategy, and budget requirements," to be submitted

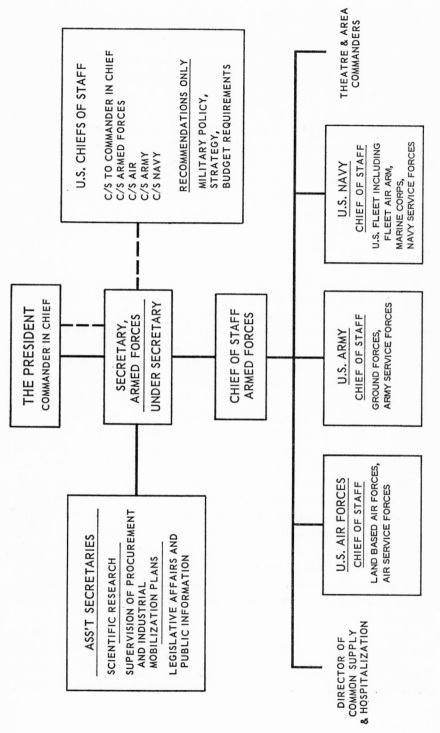

CHART 4. THE COLLINS PLAN.

"through the Secretary of the Armed Forces, who would be required to transmit them without modification to the President, together with his comments thereon." [79] The nonconcurring views of any of the Chiefs on budgetary matters would also go to the President in the same manner.[80] Collins' remarks and his chart did not agree with respect to directing the field commanders: although the chart showed them directly under the Chief of Staff of the Armed Forces, suggesting that he alone would control operations in the field, Collins denied in his statement that the Chief would have a large operating staff (something Marshall was known to be against) and maintained that the individual service chiefs would continue to act as "executive agents" for the JCS and carry out the JCS directives with their own service's operational staff.[81]

Collins assured the Committee that the War Department did not want to merge the Army and Navy into a single service and that each of these services and the new Air Force could retain maximum operating autonomy within the limits of the policies laid down at the new department echelon.[82] Collins further affirmed that there was no danger of the Navy losing its fleet air force or the Marines, although he insisted that all land-based aircraft, including the Navy's, should go to the separate Air Force. As a protection against the overall department being dominated by the views of any one service, Collins' plan provided that the Chief of Staff to the President (continuing the functions performed by Admiral Leahy) and the Chief of Staff of the Armed Forces could not be from the same service at any one time; [83] Collins also gave it as his personal opinion that both those posts should be rotated among the three services.[84]

All the Army Air Forces generals warmly endorsed unification during the hearings. They devoted most of their testimony, however, to reviewing in considerable detail the wartime exploits of "air power" (which they equated with the operations of the Army Air Forces) and to expressing their conviction that the past performance and future capabilities of the airplane justified giving its users an organizational home at least equal in status with the ground Army and the Navy. According to the moderate point of view of the wartime Chief of the Army Air Forces, General Arnold,

No one can doubt that the third element—the air—will henceforth be that from which war first comes. The warfare of the air, when it comes, cannot be auxiliary to ground or naval warfare. It can and probably will occur hundreds or thousands of miles from any ground or naval operation. Control of the air no longer means control of the air over advancing troops or ships (though that limited form of control is essential to successful ground or naval operations). It means control of the air over our own country and, probably, control of the air over an aggressor's country. Establishment of that control is no auxiliary operation. It must be the responsibility, under unified direction, of [a separate] air arm built, armed, and trained to that end.[85]

Holding to this conception of future warfare, the Army aviators went on to argue that the Air Force had replaced the Navy as the country's "first line of defense." [86] Indeed, one of the most strident of the Air Force advocates, Lieutenant General James H. Doolittle, strongly suggested that the Air Force would soon become or had already become the country's *only* necessary line of defense. As Doolittle provocatively put it,

The Navy had the transport to make the invasion of Japan possible; the Ground Forces had the power to make it successful; and the B-29 made it unnecessary. . . . I feel that the battleship has been obsolescent for the past 20 years, and obsolete for the last 10.

The carrier has reached, probably, its highest degree of development. I feel that it has reached its highest usefulness now and that it is going into obsolescence

The carrier has two attributes. One attribute is that it can move about; the other is that it can be sunk.

As soon as airplanes are developed with sufficient range so that they can go any place that we want them to go, or when we have bases that will permit us to go any place we want to go, there will be no further use for aircraft carriers.[87]

It was this kind of testimony that caused the New York *Times* to comment, "Ever since V-J Day the gloves have been discarded, and what is happening on Capitol Hill is but the beginning of what will be a brass-knuckle fight to the finish." [88]

Forrestal was the first witness to present the Navy's case to the Military Affairs Committee. He was there, he assured the chairman on October 22, not "simply in opposition to unification of the War and Navy Departments," but also "to present a comprehensive and dynamic program to save and strengthen our national security." Forrestal thought that the pending unification proposals did not provide such a program, because they failed to deal with the problems within each of the military departments and because they also failed to give attention to "the immediate integration necessary—that of the War, Navy, and State Departments." [89]

In general, Forrestal favored the Eberstadt Report recommendations (though he was not yet prepared to take a position on the separate air force), but he insisted that even they were put forth merely to provoke discussion and reiterated its suggestion that a mixed "board" of Congressmen, members of the executive branch, and private citizens should be formed to study the problem with the detachment and thoroughness it deserved.[90] Forrestal, and the admirals and Marine Corps generals who testified after him, kept emphasizing that the existing organization had, "in less time than was believed possible, attained complete victory in the greatest war of history." [91] They felt, consequently, that this war-winning system should not be changed unless the superiority of a single department were first proved by a careful and detailed weighing of its advantages and disadvantages, something that had not yet been done.[92] As the Commandant of the Marine Corps, General Alexander A. Vandegrift, summed it up,

For my own part, and based on my own personal observation, I consider that the war was skillfully and successfully conducted and that we should now be examining the record to determine the reasons for success rather than engaging in the use of innuendo to present our victories in the light of failure.[93]

In addition to these general objections to unification, the Navy Department witnesses concentrated throughout the hearings on making the following points:

1. Unity of command in the field—control over land, naval, and air forces by a single commander—as practiced in World War II had always been actively supported by the Navy, but its operation did not require a single department or a single chief of staff in Washington.

2. A unified department would be too large an organization to be effectively administered by a single overall secretary.

3. Claims of waste in procurement and excessive duplication of facilities during the war were exaggerated, and, in any event, savings through coordinated procurement and common use of facilities were not inherent in a single department nor impossible under two.

4. The parallel development of equipment and doctrines (which a single department would probably stultify) was not "wasteful duplication," as was proved by the successful use in the war by both services of radial air-cooled airplane engines, the dive bomber, and close air support for ground troops—all originally opposed by the War Department and developed only because the Navy was free to work on them independently.

5. The JCS pattern of collective decision-making in strategic planning led to wiser and more considered results than decision-making by a single chief of staff or overall commander, who also would be potentially a "man on horseback." As Forrestal explained in an indirect answer to General Marshall,

The argument has been made before this committee that a single source of decision on both military and civilian sides as opposed to the Joint Chiefs of Staff pattern is desirable. . . . I think the argument fails. It is my firm belief that victory in the Pacific was accelerated by many months and possibly by as much as a year, although no man should speculate on such abstractions as that, by the Navy's continuous and implacable insistence that a vigorous offensive against the Japanese could be prosecuted without doing injury to the success of our effort in Europe.

The eyes of the Army and its representatives on the Joint Chiefs of Staff were inevitably and quite properly fixed on Europe as the great central plain of battle, but I submit that it was a wise thing that the Navy's eyes were turned toward the Pacific and a most fortunate one that Admiral King was free to insist upon the Navy's point of view within the Joint Chiefs of Staff.[94]

6. The Collins Plan guaranteed that in the top command structure, officers with a Navy background would always be in a 2-to-3 or a 1-to-4 minority.

7. The friction between the services—often cited as an argument for unification—had almost disappeared during the war, and it was now being reintensified only because of the War Department's attempt to turn the "close partnership" that had emerged "into what might be characterized as a one-man corporation." [95]

8. The Navy "needed" and "had the right to" its own Cabinet member to handle directly its business before Congress and at high levels of the executive branch.[96]

Most of the Navy witnesses were noncommittal during the hearings on the question of a separate air force. They thought that the problem should be handled as one of splitting the War Department into two parts and consequently that it was chiefly that Department's own concern. They insisted, of course, that the complete naval air force stay within the Navy and alluded frequently to the incorporation of the British Royal Naval Air Service into the overall Royal Air Force at the end of World War I, claiming that the deprivation of its own air force had caused the British Navy to become second-rate by World War II.

Only Admiral Nimitz specifically opposed the separation of the Army

Air Forces from the War Department. Nimitz testified on November 17 after the Army Air Forces generals had made some of their more extreme claims about their particular brand of "air power" winning the war and pointed out to the Committee that "should the . . . Air Force be set up as a separate entity, with its own administrative and supply systems [as advocated by General Collins], the duplication in services and facilities frequently advanced as a reason for merging the Army and Navy, would become a possibility of triplication." [97] Nimitz also reminded the Committee in passing, that all airplanes operating in the Pacific had actually been dependent on ships both for "the flow of fuel, munitions, personnel, replacements, spare parts, and materials of all kinds which they needed" and, for the most part, for the initial capture of the bases from which they flew.[98] Nimitz explained during his testimony why he had changed his mind since his endorsement of a single department before the Richardson Committee:

At that time the advantages claimed appeared to be attainable, and, without opportunity for adequate study, I expressed to the committee my approval of a single department. . . .

With the passage of time and with greater war experience . . . I no longer favor the single department. I now believe that the theoretical advantages of such a merger are unattainable, whereas the disadvantages are so serious that it is not acceptable. . . . Our successes were more rapid than I had believed possible a year ago. I believe we should have very good reasons—better reasons than any offered so far—before we change a system that has proved itself so effective.[99]

The Navy Department witnesses advanced one other major argument against the Collins Plan. They predicted that even though the plan purported to give ultimate authority over the Department of the Armed Forces to its civilian Secretary, the actual power would become lodged in the hands of the Joint Chiefs of Staff and especially the Chief of Staff of the Armed Forces, contrary to the American tradition of civilian control of the military. To underscore this point, Assistant Secretary of the Navy H. Struve Hensel appeared before the Military Affairs Committee on November 7 with what amounted to a lawyer's brief [100] calculated to prove that "the main effect, if not the objective, of [the Collins] plan seems to be the reduction of civilian control over the armed services." [101]

Hensel pointed out that, in the first place, the number of civilian officials with secretarial rank was being reduced from eight in the existing organization to five in the one proposed. Hensel further argued that Collins' chart showed that the Secretary, the Under Secretary, and the three Assistant Secretaries would be isolated, having no contacts with the administration of their department except through the military Chief of Staff. The Secretary continued,

> The elimination of all civilians from the preparation of the budget is likewise a serious matter. . . . Instead of the budget estimates being prepared under the Secretary, and being the Secretary's responsibility to the President and to Congress as is now the case, the three services, each headed by a military man, are to originate the budget requirements. . . . Such initial budget estimates are then to pass to the United States Chiefs of Staff, a completely military organization consisting of the chiefs of the three services which prepared the budget estimates, the Chief of Staff to the President, and the Chief of Staff of the Armed Forces. . . .
>
> From such Chiefs of Staff, the budget would pass to the President. The Secretary of the Armed Forces is to be allowed to see the recommended budget as it passes by him but he will not be able to change it. He will be permitted only to comment upon it without benefit of any participation in its preparation or any facts derived from analytical examination, both of which are essential for intelligent comment. The Secretary would be lost in a mass of figures. Unless there are some glaring errors, he would be able to do little but to approve the recommendations of the United States Chiefs of Staff. . . .
>
> The proposal of the War Department makes the acquisition of information by the civilian Secretaries a most complicated and tortuous problem. Whether intended or not, there can be but one result. The civilian Secretaries will be completely dependent on the military. They will become echoes and not voices of command.[102]

Hensel's presentation was so effective that the Army decided to backtrack. When General Eisenhower—the "Conqueror of Europe" and probably even then the most popular of all the military figures—came before the Committee on November 16, he told the members that he disagreed with the place of the Chief of Staff of the Armed Forces on Collins' chart. Eisenhower thought that the Chief should be removed from the chain of command between the Secretary and the military heads of the services and should be shown set off as an "adviser" to the Secretary. Eisenhower also volunteered the information that he would not object to civilian under or assistant secretaries being placed over each service and that the War Department was prepared to accept such a change.[103]

Senator Edwin Johnson, who had been acting chairman of the Committee since the beginning of the hearings, indicated to Eisenhower that he was pleased with the two changes in the War Department's position but that he was still impressed with Hensel's argument about the Secretary being bypassed. Johnson, who it will be recalled had sponsored one of the pending unification bills, thought that

when you bypass the over-all Secretary on such matters as military policy, strategy, and budget requirements, there is not very much left for the Secretary to deal with; all he can do is, say, allocate a few lead pencils and things of that kind. . . .

It seems to me that if Congress is drafting a law on this subject they are going to have to be very careful, unless we get away from civilian control, the civilian control that we traditionally have had in this America.[104]

When Assistant Secretary of War John J. McCloy testified the following week, he brought up General Collins' remarks about the Secretary of the Armed Forces being restricted to transmitting the unchanged JCS budget to the President "with his comments thereon." "If those words," McCloy told the Senators, "appear too casual for the Secretary's actual function, they can be and should be changed." McCloy added that he personally believed that the Secretary should submit the departmental budget and that the views of the Joint Chiefs, if they differed, should be labeled " 'Comments on the Budget,' or something of that nature." [105]

McCloy did not appear before the Committee simply to make concessions, however. He struck out at the Navy Department's rejection of the Richardson Committee recommendations by summarizing the attacks that the Navy had made upon them in the following manner:

(a) Mr. Forrestal, who transmitted the committee's directive to Mr. Woodrum, now finds that the study based on the directive deals with but a fragment of the problem.

(b) Admiral King, who selected half of the committee, finds that the members lacked objectivity, were not thorough in their study, engaged in justification of prior conclusions, did not adequately examine the witnesses, and were not realistic.

(c) Mr. Hensel has the following to say about the field commanders whose testimony Mr. Forrestal so urgently called for at the Woodrum hearings:

"Without wishing to detract in the slightest from the accomplishments of our gallant and brilliant field commanders, few, if any of them, have had any experience in the operation of the governmental department during this war." [106]

McCloy concluded that "in a word, the top echelon of the Navy does not approve of the report, the men who produced it, or the overwhelming majority of generals and admirals whose opinions it represents." [107]

On December 13, Secretary of the Navy Forrestal returned to the Military Affairs Committee and formally presented with slight modifications the Eberstadt Report recommendations as the "Navy Plan for National Security." (Forrestal continued, for example, to suspend judgment on the separate air force and began to recommend that a second naval officer be added to the JCS, one of the two Navy members to be a flier.)[108] About a week later, on December 17, the hearings ended.

Throughout the Military Affairs Committee hearings it was clear that a majority of its members were sympathetic to some form of unification. Senator Lister Hill, the third-ranking majority member of the Committee and the majority whip of the Senate, was the most active supporter of the Army's plan, attending almost all the hearings, providing leading questions for the War Department witnesses, and intelligently and severely cross-examining the representatives of the Navy Department.

Truman's Special Message

Two days after the close of the Senate hearings, President Truman became an active participant in the unification conflict. On December 19, 1945, he sent a special message to Congress recommending the establishment of a "Department of National Defense" to produce "integrated strategic plans and a unified military program and budget," "extensive savings," "parity for air power," "unity of command in outlying bases," "consistent and equitable personnel policies," and a "unified system of training." [109] Since it was known that the chairmen of the House and Senate Naval Affairs Committees and the chairman of the House Military Affairs Committee were all against unification, Truman's Postmaster General, Robert E. Hannegan, had warned him that he was making a mistake to send the message, unnecessarily risking his prestige in a fight which he might lose. Truman felt, however, that it was his "duty" to do so because it represented his "conviction" and sent the message anyway.[110]

The President's plan called for a cabinet-level secretary and an overall military chief of staff to head the single department. Land, naval, and separate air forces would retain their identities and exist as "branches" under assistant secretaries and military commanders. There would also be an under secretary and additional assistant secretaries for various functional areas. The overall chief of staff and the commanders of the three services would constitute an advisory group to the overall secretary and to the President. Truman recommended that he and the overall secretary be given legislative authority to establish "central coordinating and service organizations" wherever they deemed necessary and insisted, as had the War Department witnesses, that Congress should provide only the basic framework for the new department and let the details be worked out over a period of time within the executive branch.

Apparently to try to allay the fears of the Navy, the President gave it as his opinion that "it would be wise if the post of Chief of Staff were rotated among the several services, whenever practicable and advisable, at least during the evolution of the new unified department." He said that the various staff positions should be filled by officers from all the services, and that "nothing" (presumably the Chief of Staff) should prevent the civilian heads of the department from communicating directly with any of the service commanders on questions of strategy, policy, or the division of the budget. Finally, Truman announced that the Navy "should, of course, retain its own carrier-, ship-, and water-based aviation" and that, "of course, the Marine Corps should be continued as an integral part of the Navy." He dismissed Eberstadt and Forrestal's recommendation for the appointment of a board or commission to examine the problem of reorganization with the comment, "Further studies of the general problem will serve no useful purpose. There is enough evidence now at hand to demonstrate beyond question the need for a unified department." [111]

The congressional response to the President's message was mixed: Senator Lister Hill of the Military Affairs Committee commented that, "The President's message states the need [for unification] in unanswerable logic"; Chairman Vinson of the House Naval Affairs Committee thought, on the other hand, that "the very phraseology of the scheme smacks of the Germany of the Kaiser and of Hitler, of Japanese militarism" and called the President's plan—pure "military power politics" calculated to "sink the Navy." [112]

3

War Department Coalition Goals

By the winter of 1945–46, after the Woodrum Committee hearings, the Richardson Committee and Eberstadt Reports, the Senate Military Affairs Committee hearings, and President Truman's special message, the lines of cleavage defining the unification conflict had become clear. The various plans advanced by what can be called the "War Department coalition," consisting of the Secretary of War, the senior Army ground forces generals, the Army Air Forces generals, and President Truman, essentially contained six distinct though interdependent proposals. These were opposed by a "Navy Department coalition," consisting of the Secretary of the Navy, the senior admirals, the Marines, and the naval aviators. The disputed proposals involved:

1. A single military department with a single military budget nominally under a single cabinet secretary.

2. A JCS with statutory control over the departmental budget and with direct access to the President on questions of strategy and other major matters.

3. An overall Chief of Staff of the Armed Forces with controlling influence over JCS deliberations.

4. A separate air force as a third military service.

5. Divestment of the Navy's land-based aircraft by the new separate air force.

6. Enactment by Congress of the overall structure of the single department only, with authority delegated to the executive branch to work out its details.

This listing indicates only those key proposals publicly endorsed by the War Department coalition as essential parts of its unification plan and publicly opposed by the Navy Department coalition. As shall be seen, not all the members of the first coalition were equally interested in each of the proposals, and not all the members of the second coalition were equally opposed to them.

The Ground Forces Hierarchy

"The armed forces of the United States," writes the official historian of the Office of the Army Chief of Staff,

underwent an almost continuous weakening from 1918 onward for a decade and a half. . . . The fluctuation in numbers from 1922 to 1936 was small [the Army varied between 131,959 and 166,724], but the deterioration in equipment was continuous in that the 1918 surplus, used up rather than replaced, was not only increasingly obsolescent but increasingly ineffective owing to wear and age. In the mid-thirties the Navy was permitted, by a cautious increase in appropriations, to make a start on a new shipbuilding program which by that time was acutely needed. The Army was less favored. . . . The abiding need for trained and equipped ground forces, recognized and continuously recalculated by the Army's General Staff, was generally ignored by the ultimate authority in government.[1]

In the summer of 1939, when General Marshall took over as Chief of Staff, the Army had 190,690 men. By the end of the year, the ground forces were still equipped primarily with World War I vintage Springfield rifles, 75-mm field guns, and 3-inch antiaircraft guns; none of its 329 tanks was believed capable of standing up to those Hitler's army had used against Poland that September, and the Army's total inventory of mortars amounted to 93! Fewer than 200 of the 1,800 planes in the Army's Air Corps were fit for modern combat operations. Finally, the quantities of ammunition that existed even for the obsolescent weapons available were severely limited. In short, four months after the beginning of a large-scale war in Europe that even in 1939 was perceived as likely to involve the United States, the state of the Army's equipment was such that it could not have put a single division into the field on short notice.[2] It is in this context that the unification position of the World War II ground force generals must be understood.

COMBAT EFFECTIVENESS, MILITARY CONTROL, ADEQUATE GROUND TROOPS

The overriding goal of Marshall and the other ground force leaders in the unification conflict was to prevent the United States' military forces from being cut back after World War II to the same level of inadequacy that they had reached in the interwar years—that "long period of agony," as Marshall phrased it, when our national interests were being threatened and we could do nothing about it militarily. Marshall thought that although the United States would go along as in the past "hoping and thinking about a peaceful world, . . . that is not common to all governments, and certainly is not common to all leaders." World peace and the security of the United States depended ultimately, therefore, on maintaining sufficient military strength to make contemplated aggression against this country appear unprofitable to any potential aggressor.[3]

Although this had always been the case, the necessity for forces-in-being—for "immediately available military power," in Marshall's words—was even more pressing than ever before because long-range aircraft with "the various types of bombs" now available made it possible for an enemy to destroy our industrial plant by sudden attack and thus prevent us from mobilizing powerful armed forces after the actual outbreak of war, as we had done in the past.[4]

Marshall realized, as did all the military leaders, Army and Navy alike, that the strength to be maintained by the nation would be determined in large part "by the public and congressional reaction to the appropriations required for our armed forces." [5] Or, as Marshall would put it even more simply a few years later, "The great problem—the real problem—[of national defense] was money." [6] The organizational structure proposed by the Army in its unification plans was calculated to maximize military appropriations and to insure that the kinds of military forces on which they were spent were properly "balanced" from the professional military point of view. The Army leaders believed that in the pre-World War II days there had been four major obstacles to the military's appropriations requests being translated into funds for adequately large and properly balanced armed forces: the civilian departmental Secretaries of War and the Navy, the Budget Bureau, the President, and Congress. The original Army plan, presented to the Woodrum Committee in 1944 by Marshall's deputy, General McNarney, would have substantially eliminated the future influence of any civilian secretary and of the Budget Bureau and would have seriously curtailed even Congress' influence on the granting of military appropriations.

We have seen that in the McNarney plan (and the pattern was repeated in the Collins plan), the U.S. Chiefs of Staff were to make their budgetary requests directly to the President without the civilian Secretary of the Armed Forces being allowed to make changes in them. Marshall looked back to the situation that had developed after World War I when General Pershing returned from France eventually to become Army Chief of Staff with definite ideas, budgetary and otherwise, about strengthening the Army. Marshall, who was Pershing's aide at the time, recalled that Secretary of War John W. Weeks "had only a very moderate interest in the Army; . . . would not follow Pershing's advice, and, furthermore, would not permit Pershing to see President Harding to express his views." [7]

The provision granting to the military chiefs the statutory right to make recommendations on strategy and the budget directly to the President was the result, according to Assistant Secretary of War McCloy, of Marshall's very strong feeling (no doubt widely shared within the War Department) "that the professional military men . . . should have their day in court before the President even though their views should differ from those of the Secretary of the Armed Forces." [8] Marshall himself was to admit some years later that what he had in mind was "outside of, we will say, civilian control: . . . what I was after was that period in time of peace when it is very difficult to get a correct expression from the military authorities as long as that expression is controlled politically." [9]

The Army leaders also had their grievances against the Budget Bureau. Not only had the Bureau—some might have felt without the President's active and considered approval—steadily made "crippling cuts" in the overall appropriations requests of the Army before their submission to Congress, but it had also applied the total amount cut to the various programs requested without prior consultation with the Army about the relative importance of these programs, with the result that "in effect [the Budget Director] and not the responsible head of the Department determines to some degree what . . . shall not be included in the budget." [10]

In the McNarney plan no role was mentioned for the Budget Bureau, and the Chiefs of Staff were to be expressly guaranteed the last word, subject to the President overruling them, in determining to what programs appropriated funds were to be applied. The President himself did not, of course, have to accept the Chiefs' budget as his own. But the Army leaders hoped that any cuts that the President wished to make would be left to them to apply and that their original budget would be made public so that if the President reduced it, both Congress and the general public would be so informed.[11] The Army must have realized that cutting off the Budget Bureau was an unrealistic objective, for in 1945 its continued existence and operation were conceded by both Marshall and Collins. Both generals still hoped, however, that the Chiefs' budgetary recommendations would be made public and that any cuts would be applied according to the Joint Chiefs' wishes.[12]

The Army's unification plans, it must be conceded, did not contemplate any diminution in Congress' ultimate authority over military appropriations. The generals simply wanted the legislators to take some self-denying action: In 1944 General McNarney proposed that Congress give to the JCS authority to allocate the total appropriated funds among the various services and programs, as each of the Chiefs had in effect been allowed to do for his own service during the war.[13] In 1945 the Army's proposals were more modest. The binding nature of appropriations categories was conceded, and Congress was asked merely to accept the military's recommendations as to how any particular total sum of money should be divided in writing the appropriations bill. As General Marshall told the Senate Military Affairs Committee:

One group feels that the money can very much better be spent this way and another group feels that the money can be better spent another way. Someone must balance the [programs]. I maintain, you gentlemen cannot do that. . . . You can say, "You will not get the money," but you would have an impossible technical job of judgment on your hands to determine how these military factors should be balanced. It is not easy for a man who is solely occupied with them every day and has the trained people at his disposal to analyze the various sections.[14]

An indispensable part of this balance-maximizing scheme was the Army's proposal for a single budget providing for all of the military services and, implicitly, for a single appropriations subcommittee in each house of Congress to consider it. As Marshall had explained in his testimony before the Senate Military Affairs Committee in 1945, appropriations requests from the Army and the Navy were handled separately in Congress both in the interwar period and during World War II. The Military Affairs Committees in the Senate and the House determined the Army's composition and organization and authorized strength, pay scales, allowances, and systems of recruitment and promotion, while the Naval Affairs Committees performed the same tasks for the Navy. Separate subcommittees of the Senate and House Appropriations Committees handled the budgetary requests and drafted the appropriations bills for the War Department and the Navy Department. The system, as has been pointed out,[15] was actually noncompetitive, with the size of the appropriations granted to one service having little or no bearing on the appropriations granted to the other.

The Army leaders did not perceive the system as noncompetitive, however. They appeared to feel that the total amount granted to both the Army and the Navy was what Congress was willing to spend that year in any event and that the two-budget system caused each service's share to be determined by the quality of its "salesmanship" rather than by a professional military estimate of the relative amount it required for the country to maintain the most effective overall armed forces. More specifically, the Army leaders felt that the two-budget system discriminated against the unglamorous but highly important ground Army, which Marshall specifically feared would be "starved" in another period of peace.[16] It was this system, for example, that had produced in the early 1930s a navy that stood among the three strongest in the world while the Army stood seventeenth and that as late as 1939 provided more money for a single battleship in the Navy's sizable ship-building program than the total amount granted for weapons to an army equipped with World War I rifles and 93 mortars.[17] Moreover, the Army ground force leaders were looking ahead to the day when their highly popular Air Force would almost certainly become a separate service, turning the two-budget system into what they anticipated as a still more disadvantageous, three-way competitive scramble for limited funds.

Only a single budget based on "the considered opinion of the country's leading military experts" could insure that available funds were divided so as to "buy" "the largest measure of protection for the Nation" and prevent "overlarge sums for one purpose and insufficient sums for another which must inevitably result from a lack of a single direction over the [budgetary] planning of all the constituent service elements." [18] It was also expected that a single budget formally presented by "the country's leading military experts" would make Congress more reluctant to reduce its overall amount as well as its recommended distributions among the services.

But an assumption universally held by the military was that the funds granted by Congress during peacetime would again be scarce relative to the total perceived monetary needs of the services.[19] Under such circumstances, the key questions in the formulation of a single budget would be over the distribution of "shortages" of funds among the services—questions on which a JCS organization, two or three of whose members would also be the leaders of the claimant agencies, was not likely to reach unanimous agreement. "It is here," General McNarney consequently argued in 1944, "that the [single] Chief of Staff . . . must play a very important role. It is here that intelligent decisions must replace the unsatisfactory compromises which have sometimes had to be made in the past." [20] In short, the Army plan was to retain the JCS in name but to change its character by introducing an overall Chief of Staff who would have controlling influence over its deliberations and so would himself determine the make-up of the single military budget for all of the services.

Actually, the Army's proposal of a single Chief of Staff with controlling influence over the military budget also followed from its more general theory of decision-making. Implicit in the testimony of the Army leaders was the belief that in any decision-making situation, there was an optimum solution with respect to maximizing military effectiveness that was in the "real interest" of all the services. These Army leaders further held that the optimum solution—be it on questions of strategy and the allocation of scarce resources in war or budgetary questions in peace —could never be reached through bargaining and compromise in a JCS requiring unanimous agreement. Nor could it be reached by the President, by a civilian departmental secretary, or by Congress. The civilians simply did not have the required professional expertise, and the individual members of the Joint Chiefs were prone to fight selfishly for solutions that would maximize their own service's interests instead of for the presumably readily apparent solution that would maximize their common interest in the military effectiveness of the armed services as a whole. The optimum determinations could only be reached, consequently, by an overall Chief of Staff who would be an experienced professional soldier but not be service-oriented, since his responsibility would extend over all of the services. As Marshall put it, "Once you have a single responsibility, you have a single individual who is just as much interested in that side of the house as this side of the house, and he will have them all under one roof." [21]

It was, of course, simply taken for granted that the optimum solutions would provide adequate satisfaction for the budgetary and strategic claims of the ground forces—claims that a few of the Army leaders seemed to equate with the optimum solutions themselves. It is difficult not to conclude that as a further guarantee of adequate consideration, the Army leaders looked to the single Chief of Staff wearing, at least initially, the uniform of a ground Army general.[22]

This theory of the preferability of one-man decision-making was a norm internalized by Army line officers since 1903, when Secretary of War Elihu Root had persuaded Congress to establish a Chief of Staff within the War Department. The Chief of Staff was given the power of decision over the chiefs of the various technical and supply bureaus in the Army, who had previously enjoyed a bargaining relationship with the Commanding General of the Army (the Chief of Staff's approximate organizational predecessor [23]) and who had been able to defy him in pursuit of their bureau interests, sometimes at the expense of the interests of the Army as a whole.[24] So strongly was this decision-making dogma adhered to by some of the Army generals that they were ready to criticize the effectiveness of the JCS during World War II almost as a matter of principle, even though they did not throughout the hearings take issue with the content of a single one of the Chiefs' strategic decisions. The most extreme position was to be taken by General Eisenhower in the following exchange with Senator Styles Bridges in 1947:

Senator BRIDGES.   General, were there any tragic weaknesses in the Joint Chiefs of Staff's operations during the last war?

General EISENHOWER.   Senator, I am not going back and criticising, even by indirection, what my bosses did in the war. . . . There is weakness in any council running a war. . . .

Senator BRIDGES.   On the other hand, is there not a certain strength in it: that one man who may be particularly Navy-minded or particularly air-minded, or particularly ground-force-minded would not be able to enforce his prejudice upon the Military Establishment? . . .

General EISENHOWER.   In war, you must have a decision. A bum decision is better than none. And the trouble is that when you get three [points of view], you finally get none. . . .

Senator BRIDGES.   You feel it is of advantage to get a decision, even if it is a wrong decision?

General EISENHOWER.   The whole history of warfare proves that point. . . . In warfare, any decision is better than none.[25]

In addition to determining budgetary questions and strategy, the Army leaders expected the single Chief of Staff to be useful in allocating scarce men and materials in time of war. In World War II, money had become unlimited, and the crucial problem had been to find the items to buy with it. Industrial plants, raw materials, military end-items, and personnel all became scarce and eventually had to be allocated. The process worked roughly as follows: After strategy was determined upon in the JCS and tasks assigned, each service independently procured the men and equipment to carry out its assignments. The service itself ranked the importance of its various material programs, but the overall system of direct and indirect priorities that governed allocations among both services was assigned at various times by the Army-Navy Munitions Board, the War Production Board, and the Office of War Mobilization. This was done more or less in response to the independent pleading of each of the services, with controversial decisions on key items being made by the JCS or the President.[26]

A long series of complaints during the unification hearings shows that in this truly competitive game for men and materials, the Army felt that it had suffered injustices. The Army leaders complained, for example, that the Navy and the Marines had been allowed to continue voluntary enlistments until December, 1942, which led to the more desirable personnel volunteering for these services to avoid being drafted into the Army, and that even after the President had prohibited further voluntary recruitment of men of draft age (eighteen years and older), the Navy and Marines were still allowed to continue recruiting seventeen-year-olds. These recruitment practices had given the Navy and the Marine Corps a disproportionately large share of the younger and more desirable age groups. Similarly, the Navy was alleged to have had a larger proportion of nurses than the Army, better allowances for officers overseas, Coca Cola and beer at times that the Army had none, and as many five-star admirals as the Army had five-star generals, even though the Navy had only one-third of the total armed forces personnel. Finally, it was pointed out that in the early part of the war, the Navy had been given higher priorities for the production of landing-craft engines and naval guns than the Army had been given for jeep engines and field artillery.[27]

Although the Army witnesses admitted during the hearings that the problems of hoarding, competitive procurement, and allocation of scarce materials had been largely settled through the work of various joint bodies, these joint bodies equally represented the Army and the Navy and involved negotiations, bargaining, and compromise. The Army witnesses strongly implied that what they actually desired was a setup that would guarantee top priority for their own requirements, unilaterally determined. Their point of view was summed up by General Somervell, who as Commanding General of the Services of Supply (later the Army Services Forces) had been in direct charge of Army procurement during the war:

All of these [joint committees] were helpful, but desired results were accomplished only through an inordinate amount of effort that would have been unnecessary if these activities . . . had been coordinated on the basis of command rather than through the slow and cumbersome committee action, requiring agreement.[28]

In any future war, that kind of command could be provided by the Chief of Staff of the Armed Forces.

RESTRICTION OF THE MARINE CORPS

The Chief of Staff system of decision-making was expected to promote still another Army goal: the permanent restriction of the Marine Corps to a size and to functions that would not again resemble those of a regular ground army. The Marines had first been organized during the Revolutionary War and were established on a permanent basis in 1798 soon after the creation of the Navy Department. Among the original functions of the Marines were to keep order aboard ship, to snipe at enemy personnel from the rigging during sea battles, to spearhead boarding parties, and to help repel enemy boarders.

In later years the Corps regularly provided landing parties to enforce American rights, protect American citizens, or otherwise intervene in foreign countries. On occasion, the Marines also participated in extended land operations with regular Army ground troops, as in World War I. In the interwar period the Marine Corps had averaged about 15,000 men, and its main fighting elements had been two understrength brigades stationed on the Atlantic and Pacific coasts. It was during these years that the Marines applied themselves to the problems of assaulting fortified beaches (which they predicted would be necessary in any war with Japan) and developed tactics and equipment for amphibious warfare. Following the outbreak of the war in Europe, the two Marine brigades were expanded to divisions. This was the first time that Marine units had existed in division strength since the Corps was established in 1798. The Marine divisions were sent to the South Pacific after Pearl Harbor, and in August, 1942, they amphibiously assaulted Guadalcanal in the Solomons, which was the first American offensive action of the Pacific war.[29]

To control their forces in the South Pacific, the Marines established in 1942, also for the first time, a command and administrative echelon higher than the division, which they called the I (later the III) Marine Amphibious Corps. In the summer of 1943, a V Marine Amphibious Corps was set up at Pearl Harbor to command the planned amphibious campaign across the central Pacific that eventually led to Tarawa in the Gilbert Islands, Kwajelein and Eniwetok in the Marshalls, and, with Army troops, Saipan, Tinian, and Guam in the Marianas. The overall force that assaulted the Marianas in June, 1944, consisted of three Marine divisions, a Marine "provisional brigade," and two Army divisions, constituting the equivalent of about two "corps," or, in War Department terms, an "army." All these troops were commanded by Major General Holland M. Smith, a Marine Corps officer.[30]

Marshall and the other Army ground-force generals resented the creation of a Marine Corps that by the Marianas campaign had reached five divisions and would reach six divisions and almost half a million men by the end of the war. Such a force competed directly for men and ground-force equipment that they felt could be put to better use within the Army. The Army generals still conceived of the Marines strictly as an auxiliary to the Fleet, to serve as landing parties to protect Americans during disturbances in foreign countries and, in wartime, as an expeditionary force to seize advanced naval bases that were of exclusive interest to the Navy and could be overcome by small units.

The Army leaders had been trained to believe that the basic ground-force battle unit was the corps: two or more divisions with supporting troops such as heavy artillery, engineers, signal troops, and tanks—all coordinated and controlled by the corps commander and his staff. They also believed that control of a corps or a larger unit was an extremely complicated task, requiring long previous training, which the Marines, who had never been larger than brigade strength before 1939, simply did not have. The Army consequently had opposed the original establishment of both the I and V Amphibious Corps and had repeatedly proposed that command of units larger than single divisions in the drive across the Pacific go to Army commanders and staffs, who were experienced at the corps echelon. Admiral King was able to defeat these proposals in the JCS by pointing out that the Central Pacific campaign was primarily a naval undertaking, under an overall naval commander, Nimitz, and in which for a long time the Marines provided most of the ground troops.[31]

But the Army's objection to large forces under Marine officers was not due entirely to organizational dogma. General Marshall and other Army generals personally disliked General Holland M. Smith, the commander of the V Amphibious Corps and of the overall Marianas assault force. This was the result in part of certain characteristics of Smith's personality, which had not unjustifiably earned him the nickname "Howlin' Mad" (from Holland M.), and, in Marshall's opinion, to Smith's lack of ability as a commander. An incident during the Marianas campaign served to magnify greatly the underlying hostility that had been developing within the Army against both Smith and the Marines. In the long, hard-fought battle for Saipan, Holland Smith relieved from his command Army Major General Ralph B. Smith, whose Twenty-seventh Division was slowing down the general advance because of, among other things, "lack of aggressive spirit."

After the Army had leaked its own version of the event to the press, a *Time* correspondent in Holland Smith's headquarters wrote a story that was interpreted as imputing cowardice as well as ineffectiveness to the Army commander and his troops.[32] Marshall was so annoyed by the Saipan controversy that reportedly he lost his temper in a JCS meeting and declared that he would never again tolerate command of Army troops by Marine officers, rejecting implicitly the whole principle of unity of command in the field.[33] Marshall later repeated the statement to Rear Admiral Forrest P. Sherman, who was Nimitz' chief planner in the Pacific.[34] This removal during battle of an Army division commander by a purportedly less experienced Marine officer strengthened the Army's determination not to let the Marine Corps again reach a size that would permit it to contribute the majority of the forces in any major amphibious assault and thus justify placing the command of the operation in Marine hands.*

* Just after Holland Smith's removal of Ralph Smith, Lieutenant General Robert C. Richardson, the top Army commander in Nimitz' Pacific Ocean Areas, went to Saipan, where he reportedly berated Holland Smith in the following fashion:
"You and your Corps commanders aren't as well qualified to lead large bodies of troops as general officers in the Army. . . . We've had more experience in handling troops than you've had and yet you dare . . . remove one of my Generals. . . . You Marines are nothing but a bunch of beach-runners, anyway. What do you know about land warfare?" Holland M. Smith and Percy Finch, *Coral and Brass* (New York, Scribner, 1948), p. 177.

Although the ill-feeling between the Army hierarchy and the Marines continued until the end of the war, the Army's specific plans for the Corps did not become evident until the height of the unification conflict. In June, 1945, Secretary of the Navy Forrestal sent proposed legislation to President Truman through the Budget Bureau increasing the authorized peacetime strength of the Navy and Marine Corps. Two months later, on the advice of his Budget Director, the President asked the JCS to review the Navy's request in relation to the contemplated peacetime requirements of all the armed forces. The Chiefs assigned the problem to one of their subordinate staff groups, which studied it for the next six months. In February, 1946, the staff group reported to the JCS that it could not agree either on the size or the functions of the various elements of the postwar Army and Navy.[35]

In the course of these staff considerations, which overlapped the Senate Military Affairs Committee hearings, and in later discussions at the JCS level itself, the Army leaders made clear their view of the proper role of the Marines. Generals Eisenhower and Spaatz, for example, recommended in their so-called Series 1478 JCS papers that the Corps be restricted in the future to "small, readily available and lightly armed units, no larger than a regiment, to protect United States citizens ashore in foreign countries and to provide interior guard of naval ships and naval shore establishments." They argued that Marine units possessing their own tanks, artillery, and air support as in World War II and organized in division strength or larger constituted, by definition, a land army that duplicated the regular Army and should therefore never again be allowed to exist.* With respect to amphibious warfare, whose techniques the Marines had developed, Eisenhower and Spaatz proposed that the Corps be restricted to "minor shore operations in which the Navy alone is interested" and that all "major amphibious operations in the future . . . be undertaken by the Army" with the Marines serving as boat crews for the landing craft. The Army leaders consequently saw no need for the Marine Corps to "appreciably expand in time of war" and urged that it be limited permanently "to some 50,000 or 60,000 men."[36]

Since the Navy member of a JCS of the World War II type could

---

* Strongly supporting this point of organizational dogma was probably also the unexpressed fear that the 100,000-man peacetime Marine Corps that the Navy was thinking about (see Admiral King's testimony in *Universal Military Training*, Hearings before the House Committee on Military Affairs on H.R. 515, 79th Cong., 1st Sess. [1945], p. 93)—a force only slightly smaller than the total interwar Army —might be seen in Congress as obviating the need for any sizable regular Army ground forces during the postwar period.

never be expected to agree to such a permanent restriction of the Marines—Admiral Nimitz characterized one of Eisenhower's JCS papers as a proposal "to eliminate the Marine Corps as an effective combat element" [37]—the Army once again looked to the proposed overall Chief of Staff of the Armed Forces to recognize the duplicatory nature of a sizable Marine Corps and to restrict it accordingly.

ECONOMY

It is difficult to evaluate the degree to which Secretary of War Patterson, General Marshall, and the other ground-force leaders actually believed that great savings would result from unification, although that was one of their professed goals. Patterson, who as Under Secretary had general responsibility for War Department procurement during the war, repeatedly alleged that the economies would take place through the elimination of "two lines of supply, two hospital systems, two procurement agencies, [and] two air transport systems, where one will do the job as effectively and for less money." These were "duplications that no joint board with equal representation of the Army and the Navy has been able to eliminate." [38] Yet, given General Collins' specific assurance that not only the Army and the Navy but the new Air Force as well would be allowed to maintain their own service forces for supply and support functions, thus increasing the "lines of supply," etc., to three, it is difficult to believe that economy was one of the predominant goals of the War Department unifiers.

This is not to say that the Army leaders did not have some vague feelings that money could be saved under a single department. Patterson had "guessed," no doubt sincerely, for the Senators in 1945 that "billions" could have been saved if the war had been fought with a single department. Eisenhower had given his opinion that with respect to personnel, "you could develop a more efficient fighting force with unification, with 75 percent of the men that you would have if you had separate forces," admitting, however, that his estimate was only a "flash guess." Eisenhower had also claimed in his opening statement that with unification "we can buy more security for less money" and that "without it we will spend more money and buy less security." But when he was asked about the size of the savings that he anticipated, the General replied that he had no idea and simply reiterated his belief that some "saving is there." [39] It is probably significant that throughout the unification hearings no Army witness ever gave a single concrete relevant example of where savings might result.

To summarize, the Army ground-force leaders' chief goals in the unification conflict were combat effectiveness, military control, adequate ground troops, restriction of the Marine Corps, and economy. Since maintaining the powerful military forces required for combat effectiveness took money, the Army leaders proposed an organizational solution calculated to preserve, as much as possible, the almost controlling influence that the military chiefs had acquired over the military budget during World War II with their direct access to the President and with a Congress that followed the recommendations of the Chiefs almost blindly and "was willing to give [practically] without argument the money that was requested," with "the War Department, or . . . General Marshall, . . . virtually dictating the [Army] budgets." [40] Their desires and expectations were probably best expressed in the following passage written by the Richardson Committee majority:

As the Nation returns to peacetime pursuits, interest in the armed forces will decline sharply and Congress and the President will be reluctant, as in the past, to appropriate funds which the armed forces believe to be adequate for their proper maintenance. It is believed that an over-all estimate of expenditures showing the amounts required by each major component submitted to the President by the United States Chiefs of Staff, at least annually, will have great weight with the President, the Congress, and the Nation as a whole, representing as it does the combined views of all the components. . . . Beyond this, the strength and prestige of the United States Chiefs of Staff, may, in many instances, result in the adoption of sound military policies which might otherwise be inadequately presented.[41]

Besides maximizing overall military appropriations, a single military budget controlled by the JCS would prevent the more glamorous Navy and Air Force from approaching Congress independently and getting a larger share of the total funds than was justified from the overall military point of view. Predicting, however, that the JCS would have a hard time agreeing among themselves on the distribution of "shortages" among the services, the Army leaders proposed to add an overall Chief of Staff (a position also in line with War Department organizational tradition and theory) to the JCS to insure that available funds were allocated in a way to provide "balanced forces" that included adequately equipped and sizable ground troops.

Since a single budget and a single chief of staff implied a single military department, and since a cabinet-level department was traditionally headed by a civilian secretary, such a secretary also had to be proposed. In both the McNarney and the Collins Plans, however, the civilian Secretary of the Armed Forces was expected to content himself with "administrative matters" and be forbidden *by law* from effectively influencing either matters of military strategy and operations or of appropriations. Though not openly stated in the hearings, there is little doubt that the Army leaders also looked to the single-chief-of-staff mechanism to impose their version of equitable allocations of personnel and equipment in case of war and to restrict the Marine Corps to functions that would be strictly noncompetitive with those of the ground Army. Finally, the Army ground-force leaders had some unstructured and unsupported beliefs —at least hopes—that economies would result under the single department, not in the sense that the country could spend less for defense, since the generals were convinced that the President and Congress would never provide adequate funds in peacetime but in the sense that a greater part of each dollar could be made available for the creation of military power.

REORGANIZATION THEORY

It will be recalled that in the unification conflict, the War Department proposed not only the form for a reorganized military establishment, but also a method for bringing it about. As we have seen, the Army witnesses argued in favor of the speedy enactment by Congress of the "principle" of unification. This meant, presumably, the statutory establishment of the principal offices such as the Secretary, the Chief of Staff, and the JCS, with delegated authority to prescribe their own detailed functions and to work out the rest of the departmental structure. The Army's point of view, in the words of General McNarney, was that "If . . . the committee or the Congress tries to work out and prescribe how all the complicated pieces [of the single department] will fit together, I am sure that there will be such confusion over details as to becloud the entire issue." [42]

The Army had brought about a radical reorganization of the War Department with this "agreement in principle" approach in February, 1942. McNarney, who had been one of the active proponents of that reorganization plan also, persuaded Marshall that if the plan were submitted for comment to the "various staff divisions" and other "interested parties" concerned, it would run into "numerous non-concurrences and interminable delay." McNarney got Marshall to approve the plan "in principle" and only later promulgated it generally through the War Department while appointing a committee to work out the details and draw up the necessary regulations for putting it into effect.[43] The War Department reorganization proved generally successful for the rest of the war. The Army leaders calculated, therefore, that if they could get Congress quickly to enact their unification plan in general statutory language, the expected controversy over its details could not prevent its overall operation, since the President, the Secretary, and the Chief of Staff would have the power to put the preferred detailed structure into effect despite opposition from any of the services.

Army Air Forces Hierarchy

SEPARATE AIR FORCE

The overriding goal of the Army Air Forces hierarchy in the unification conflict was its separation from the War Department and its establishment as a third military service equal in status to the ground Army and the Navy. This was not a new goal for the Army aviators. Billy Mitchell and most of the other Army Air Service officers had been arguing for "separation" or "independence" at least since the end of World War I. This aspiration can in large part be traced to their unsatisfying experience in that conflict.

Soon after the United States entered the war against Germany in 1917, the civilian and military leaders of Army aviation, abetted by the public press, made extravagant predictions of the potential of American air power for successfully ending the war in Europe. To justify a request for the $640-million air program passed by Congress in July, 1917 (without the concurrence, incidentally, of the War Department General Staff), the air power enthusiasts generated a high-powered publicity campaign, promising among other things, "an enormous number of flying fighters to raid and destroy military camps, ammunition depots, and military establishments of all kinds, . . . winged cavalry sweeping across the German lines and smothering their trenches with a storm of lead, . . . clouds of planes" providing a "million roads to Berlin." [44] The Washington *Post,* in a not untypical comment on the passage of the huge air program by the House of Representatives, speculated that "a fleet [of aircraft] three months from now may bring the war to a successful end." [45]

The Air Service's procurement program ran into difficulties, however. Not only did American aviation not "win the war," but by the time of the Armistice in November, 1918, only 696 of the 4,500 aircraft promised for the previous spring had arrived in the American Expeditionary Force's Zone of Advance, and the total "rain of bombs" dropped by American units on the Germans amounted to 138 tons.* As the official Army Air Forces historians have put it,

The story of the Army air arm in World War I was one of promise rather than of achievement. The combat record was excellent, but brief and on a scale far more modest than the public had been led to expect. . . . Six months more of war might have seen an Army air force such as had been promised in June 1917; but actually the "regiments and brigades of winged cavalry mounted on gas driven flying horses" never arrived to "sweep the Germans from the sky."[46]

As a result, the Army aviators came out of World War I severely frustrated. They "knew" what air power could do, yet the production failure at home and the Armistice had stopped them from proving it. The regular Army ground-force officers, furthermore, tended to look back to the Air Service's actual performance and to remain skeptical of the fliers' claims. This differential interpretation of past experience caused a cleavage between the Army fliers' and the ground-force-dominated General Staff's conception of the role of the airplane that was to persist for almost two decades. The General Staff viewed the airplane as a new weapon that had proved useful in support of land operations, particularly in such strictly auxiliary functions as observation and spotting of artillery fire. The aviators viewed the airplane, on the other hand, not merely as a weapon but as creating a completely new form of warfare, different, independent, and more telling than that practiced by the ground Army and the Navy and perhaps even making those services unnecessary for future national defense. The General Staff's refusal to accept such a role for the airplane and to support it with funds accordingly the aviators attributed to prejudice, ignorance, and hostility. The aviators argued,

---

* Meanwhile, the announcement of the $640-million program in 1917 had caused the Germans to institute the *Amerikaprogramm,* substantially increasing their own aircraft production. U.S. Dept. of the Air Force, Office of Air Force History, *The Army Air Forces in World War II.* Vol. I: *Plans and Early Operations, January 1939 to August 1942,* ed. by Wesley Frank Craven and James Lee Cate (Chicago, University of Chicago Press, 1948), p. 9.

consequently, for a separate organization in which military air power could develop fully, free from the unsympathetic and short-sighted control of nonfliers.[47] The aviators' specific organizational model was Britain's Royal Air Force, which was constituted in 1918 out of the Army's Royal Flying Corps and the Navy's Royal Naval Air Service and placed under a separate, cabinet-level Air Ministry.

The Army aviators used a "strategic doctrine" to justify their separation from the Army, although there is some question as to whether the doctrine came before the desire for separation or after it. In 1919, only months before he was to advocate publicly an independent Air Force before the Senate Military Affairs Committee, General Mitchell published an article describing the "theory of operations" that guided the Air Service in World War I as one dedicated to the immediate support of ground troops, as had been in fact the case.[48]

It was only in the course of the next few years, after repeated failures to get Congress to establish a separate air force, that Mitchell began to expound explicitly the theory of "strategic air bombardment." This theory held that the primary function of military aviation was not the support of armies or navies but independent operations against the enemy's homeland in order to destroy his industry and possibly his whole social organization to such a degree as would bring about total national collapse. Major General Hugh Trenchard, the first commander of the RAF, had implied this theory in building an Inter-Allied Independent Air Force in 1918 for contemplated use against German industries and cities, but the end of the war cut off his efforts before the raids could begin.[49] The theory was most fully set forth in 1921 by Giulio Douhet, an Italian air force general, in his book, *The Command of the Air*. Douhet's thesis was that the defense in ground operations had gained a permanent ascendancy over the offense and that, consequently, the land battle would be stalemated in future wars. The decision would go, therefore, to the country that could first gain "command of the air" through the destruction of its enemy's air force and then proceed to "take out" the enemy's industry and demoralize his population. This could all be done, according to Douhet, in short order: "A really strong Independent Air Force . . . could inflict upon an unprepared enemy such grave damage as to bring about a complete collapse of his forces in a very few days." [50]

Given the maximum range of about 350 miles for the stick-and-wire bomber of the immediate post-World War I period, the claims for total destruction through strategic bombardment did not seem very plausible to the emotionally uncommitted. As one of the leaders of naval aviation summed up in 1925 the dominant reaction to the Army aviators' theory of strategic air bombardment,

It isn't even their own idea, but the nonsense preached by that Italian General Douhet in a book called *Command of the Air*. And on his say-so, these wild-eyed enthusiasts want to scrap the Army and Navy, on no other grounds than their personal opinions, unsupported by experience or fact.[51]

The War and Navy Departments were therefore able to block any independent Air Force with the general argument that ground and naval forces must have control of their own supporting aviation. In response to this situation, the Army fliers sought quite consciously from the early 1920s on to develop a heavy bomber with sufficient range and bombload to apply the doctrine of strategic bombardment and thus fortify their demands for organizational independence. The first such bomber was the B-17, which had a range of over 1,000 miles and was successfully tested in 1935.[52]

Strategic bombardment was practiced extensively in World War II. The Army Air Forces sent huge fleets of B-17's, B-24's, and B-29's against Germany and Japan, dropping tonnages of bombs that exceeded by factors of 1,000 the amount postulated by Douhet for ending a war in a matter of days. Strategic bombing by the winter of 1944–45 (at which time the Allied ground armies had also begun their land conquest of the German home territory [53]) brought portions of the German war economy to "virtual collapse" and, with the dropping of the two atomic bombs, precipitated Japan's surrender; [54] but it is quite clear that strategic bombing did not "win the war." As one leading military analyst concluded on the basis of his detailed examination of the findings of the U.S. Strategic Bombing Survey,

Air power had a mighty vindication in World War II. But . . . it was in tactical employment that success was most spectacular and that the air forces won the unqualified respect and admiration of the older services. By contrast, the purely strategic successes, however far-reaching in particular instances, were never completely convincing to uncommitted observers. Against Germany they came too late to have a clearly decisive effect; against Japan they were imposed on an enemy already prostrated by other forms of war.[55]

Put very simply, the Bombing Survey found (1) that high-explosive bombs did not have anywhere near the irreparable destructive effects on machines and factory buildings predicted by Douhet and the Army aviators, and (2) that any demoralization inflicted upon the civilian population could not be transformed into effective influence on its government to end the war.[56]

Despite the findings of the Strategic Bombing Survey, the Army Air Forces generals did come back to argue during the unification conflict that they had, in effect, "won the war." They claimed therefore that now, more than ever, they deserved an organizational home equal in status to that held by the ground Army and the Navy. But their clinching argument in 1945 was the existence of the atomic bomb—a bomb with about 10,000 times the power of the typical World War II high-explosive projectile.[57] As General Arnold concluded in his final report to the Secretary of War released on November 12, 1945,

> The influence of atomic energy on Air Power can be stated very simply. It has made Air Power all-important. . . . [The] only known effective means of delivering atomic bombs in their present state of development is the very heavy bomber. . . .
>
> This country . . . must recognize that real security . . . in the visible future will rest on our ability to take immediate offensive action with overwhelming force. It must be apparent to a potential aggressor that an attack on the United States would be immediately followed by an immensely devastating air-atomic attack on him.
>
> The atomic weapon thus makes . . . Air Power (in a state of immediate readiness) the primary requisite of national survival.[58]

It was thus unthinkable that the "all-important . . . primary requisite for national survival" should continue subject to even the nominal control of those who had not been fully initiated into its mysteries.

Actually, by 1945 the goal of a separate Air Force had become almost entirely a matter of tradition for the Army fliers. They could no longer complain (and did not, in fact, complain during any of the hearings) that they were being unduly restricted either in their careers or in their development of air power by a nonflying, unsympathetic General Staff. To begin with, they were at the end of World War II for all practical purposes completely independent of General Staff control, feeling at most only some slight subordination to the Chief of Staff of the Army himself and to the Secretary of War.[59] Second, the aviators' share of the first peacetime budget (fiscal 1948) was over half of the total for the whole War Department.[60] Third, by early 1946 Air Force officers had held at various times the posts of Deputy Chief of Staff of the Army, Chief of the War Plans Division, and Chief of the Operations Division of the

General Staff, and they were fully represented in all the General Staff divisions at the working level. Indeed, there was no reason that an Air Force officer could not look forward to becoming Chief of Staff of the Army in the very near future.[61] Admiral Sherman, himself a leading naval aviator who would be appointed Deputy Chief of Naval Operations and eventually reach the top Navy post during the Korean War, pointed out to the Senate Military Affairs Committee that he was

personally inclined to the view that through the process of evolution if the present organization should continue, the air forces would dominate the Army. . . .

We would see the day when the Chief of Staff or at least many of his principal subordinates, would normally be flying officers. . . .

The question will really be reversed and become whether or not the ground forces should have autonomy. . . .

I personally, if asked to give advice, . . . would retain the War Department as one department, and let the air reach dominance in that department.

That is what I have advocated in the Navy.[62]

But the Army Air Forces generals, who had been junior officers in Billy Mitchell's day, had completely committed themselves to the goal of independence when it had had some instrumental value, and they could not now abandon it.[63] They still recalled with a sense of injustice the "martyrdom" of their leader and, as they saw it, their having been short-changed at least until 1939 in promotions to high rank and in the General Staff's determination of the overall War Department budget (even though from the middle 1930s on they were actually receiving 60 to 80 percent of the Department's funds for research and development).[64] They remembered that even after Congress had authorized, in the Air Corps Act of 1926, a substantial five-year expansion program for Army aviation, the nonflying War Department hierarchy, abetted by the Budget Bureau, had proceeded to make cuts in the aviators' appropriations requests for the next five years averaging some 40 percent.[65] They frequently referred to the fact that after the successful flight of the B-17 in 1935, the first true strategic bombardment plane, the General Staff cut the Air Corps' 1936 request for 65 additional B-17's to 26 and their 1937 request for 60 B-17's to 26 and then to 20 and that for one short period in late 1937 and early 1938 the General Staff decided against authorizing any additional four-engined bombers at all.[66]

The Army aviators were firmly convinced that Congress had been ready to appropriate larger funds for aircraft throughout the interwar period and that only the Air Corps' lack of direct access to the legislators because of its subordinate position in the War Department had prevented the Corps from getting those funds. Such a situation the fliers were determined to prevent in the future through independence. The Air Force leaders were aware of the privileged organizational status they enjoyed within the War Department at the end of World War II, but they were also conscious that it was the result of an executive order based on the First War Powers Act, whose authority was due to expire automatically six months after the formal end of the war. Although reduced status was highly unlikely, the aviators could not be absolutely certain that "hostile" elements would not again capture the General Staff and try to bring them under strict control and deny them adequate funds.

CONTROL OF ALL LAND-BASED AVIATION

Although the Air Force based its claim to independence in the unification conflict on the overwhelming importance of strategic bombing with atomic weapons, its leaders argued that, furthermore, not only the strategic air warfare planes, but also "all land-based air must be under the [separate Air Force]. We cannot efficiently split our forces. . . . Carrier-based aviation should remain under Navy control but all land-based aviation must be under one agency." [67]

The nonstrategic land-based aircraft in question involved two categories: (1) those used by the Army for close support of ground troops and for transport purposes, which were already controlled by the Army Air Forces, and (2) those used by the Marines for close-support purposes and by the Navy for antisubmarine warfare, long-distance overwater reconnaissance, and protection of shipping. Since the ground Army was not opposing inclusion of its support and transport aircraft within an independent Air Force, the aviators' claim for complete control of land-based aircraft had reference to the Marine and Navy land planes and particularly the bomber-type aircraft that the Navy had been using for reconnaissance and antisubmarine warfare.

By the end of World War II, the Navy had acquired about 1,000 B-24 four-engine bombers as well as a smaller number of multiengine land-planes of its own design. The Navy had begun to acquire the B-24's, planes that the Air Corps had originally developed for strategic bombing, in 1942 for use in the antisubmarine campaign in the Atlantic, which was under the Navy's general responsibility. The Navy found that the seaplanes it had been using for patrol and attack purposes tended to become icebound in northern latitudes and that landplanes also had advantages with respect to range, ease of operation, firepower, and invulnerability, making them generally more desirable than seaplanes for anti-submarine work. The Army Air Forces, which controlled the production and allocation of bomber-type planes during the war, at first simply dismissed the Navy's requests for its bombers, but after prolonged negotiations between Admiral King and General Marshall and the mounting submarine sinkings in the Atlantic, the Air Force, at Marshall's insistence, provided certain of its bomber-type landplanes to the Navy. In the course of the war the Navy also proceeded to organize land-based aircraft into "fleet air wings" in the Pacific to provide long-range over-water reconnaissance for the fleet which could not be carried out so effectively by carrier-based planes or by seaplanes.[68]

Although the Army Air Forces complied with the direction of their Chief of Staff and diverted some of their landplanes to the Navy, the aviators never ceased to object, arguing that as a matter of organizational principle,* all land-based aircraft should be controlled by the Air Forces. The organizational principle had, no doubt, been buttressed in 1942 by the Army aviators' reluctance to let any of the limited number of aircraft available for strategic bombing against Germany be used for other functions, especially functions that they did not directly control. By the end of the war, the Army aviators claimed actually to fear that the Navy might use the landplanes to develop its own long-range strategic bombing force and so challenge the very basis on which the Air Forces expected to be staking its postwar claims for independence and budgetary preferment.[69] But the overriding consideration in attempting to gain control of all land-based planes was probably the normal bureaucratic desire to maximize the size of one's organization. The great destructiveness of atomic bombs, in addition to making the strategic air force "all-important," had also made it possible, as some of the admirals pointed out, for it to be relatively small.[70] Unless the separate Air Force could capture

---

* The Army aviators could not argue on the basis of concrete examples of Navy misuse of land-based aircraft, because they apparently knew of none: as late as Jan. 29, 1946, a senior officer attached to "Headquarters, Army Air Forces," in Washington would complain that in connection with the "battle over land-based air," more research would have to be done because the "surprising thing" was that it had been impossible "to find in this building anything other than the merest scraps of information as to what the Navy had and what it did with it." Memorandum in Norstad Files.

land-based aviation in general, its leaders would most likely be presiding over the smallest of the three services.

The more "imperialistic" of the Air Force generals tried to include within the exclusive cognizance of the independent Air Force not only all land-based aircraft but all "air weapons." According to General Doolittle, an air weapon was

any weapon, any directed weapon that uses air as a medium of travel . . . , whether an airplane with a pilot or an airplane without a pilot; whether it had wings, complete wings, rudimentary wings or whether the wings are entirely absent. If it is directed after it starts off and uses air as a medium of travel, it is, then, an air weapon.[71]

Such a definition was intended to capture for the Air Force control of guided missiles, which were seen in 1945 as the weapon of the future. Even General Doolittle, however, was not prescient enough to foresee that ballistic missiles rather than guided missiles would become the real key to unlock congressional larders from the middle 1950s on, and his discussion of air weapons specifically excluded artillery shells and bazookas, to which the ballistic missiles (being undirected in flight) are most akin in principle.[72]

To sum up, the overriding goal of the Army Air Forces hierarchy in the unification conflict was the separation of their organization from the Army and its establishment as a third military service controlling all land-based military aircraft, including those being then used by the Navy. Another goal, revealed by Assistant Secretary of War for Air Robert Lovett before the Woodrum Committee but not being pressed by 1945, was to control the research and development, the procurement, the recruitment organizations, and all but the most advanced flight-training schools for all aviation including carrier-borne. The Army aviators' ultimately preferred objective was, of course, the post-World War I status of the Royal Air Force—an organization controlling all military aviation and determining by its overall allocation of funds and personnel the relative emphasis to be given to the various types of air warfare. But such a goal was impossible to achieve in 1945, and it was useless to advocate it officially. That this ultimate objective would persist was indicated by General Spaatz' speech to the pro-Army Air Forces Wings Club in 1946. As the General continued to see it,

Control of the air has always been split up among a number of agencies. Our point is this: You can have an air element in the Army and another air element in the Navy. That would make the air elements serving the surface. Or, you can have an air force serving Air Power in the full expanse of the third dimension, its own medium. The Air Force will never reach its full stature so long as it remains the divided responsibility of agencies whose major interests lie in other fields.[73]

The Army aviators' line of argument in justification of the kind of separate Air Force that they proposed in 1944 and 1945 could be reconstructed as follows: Strategic air warfare is the overwhelmingly decisive warfare of the future. An organizational entity must therefore be set up with primary responsibility for this kind of warfare, since such organizations already exist for the less important, if not completely obsolete, forms of land and sea warfare. But since the strategic air warfare organization will be the most important, if not necessarily the largest, user of land-based military aircraft, all land-based aircraft must belong to that organization because their possession by the Army or the Navy would constitute "duplication," an unquestionable and expensive evil.

Similarly, since the overall Air Force would become, through this line of reasoning, the largest developer and procurer of aircraft and the largest recruiter and trainer of pilots, any development, procurement, and training establishments in the Army or the Navy would also amount to duplication and should therefore not be allowed to exist. Finally, since aircraft are essentially weapons using air as a medium and being directed in flight, and since the Air Force will be the preponderant user of such directed air weapons, all air weapons, including guided missiles, should belong to the new Air Force.

After tracing the attempts of the Army aviators to achieve organizational independence in the interwar period, their official historians felt forced to comment, "Read out of context, the story of the struggle can be made to appear . . . an attempt of ambitious officers to further their own petty interests by escape from the salutory control of a beneficent General Staff." [74] The historians' observation is accurate and could be extended to the immediate postwar period as well. The only question is whether the opening qualifying phrase was absolutely necessary.

President Truman

When Harry Truman became President in April, 1945, he already held the "strongest convictions" that the country's defense setup was "antiquated" and needed quick reorganization.[75] Truman had begun to study military organization in World War I, when he served with the Army in France, and he continued his interest while rising to the rank of colonel in the Army Reserve during the interwar period.* When Truman entered the Senate in 1937, he maintained his contact with the Army and its problems through service on the Military Affairs Committee and the Subcommittee on Military (War Department) Appropriations. From March, 1941, until his election to the Vice Presidency, Truman also headed the "Special Committee to Investigate the National Defense Program," which was studying industrial mobilization and military procurement matters. All these experiences had served to give him "some very definite ideas on what the military department of a republic like ours should be"—ideas that he had published [76] during the 1944 presidential campaign.[77]

SHARING OF ARMY GROUND FORCES GOALS

Truman recommended, as we have seen, what was essentially the War Department's plan for unification in his special message to Congress in December, 1945. His long and apparently gratifying contact with the Army had thoroughly imbued him with the War Department's organizational theory of straight-line military command for furthering combat effectiveness. Indeed, Truman had gone farther in his magazine article than the Army generals themselves, calling for the complete elimination of the JCS and its replacement by an overall General Staff under a single commander.[78] Identifying himself with the Army, Truman also shared its sense of injustice over the favored treatment perceived to be accorded to the Navy in personnel and budgetary matters and looked to a single department to enforce "equitable" policies. Finally, Truman's investigations in the Senate had convinced him that there had been "wastes" and "duplications" in military procurement during the war,[79] and at some point he must also have become convinced that, as the War Department had been contending, a single department would eliminate them by forcing better coordinated purchasing and common use of facilities.

Truman had one other argument in favor of unification that had not

* After talking to the President about unification in July, 1945, Forrestal thought "it was clear that most of his thinking was predicated upon his experience in the Army during the last war and in the National Guard since then." The President "remarked that he had gone every year to a refresher training course and had read and thought a great deal about military problems." In one of his rare misjudgments about people, Forrestal gained the impression from the conversation that Truman was "not close-minded [about unification] nor will he hold rigidly to his own views." Forrestal Diaries, p. 89.

been used by the Army generals. The President claimed that in addition to its other faults, the two-department system of military organization had been largely responsible for the success of the Japanese surprise attack against Pearl Harbor on December 7, 1941. Writing three years later as the vice-presidential nominee, Truman asked rhetorically,

Granting neglects and derelictions, what stands clearer than that the root cause of the Pearl Harbor tragedy was the lack of a single security set-up, and the fact that two Secretaries in Washington issued their separate commands to two field commanders, each reared in the tradition that cooperation carries the risk of endangering independence? [80]

It was probably Truman's article that originated the belief that the Army and Navy commanders at Pearl Harbor were personal enemies. As he had put it, "In Hawaii, General Short and Admiral Kimmel could meet, if they happened to be on speaking terms, or exchange cables and radiograms" to coordinate their preparations in late 1941 for meeting the expected Japanese attack in the Pacific.[81] Whatever the lack of fullness in their exchange of information, Short and Kimmel had actually been good friends and, besides seeing each other socially, had held routine conferences as late as December 1, 2, and 3 to discuss the defense situation.[82]

SPECIAL PRESIDENTIAL STAKES

Although Truman's sharing of the Army's organizational goals and theories would have caused him to support the War Department's plan in any event, his conception of his own role as President gave him independent incentives to press for some sort of unification of the Army and Navy into a single department. As President in the immediate postwar period, Truman felt that he had many more pressing problems than military affairs. He did not wish, therefore, to devote much of his limited time and energy to the coordination of two separate military departments —a situation that would become even more demanding, as he saw it, with the inevitable establishment of the Air Force as a third Cabinet-level military department.[83] Truman's overriding consideration in favor of unification was that

The President, as Commander in Chief, should not personally have to coordinate the Army and Navy and Air Force. With all the other problems before him, the President cannot be expected to balance either the organization, the training or the practice of the several branches of national defense. He should be able to rely for that coordination upon civilian hands at the Cabinet level.[84]

Furthermore, Truman had the normal presidential desire to maximize his own control, as opposed to that of Congress, over the various parts of the executive branch. He resented that under the existing system, as he saw it,

The chairmen of the Military and Naval Affairs committees, especially in the House, where appropriations originate, tended to become Secretaries of War and Navy. There were a couple of House members, chairmen of the Military Appropriations Subcommittee and Naval Affairs Committee, who had to have seventeen-gun salutes, parades, etc., as often as they could find excuses to visit Army posts and naval bases.[85]

Truman thought that a single cabinet officer over all the armed forces and a single military budget, by presenting a common front to Congress, would maximize presidential control over the military establishment. Similar considerations led him to endorse the War Department demand for congressional enactment only of the overall framework of the single department with authority to prescribe the details delegated to the executive branch.

4

Navy Department Coalition Goals

The Navy Department coalition in the unification conflict centered around the goal of preserving the Navy and all its constituent parts as they had developed during World War II, that is, a sizable fleet based primarily on the naval air power of fast-carrier task forces and including a "Fleet Marine Force" as the country's combat-ready landing force and as the trustee and refiner of amphibious warfare expertise. Secretary of the Navy Forrestal personally also gave high priority to the creation of governmental bodies to consciously coordinate military policy and programs with foreign policy objectives and to prepare and keep up-to-date plans for mobilizing the economy to support the adopted military programs in case of actual war. Forrestal had explained to the Senate Military Affairs Committee in 1945, when he brought along an organizational chart showing the National Security Council and National Security Resources Board as part of the Navy's suggested unification plan, that it was a "fetish" of his that

the question of national security is not merely a question of the Army and Navy. . . .
We have to take into account our whole potential for war, our mines, industry, manpower, research, and all the activities that go into normal civilian life. I do not think you can deal with this only by the War and Navy Departments. . . .
I think the State Department is [also] part of the team.[1]

A State-War-Navy Secretaries Committee, which on a very informal basis resembled Forrestal and Eberstadt's National Security Council, and a more formalized lower-level State-War-Navy Coordinating Committee (SWNCC) had already been in operation since the last stages of World War II.[2] The War Department offered no real objections to the Navy proposals for superdepartmental coordinating committees, simply arguing that they were on a different organizational level from their own and hence neither incompatible nor substitutable.[3] Thus, these proposals did not provide a significant basis of cleavage in the conflict over unification.

Combat Effectiveness and a Strong Navy

At the end of World War II, the Navy leaders still considered axiomatic the Mahan thesis that a strong navy and command of the sea were indispensable elements in maintaining overall combat effectiveness and national security. As Admiral King articulated the Navy interpretation of the war experience, sea power had proved essential in the defeat of Germany "because of the necessity of transporting our entire military effort across the Atlantic. . . . Without command of the sea, this could not have been done."

The war in the Pacific, furthermore, had been "primarily a naval war," with Japan surrendering after her navy and merchant fleet had been destroyed even though her armies were still intact and her air forces only weakened:

Dependent upon imported food and raw materials and relying upon sea transport to supply her armies at home and overseas, Japan lost the war because she lost command of the sea, and in so doing lost—to us—the island bases from which her factories and cities could be destroyed by air.[4]*

Consequently, one yardstick by which to measure any proposal to change the existing military organization had to be, in the words of Admiral Nimitz, "How does it affect our seapower?" "Our country," he continued, "is dependent on our seapower for its external influence. With the control of the sea lanes we have influence; without that control

---

* "The Army," Admiral Leahy has written, never appeared "to be able to understand that the Navy, with some Army air assistance had [by the fall of 1944], already defeated Japan. The Army not only was planning a huge land invasion of Japan, but was convinced that we needed Russian assistance as well to bring the war against Japan to a successful conclusion." William D. Leahy, *I Was There: The Personal Story of the Chief of Staff to Presidents Roosevelt and Truman* (New York, McGraw-Hill, 1950), pp. 304–05.

we are limited to the boundaries of our continent." [5] Nimitz amplified his thought a few minutes later:

I do not oppose change out of the feeling that the old ways are the best ways. If I were a conservative of that kind I could not have formed and stated the opinions I held a year ago [favoring unification]. If the Navy were conservative in that way, it would never have developed effective amphibious and carrier warfare. I do value the history and tradition of the Navy. That, however, is no superficial affection for seagoing vocabulary and customs, but a deep sense of what sea power has meant to our country and to England in controlling vital sea lanes in time of war. I do not believe our people are sufficiently aware of the importance to America of the control of the seas. Perhaps this is something well understood and valued by the Navy's sister services, but if so we are not often given that assurance. [6]

Little attempt was made by the Navy leaders during the unification hearings to provide an explicit justification for a strong fleet in the emerging atomic age, either from the point of view of its possible vulnerability or of its necessity in the face of the overwhelmingly destructive nature of bombardment with atomic weapons. [7] Vice Admiral Charles M. Cooke, Jr., the Deputy Chief of Naval Operations (Operations), made the most detailed attempt to provide a rationale for the postwar Navy:

It is true that with the developments the future is apt to bring, long-range aircraft . . . and long-range rockets may be utilized to bombard the United States. Similarly, the United States can retaliate with long-range aircraft and rockets. What do we have to do in such a stalemated situation? We have to advance our bombing platforms or bases to positions closer to our overseas enemy while preventing him from using the seas to close the range for increasing the power of his attack against us. We have to be prepared to cut off his supplies by sea. We must be ready to project ground forces and air forces overseas to seize the positions from which we are being bombarded. In no other way can such a war, if it becomes a total war, be successfully concluded.

To accomplish these missions, to maintain the singularly potent advantages that our island position gives us, we must develop and maintain a powerful navy. This navy must be stronger than any possible combination of navies in the Pacific and Atlantic, not only those possible enemy navies now existing, but any that foreign building capacity can produce in the future. [8]

In other words, the Navy did not see the atomic bomb as making a qualitative difference in warfare. Unable, like the ground Army and the Army Air Forces, to foresee limited wars of the Korean or Viet Nam type, the Navy conceived of any future war as another World War II, only with much more destructive (though still indecisive) bombing. To end the war, therefore, the Navy would again have to carry out its traditional roles at sea and support the Army in invading and capturing the enemy's territory.

Only Admiral Sherman mentioned the possibility of a radically new role for the Navy. Commenting on some of General Doolittle's remarks about the obsolescence of any kind of Navy, Sherman briefly speculated that one of the key weapons of the future might actually be "a large armored [naval] vessel firing guided missiles with atomic warheads." He argued that no possibly fruitful approaches to the development of new weapons systems should be cut off by granting a monopoly of the airplane, the guided missile, "or any other weapon or technical device [read, 'the atomic bomb']" to a single service. But even Sherman emphasized the World War II functions of the Navy. He reminded the Senators that if a war came in the near future, it would have to be fought for the most part with existing weapons and tactics, including carriers, submarines, and even battleships. As Sherman put it, "while planning for the conditions of 10 or 20 years hence we must not overlook tomorrow." [9]

Given the Navy's intense feeling about the continued value of seapower and the need for an effective fleet, its leaders were not predisposed to seek major changes in the organizational system that had allowed it to become stronger than all the other navies of the world combined. Of course, the Navy's growth had been primarily a wartime phenomenon and, like the Army, it too had had slim budgetary pickings in the interwar period. Before the passage of the Vinson-Trammell Act in 1934, the Navy had not even been authorized to build up to the tonnage limits imposed by the Washington Conference of 1922 or the London Naval Conference of 1930. Moreover, funds were not provided to achieve authorized treaty strength until the late 1930s, and not until 1940 were the vessels actually on hand.[10] Throughout the 1920s and 1930s, the planners in the Navy Department were repeatedly pointing out that "strengthening the fleet, especially with respect to auxiliary ships and naval aviation, was essential to the carrying out of [the Navy's] mission in any future war in which the United States might find itself engaged, particularly a war in the Pacific." [11] So serious was the situation that, even before the fleet was severely damaged at Pearl Harbor, the Navy was calculating that weakness would prevent it from taking offensive action in the western Pacific for from six to nine months after the beginning of war.[12]

Nevertheless, the Navy leaders had not developed any sense of unjust deprivation as a result of their interwar experience, and they especially did not hold the organizational system responsible for their past difficulties. First of all, although funds had certainly been short relative to the perceived needs of the Navy to carry out its tasks, between 1922 and 1939, with one exception, they always exceeded those granted to the Army.[13] Second, it was common knowledge that during the careers of the Navy's World War II leaders, the Navy had been the favorite service in Congress. Not only did it get more money, which might be justified on the ground of the Navy's having been regarded the country's first line of defense, but it had established such excellent relations with the Naval Affairs Committees, especially the one in the House, that the details of its promotion and retirement policy and its pay scales and allowances were all considered as good or better than the equivalent benefits in the Army.

Finally, the Navy's Commander in Chief from 1933 to 1945 had been Franklin D. Roosevelt. Roosevelt had been Assistant Secretary of the Navy (at a time when there were no other under secretaries or assistant secretaries) for the eight years of Woodrow Wilson's administration and had formed lasting friendships with many of the officers who were to rise to high rank during his own Presidency. He was known to be a lover of ships and the sea.* If Roosevelt as President did not always fully press the Navy's claims before Congress, the admirals knew that it was not because he was unsympathetic to them.

In short, the Navy during and immediately after World War II was a satisfied service. It wanted nothing more than to be left undisturbed,

---

* After visiting Roosevelt in the White House in 1935, Billy Mitchell told a friend about the President's desk being covered with all sorts of "gimcracks," including miniatures of ship's clocks, steering wheels, life preservers, etc. "I wish," Mitchell is supposed to have said, "I could have seen an airplane model in that collection." R. Earl McClendon, *The Question of Autonomy for the United States Air Arm, 1907–1945* (Maxwell Air Force Base, Ala., 1950), pp. 152–53.

Although Roosevelt loved the Navy, he did not unreservedly love the admirals. After once complaining to a friend about the difficulties of getting the action he wanted from the Treasury and State Departments, Roosevelt explained,

"But the Treasury and the State Department put together are nothing compared with the Na-a-vy. The admirals are really something to cope with—and I should know. To change anything in the Na-a-vy is like punching a feather bed. You punch it with your right and you punch it with your left until you are finally exhausted, and then you find the damn bed just as it was before your started punching." Quoted in Marriner S. Eccles, *Beckoning Frontiers: Public and Personal Recollections,* ed. by Sidney Hyman (New York, Knopf, 1951), p. 336.

with its own Secretary dealing with its own committees and appropriations subcommittees in Congress and presenting its case to the President. As one of the top Pacific commanders would put it, the Navy "just wants to hold what it has. . . . [It] has never made any effort to take Army transports over from the Army or interfere with the Coast Guard. All we want is the tools that we need to do the job, that properly belong to us." [14]

The Navy believed that its difficulties during the interwar period had been due to the general public's unwillingness to maintain adequate armed forces in time of peace. If any major organizational change were desirable, it would be the establishment of the Eberstadt Report's National Security Council, whose high-status members (including the President and the Secretary of State) could authoritatively set concrete foreign policy objectives to which the services could refer in justifying their requests for funds. Eberstadt had specifically recommended that the Council make annual reports to the President and to Congress and, to the extent that absolute secrecy was not required, that the reports also be released to the public so that the "Council could aid in building up public support for clear-cut, consistent, and effective foreign and military policies." [15] The Navy realized that the Air Force had come of age and would become increasingly more popular with both Congress and the general public; but the Navy was content, indeed insistent, that it be left alone to take its chances of independently persuading Congress to appropriate sufficient funds to allow it to fulfill its given missions.

Despite the Navy's general satisfaction with the organizational *status quo,* not all its leaders at the beginning of the unification discussions were opposed to a single military department. It will be recalled that Admiral Stark had proposed a Navy General Board plan for a joint general staff to the old Joint Board in early 1942 and that Admiral Yarnell had publicly advocated unification in 1943.[16] Even in 1944, Admirals Nimitz, Halsey, Kinkaid, and Sherman, among others, had endorsed unification as a general principle before the Richardson Committee, and Secretary of the Navy Frank Knox had told Secretary of War Stimson and Representative Woodrum just before the Woodrum Committee hearings that he too was not opposed to a single department.[17]

Unity of command in the field under a single commander with a joint staff had worked well, and it appeared plausible to carry that unity of command to a higher level in the form of a single department in Washington. Besides, the Navy too would probably have liked to bypass the

Budget Bureau if possible. Admiral Sherman would explain in 1947 that it was a "practical problem" for the Navy Department "that our budgetary requirements are reviewed by people in the Bureau of the Budget, and adjustments are made . . . by people . . . who do not have access to our strategic concepts and our military plans." [18] By that time the concept of a Secretary of Defense had finally been accepted, and Sherman admitted the hope that the new Secretary would constitute an official responsible for that "adjustment" who is "fully informed as to our foreign policy and as to our international situation, . . . and who has at his disposal all of the information that is available to the Joint Chiefs of Staff." [19]

It became increasingly clear to the Navy field commanders in early 1945, however, as it had been clear to Forrestal, and perhaps to King, in Washington all along, that one of the chief goals of the Army's unification plans was the weakening of the Navy's relatively satisfactory position in the appropriations process and that the goal of some of the War Department coalition's more extreme elements was the virtual destruction of the Navy. Admiral Sherman told the Military Affairs Committee about the "general change of feeling about the feasibility of a single department" that took place among naval officers in the Pacific in the spring of 1945:

As the war against Germany under an Army commander drew to a close, the policy of the War Department with respect to unity of command appeared to change and the Army forces in the Pacific Ocean areas were gradually but completely withdrawn from command by a naval officer.[20]

The two major events that disillusioned the admirals were the establishment of the Twentieth Air Force on the Marianas for attacks against Japan, with its commander directly responsible to General Arnold in Washington even though both the base and the target were within Nimitz' Pacific Ocean Areas, and the issuance of a JCS directive, upon the insistence of the Army, that had transferred to General MacArthur control of all Army ground and service forces in the Pacific. It thus appeared to the Navy leaders that as soon as the Navy's cooperation in Europe was no longer necessary, the Army was rejecting the principle of unity of command if it could not appoint and control the unified commander.[21]

Furthermore, after the end of the war in the Pacific, the former Navy field commanders were able to pay some attention to the testimony of the

War Department witnesses in the unification hearings. The admirals noted (with Admiral Halsey quoting in his own testimony) Secretary Patterson's statement about not tolerating "in our military budget over-large sums for one purpose and insufficient sums for another which must inevitably result from lack of a single military direction." [22] It is unlikely that they missed General Marshall's remarks about the necessity of a single budget to insure a "balanced program" and prevent the best "salesman" from getting the largest appropriations through independent presentations to Congress.

Now what did this "balanced program" mean? The Navy calculated that the persons trying to effect an organizational change to bring it about must obviously have felt that previous programs had been "unbalanced" to their disadvantage. The balance, the Navy leaders realized, was to be effected according to the ground Army's point of view at Navy expense and be guaranteed primarily by the overall Chief of Staff who, even if, as the President had suggested in his 1945 message, he were to be rotated among the services, was expected almost certainly to be an Army general for the immediate future. Admiral Cooke stated the Navy's perception of the situation quite simply:

The urgers [of unification] appear to feel that, on the one hand, the budget of the Army air component of the land forces would not receive adequate consideration unless this air component was divorced from the Ground Forces and, on the other hand, that the Navy budget would not be properly integrated and adjusted to the needs of the land components unless it was married to the land forces.[23]

The Navy too was in favor of a "balanced program," [24] but to the Navy leaders this term meant an overall military program that included as strong a fleet as its own leaders could persuade Congress to support in order for the Navy to carry out the missions assigned to it by the JCS and the President. As Admiral King expressed the thought in language that was also not likely to lose any goodwill among the legislators:

Under the Constitution, it is the duty of Congress to "provide and maintain a Navy." Granted that the requirements of the Navy, translated into dollars and cents and transmitted to Congress through the budgetary machinery now provided, are dependent upon our approved military strategy, recommendations for which originate with the Joint Chiefs of Staff, the final decision as to the amount of money necessary will be made by Congress. . . . The needs of the Navy should not be subject to review by individuals who do not have informed responsibility in the premises. In my opinion, once the functions of the armed services have been coordinated by strategic decisions and allocation of tasks, there should be no real impediment to presentation of estimated requirements to Congress.[25]

A few minutes later, in response to Senator Lister Hill's criticism about the Navy not having submitted its plan in 1945 for the size of the post-war fleet to the War Department before presentation to the Senate and House Naval Affairs Committees, King put in even plainer terms what the Navy was resisting:

[The plan] is a pattern. It can be adjusted. I do not think it will be adjusted upward. But it can be adjusted downward if the Congress sees fit to do so. But may I be perfectly blunt: I am not ready to say it should be adjusted downward by the Army.[26]

Erecting one or two extra echelons—the Secretary of the Armed Forces or the overall Chief of Staff or both—in the chain of communication and command between the Navy, on the one hand, and the President and Congress, on the other, would at best introduce an unpredictable element into an otherwise satisfactory relationship and could, at worst, put the fortunes of the Navy into the hands of those ignorant or hostile to seapower. "We believe," Forrestal testified in 1945,

that the efficacy of the Navy's needs can well be left to a man who is an advocate for the Navy rather than going through a man who might be completely unaware of what seapower means. . . . I am completely convinced right now that it is of the utmost urgency that we keep our seapower. But I am afraid a civilian or a man coming from the Army would not have the time for the education that is necessary.[27]

A similar line of reasoning was behind the Navy's opposition to the elimination of the separate committees and subcommittees in Congress that was almost certain to result from unification. In a statement that once again could not fail to warm the hearts of the Navy's key congressional friends and also suggest bases for opposition to unification to Congressmen who might stand to lose organizational status through committee consolidation, Forrestal spoke of his belief

that one of the major reasons for the effectiveness of the various parts of our armed forces lies in the fact that there are in the Congress separate committees composed of men who through study and contact with each separate part have quite intimate knowledge of the needs of that part or service. It is my belief that no consolidated committee of the Congress could master the intricacies of both the Army and the Navy in their many ramifications to the extent that is now possible in the separate committees of naval affairs and military affairs.[28]

Separate committees that could best master the "intricacies" and acquire "intimate knowledge" of a service would be both better motivated and better able to convince Congress of the reasonableness of that service's requests to the mutual benefit of the Army and the Navy. Unlike the Army generals, the Navy leaders did not view the multiple-budget–multiple-committee system as competitive but as augmentative: two or three good advocates to press for military appropriations in each house of Congress were expected to obtain a larger total sum than one.

Organizational Integrity

In addition to the unpredictability to be introduced into the Navy's appropriations process by the single-budget aspect of the single military department and the consequent elimination of direct Navy justification of its monetary requests to the President and Congress, the War Department leaders caused the Navy to perceive as also inherent in unification the divestment of two of its parts: a World War II type of Fleet Marine Force and land-based aviation. This proposal ran directly against the Navy Department coalition's desire for continued integrity of their existing organization and for maximum combat effectiveness.

The Navy leaders shared, of course, the typical bureaucratic disinclination to lose any part of their organization or functions to a competitor, but they also were convinced that without amphibious forces to seize advanced naval bases from which to operate and to deny them to the enemy (the Navy was still thinking in terms of the World War II island-hopping campaigns of the Pacific) and without land-based aircraft to fight submarines and conduct long-distance overwater reconnaissance, the Fleet could not perform its functions in wartime properly. The Navy leaders denied that, because the War Department maintained large ground forces and large fleets of land-based aircraft to fulfill its own principal functions, the Navy as a matter of principle should not be allowed to maintain similar units when these were necessary to insure control of the seas. The Navy had never objected, for example, to the War Department's operating a fleet of over 1,500 ships by the end of the war to transport men and supplies. As Admiral King explained in his memoirs after recounting the conflict with the Army Air Forces over possession of land-based bombers for antisubmarine warfare, there existed a "basic difference in organizational concepts between the Army and the Navy":

> The Navy concept maintained that the *function* should be the basis for organization; that the Army, Navy, and air components of the Army should be assigned basic functions and given the bases and weapons to fulfill those functions in a unified manner regardless of whether the weapons operated on land, or sea, or in the air . . . and that no service should be artificially restricted in the employment of its weapons. . . . This was the principle of operational unification.
>
> The Army–Air Corps concept maintained that the *weapon* should be the basis for organization; that the Air Corps, for instance, should control and operate all aircraft and all functions of which aircraft are capable; that the Navy should control and operate all ships, and so forth.
>
> Of the two concepts, the Navy's was in accord with the generally accepted methods of business and government. The Army–Air Corps concept on the other hand was a purely military one, devised by the authorities of the German Army and of the Royal Air Force in England.[29]

In other words, the Navy thought that there were a number of differentiated general functions to be performed in wartime, such as extended land operations, control of the seas, and strategic bombing. It further held that although each function or kind of warfare required many of the same types of weapons for its success, the success of each was best assured when all the weapons needed were controlled by the one service responsible for the function, whose personnel possessed common loyalties and had undergone common training, thus maximizing cooperation in battle. Differently put, the Navy did not want to have to negotiate with the Army or with a separate Air Force for the weapons and units without which it could not accomplish its basic functions in a naval campaign.

The Navy leaders were also concerned that divestment of their land-based aircraft was but a first step and that a separate Air Force might eventually extend its control even to carrier-based aviation—the Fleet's major offensive weapon—thus completely destroying the effectiveness of the Navy. Assistant Secretary of War for Air Lovett had said almost as much before the Woodrum Committee in 1944, and it was common knowledge that an organizational set-up that would duplicate the post-World War I Royal Air Force had for years been the Army fliers' ultimately preferred goal.

Forrestal and the admirals were familiar with the British Navy's dissatisfaction over not having its own Fleet air force until war broke out in 1939. Throughout the interwar period, the high-status units in the RAF had been the Fighter Command and the Bomber Command. Their leaders had dominated the RAF–Air Ministry structure and controlled the funds, the types of aircraft, and the personnel made available to the Fleet. Since service with the Fleet air force was an unprestigious and infrequent tour of duty for the RAF fliers, none of them built up extensive experience in carrier operations and naval warfare. Similarly, since the Royal Navy had no aviators to work themselves up to the high ranks, its captains and admirals did not have flying experience and thus were not particularly air-minded. The aircraft developed by the Air Ministry for the Fleet air force, moreover, were not suitable for carrier warfare. In the eyes of the American Navy, it was these factors that led to some disastrous British warship losses because of lack of proper air cover, the most frequently cited of which were the sinking of the *Prince of Wales* and the *Repulse* off the coast of Malaya by the Japanese in December, 1941.[30]

The Navy leaders believed that the success that had characterized their own naval operations was the result of American naval aviation having been completely integrated with the rest of the Fleet and of air operations consequently having been planned, directed, and executed by naval aviators who were also line naval officers.[31] A strong separatist movement for air had never developed within the Navy as it had in the Army. Only once, in the 1920s, had a few of the younger naval aviators, who were discouraged by the lack of appreciation shown for the capabilities of carriers and carrier warfare by some of the entrenched "battleship admirals," begun talking seriously about "seceding" from the Navy. The dominant point of view was always that expressed by Rear Admiral William A. Moffett, long-time Chief of the Bureau of Aeronautics and recognized as the "father of naval aviation," when in cutting off the revolt, he admonished his younger colleagues, "Hell, we won't secede from the Navy. If we are half as good as we think we are, we'll take it over." [32] During World War II and immediately thereafter, they were doing just that.

The Navy's very real fear of a repetition of the RAF experience in the United States, leading to a divestment of its own air force, was highlighted in the following exchange between Senator Lister Hill and Secretary Forrestal before the Military Affairs Committee:

Senator HILL.   You realize this, don't you Mr. Secretary, that if you had these three services—land, sea, and air—on a parity or on an equality, that would not necessarily mean that the fleet would not have its air arm, would it, as it has today?

Secretary FORRESTAL.   All I know, Senator, the same statement was made about the RAF, regarding the British [naval] air arm . . . but I say at the beginning of the war the British Navy was stripped of air power, and it found the lack of air power a most costly and dangerous business. . . . You say the preservation of the use of air to the Navy can be guaranteed. You cannot guarantee areas of responsibility to ambitious men when they are assailed by men who quite properly want to exploit their weapons.[33]

Collective Strategy-Making

The Navy leaders saw still another part of the Army's unification plan as not conducive to combat effectiveness—the substitution of a single Chief of Staff for the JCS system of collective decision-making on matters of strategy. The Navy believed that there was a basic difference in the weight to be assigned to the factors of speed and thorough consideration in the combat theater and at the seat of the government. The Navy supported unity of command under a single theater commander in the field, where immediate decisions were often necessary to meet enemy action and to take advantage of tactical opportunities; but it denied that such unity of command necessarily required either a single department or a single chief of staff in Washington (something that the World War II experience would appear to have demonstrated) and that a single chief could make better strategic decisions than the JCS.

Forrestal testified before the Military Affairs Committee that in his opinion the war in the Pacific had been shortened because the Navy had been free to keep insisting in the JCS that a "limited offensive" in the Pacific would not interfere with victory in Europe. Throughout the war, King and the Navy had accepted the overall Allied strategy of concentrating the great preponderance of forces on the defeat of Germany first. The conflict between the Army and Navy strategists was a more peripheral one: The Army was willing to take risks of further losses to the Japanese in the Pacific for the sake of maximizing the forces in Europe; King and the Navy at first argued for the diversion of sufficient resources to the Pacific to be certain that no further losses occurred and later argued for sufficient forces to begin the "limited offensive" that by the time of the German surrender had carried American forces thousands of miles across the Pacific to Okinawa, within 350 miles of the Japanese home islands.[34] A more general defense of the JCS was made by Admiral King:

The strength of the Joint Chiefs of Staff lies in the combined knowledge possessed by the members and in the "checks and balances" that tend to prevent domination of any one person. When the history of the Joint Chiefs of Staff comes to be written, the record will show how many proposals—including some of my own—had to yield to the cogent reasoning of one or more members. As for rapidity of decision, the recent biennial report of the Chief of Staff of the Army relates a major decision made—when the premises were all available—and in the hands of General MacArthur and Admiral Nimitz in 90 minutes. This was the decision to attack Leyte 2 months ahead of schedule. I can say that while such speed was rare, the case is not an isolated one.[35]

The Navy leaders implied a theory of decision-making which held that strategic decisions—what objectives to attack and in what order, the size and types of forces to be used, the allocation of limited forces and equipment among competing theaters and kinds of warfare—were extremely complicated and were not susceptible to optimal determination. They argued that the ultimate test was success in battle, which could be best assured in a JCS system for strategic planning and direction consisting of a number of persons with equal status free to propose solutions and criticize the solutions of the others from the point of view of their special knowledge of the capabilities and limitations of their own service until a solution appeared that was not deemed unsatisfactory by anyone. No single officer, the Navy contended, would have the sufficient background in land, sea, and air operations to make the complete decision, because his previous experience and training had been restricted within either the Army or the Navy.

The Navy conceded that speed would often have to be sacrificed but argued that whereas a faulty tactical judgment could lose a battle, a hasty and ill-considered strategic one could lose the war. As Assistant Secretary of the Navy Kenney put it in a biting attack on the Army's stress on the need for eliminating delays,

If that is the all-important thing, to have the decisions made by one man who doesn't definitely know all the details, then, for heaven's sake, just toss a coin. Get a coin-tossing machine and you will get your decision. If you want an intelligent set-up and want to have a body than can get a grasp of all these things, don't rely on one man.[36]

Apart from their more theoretical objections to one-man strategic decision making, the Navy leaders were also concerned that the overall Chief of Staff might in time be an Air Force officer, who would unwisely commit the country exclusively to a strategy of air bombardment and restrict the Navy to transport duty. The Navy leaders recalled that as early as 1919 General Mitchell and his followers were already arguing that the airplane was making navies superfluous.[37] Just after the end of the war in the Pacific it was reliably reported that almost any important Army Air Forces officer was willing to say privately "that naval aviation is useless and that the carrier is 'dead.'" [38] Some, of course, like General Doolittle, were willing to say so publicly. The Army fliers were also beginning once again, with the advent of the atomic bomb and the planned development of a long-range bomber that could eventually reach any potential enemy from bases within the United States, to question seriously the necessity for any Navy at all. General Carl Spaatz, who had succeeded Arnold as Chief of the Army Air Forces and as a member of the JCS, openly asked in a speech before the Aviation Writers Association in March, 1946,

Why should we have a Navy at all? The Russians have little or no Navy, the Japanese Navy has been sunk, the navies of the rest of the world are negligible, the Germans never did have much of a Navy. The point I am getting at is, who is the big Navy being planned to fight? There are no enemies for it to fight except apparently the Army Air Force. In this day and age, to talk of fighting the next war on oceans is a ridiculous assumption. The only reason for us to have a Navy is because someone else has a Navy and we certainly do not need to waste money on that.[39]

With views like Spaatz' known to be held by many officers who could conceivably be appointed Chief of Staff of a unified department, the Navy leaders felt that their safety in preserving an effective fleet lay in a JCS organization where the Navy member by nonconcurring could prevent the adoption (subject to the President approving it anyway) of any policy seen to be disastrous for either the country, the Navy, or both.

Civilian Control

The chief-of-staff part of the Army unification plan was perceived to be incompatible with another of the Navy Department coalition's goals: civilian control of the military on the secretarial level of organization. This kind of civilian control required, from the Navy point of view, that (1) any civilian secretary have all-inclusive authority over his department, particularly with respect to the budget, and (2) the secretary have more than one formal line of communication and control to subordinate parts of his department.

The first requirement was fairly simple. Putting authority to formulate the departmental budget into the hands of the military chiefs and prohibiting the civilian secretary by law from changing it was clearly a radical departure from traditional practices. Even the old Commanding General of the Army, who had been independent of the Secretary of War before 1903 on questions of military policy, did not control the department's budget.[40] As Forrestal explained in his criticism of the Collins Plan, "the preparation of the budget, . . . after all is the most important function of the civilian Secretary of the War or Navy Department." [41] At the very minimum, the Navy leaders felt that in order to maintain civilian control, any cabinet secretary should have the right to formally recommend the departmental budget to the President through the Budget Bureau and to Congress.

The second requirement was more complicated. The Navy Department coalition insisted that even given all-inclusive authority, a civilian secretary still could not in fact control his department unless he had more than a single direct, formal source of recommendation and information. This precluded, consequently, an overall chief of staff, whom the War Department witnesses extolled, in Assistant Secretary McCloy's words, for the very reason that he would give the secretary "a single responsible source of information. . . . I think that is an important point. It gives him a single responsible source of information." [42]

Just as we have seen that there had been a tradition favoring a single Chief of Staff in the War Department since 1903, the dominant tradition in the Navy Department since the turn of the century had been against such an officer. Navy Department organization did not differ greatly from that of the War Department in 1900. A number of powerful bureaus, responsible for the construction, repair, manning, and provisioning of the Navy's ships, reported directly to the Secretary of the Navy.[43] The bureaus were independent of the sea-going Commander in Chief of the Fleet, who, unlike the Commanding General of the Army, also reported directly to the civilian departmental secretary.[44]

About 1900, a movement began among naval line officers to establish a general staff system in the Navy Department under a line officer with authority to coordinate the work of the bureaus from the point of view of the needs of the Fleet and to plan and direct the Fleet's operations in case of war. Up to and including the war with Spain, whenever the Fleet was likely to engage in combat, *ad hoc* arrangements had been made in Washington for its direction.[45] In 1900, McKinley's Secretary of the Navy, John D. Long, rejected the general-staff idea and established the General Board of the Navy, which consisted of a group of senior line officers who served in a purely advisory capacity to the Secretary on such matters as war plans, ship construction programs, and the characteristics of new ships.[46] Writing a few years later, Long explained that he had not wanted to "lapse into a figurehead [with] no other function than to sit . . . at the cabinet table." [47] The general-staff movement persisted, however, and in 1909, Taft's Secretary of the Navy, George von L. Meyer, responded to it once again by establishing the so-called "naval-aide system"—four senior line officers who would "aid the Secretary in efficiently administering" the fields (including the relevant bureau activities) of fleet operations, personnel, material, and inspections but who themselves would hold no independent authority.[48]

The Navy chief-of-staff men were still not satisfied, and the issue finally came to a head under Wilson's Secretary of the Navy, Josephus Daniels. Daniels' Aide for Operations, Rear Admiral Bradley A. Fiske, was a leading advocate of the general-staff system and repeatedly recommended it to the Secretary. Daniels, however, refused to be persuaded, believing that the "alleged need for a General Staff [was] mere camouflage for the elimination of civilian control." [49] In 1915, Fiske managed to get Representative Richmond P. Hobson, a retired naval officer and a hero of the Spanish-American War, to introduce a bill that Fiske had principally drafted establishing "a Chief of Naval Operations [with fifteen assistants], . . . who, under the Secretary of the Navy, shall be responsible for the readiness of the Navy for war and be charged with its general direction." [50] The House Naval Affairs Committee voted unanimously to incorporate the bill as a rider to the Naval Appropriations Act of 1916 that it was considering, but the provision was struck on the floor of the House on a point of order.[51]

When Daniels was shown the Hobson Bill, he threatened to "go home" if it were enacted in its original form and managed to persuade the Senate Naval Affairs Committee, which had been ready to reincorporate the CNO provision into the appropriations bill, to change its language to "There shall be a Chief of Naval Operations, . . . who shall, under the direction of the Secretary, be charged with the operations of the fleet, and with the preparation and readiness of plans for its use in war." [52]

This version, which was eventually enacted, while creating for the first time a professional military officer in Washington with direct authority over the operations of the fleet, clearly subordinated the CNO to the Secretary of the Navy and also denied him any authority over the bureaus on which he would have to rely for support of his plans and activities. The bureaus remained directly under the Secretary, with the Assistant Secretary taking over their supervision during World War I. Testifying before the Senate Naval Affairs Committee in 1920, when Fiske and a few others had once again brought up the proposal to give the CNO all-inclusive authority over the Navy Department, Daniels recounted his earlier conflict with the Admiral:

I may add that Admiral Fiske talked with me many times about this, and rarely about anything else that he did not bring this in, and I was very glad at first to hear him, because I always give very patient and careful consideration to anything that the naval officers bring to me; and I told him to draw me up a diagram pointing out how his plan would work. He did so, very elaborately, and when he finished I said, "Well, what power has the Secretary in all your organizations?" "Oh," he said, "he is above everything. He is over everything." I said, "well, what power has he got?" And, of course, the whole program, and the whole program of this organization, is to place the Secretary of the Navy on the Washington Monument and not give him a telephone, so that he will not know anything that is going on, but will just "sign here." Un-American![53]

By 1945, the CNO still had only the statutory authority granted to him by the 1915 act. During World War II, Admiral King, as Chief of Naval Operations–Commander in Chief United States Fleet (CNO-COMINCH), acquired controlling influence over many aspects of bureau activities, but the bureau chiefs still retained their direct access to the Secretary through his civilian assistants and felt themselves responsible for the performance of their overall job only to him.[54] Between World War I and World War II, proposals were made a number of times to extend the CNO's authority over the bureaus, but the Secretaries of the Navy (and, as might be expected, the bureau-chief admirals) consistently and successfully opposed such a development,[55] arguing that an all-powerful CNO would turn them into "rubber stamps" or "figureheads." According to one student of naval administration, "one or the other of these two descriptive figures has been used by every single Secretary who considered the problem from [1913] until 1940, and Josephus Daniels, who had more ingenuity with words than most men, succeeded in bringing both into the same sentence."[56]

To sum up, the dominant tradition within the Navy Department since the question was raised around 1900 had been that a single military officer under the Secretary responsible for all parts of the Department would usurp the Secretary's control through the military chief's near monopoly of relevant knowledge about possible alternative lines of action. When such an organizational unit was proposed during the unification conflict, not only for the Navy Department but for a department that would control all of the armed forces of the country, the Navy leaders viewed the proposal in their traditional frame of reference as an attempt to eliminate civilian control and reacted accordingly.

The arguments that the Navy used were stock: Secretary Forrestal contended that the Army's plan would give the Secretary of the Armed Forces "authority without knowledge, and authority without knowledge must inevitably become impotent," while Assistant Secretary Hensel attacked the Collins plan chiefly on the grounds that it would make "the acquisition of information by the civilian Secretaries a most complicated and tortuous problem," thus turning them into "echoes" instead of "voices" of command.[57] *

Economy

The Navy Department coalition shared the War Department's professed goal of economy in the unification conflict, but the Navy denied that economy would necessarily be furthered by the Army plans. The

---

* Franklin D. Roosevelt, who had served as Josephus Daniels' Assistant Secretary during the battles with Admiral Fiske and the other Navy "Chief of Staff" men, obviously shared the dominant Navy organizational philosophy. Writing as President in 1934 to the Acting Secretary of the Navy that he would not approve of any reorganization of the Navy Department giving the CNO all-inclusive authority, because "in my judgment [the Secretary of the Navy] would too greatly delegate [his] power if he delegated to the CNO the duty of issuing direct orders to the bureaus and offices," Roosevelt closed his letter by explaining the "compelling principle" behind the conclusion he had reached: "because civilian control of the Army and the Navy has always been regarded as essential . . . , it is of the utmost importance that the Secretary of the Navy himself shall know what is going on every day in all major matters affecting all bureaus and offices." Reprinted in Navy Department, *Naval Administration: Selected Documents on Navy Department Organization, 1915–1940*, V, 54–55.

Roosevelt continued to oppose a chief-of-staff type of CNO in 1940 and again when Admiral King tried to establish one at various times during the war, finally indicating in 1943 that "Ernie" should stop trying to reorganize the Navy and concentrate on winning the war. Robert H. Connery, *The Navy and Industrial Mobilization in World War II* (Princeton, N.J., Princeton University Press, 1951), pp. 415, 418.

Navy leaders accepted the Eberstadt Report's findings that there had been some hoarding and uncoordinated competitive buying between the services, particularly early in the war. They recommended, therefore, that the various joint procurement boards in existence be strengthened and that a Munitions Board be established, whose chairman, unlike the chairman of the existing Army-Navy Munitions Board, would have actual power of decision over the coordination of Army-Navy procurement, production, and personnel programs. The Navy pointed out that throughout the war there were many instances of one of the two services purchasing a commonly used item for both and that that practice could be extended under the two-department system.[58] In short, with renegotiation provisions and excess profits taxes to offset purchasing at overly high prices, the Navy leaders simply did not believe that a major portion of the money wasted by the services had been due to uncoordinated buying.[59]

The Eberstadt Report had found that waste and duplication of resources occurred for the most part within each of the two departments. Specifically, it found that the major source of waste was the result of each department's logistics and procurement agencies not receiving adequate guidance from the JCS about what would actually be required for future military campaigns. In order to insure timely delivery, contracts had to be placed for supplies and equipment long before the Chiefs had formulated specific operational plans for their use; and institutionalized lines of coordination between the JCS and the logistics and procurement agencies in the two departments were either weak or nonexistent, so that even the maximum guidance possible was not being given. To oversimplify the actual situation, logistics-procurement agencies in each department pretty much had to guess about quantities and types of equipment that the military command structure would require months and even years in the future and place their orders accordingly. Their more-or-less informed guesses sometimes turned out wrong, and equipment and supplies were purchased that were never used.[60]

The Navy felt that the major change necessary to save money in any future war was that those responsible for logistics and procurement be brought closer to the process of strategic planning by institutionalizing lines of coordination between the new Munitions Board and the JCS.[61] To the establishment of such lines of control, the Army's unification plans appeared irrelevant.

Furthermore, even with respect to the relatively minor savings that could be gained through the elimination of uncoordinated purchasing, the Navy did not think, in Forrestal's words, "at all that consolidation insures [its] elimination. I think it may add to it." Forrestal explained,

The business of the Navy alone in 1944 was three times that of General Motors, U.S. Steel, Sears-Roebuck, Westinghouse, and Curtiss-Wright put together. That of the Army was even greater. . . .

In organizing procurement for that part of the business conducted by the Navy, I found it necessary, in order to buy with any confidence of economy and business judgment, to disperse the procurement functions through the bureaus rather than try to consolidate the business in any one place. I am satisfied that we saved money by so doing.

If you put the Army, Navy, and Air Force procurement under one head, it cannot possibly work, except by the immediate splitting and resplitting of functions.[62]

Forrestal pointed out that even within the War Department, the Army Air Forces had found it necessary to separate their procurement agency from that of the ground forces in order to provide for their own specialized needs. "Certainly," he concluded, " 'single command' should not be swallowed as the cure-all for duplications in procurement." [63]

The Navy Department leaders also denied that the maintenance of separate facilities such as airfields and hospitals by the two services necessarily constituted "wasteful duplication" that could be eliminated by a single department. As Admiral King testified in 1945,

Will you permit me, please, Senator, to say that I have read a good deal about duplication of facilities, and I am surprised to hear that there was any locality in which the facilities were in excess. That is not my information. Certainly during the war it was not a case of duplication to excess, where all facilities were all in use. . . .

Frankly, to my mind, a great deal has been made out of the relatively minor things, which, as I say, are susceptible to correction under the two-department system. May I repeat, and emphasize by repeating, that a lot of this duplication merely means additional facilities were made available, and just because they didn't come wholly under the Army or Navy really had nothing to do with it. The services were needed to get on with the war. Now that the war is over, we can come down to what one service can do for the other, whether they can do is satisfactorily and completely, and I believe that that is another field in which a great deal has been done.[64]

In short, the Navy believed that wasteful duplications could only be eliminated on an *ad hoc* basis. Forrestal had told the Woodrum Committee in 1944 that it required "the daily dustpan operation of many men" to prevent duplications even within the Navy Department. He then posed the following question to the Congressmen: "Do you prevent those duplications by simply dumping into a larger basket all these function? I do not know. Maybe you will. Maybe there are genii that can do that." [65]

Finally, the Navy was concerned that, in the name of economy, a single department might impose a destructive orthodoxy on the armed forces in the field of research and development and curtail desirable parallel efforts by the two services that in the past had led to important weapons discoveries. The Navy brought up repeatedly that the development of radial air-cooled airplane engines, dive bombers, and other widely used World War II weapons had originally been opposed within the Army and that they had been available for both the Army and the Navy to use in the war only because the Navy maintained its own independent research organization free from Army control.

Similarly, the Navy feared that a single department might enforce standardization on one out of a number of items that appeared superficially alike but that were not from the informed technical point of view. The sort of thing the Navy had in mind was illustrated by Senator Chan Gurney's contention in 1945 that if the Army and the Navy, which had been using 4.5-inch and 5-inch rockets, respectively, had agreed to standardize on one or the other, it would "save a tremendous amount of money and effort." [66] The case of the rockets was brought up repeatedly by the Army witnesses in 1945 and in later hearings as a classic example of wasteful duplication. It was not finally disposed of until Forrestal had the matter studied and testified in 1947 that the two rockets were in no sense interchangeable: The Navy rocket, although only ½ inch larger than the Army's in diameter, was four times as heavy, carried five times the weight of propellant, and had approximately twice the velocity—all of which made it an altogether different weapon with respect to destructive effect.[67] In order to bring the distinction between desirable parallel effort and wasteful duplication even closer to home for the Congressmen, Assistant Secretary Gates remarked in 1944,

Specifically, you gentlemen of Congress realize more fully than I, that a bicameral legislature is termed by some professors of political science as unnecessary duplication. Committees of the House of Representatives investigate urgent problems, while similarly constituted committees in the Senate examine the same problems. This is duplication, but in my opinion, necessary duplication to carry out the precepts of our Government. I feel much the same about the Armed Forces.[68]

To sum up, the Navy Department coalition's overriding goals in the unification conflict were combat effectiveness and its perceived indispensable prerequisite—a strong Navy with the World War II functions of its naval aviation and Marine Corps components unimpaired. Since the Navy leaders had never regarded the existing organizational system as presenting any serious obstacles to the achievement of either of those goals, they were not favorably predisposed toward changes that introduced a new echelon of control and, consequently, at best an element of unpredictability into the favorable relations that they enjoyed with the President and particularly with Congress. Nevertheless, when unification was first proposed, not all the Navy leaders were opposed to a single military department. They did begin to oppose such a department almost unanimously when they realized that the War Department coalition's specific unification plans also entailed a single military budget under, in effect, the controlling influence of an overall chief of staff, who, the Navy leaders were convinced, was not likely to be a person sympathetic with or understanding of the Navy's needs and who could very well be positively hostile to them.

In addition to these budgetary considerations, the Navy also opposed unification because it soon became identified and inextricably connected with the War Department coalition's campaigns to divest the Navy of its land-based aviation (and eventually, the Navy feared, of naval aviation in general) and to restrict severely the combatant functions of the Marines. Not only did such proposals run counter to the Navy hierarchy's normal bureaucratic goal for organizational integrity, but, given the Navy's theory of "functional" organization, they were also interpreted as trying to deprive the Fleet of the supporting units absolutely necessary to carry out its primary task of control of the seas.

Still another reason for opposing the War Department's unification plans was the Navy's insistence that the proposed single-chief-of-staff system was not so effective as the JCS in strategic decision-making and was more prone to mistakes. The Navy also held that the chief's position in the organizational chain of command between the overall Secretary and all other parts of the department (let alone the Secretary's statutory bypassing in budgetary and strategic matters) usurped the Secretary's authority over his department's affairs and thus defeated the traditional goal of civilian control of the military to which the Navy adhered. Finally, the Navy denied that unification was either a sufficient or a necessary condition for any increased economy in logistics and procurement matters through improved interservice coordination, while at the same time it feared that a single military department might, in the guise of economy, prevent the Navy from maintaining all the separate facilities that it considered necessary to carry out its assigned tasks and from engaging in independent research and development efforts that in the past had paid off in important weapons discoveries.

Reorganization Theory

Apart from opposing the content of the Army's unification plans, the Navy also opposed the War Department's reorganization theory of agreeing on an organizational form "in principle" with the details to be worked out later. Assistant Secretary Hensel explained the Navy's reorganization approach:

First, mergers cannot be approved in the abstract. With all due deference to the standing of the men who have urged that we decide on an abstract merger and let the details take care of themselves, there is nothing in that argument. Even if merger were a principle instead of a method, there are very few principles unrelated to the details of the situation. . . .

If any of us were to suggest that two great industrial corporations merge in principle and work out the details later, we would not be very popular with the stockholders or the employees of such a corporation. We would probably never again secure an audience

Second, there are advantages and disadvantages in every organization. It is a mistake to portray either the several-department system or the single-department system form as all good or all bad. A proper decision requires a listing and a balancing of the advantages and disadvantages of the various proposals. The final conclusion should not be reached until we are satisfied that the advantages definitely outweigh the disadvantages, and that the advantages cannot be more satisfactorily attained by other means, and that impulsiveness has been definitely eliminated from out thinking.[69]

Although the tactical advantages for the Navy of such an approach in the unification conflict are clear, the reorganization theory did happen to coincide with standard Navy practice. Secretary of the Navy Knox had hired a firm of management consultants to make a survey of the Navy Department when he took over in 1940. Throughout the war, the Navy continued to use management engineers and other outside consultants, and surveys were eventually made of practically all the offices and bureaus of the Department, with recommendations for improving their organization and practices.[70]

Kinds of Cleavage

It might be noted at this point that the lines of cleavage between the War and Navy Department coalitions in the unification conflict were not all of the same kind. For example, only the disputes over the proposals for divestment of the Navy's land-based planes and JCS control of the budget and part of the dispute over the proposal for a single chief of staff were based on what might be called "pure goal conflict" in the sense that the goals directly to be furthered by the War Department coalition—separate air force control of all land-based planes, military control of the budget, and restriction of the Marine Corps—and certain goals of the Navy coalition—Navy Department organizational integrity and civilian control on the secretarial level—were mutually exclusive.

Most of the other lines of cleavage discussed were based on what might be called "goal incompatibility" or "means-end disagreement." Goal incompatibility existed where, although no goals of the two coalitions directly affected by a proposal were mutually exclusive by definition, the Navy coalition nevertheless expected the pursuit of the War Department's goals through the proposals advanced to develop adverse consequences or side effects for its own goals in the particular empirical situations anticipated.[71] Thus, to spell out just one example, the Navy coalition did not oppose the single-military-department–single-budget proposal because the goals primarily sought by the War Department coalition—combat effectiveness, economy, adequate ground troops, and the special presidential stakes in Cabinet-level military coordination—were inherently contradictory to any of the Navy's own goals. The Navy opposed the single-department proposal mainly because it was coupled with additional proposals amounting to control over the single department's budget and general administration by an overall chief of staff. The Navy expected that all the proposals together would operate to render the War Department goal of adequate ground troops incompatible with its own goal of a strong Fleet, in the sense that the first would be furthered chiefly at the expense of the second in the expected postwar situation of extreme budgetary scarcity.

The lines of cleavage were based on means-end disagreement, finally, when the two coalitions simply disagreed over the effectiveness of a proposal for advancing goals that they both shared.[72] Thus, the War and Navy coalitions disagreed both over the consequences of a single-chief-of-staff system of strategic decision-making and of a separate air force for their shared goal of combat effectiveness and over the consequences of a single department generally for their goal of economy. As will be explained at a later point, these different bases of cleavage in a conflict have an important bearing on the possibility and manner of its resolution.

Submerged Intra-Coalition Cleavages

The analysis of the bases of cleavage between the War and Navy Department coalitions has proceeded as if each of them was perfectly cohesive during the unification conflict. Although such was the impression they tried to convey, there is good reason to believe that, as in other kinds of coalition politics, important cleavages existed within the coalitions for reasons the members managed to keep submerged.

WAR DEPARTMENT: GROUND FORCES–AIR FORCES

The most important submerged cleavage within the War Department coalition was apparently between the Army ground and Air Forces leaders on the question of a separate air force. It will be recalled that

Before World War II the idea of a separate Air Force was unacceptable to the Army as a whole. Certain air functions such as local liaison and artillery observation were recognized . . . as an essential part of ground force responsibility. Others, such as local tactical support for the infantry, it [was] argued, were subject to full control by the commander of the ground forces concerned, under the tactical theory then prevalent. That there was a semi-independent character in long-range bombing was recognized as early as 1923, but performance of the semi-independent function was not regarded as a sufficient cause for giving the Air Force autonomy in all functions, or any.[73]

As late as September, 1941, when there had been talk in Congress of establishing a separate air force purportedly to speed up aircraft production, Secretary of War Stimson sent identical letters (drafted in General Marshall's office) to the chairmen of the Senate Military Affairs and House Expenditures Committees,[74] telling them that

The War Department in previous reports to the Congress has opposed the proposal to separate the aviation forces from the Army or the Navy, either as one of three components charged with national defense or as one of the three components of a single department of national defense. To date, nothing in the current European war has caused the War Department to alter its opinion.[75]

Indeed, at the level just below the Army Chief of Staff, not only separation but even increased autonomy for the Air Corps was opposed by elements of the ground Army. When asked to comment on a 1940 Air Corps proposal for a Deputy Chief of Staff for Air with his own air staff and control over substantially all Army aviation activities, Marshall's two existing Deputy Chiefs strongly opposed the "tendency" toward a "separate Air Corps responsible to the Chief of Staff alone." The Deputy Chiefs thought that the proposal was based on an incorrect view of the role of the airplane: "The Air Corps believes that its primary purpose is to defeat the enemy air force and execute independent missions against ground targets. Actually, its primary purpose is to assist the ground forces in reaching their objective." [76] The plan was, in effect, approved the following year, but over the objection of the Chief of the General Staff's War Plans Division.[77]

The major 1941 and 1942 reorganizations of the War Department provided that the Army Air Forces still remain under General Staff control with respect to strategic planning and direction of theater operations. In the course of the war, however, the General Staff, and specifically its Operations Division, fought a losing battle with Arnold's air staff for control of the overseas air units. The General Staff's defeat was most dramatically illustrated by the establishment in 1944 of "Strategic Air Forces" in Europe and in the Pacific responsible directly to the CCS and the JCS with General Arnold and his Air Forces staff acting as executive agent and the General Staff's Operations Division completely bypassed.[78] Similarly, during the war, in the face of repeated protests by the Army's Service of Supply, the Army Air Forces proceeded to develop a separate logistics establishment, "not only for technical supplies [peculiar to the needs of the Air Forces] but also for all regularly issued equipment procured by the AAF." [79]

With Arnold's membership in the JCS on a basis of equality with his nominal superior, Marshall, and with representatives from Arnold's own Air Staff (rather than flying officers from the War Department General Staff) sitting as equals with ground Army and Navy officers on the important JCS subordinate committees, the Army fliers had attained virtually complete autonomy vis-à-vis the General Staff by the end of the war. This development had come about only because of Secretary of War Stimson's [80] and General Marshall's tacit or explicit approval, and there had been opposition among high officers in the ground-force hierarchy.

At the end of World War II there was probably still substantial opposition within the ground forces to a separate air force, particularly one including the tactical air units used for close support of ground troops.[81] After all, the Air Force doctrine of the all-sufficing nature of strategic bombardment with atomic weapons jeopardized the future of the ground Army just as much as that of the Navy. The ground-force generals could not have been unaware that certain of the aviators believed that in any future war the ground forces "will be an army of occupation, that's all, just as we now have two armies of occupation in Germany and Japan, both of which were essentially defeated by the Army Air Forces." [82]

General Arnold, who himself was a moderate on the issue, had pointed out just after the war how "entirely possible" it was that the development of the air arm "especially with the concurrent development of the atomic explosive" would reduce the requirement for "mass armies and navies" and then proceeded to call for the "ruthless elimination of all arms, branches, services, weapons, equipment or ideas whose retention might be indicated only by tradition or sheer inertia." [83]

Given these assertions by their Air Forces colleagues, the Army ground-force leaders found it necessary to argue explicitly at various times for the indispensability of sizable ground troops in the atomic age. During hearings before the House Military Affairs Committee in the fall of 1945 on the question of universal military training, Secretary of War Patterson, for example, spoke of the "many Americans, awed by the tremendous capabilities of atomic energy," who "have convinced themselves that all we shall need in a future crisis are a supply of atomic bombs and a comparative handful of trained men to push the buttons that will set off the bombs." Patterson hastened to add that he knew

of no responsible military authority who shares that belief. On the contrary, . . . the bomb's capacity . . . enormously increase[s] the need for maintaining in every section of the United States trained citizen-soldiers. . . . I make that statement with full knowledge that it is the fashion to dismiss as "reactionaries" and "die-hards" all who express doubt that the atomic bomb has already rendered every other weapon obsolete.[84]*

Even in the unification hearings, a few chance remarks indicated the ground Army's submerged concern over Air Force independence and

* The President himself felt called upon to refer in his 1945 Navy Day Speech to the "talk about the atomic bomb scrapping all navies, armies and [nonstrategic?] air forces. For the present I think that such talk is 100% wrong." New York *Times*, Oct. 28, 1945.

its strategic theory. Assistant Secretary of War McCloy, for example, after telling the Senators in 1945 that the Navy could no longer "insist on the same treatment it would be entitled to were it clearly our first line of defense as it has been in the days past," quickly added that neither could the Air Force "sensibly claim that it is our only necessary line of defense." [85] A few minutes later, while criticizing the Navy's resistance to unification because of its fears that its appropriations requests would be discriminated against, McCloy declared,

I would think that of all branches if such considerations were to apply, the group most concerned should in reality be the Ground Forces. . . . They will be sandwiched in between these two high-powered propagandists—and I have seen them operate—namely, the Navy and the Air Forces. If anyone is in the dangerous minority with the popular appeal that the Navy and the Air Forces can exert, it is the Army Ground Forces.[86]

Even General Eisenhower, who was the most outspoken ground-force supporter of a separate Air Force, voiced similar fears in later hearings when he was Chief of Staff of the Army:

Now, can you conceive, with the glamor that attaches to the Navy and to the Air Forces, that the ground forces, the boys who finally have to wade in and fight and take the losses, and win the battles, are going to get anything out of this? Not for an instant. The tendency is going to be to give appropriations and great concern to these more glamorous people, those who would win wars by pushing buttons. And the poor doughboy who finally has to trudge in and take his losses and win his battle, is the one who will suffer.[87]

Occasionally, an Army general would rebel during the hearings and even try to set the record straight with respect to some of the Air Forces' claims. When General Spaatz testified on November 15, 1945, besides his more general claims for the performance and capabilities of strategic bombing, he explained to the Military Affairs Committee how the only way that a weapon such as the German V-2 had been defeated was by "destroying the launching platforms . . . the communications . . . the factories where they were made" by means of air bombardment. General Omar N. Bradley, who had been one of Eisenhower's immediate ground force subordinates in Europe as commander of the Twelfth Army Group, took the witness chair a few minutes later and took issue both with Spaatz' strategic doctrine and with his explanation of the destruction of the V-2's:

I have heard many statements as to what service won the war. In my opinion, no one service won this war or is going to win any future war of any magnitude. It takes all our services together, plus the industrial effort of our Nation to win any major war. The question was asked here a moment ago about the Air Forces knocking out the launching sites of the V-2. There is no doubt that the Air Forces had a great deal to do with cutting down the V-2's. However, I would like to call your attention to the fact that not until the Navy and the Army forces got together and went over and captured the launching sites did the V-2 attacks completely come to a stop. It was not until then that the V-2's stopped falling over England.[88]

The question might be raised why the ground-Army civilian and military hierarchy was willing to support (or at least not oppose) [89] a separate air force during the unification conflict: First of all, the Army generals, as has been explained, had already lost almost all control over their Air Forces component, and it is not unlikely that they calculated that because of public and congressional sentiment, formal separation of the air force was inevitable within the immediate future regardless of their opposition. As Senator Johnson had put it during the 1945 Senate Military Affairs Committee hearings,

The importance of air power in this war, it seems to me, has developed a sentiment in this country, and in the Congress, not to relegate the Air Forces to a subordinate position. . . . I do not think there is any escape from it. I do not think the Congress, or the country, will take any chances of having the Air Forces squeezed between the Navy and the War Department. So this is a matter in which we have to take a chance between having a three-headed situation or unity. At least, that is the way it occurs to me.[90]

Consequently, any attempt by the ground-Army generals to obstruct air force separation would probably have been fruitless and only earned them the hostility of the new Air Force, on which the ground Army would be depending for various types of air support. Furthermore, even if an attempt to prevent the separation of the Army Air Force could have been successful, it would have involved the costs of continuous conflict with an organization whose leaders publicly testified that "the controversy will be continued, ad infinitum, until the Air Force finally reaches its proper [i.e., separate] stature." [91]

Second, by supporting a separate Air Force, the ground-force leaders got the Army fliers to endorse the rest of the War Department's unification plan with the single-chief-of-staff–single-budget provisions. The Army Air Forces witnesses made it perfectly clear that they were prepared to oppose unification if it did not also provide separation for them from the Army. One need merely recall General Hansell's revealing reply to Congressman Vinson that "unity" could be brought about only "by further separation." Assistant Secretary of War Lovett reiterated that position, also in an exchange with Vinson:

> Mr. VINSON.   Why not just put the Army and the Navy and all of its units under this single department? . . . Would you support a proposition in which the Army and all of its units, and the Navy and all of its units were under a single head?
> Mr. LOVETT.   No, sir; I would not.
> Mr. VINSON.   Of course, not.[92]

Third, just as the ground-force leaders believed that the single-chief-of-staff–single-budget mechanism would insure adequate funds vis-à-vis the Navy, they no doubt also relied on it to prevent Air Force over-expansion and "unbalance." * One suspects that Marshall's critical allusions in the hearings to the lack of "balanced" development of the armed services during the immediate prewar and early war years had been directed at least as much against the Army Air Forces as the Navy. The official historian of the Office of the Chief of Staff reports that Marshall and the General Staff had been violently against the 10,000-airplane program announced by President Roosevelt in November, 1938:

> The President's apparent desire in November 1938 to concentrate almost wholly upon airplane construction ran counter to the judgment of his military advisers who favored airplanes . . . in balance with supplies and training and ground force requirements.

Although the Army leaders managed to persuade the President to modify his objective somewhat in the interest of "balanced forces," the basic conflict continued "between the Army's tenacious desire to attain a balanced force, which professional training recognized as essential and the President's insistence upon air additions first of all." [93] Similarly, discussing in 1949 his original views on the need for unification, Marshall would point to "Air in particular" and to the Navy and the ground forces "to a less degree" as having proposed appropriations immediately after the end of World War II that were "entirely too high." [94]

Finally, according to two leading World War II ground-force commanders, both of whom later became Chief of Staff of the Army, the

---

* One hears of responsible Army Air Forces officers who argue that the overriding objective of a single Chief of Staff was precisely to reestablish ground-force control of the Army Air Forces.

ground forces had been generally satisfied with the air support they had received during the war and expected it to continue. Furthermore, ground-Army leaders looked to the World War II tactical air force generals to have major influence within the new Air Force—men whom the ground Army knew to be sympathetic to its needs. Whatever the exact reasons, the highest echelons of the ground Army simply did not take seriously the possibility of a separate air force being dominated by strategic bombardment enthusiasts who might refuse to maintain either the force levels or the kinds of aircraft for tactical air support and air transport deemed necessary by the Army.[95]

The Army aviators, on the other hand, were willing to support the remainder of the War Department's unification plan, and specifically the single-chief–single-budget provision that the Army could obviously use against them, probably for the following reasons:

1. Ground Army support for a separate air force was clearly contingent on the aviators' support for and the simultaneous establishment of a single military department.[96] Although "independence" for the Air Forces was highly probable regardless of ground-force opposition, lack of such opposition made it certain and insured that all, rather than just the strategic air portion, of the Army Air Forces would go to the new Air Force.[97]

2. The Army Air Forces leaders had also been imbued with the standard War Department single-chief-of-staff ideology and, all other things being equal, were predisposed to support it.

3. The Air Forces generals were very likely also not unmindful that the single-chief-of-staff–single-budget mechanism, instead of serving to protect the ground forces, could eventually be captured and used to promote armed forces that were "balanced" according to the Air Force strategic bombardment point of view.

We thus find the curious paradox of the ground forces and Air Forces members of the War Department coalition holding certain conflicting or, at least, incompatible goals—ground forces budgetary and strategic preferment as opposed to Air Forces budgetary and strategic preferment—yet able to maintain what might be called an "antagonistic partnership," primarily because they also had a means-end disagreement over the effects of the single-chief–single-budget mechanism, which allowed each of them to expect that it could be used ultimately to protect his own goals at the expense of the other.

NAVY DEPARTMENT: CIVILIANS—MILITARY

The submerged cleavage within the Navy Department coalition was between Forrestal and his civilian assistants, on the one hand, and some of the admirals, on the other hand, over the question of a JCS with direct access to the President on budgetary and strategic matters and over the inherent desirability of a single military chief of staff. Admiral Leahy writes that the "one point" on which both he and Admiral King (and from the findings of the Richardson Committee, most of the other admirals) agreed with their War Department colleagues in the JCS discussions of unification was that the "Joint Chiefs of Staff should be a permanent body *responsible only to the President,* and that the J.C.S. should advise the President on the national defense budget." [98]

Similarly, King and, no doubt, other senior naval officers did not share the dominant Navy tradition against an Army-chief-of-staff kind of Chief of Naval Operations as improperly interfering with civilian control. King had been in favor of the original Hobson bill in 1915 and during World War II had tried a number of times without success to reorganize the Navy Department so as to bring all aspects of bureau activities under his direct control as CNO-COMINCH.[99] Indeed, even while the unification conflict was raging in the fall of 1945, King, about to be relieved, drew up still another reorganization plan for the Navy Department. This plan eliminated the separate office of Commander in Chief U.S. Fleet, but retained for the CNO some of the exact language of the 1942 executive order that had made King as COMINCH "directly responsible, under the general direction of the Secretary of the Navy, to the President" for the operating forces of the Navy.[100] Forrestal opposed making the World War II short-cutting of the Secretary's authority permanent, and after weeks of argument between himself and King, Forrestal's view prevailed.[101]

This disagreement between the civilian and some of the military members of the Navy Department coalition over the proper relations among the military chiefs, the President, and the civilian departmental secretary or secretaries and over the desirability of a single Chief of Staff managed to remain submerged. For one thing, Forrestal conceded in his second appearance before the Senate Military Affairs Committee in 1945 that even under the Navy plan, the JCS would retain their "direct line" to the President on strategic planning and the direction of military forces.

Forrestal added, however, that he expected that situation to arise "more in wartime than in peacetime because in peacetime the necessity for immediate relationship to the President is not so paramount." [102] On the other hand, the admirals never pressed their claim for JCS control of the budget and argued against a single chief of staff as a matter of principle, having probably calculated that

1. The benefit to the military generally, through a dominant JCS on budgetary and strategic matters and a powerful single Chief of Staff, was outweighed by the probable harm to the Navy as a result of having its share of the total budget and the combatant functions and allowed equipment of its component parts controlled by a non-Navy Chief of Staff.[103]

2. An open split within the Department on either of the issues might critically weaken its ability to block any of the War Department's proposals and also give up the tactical advantage of maintaining the "civilian control" position in the overall conflict.*

Thus, active conflict on the basis of actually conflicting goals between the Navy civilians and some of its military leaders was precluded because of the reluctance of both potential participants to increase the risk to the goal that they shared and to which they both assigned overriding importance—a strong and unimpaired Navy.

WAR DEPARTMENT: CIVILIANS–MILITARY

There was, finally, the basis for a cleavage within the War Department coalition between the civilians and the generals. After all, the McNarney and Collins plans did effectively remove the civilian secretary from any significant influence over matters of military strategy or appropriations in the unified department. Yet Stimson and Patterson both supported the plans, with only Assistant Secretary of War McCloy expressing his personal opinion that the secretary should be responsible for the departmental budget.

Stimson had not always been so unheedful of the prerogatives of the civilian secretary of a military department. When General McNarney and the General Staff committee that were formulating the plan for the major reorganization of the War Department in 1942 proposed that the

---

* King, for example, found himself, perhaps uncharacteristically, speaking disapprovingly during the Military Affairs Committee hearings of the possibility of "military personnel" exerting "an undue influence on our national affairs" under the War Department plans and referred to a "single commander of all the armed forces" as "potentially, the 'man on horseback.'" 1945 Hearings, pp. 120, 121.

designation of the Chief of Staff of the Army be changed to that of Commanding General, Stimson writes that he threw his "influence pretty heavily in order to keep the committee from going astray on some of the old principles that I learned thirty years ago under Mr. [Elihu] Root's regime." Stimson thought that although the matter was "largely one of nomenclature" and the Chief of Staff very often acted "virtually as a commander," the title "Chief of Staff" made it clear that the head of the military hierarchy had "no real independence of command" and acted only on behalf of the President or the Secretary of War.[104] The McNarney Committee accepted Stimson's views on this particular point, but the Secretary was not able to prevent the executive order putting the reorganization into effect from stipulating that "in relation to strategy, tactics, and operations," the President would exercise his functions as Commander in Chief not through the Secretary of War but "directly through the Chief of Staff." [105]

At some point Stimson—an elderly and increasingly tired man as the war continued [106]—must have adjusted to this removal of military matters from his office and accepted as legitimate the World War II pattern of military control over strategy and operations, even willing to see it institutionalized and extended to control over the budget within the proposed unified military department in the postwar period. Stimson admits in his published memoirs to not having minded being restricted during the war chiefly to "housekeeping" functions:

In late November, 1942, after the Joint and Combined Chiefs of Staff had been created and had begun to function, one of the less tactful hangers-on of the administration asked Stimson how he liked being relegated to the position of housekeeper for the Army. The question was a foolish one, betraying a fundamental ignorance of the functions of the Secretary of War. . . . A further foolishness lay in the assumption that Stimson did not like Army housekeeping or thought it unimportant.[107]

Nevertheless, when Stimson learned of the War Department's unification plan before the beginning of the Woodrum Committee hearings, even he raised some objections:

The main trouble . . . was the cleavage between Marshall's and my opinion with regard to the relations of the Secretary of the Armed Forces in the new arrangement to the President's Chief of Staff and the Joint Chiefs of Staff. It is a rather narrow question but both of us think it is important, each in his own mind. Marshall evidently would like not to have the Secretary have anything to do with the meetings of the Joint Chiefs of Staff or anything to do with the conferences with the President on the subject of their jurisdiction. However, he realizes that the Secretary must have knowledge of it and he has no objection to this.[108]

After having it "back and forth pretty heavily," Stimson was apparently satisfied with getting Marshall to agree that he "would have no objection to having copies of [the JCS's] written reports go [to] the Secretary whenever they report to the President or to [having the Secretary] confer with them separately, call them into his room, and ask what they are doing." [109] Stimson's Under Secretary and eventual successor, Patterson, was even less bothered by the military control aspects of the Army's unification plan. In the spring of 1946 he told Forrestal that "he did not see much use for civilians in this [unified] organization except on essentially civilian matters such as public relations." [110] The Navy Secretary noted in his diary that "it was rather astonishing to me to see the extent to which [Patterson's] mind had been pervaded by Army thinking." [111]

Finally, Stimson's and Patterson's acquiescence to the single-chief-of-staff aspect of the McNarney and Collins plans could probably be attributed to the conception they shared with their predecessors in the War Department of the organizational requirements of secretarial control. Whereas the Navy Secretaries traditionally recognized the necessity of participating actively in the formulation of decisions while alternative lines of action were still open—a system that might be called "participant civilian control" and that requires multiple channels of information and recommendation—the War Department Secretaries wanted to get their advice from a single source, retaining primarily the right to reject it if they found it unsuitable. To this, the War Secretaries also claimed the right to go to lower levels of the hierarchy and inquire about matters that particularly interested them. Assistant Secretary McCloy, for example, explained the workings of civilian control in the War Department as follows:

If we were to consider only the printed lines on the War Department organization chart, [the Chief of Staff] would appear to be the only military man reporting to the Secretary. . . .

The point is that no matter what the chart looks like, the fact is a good secretary of the Armed Forces not only can but will reach down into all of the departments and divisions as he sees fit. The chart of a regiment which shows lines moving through lieutenant colonels and majors does not preclude the colonel from maintaining contact with his captains.[112]

That this was a somewhat idealized version of the effectiveness of civilian control through "reaching down" is, however, suggested by the following incident: In September, 1940, Assistant Secretary of War Patterson sent a memo endorsing the then current staff proposal for making General Arnold Deputy Chief of Staff for Air to Secretary of War Stimson, who in turn approved it and sent it on to Marshall. The official historian of the Office of the Chief of Staff reports that Marshall received Stimson's communication "with some irritation, not because of any opposition to General Arnold, but because he disliked 'outside' interference with his staff." [113] In short, this War Department concept of what can be called "supervisory civilian control" contented the civilian department Secretary with the role of actively exercising influence only when a policy already formulated on the chief-of-staff level did not meet with his approval, and, in view of the Secretary's limited source of other alternatives, this would be seldom.*

We have examined in Part II the development of the unification conflict from the time of General Marshall's JCS proposal in 1943 to President Truman's special message in December, 1945, and have tried to account for the specific points at issue between the War and Navy Department coalitions at the time of their maximum disagreement. Beginning in the spring of 1946, the unification conflict began to become resolved until by the summer of 1947 it could finally be cut off with the passage of the National Security Act. To an examination of this resolution of the unification conflict we now turn.

* Perhaps the most striking illustration of Stimson's insulation from the policy-making process in the War Department was that although various proposals for eliminating his own office and that of the Secretary of the Navy and establishing a single military department had been discussed on the Army staff level at least since 1943, the Secretary of War first learned of them on April 17, 1944, precisely one week before the opening of the Woodrum Committee hearings, during which he was expected to testify in their support. See Stimson Diary, April 17, 18, 1944.

Part III

The Conflict Becomes Resolved

5

Intra-Executive Branch Bargaining

It will be recalled that the 1945 hearings before the Senate Military Affairs Committee were suspended on December 17 and that two days later President Truman sent his special message to Congress. Also in December, Chairmen Vinson and May of the House Naval and Military Affairs Committees, in a fairly obvious attempt to detach the Army Air Forces from the rest of the War Department coalition, introduced identical bills establishing a "United States Air Force" under its own cabinet secretary and authorizing the creation of a "United States Aviation Academy." [1] Soon thereafter Navy leaders were reported confident that the Army aviators were ready to cease supporting a single military department in exchange for Navy endorsement of the separate air force bills. [2] The Navy leaders turned out to be wrong, and no such arrangement was ever brought off.

That this kind of a "deal" was at least being considered is evidenced by the record of the agenda of a policy meeting held on January 14, 1946, at apparently just below the highest level of the Army Air Forces hierarchy. [3] Chairman Carter Manasco of the House Committee on Expenditures in the Executive Departments, to which Vinson's and May's bills had been referred, had written to Secretary Patterson, asking for the War Department's position on the pending separate air force measures. The topic before the policy meeting was what position the Air Forces itself should take on the bills and specifically whether it should concur in the expected reply from the Secretary of War to Manasco opposing them. No decisions were actually reached at the meeting, but the questions raised illustrate the general ambivalence of the Air Forces' position:

2. . . . on AAF action on the Manasco letter or May-Vinson bill?
    (a) Are there any commitments to the War Department?
    (b) If so, should steps be taken to terminate the commitments?
    (c) Are officers now in Washington under any orders from CGAAF [Commanding General, Army Air Forces] as to a course of procedure?
    (d) If so, should steps be taken to have the orders changed?
3. Immediately upon Gen. Spaatz's return he will be asked to confer with Gen. Eisenhower for the purpose of agreeing on the terms of a letter for the Secretary in which it will be stated that General Arnold concurs.
    (a) Should negotiations on the Manasco letter and May-Vinson bill be carried on by personal conversations between Gens. Spaatz and Eisenhower?
    (b) Is it advisable that the AAF should concur in a letter sent by the Secretary?
        (1) If so, should we accept a letter which states that a two-department system is a possibility?
        (2) Should we accept a letter which states directly or indirectly that the difficulties of coordinating three departments are greater than the difficulties of coordinating two?
4. Should steps be taken to insist upon a reply to Gen. Spaatz's memorandum requesting assurances of WD support for a separate air force if unification fails?
    (a) If so, what should be done in the event that the WD states that no such assurances can be given?[4]

The letter that was actually sent on January 17 from Acting Secretary of War Royall to Manasco, in which it was stated that General Arnold did concur, skirted the issue that was troubling the aviators. It reframed the pending question into "whether the most effective use of all our military arms can be obtained in three independent departments or in one under unified direction" and gave the War Department's conviction "that the answer to this question is a single department." [5]

During the congressional Christmas recess in December of 1945, the chairman of the Senate Military Affairs Committee, Senator Elbert Thomas, had proceeded to draft a new unification bill with the help of the Committee's legislative counsel, taking into account the information gathered in the fall hearings and the recommendations in the President's special message.[6] Thomas then appointed a subcommittee consisting of himself, Senator Lister Hill, and Senator Warren B. Austin (the ranking minority member of the full committee) to work over the draft. Thomas also wrote to the Secretaries of War and Navy, asking each of them to "appoint one of your best or your best officer or member of your Department" to meet with the subcommittee and represent the views of his service.[7] The War Department designated Major General Lauris Norstad,* the Assistant Chief of the Air Staff for Plans and soon to be appointed Chief of the War Department General Staff's Operations and Plans Division, and the Navy sent Vice Admiral Arthur W. Radford, the Deputy Chief of Naval Operations (Air).

On April 9, 1946, after about three months of intensive conferences among themselves and with Norstad and Radford and after meetings with Patterson, Forrestal, Eberstadt, the Secretary of State, and the Budget Director,[8] Thomas, Hill, and Austin together introduced a new unification bill, S.2044. It was the ninth version they had drafted,[9] and it had been shown to the President. Norstad has described that meeting as follows:

At 1030 Thursday, 4 April, Senator Thomas, Senator Austin and myself . . . submitted Confidential Committee Print #9 to the President.

Senator Thomas briefly outlined the background . . . then proceeded to go over the Bill, paragraph by paragraph while the President followed a copy on his desk. . . .

On all important paragraphs [the President] indicated a favorable reaction. On the conclusion of Senator Thomas' presentation the President indicated that he was highly pleased with the legislation. . . .

A short discussion followed during which the President asked the opinion of the Senators as to whether the Bill could be gotten through. Senator Austin answered this by saying yes, without qualification. Both Senators indicated that the early and successful passage of the Bill depended to a considerable extent on the weight the President would put behind it. He answered that all the resources at his disposal were available, and that he would do everything that he could.

Senator Thomas suggested that a word to Senator Walsh and Congressmen May and Vinson encouraging support, would be helpful. The President stated that as soon as he had read the bill personally he would write letters to these gentlemen. The conference was concluded at 1120 by the President congratulating the Sub-committee on the excellent job that had been done.[10]

S.2044 and the "Gagging" of the Navy

The Thomas-Hill-Austin bill set up the single military department, the single secretary, and the single chief of staff advocated by the President

---

* Norstad received Thomas' letter from the Secretary of War with the words, "one of your best or your best officer," underlined in ink and with a memo slip attached, saying simply, "Here is your invitation." Norstad Files.

and the Army. It gave the "Secretary of Common Defense" an under secretary and four assistant secretaries, who were charged with "supervising" and "coordinating" scientific research and development; military intelligence; procurement, logistics, hospitals, and medical care; and education and training. The bill explicitly abolished the War and Navy Departments and transferred all their functions, duties, and responsibilities to the Secretary of Common Defense, who could delegate them to any of his subordinates as he saw fit. It designated the Army, the Navy, and a new separate Air Force as "arms" to consist of whatever components were assigned to them by future law or executive order. The bill defined, finally, the overall department and its Army, Navy, and Air Force arms as "agencies" and made them subject to reorganization (but not abolition) under the Reorganization Act of 1945.[11]

On the military side of the department, a "Chief of Staff of Common Defense" was designated the "military adviser of the President and the Secretary" and directed to execute whatever orders either of those two officials assigned to him. The bill also gave statutory sanction to the Joint Chiefs of Staff, which it renamed the "Joint Staff," with a membership consisting of the overall Chief of Staff, the "Commanding Generals" of the Army and Air Force, and the Chief of Naval Operations. The Joint Staff was given no duties except to submit its recommendations on military policy, strategy, and the composition of the budget to the President through the Secretary of Common Defense at least once a year, together with the views of any nonconcurring members. With respect to military policy and strategy, the Secretary was required to transmit the recommendations to the President without change and "with comments deemed appropriate," as had been recommended by General Collins. In the case of budgetary recommendations, however, the bill reserved to the Secretary the right, "after consideration and review thereof," to "submit to the President the annual budget of the Department together with the recommendations of the Joint Staff." Each of the "arm" commanders was given the right to submit to the Joint Staff for eventual presentation to the President through the Secretary of Common Defense "any report or recommendation relating to the component commanded by him which he shall deem desirable." [12]

The Thomas-Hill-Austin bill also provided, apparently to please the Navy, a "Secretary for the Army," a "Secretary for the Navy," and a "Secretary for the Air Force," who were charged, under the direction of the President and the Secretary of Common Defense, with the "administration" of the three military arms. The bill established, finally, the Eberstadt Report's National Security Resources Board, Central Intelligence Agency, and National Security Council, with the last being renamed the Council of Common Defense and the Secretary of Common Defense substituted for the Secretaries for War, the Navy, and the Air Force in its membership.[13]

Between the President's message in December and the introduction of the Thomas-Hill-Austin bill in early April, the public controversy over unification had tended to subside, almost disappearing from the front pages of the nation's newspapers.[14] The day of Truman's message, Secretary of the Navy Forrestal sent a naval communication to "all hands" telling them that in view of the President's announced stand in favor of unification, they were expected "to refrain from opposition . . . in their public utterances." They were permitted, "of course, [to] give frankly and freely their views and . . . respond to any questions asked" if called by congressional committees and to continue "to advocate at all times the importance of the Navy as one of the major components of national defense and the great importance of sea power to the national security and welfare." [15] The President endorsed Forrestal's position and appeared to go even further in a news conference the following day. In response to a question, Truman denied that he wanted to "muzzle" the Navy and came out "entirely in favor of a free and frank discussion of the pros and cons of the issue as long as the protagonists made it clear they were expressing their own views and not those of their respective departments or of the Administration." [16]

As soon as S.2044 was formally introduced, the Navy leaders took the President at his word and immediately opposed it both privately and, at times, publicly, causing the controversy to hit the front pages once again. Forrestal himself had seen a draft of S.2044 in March and expressed his opinion to the President that it was "completely unworkable" and that "while it might pass the Senate by a slight margin, it was certain to fail in the House." [17] At his April 11 news conference, the President reacted to the newspaper "leaks" of Navy opposition by bitterly denouncing what he termed "lobbying" by the Navy admirals and "others" against unification. Truman told the reporters that the Navy was wrong in continuing to oppose unification after he, as Commander in Chief, had announced it as Administration policy. He warned that unless the Navy's official leaders "got into line," he might have "to alter the situation." The President believed that such steps would not be necessary, however, and reiterated his conviction that individual officers were still free to oppose unification as a matter of personal opinion.[18]

About a week later, the President became "really stirred up" over an interview given by Rear Admiral A. S. Merrill, the Commandant of the Eighth Naval District at New Orleans and a former Pacific combat commander. Merrill had expressed his personal opinion that S.2044 contained all "the objectionable features of the original Army merger bill" with the Navy's proposals for super-departmental coordinating bodies simply grafted on to it. He had also predicted that "when the next war comes we will need the finest army and air force in the world because, with a greatly weakened navy, submerged under army control, the fighting will be on our own shores." Truman told his news conference that the Admiral "didn't know what he was talking about" and repeated his previous denunciation of Navy lobbying, being careful this time, however, to exonerate Forrestal and the Chief of Naval Operations, Nimitz, from responsibility.[19]

Truman met later in the day with Forrestal and Nimitz, and at the conclusion of the conference the Secretary issued a statement agreeing with the President that "further debate by means of speeches and propaganda" should be foregone and that officers "should make known their opinions only to appropriate committees of Congress." [20] During his news conference, the President denied any knowledge of War Department "lobbying," although just a few days before, in response to his own April 11 statements, Senator Edward V. Robertson had made a long speech on the floor of the Senate documenting the crassest form of pressure tactics by certain Army Air Forces commanders.

S.2044 was eventually reported favorably to the Senate by the full Military Affairs Committee on May 13. Two of the Committee's members, Styles Bridges and Thomas C. Hart, filed a lengthy minority report, however, attacking the bill as "bringing about the prussianization of our military system" and being infused with "militaristic and totalitarian doctrines in spirit and form." [21]

Forrestal had not been surprised by the Thomas-Hill-Austin bill. All along the Secretary of the Navy had been convinced that the Military Affairs Committee was "a highly prejudiced body which had reached a conclusion in advance" in favor of the Army plan.[22] He had already approached Senator Walsh in the fall of 1945 about the Senate Naval Affairs Committee holding additional hearings on the unification question, in effect to give the Navy a chance fully to develop and publicize its fears and objections within a legitimate and sympathetic forum.[23] Senator Walsh must have agreed, for on April 30 the Naval Affairs Committee began its own unification hearings, purportedly on S.2044.

1946 Senate Naval Affairs Committee Hearings

The Naval Affairs Committee hearings achieved Forrestal's objective with considerable success. With the exception of Thomas, Hill, and Austin, who testified the first few days, all the witnesses who were called were either representatives of the Navy Department or, like Eberstadt, closely identified with its general position. All of them opposed S.2044.

Secretary Forrestal began the Navy Department's presentation on May 1. "The Navy," Forrestal told the senators, "from loyalty and conviction" was "solidly behind" what it believed to be "the basic objective of the President, namely, an integrated military–diplomatic relations, industrial–economic organization which will meet the security needs of the Nation." [24] The only question was whether the Thomas-Hill-Austin bill was calculated to do the job. Forrestal obviously thought it was not.

Forrestal proceeded to develop the by now standard Navy arguments against a single military chief of staff and any restriction of the Marine Corps or of naval aviation, but his chief theme was that the particular bill pending was not well thought out and could never work in practice. The Secretary referred to the complexity of the organizational machinery and to the "cross currents" and "vacuums" of authority among the Secretary of Common Defense, the Under Secretary, the four functional Assistant Secretaries, and the three Secretaries for the Army, Navy, and Air Force. Forrestal was also particularly concerned with the status of the new Secretary for the Navy. Forrestal objected that this Secretary was assigned no statutory duties (while, on the other hand, the functional assistant secretaries were assigned responsibilities in all of the key administrative fields), that the existing Under and Assistant Secretaries of the Navy would be eliminated, that the Secretary for the Navy was not given any statutory right of direct access to the President, the Budget Bureau, or Congress and was thus implicitly denied the opportunity directly to justify the Navy's appropriations requests, and that this Secretary was denied membership not only in the Cabinet but also in the Council of Common Defense. Forrestal opposed, finally, the overall department being made subject to executive reorganization, with the consequent standing threat to the continued integrity of naval aviation and the Marines. At the end of his presentation, Forrestal was asked by Senator Harry F. Byrd whether the Secretary for the Navy provided by the bill was not "really an Assistant Secretary," to which Forrestal replied, "I don't want to be flippant about it, but I think he is a zero." [25]

It should be noted that during these Naval Affairs Committee hearings, Forrestal was not insisting on retention of the wartime *status quo*. He, too, was in favor of "unification." Indeed, when a questioner implied to the President in a news conference the following day that Forrestal was continuing to defy him, Truman answered somewhat testily that he had read in advance and authorized Forrestal's prepared statement, that "when read carefully," it was not to be interpreted as opposed "to a merger," and that the questioner would "not have so much trouble if he studied these things carefully." [26] Forrestal recommended in the place of a single military department, a "Director of Common Defense—call him a Secretary, if you will," to serve as chairman of the Council of Common Defense and to decide issues in dispute between the services, lay down common procurement policy, coordinate research, training, and intelligence activities, and supervise the preparation of the military budget. Forrestal's Director would be provided with a small staff, "emphasizing quality rather than quantity, and have somewhat the same type of supervisory jurisdiction as that exercised during the war by Justice Byrnes, Mr. Vinson and Mr. Nelson." [27] "In other words," the Director would function as "an *alter ego* of the President, and . . . be the source of decisions upon matters which otherwise would have to be decided by the President himself, and which the President simply does not have the time to decide." [28]

What Forrestal definitely continued to oppose was "the Army's concept of an overlord of all the services, who not only would make decisions of the kind I am talking about . . . , but who would actually operate this vast colossus of government called the Department of Common Defense." [29]

Admiral Nimitz, General Vandegrift, Admiral King, and Eberstadt followed Forrestal before the Naval Affairs Committee. In general, Nimitz repeated Forrestal's objections to S.2044, but the Admiral managed, in response to a specific question by Chairman Walsh, to make public for the first time Eisenhower's and Spaatz' still highly classified JCS proposals on the functions of the Marines and naval aviation in the following paraphrase:

General Eisenhower has expressed his belief that the Marine Corps should be limited in size and organized in units no larger than a regiment and lightly equipped, for minor operations against objectives in which the Navy is primarily interested, and for employment as interior guards of naval vessels, and for the guarding of shore establishments. He has stated that Marine Corps units as large as divisions should not be in existence. He believes that when a Marine Corps unit reaches the size of a division it is encroaching on an Army function.

General Spaatz has expressed the view that all land-based aviation other than carrier-type planes should be a function of the Army Air Forces.[30]

Nimitz told the senators that the Army Air Forces were also proposing that they be granted exclusive control of guided missiles, and that he personally believed that "the ultimate ambition of the Army Air Force [is] to absorb naval aviation in its entirety and set up one large air force." [31] Consequently, Nimitz "hoped" that in any unification bill, Congress would "define the functions of the services in sufficiently explicit terms so that there would not be a possibility of . . . trouble arising" and include the following provision from the most recent edition of *Joint Action of the Army and Navy,* which had been approved by the Joint Board and the Secretaries of War and Navy in 1935:

(a) No service will attempt to restrict in any way the means and weapons used by another service in carrying out its functions.

(b) No service will attempt to restrict in any way the areas of operations of the other services in carrying out their functions.

(c) Each service will lend the utmost assistance possible to the other services in carrying out their functions.[32]

When Admiral King, now an elder statesman, testified on May 7, his chief contribution to the discussion was a redefinition of "sea power." Replying to those who were saying "that there is little need for a United States Navy, because, at the moment, Britain has the only other Navy of any consequence," King noted for the Committee that the Navy's functions and capabilities were not restricted to dealing with seaborne objectives and keeping clear the lines of supply for ground and air forces overseas—both of which presupposed some sort of enemy fleet. According to King, dealing with "land objectives that can be reached from the sea" was also a function of sea power.[33] * In one of the first allusions to the validity of military capabilities other than the waging of all-out war even in the atomic age, King explained the value of self-contained, relatively self-sufficient naval task forces, which could be kept near trouble spots and were capable of exerting constant pressure in behalf of the United States or of the United Nations.[34]

The most bitter witness to testify before the Naval Affairs Committee was the Commandant of the Marine Corps, General Alexander Vandegrift. The General predicted that "passage of the unification legislation as now framed will in all probability spell extinction for the Marine Corps" because "the War Department is determined to reduce the Marine Corps to a position of studied military ineffectiveness—and the merger bill in its present form makes this objective readily attainable." [35] He alluded, as had both Nimitz and Forrestal, to Eisenhower's JCS proposals and even identified them by their formal designation, "Series 1478." Vandegrift stressed the need for an "effective, mobile, amphibious fighting force, in peace and war—a force ready to act as a part of the fleet at any time." He thought that if the responsibility for amphibious warfare were given to the Army, which had "a myriad of other more general, and perhaps more vital, concerns related to the security of the United States," the country would lose the preeminence that it enjoyed as a result of having an organization that considered amphibious operations to be its major specialty.[36] General Vandegrift reminded the Committee that Congress had acted to save the Marine Corps from extinction five times since 1829 and then appealed to it to come to the rescue once again:

In placing its case in your hands the Marine Corps remembers that it was this same Congress which, in 1798, called it into a long and useful service to the Nation. The Marine Corps feels that the question of its continued exist-

* King had already pointed out in his "Third Official Report" that "our fleet in World War II was not solely engaged in fighting enemy fleets":

"On numerous occasions a large part of the fleet effort was devoted to operations against land objectives. A striking example is the capture of Okinawa. During the three months that this operation was in progress our Pacific Fleet . . . was engaged in a continuous battle which for sustained intensity has never been equalled in naval history; yet at this time the Japanese Navy had virtually ceased to exist—we were fighting an island, not an enemy fleet." "Third Official Report to the Secretary of the Navy," Dec. 8, 1945, in *The War Reports of George C. Marshall, H. H. Arnold, and Ernest J. King,* ed. by Walter Millis (Philadelphia, Lippincott, 1947), pp. 655–56.

ence is likewise a matter for determination by the Congress and not one to be resolved by departmental legerdemain or a quasi-legislative process enforced by the War Department General Staff.

The Marine Corps, then, believes that it has earned this right—to have its future determined by the legislative body which created it—nothing more. Sentiment is not a valid consideration in determining questions of national security. We have pride in ourselves and in our past but we do not rest our case on any presumed ground of gratitude owing us from the Nation. The bended knee is not a tradition of our corps. If the Marine as a fighting man has not made a case for himself after 170 years of service, he must go. But I think you will agree with me that he has earned the right to depart with dignity and honor, not by subjugation to the status of uselessness and servility planned for him by the War Department.[37]

The President Intervenes

By the beginning of May it was becoming increasingly clear that a bill to which the Navy and the Marines were so bitterly opposed would have great difficulty passing Congress, at least in that session. At a meeting on May 7, Clark Clifford, President Truman's naval aide and later special counsel, who had been given White House staff responsibility for the unification legislation, told Norstad and the newly appointed Assistant Secretary of War for Air, Stuart Symington, that he was personally "convinced that the Thomas Bill could not pass in the near future or, in fact, at any time" and that they were "actually losing ground." [38] Furthermore, Clifford revealed that he too shared some of the Navy's misgivings about the single Chief of Staff and about the functions of the Assistant Secretaries of Defense and that he himself had worked on the statement Forrestal had presented to the Naval Affairs Committee. Clifford told Norstad and Symington that he had talked to the "Boss" about unification on two occasions and that he planned to raise the subject again. He would recommend that the President call the Secretaries of War and the Navy with two or three of their military advisers to a conference and direct them to report to him within a specified time on their areas of agreement and their specific points of disagreement. Apparently Clifford's advice was taken, for Truman called just such a conference at the White House on May 13 and asked Patterson and Forrestal to make their report by May 31.

In the course of the discussions at this May 13 White House meeting, the President asked Admiral Leahy, who had stayed on as his personal

Chief of Staff, for his views on the matters at issue. Leahy thought "something could be worked out," provided the proposed bill eliminated the single Chief of Staff. The Admiral explained that his experience during the war convinced him that "the idea of a single Chief of Staff was dangerous—that had he wanted to secure power for himself during the war he could have arrogated a great deal to himself." President Truman then announced, somewhat surprisingly, that while he would not be too much concerned "if the nation could always count on having someone like Admiral Leahy in the position," he too had now become convinced that the idea of a single Chief of Staff "was a dangerous one, that it was too much along the lines of the 'man on horseback' philosophy, and that he had finally made up his own mind against it." [39] Secretary of War Patterson expressed his own continued preference for the single Chief of Staff, but admitted that he was not prepared to "jump into the ditch and die for the idea." [40]

It should be noted that two days after this White House conference, Chairman Walsh of the Senate Naval Affairs Committee and Chairman Vinson of the House Naval Affairs Committee sent a joint letter to Forrestal warning him that Congress was not likely ultimately to approve any compromise that might be reached with Patterson that provided for

(a) A single Department of Common Defense. . . .

(b) The placing of a single military officer in supreme command of all the armed forces

(c) Divesting the Marine Corps of its important functions. . . .

(d) Transferring the vital functions of naval aviation to the Army Air Corps or to a separate Air Corps.

(e) Removing from the Secretary of War and the Secretary of the Navy the responsibility of initiating the budget of their respective Departments and supporting these budgets before Congress.[41]

On May 31 Patterson and Forrestal reported in writing to the President that they had been able to identify eight points of agreement and four of disagreement. The two Secretaries agreed that there should be a Council of Common Defense (with the civilian heads of the separate services as members even if there were to be a single Secretary of Common Defense), a National Security Resources Board, a statutory JCS to head the military command and planning structure and to advise on the budget, no single Chief of Staff over the JCS, a Central Intelligence Agency, and three other agencies to coordinate procurement and supply, research and development, and military training. These last three agencies were to be within the single department if one were established and joint Army-Navy (or Army–Navy–Air Force) agencies if one were not.

Patterson and Forrestal still could not agree on the key question of whether there should be a single military department under one Cabinet-level secretary, as desired by the Army, or whether the unification should take a "less drastic and extreme form" by placing a "Presidential deputy with clearly defined powers of decision over specified matters at the head of the Council of Common Defense," as desired by the Navy. They could also not agree on whether the Army Air Forces should be given a separate status: the Navy view was that although this would not be "in the best interest of our national security, . . . if the alternatives were three departments or one, the Navy would prefer three departments." The other two points concerned the roles of naval aviation and the Marine Corps. The Navy held out, against Army opposition, for the continued procurement, control, and operation by the Navy of its land-based planes for long-range reconnaissance, antisubmarine warfare, and protection of shipping, and for the continued responsibility by the Marines (1) for the development of techniques and weapons for all rather than just the "waterborne" (i.e., ship-to-shore) aspects of amphibious warfare and (2) for the conduct of such "limited land operations" as prove to be essential to the prosecution of a naval campaign even if they involved "sustained land fighting." [42]

President Truman called another meeting of the key unification participants on June 4 and listened to further argument on the points at issue between the Army and the Navy. After the two sides had made their presentations, Patterson and Army Chief of Staff Eisenhower emphasized that no matter what the President's decision would be on the disputed points, they would accept it "cheerfully and loyally and do their best to support it." [43] Although Nimitz immediately volunteered that the Navy would do the same, Forrestal made no such observation until later, thinking that "Patterson's and Eisenhower's remarks flowed from the realization that the President was already pretty much on the Army's side of the case and that they had nothing to risk in volunteering such a statement." [44]

On June 15 President Truman sent a joint letter to the Secretaries of War and the Navy and substantially identical letters to the chairmen of the Senate and House Military Affairs and Naval Affairs Committees, indicating his position on the four unresolved points and recapitulating the eight points already agreed upon. Truman upheld the Navy only with respect to the functions of the Marine Corps. He decided that a separate Air Force should be constituted as a third military service and that the non-Marine land-based planes in dispute "can and should be manned by Air Force personnel," although he also added that "within its proper sphere of operation, naval aviation must not be restricted but must be given every opportunity to develop its maximum usefulness." On the main point, the President reaffirmed his position in favor of a single military department under a single Cabinet-level secretary. He did agree, however, to each service being headed by a civilian with the title of "Secretary," who would sit on the Council of Common Defense and thus have an opportunity to represent the views of his service before the President. Truman also announced that he had been recently advised that both services now believed that the four Assistant Secretaries of Defense provided in S.2044 were unnecessary and that he agreed, since such Assistant Secretaries "would greatly complicate . . . administration" and "deprive the secretaries of the respective services of functions which are properly theirs." [45]

Throughout his June 15 letters the President emphasized that, subject to the overall authority of the Secretary of Common Defense, each of the services should retain maximum "autonomy" and "integrity" in order "that the high morale and esprit de corps of each service can be maintained." The President concluded his letter to the two Secretaries with a hammerblow for the Navy. Picking up Forrestal's reluctantly given and largely formal promise to abide by the President's decision, Truman announced that

It was gratifying to have both of you and General Eisenhower and Admiral Nimitz assure me that you would all give your wholehearted support to a plan of unification no matter what the decision would be on those points upon which you did not fully agree. I know that I can count upon all of you for full assistance in obtaining passage in the Congress of a bill containing the 12 basic elements set forth above.[46]

The President also concluded his letters to the committee chairmen by telling them that Patterson, Forrestal, Eisenhower, and Nimitz had assured him that they would support his plan before Congress.[47]

A few days after the President's letters were released, a close observer of the Washington political community reported that high Navy officials were "boiling" over this last bit of Presidential lettermanship.[48] Secretary Forrestal refused to see reporters or to issue a statement either confirming or denying his support for the President's plan. The Navy's silence was highlighted on June 18, when Secretary Patterson sent the President a letter reaffirming his own and the War Department's support for the President's decision.[49] The following day Forrestal asked to see the President to discuss the letter that he was preparing to send.

When Forrestal met with the President, the Secretary explained that his letter would express gratification that many of the Navy's ideas were in the President's latest plan and that the President had stressed the concept of *"autonomy* and *integrity* for the Navy." Forrestal told the President that Admiral Nimitz was, however, concerned that the June 15 letters created the impression that the Navy was "foreclosed from expressing opinions on any bill that was sent in." Forrestal immediately added that he was confident that such was not the case and that the Navy was still free to express its views on any particular legislation, so long as it kept within the President's major objectives. Truman "agreed fully" with that view. Forrestal then proceeded to tell the President that the "Navy air people" were greatly disturbed with his decision on the control of land-based aircraft and that they "felt so strongly as to be fanatic" that the Navy must have the tools to carry out its mission. It was his own impression, Forrestal stated, that the President's language had not intended "to convey a denial to the Navy of sufficient land-based planes for reconnaissance and 'search and strike' purposes," which the President also confirmed in an inexplicable apparent reversal of his June 15 decision.[50]

Forrestal summed up his position by telling the President that while he had been "against the single Secretary all along" and found it hard to shake himself "loose from those misgivings," the essence of the matter now was whether a bill could be drawn which would "clearly leave the Secretary of the Navy free to run his own Department without kibitzing from above . . . while at the same time giving the Secretary of National Defense the global authority to make decisions on broad issues." Forrestal wrapped up the discussion by explaining to Truman that his general view of a Cabinet member's responsibilities was to support his President's policies up to the point where he encounters "sincere and *major* disagreement" and then "ask to withdraw from the Cabinet." [51]

Forrestal dispatched his promised letter to the President on June 24 and showed that he too could try to commit his opponent publicly to positions that he did not altogether hold. He gave it as his understanding that the President's principal objectives were "(1) the creation of a single department of national defense under a civilian head, with broad powers of overall supervision and control, while leaving full administration of their respective services to the Secretaries for War, Navy, and Air; and (2) with particular regard to the Navy—the preservation of its integrity and autonomy." [52]

Forrestal wrote that he considered those "objectives attainable, and the recognized difficulties in drafting legislation which will insure their success, surmountable." The Secretary assured the President of his own and Admiral Nimitz' desire to cooperate fully in the effort to achieve "the objectives of your program" and noted how glad he was that the Navy was to have "a continuing part" in naval reconnaissance, anti-submarine warfare, and protection of shipping by means of land-based planes. [53]

On June 26 the Senate Military Affairs Committee reported a revised version of S.2044, which was substituted for the bill on the Senate calendar. It carried the printed notation: "Printed with the Amendments of the Senate Carrying Out the Recommendations of the President in His Letter to Senator Thomas of Utah of June 15." Essentially the revised bill (1) eliminated the provision for a Chief of Staff of Common Defense, (2) changed the language stipulating that the Department of Common Defense "shall be administered" by the Secretary of Common Defense to "shall be under the control and supervision" of the Secretary, (3) changed the titles of the four functional assistant secretaries to "directors" and labeled their organizational units "agencies," and (4) added the Secretaries for the Army, Navy, and Air Force to the Council of Common Defense. [54]

Resumption of Naval Affairs Committee Hearings

The Senate Naval Affairs Committee resumed its hearings on July 2, taking under consideration the revised version of S.2044. Since Forrestal was away observing the first series of postwar atomic bomb tests at Bikini (Operation Crossroads), Assistant Secretary of the Navy W. John Kenney led the Navy witnesses. It was Kenney's contention that S.2044, even as amended, did "not attain or, as I say, even attempt to attain, the expressed desires of the President." [55] Kenney pointed out that the new language defining the Secretary's authority still did not restrict him to the role of a coordinator, that the bill still abolished the offices of the Secretaries of War and Navy and their assistants and transferred the statutory responsibilities of all those officials to the single Secretary, that the functions of the various components of the Navy were still not specified in the bill, and that the overall department and the three services were still made subject to executive reorganization—all of which meant that the Navy continued to have in the revised S.2044 no guaranteed statutory base whatever. In view of this situation, Kenney concluded that

> This is certainly not a retention of autonomy and integrity and represents, in my opinion, a fundamental difference between the concept of the War Department which is incorporated in this bill, and that of the Navy, and the concept of the President.
> The Secretary of Common Defense should be charged with powers of coordination and not of administration and operation of these three great services. [56]

The Naval Affairs Committee members agreed with Kenney's criticism of the revised Thomas-Hill-Austin bill, but they were clearly very displeased over the concessions that Forrestal had appeared to make in his June 24 letter to the President. Before Kenney had finished reading the first page of his somewhat lengthy prepared statement, Chairman Walsh interrupted him to ask specifically whether the Navy had agreed in Forrestal's letter to a single Secretary of Common Defense and to the Secretary of the Navy's being removed from the Cabinet. When Kenney tried to explain that Forrestal was agreeable, providing only that the Navy retained its autonomy and integrity as promised by the President, Walsh cut him off and dismissed that explanation with the following comment:

> The moment you agree on a Secretary of Common Defense your autonomy and protection are gone. . . .
> When you give up the Secretary of the Navy's being a Cabinet official and make him a clerk under the Secretary of Common Defense, you have given up your integrity and autonomy.[57]

Senator Byrd also kept interrupting Kenney to insist that Forrestal's letter not only approved the single Secretary, but that the language Forrestal had used to define the Secretary's powers ("broad powers of over-all supervision and control") also appeared to support the substantially equivalent language in the revised Thomas-Hill-Auston bill ("control and supervision"). Byrd thought, as did Walsh and Robertson, that Forrestal's term "control" connoted unlimited authority for the overall Secretary, including the right to raise or lower the Navy's appropriations requests and to prevent the Secretary of the Navy from going before Congress to defend his budget. The Senators made it plain that they strongly objected to such developments. Kenney immediately agreed that the word "control" in the bill would have to be qualified in order to limit the Secretary to the coordinator's role envisaged by the Navy, but Byrd kept hammering the point that it had not been qualified in Forrestal's letter, and "that is what we have got to fight on." Byrd continued,

> Don't you think that this is a very tragic thing because this is the whole crux of the thing, and he [Forrestal] has agreed to it. He has gone to the Pacific, and if this bill comes up it will come up within the next 10 days, if it comes up, and he is not clear as to what he does think.
> If you take his reasoning, and that is all Congress can take, as expressed in his language, that is all it can be. . . .
> "Control" is very well defined in the dictionary.[58]

Chairman Walsh and Senator Byrd were also displeased that the Navy had allowed its opposition to S.2044 to rest on the very precarious argument that the bill still did not meet the President's objectives. "Let me ask you this," Byrd said to Kenney,

> Suppose the President should issue a statement that this bill of the Military Affairs Committee meets, in his judgment and in his opinion, his letter of June 15. What would be the attitude of the Secretary of the Navy then? . . .
> It seems to me that the Navy has been maneuvered into a very untenable position.

Kenney admitted that "if that were done we would be placed in an extremely difficult position." [59]

The famous World War II fleet and task force commanders who followed Kenney before the Naval Affairs Committee were more forthright in their opposition to S.2044. Admiral Halsey came out flatly against a single Secretary of Common Defense, and all the admirals who testified —Kinkaid, Spruance, Towers, Turner, Mitscher—thought that whatever kind of subpresidential decision-maker were set up, the Secretary of the Navy should remain in the Cabinet.

The admirals most violently resented, however, the proposed assignment to the Air Force of the Navy's land-based planes. Their experiences in the Pacific, which they recounted in detail, had convinced them that the Army Air Forces had been either unwilling or unable to carry out overwater reconnaissance or protection of shipping effectively. Admiral Thomas C. Kinkaid, who had been commander of the Seventh Fleet under MacArthur during the war, told the senators how Army fliers had bombed our own cruisers (fortunately scoring no hits) in the battle of the Coral Sea as a result of recognition errors. The Army fliers were also allegedly inept at Navy communications practices. Furthermore, the admirals did not think that even with additional training the Army Air Forces could perform much better, for the Army aviators simply were not sailors. As Kinkaid explained,

[The land-based] planes are a definite part of a fleet disposition, an extremely important part of it. They have got to not only be trained in the mechanics of flying and covering an area, observing ships on the surface, observing other things in the air, but they have got to have an understanding of the operations themselves. What they see with their eye on the surface will mean quite a different thing to one man from what it will mean to another. If he is part of the Navy, trained in naval warfare, trained in naval operations, he will understand what he sees.

Furthermore, he will function in a much more loyal manner.[60]

In order to guarantee that the fleet would have all the tools necessary to carry out its tasks in any future war, all the admirals advocated that the detailed functions of the Navy and the Marine Corps be written into any unification bill.

The Senate Naval Affairs Committee hearings ended on July 11. On that day Chairman Walsh inserted into the record a telegram from Forrestal, which held that S.2044 continued to create an "organizational monstrosity," denied that the "President's plan" could ever be incorporated "into [the] framework of the Thomas bill," and called for an "entirely fresh approach" to the unification problem.[61]

In any event, by July the Seventy-ninth Congress was drawing close to its final adjournment. S.2044 had been on the Senate calendar during most of the Naval Affairs Committee hearings without any attempt being made to call it up for consideration on the floor. On July 17 President Truman informed Senator Thomas through the Senate Majority Leader, Alben Barkley, that on the advice of the legislative leadership, he had decided to put off any request for further consideration of unification legislation until the next Congress.[62]

Presidential-Secretarial Strain: An Analysis

The events described in this chapter illustrate the strain that often develops between the President and his cabinet secretaries.[63] From December of 1945 to July of 1946, President Truman and Secretary of the Navy Forrestal were actively heading opposed political coalitions in the unification conflict, with Forrestal doing all he could to obstruct the unification plan that the President had officially endorsed in his special message to Congress. Yet the President, except for the one veiled threat in his April 11 news conference, did not indicate that he considered firing Forrestal and replacing him with a more tractable Secretary. What Truman did was to use his influence in a bargaining context, to get Forrestal to give in on certain specific points. We have seen that by the time of Forrestal's June 24 letter, the President had persuaded the Navy Secretary to agree publicly to a single Secretary of Common Defense with "control" over the military services and, as Assistant Secretary Kenney and the Naval Affairs Committee construed the letter, to the Secretary of the Navy being removed from the Cabinet.

The first was a vital concession. Indeed, as late as May 14, Forrestal had been telling Secretary of War Patterson that "we would never agree to *administrative control* over the Navy. . . . We might consider the word 'supervise' but that was as far as we could go." [64] The President's costs for these concessions were to agree that the individual services could retain considerable organizational autonomy within the overall department and that the Marines could keep their World War II function, to withdraw his support for a single chief of staff, and to withdraw partially from his endorsement of Army Air Forces control of all land-based aviation.

The question might be raised why Truman should have paid any price at all for concessions by Forrestal, who was his legal subordinate and whose continued tenure in office depended on the President's acquiescence. First of all, this study of the unification conflict abstracts severely from reality. From December, 1945, to July, 1946, the President was pursuing many goals which he ranked higher than unification; indeed, even in the military field, universal military training and then extension of selective service appear to have taken priority over the reorganization of the military establishment.[65] Forrestal was an active supporter of the President on these latter campaigns and on the question of adequate military preparedness generally. Overall, consequently, the Secretary of the Navy may have been contributing a net balance of support for the President's total programs even though he opposed him on unification. Moreover, Forrestal's support was valuable: his very ability to resist the President's wishes on unification demonstrated that he had considerable influence in Congress which he might be able to use on other occasions to help the President.

Secondly, Forrestal's opposition was not simply a personal matter. It also reflected (and in a more moderate form) the views of the preponderant majority of high naval officers, all of whom could not be dismissed and replaced.[66] The President's best method of converting these officers was first to convert Forrestal, who held their confidence as a result of having been in the Navy Department since 1940. The admirals were much more likely to adhere out of personal loyalty to an agreement negotiated by Forrestal than they were to a *diktat* of a new Secretary.

Similarly, converting Forrestal was also the best, if not the only, means of overcoming the very powerful resistance to unification in Congress. We have noted that the chairmen of the House Military Affairs and Naval Affairs Committees and the chairman of the Senate Naval Affairs Committee were all opposed to a single military department. This was not Forrestal's doing. They had all been in Congress and developed their views long before Forrestal arrived on the Washington scene. Carl Vinson, for example, the chairman of the House Naval Affairs Committee, had opposed unification in 1925 as a member of the Morrow Board and again in 1932 when he was one of the leaders in the floor fight to strike the unification title from the Economy Act of 1932.[67] The President was probably convinced that Forrestal was correct when the Secretary of the Navy told him that, "if we arrived at a compromise which the Navy believed in, . . . I believed we could sell it even to Mr. Vinson, but it would have to be something that we could really put our hearts into." [68] A compromise agreed to under duress was not one that Forrestal and the Navy could have put their hearts into.

Finally, the rules of the game in American politics generally and the norms of Congress in particular protect independence and freedom of expression within the subordinate parts of the executive branch. The President's denunciation of Navy "lobbying" in April brought him unfavorable comment in a majority of the nation's newspapers, almost all of which had previously been supporting his stand on unification.[69] Indeed, an informed observer of the Washington military scene gave it as his opinion that the President's news conference statements had effectively killed any chances for passage of a unification bill that session of Congress: [70] An attempt to curb freedom of expression within the executive branch is very readily interpreted as an attack on Congress' authority to seek information for the purpose of legislating. Vinson was probably not speaking only for the opponents of unification when he did not see "how the President can keep the Army and Navy from talking. . . . If Congressional committees call admirals and others before them for questioning, they have a duty to Congress to give the information the committees seek." [71] If the mere application of a "muzzle" cost the President so much support, the removal of a popular Secretary of the Navy for trying to keep the Navy "from being sunk" would have cost him even more in "public prestige" [72] and might have permanently frozen opposition against unification in Congress.

On the other hand, Forrestal too was vulnerable, and his opposition therefore had to operate within limits. For one thing, "unification" was accepted as desirable by a large majority of newspaper and public opinion, which made it almost inevitable in the intermediate or long run. Forrestal himself was not opposed to some form of unification: in November, 1944, he was telling Harry Hopkins that the functions Hopkins had performed early in the war as a sort of Presidential alter ego on military and foreign policy matters should be continued in the postwar period and partially formalized; [73] on April 17, 1946, at the height of the conflict over the Thomas bill, Forrestal could write in his diary, "Speaking personally, I am for unification." [74]

Given the inevitability of some military reorganization, Forrestal could help the Navy best and promote his overriding goal—"to keep the Navy intact as a Service as distinct from a merely subordinate branch of a vast Department" [75]—by using his very considerable political talents to bargain for a solution that was at least minimally acceptable from the Navy's point of view. All along, Forrestal was able to define the conflict with the President as being over means and not over the ultimate objective of "unification." Complete and inflexible opposition to any change at all would very likely have cost him his job eventually and deprived the Navy of his very astute leadership in its crucial battle.

Furthermore, although any cabinet secretary may find it necessary at

times to oppose the President, the Secretary, with possibly a few striking exceptions like Franklin Roosevelt's Secretary of Commerce Jesse
Jones,[76] generally has internalized the norm—strongly or weakly in any
individual case—of loyalty to his formal superior, the Chief Executive.
This imposes an internal psychological pressure to conform to some
extent to the President's wishes, which it may be painful to resist. We
have seen that Forrestal had internalized this norm rather strongly and
felt that it would be necessary to resign if major disagreement between
himself and the President persisted.

Finally, a cabinet officer too has goals besides the ones involved in
the particular conflict with the President. The President can help him
to advance many of these, including the desire for the President's esteem
and approval and for holding on to his Cabinet position.* Although
leaked stories of possible mass resignations in the Navy Department
secretariat made the pages of the New York *Times* regularly whenever
the President had just taken or was about to take action disadvantageous
to the Navy, the resignations never eventuated. Aside from Forrestal's
self-perceived usefulness in leading the Navy's fight on unification, the
Secretary of the Navy's diary reveals very clearly (as did his tragic death
in 1949 after his forced resignation as Secretary of Defense) that government service in a high post had become a central part of Forrestal's
life and that it would be extremely painful to be separated from it,[77] regardless of what he might leak to reporters or say to the President as a
matter of form.

Agreement Is Reached

On September 10, after the adjournment of the Seventy-ninth Congress, President Truman called still another conference of the unification
participants at the White House to consider plans for the introduction

---

* As Forrestal would explain to one of his correspondents the following spring,
when the unification conflict was coming to a close not too disadvantageously for
the Navy, keeping his job had taken "a good deal of toe-dancing and particularly
in view of the fact that the President, before he became president, had committed
himself to the general principle of consolidation." Forrestal added, "To be fair to
him, however, I must say that he has exhibited a most extraordinary degree of pa-
tience and tolerance and understanding, in addition to which he has acquired a good
deal more fundamental knowledge of the Navy. . . . If it had been anyone else but
Mr. Truman I think I would have been fired long ago." Letter to General Thomas
B. Holcomb, U.S. Marine Corps (Ret.), March 1, 1947, in Forrestal Papers, Firestone Library, Princeton University.

of new legislation in the next Congress. Present in addition to the President were Secretaries Patterson and Forrestal, General Eisenhower, Admiral Nimitz, Admiral Leahy, and Clark Clifford. The President announced that he proposed to have a unification bill drafted in his own office by Leahy and Clifford, which would then become the "doctrine of the administration, and after it had been mulled over by all interested parties," he would expect to have supported in Congress.[78]

Forrestal indicated to the President during this meeting that he was still ready to support a single Secretary providing that Secretary was limited to being a source of decisions on fundamentals and did "not try to get down into the administration of each Department, and by that I meant he should not have the power to oust a bureau chief in the Navy or the head of a branch in the Army." Forrestal explained, however, that he could not agree beforehand "to support by testimony before committees of Congress" a bill which might do violence to the principles he had outlined. The Secretary told the President that he "recognized clearly" that a member of the President's Cabinet should support his policies, and Forrestal then promised that if he could not support "with conviction and sincerity" a bill introduced by the Administration, he would ask the President "to accept my resignation." Truman replied that he expected no such necessity to arise.[79]

Between the September White House conference and the convening of the Eightieth Congress in January, 1947, there were numerous meetings among the Army, Army Air, and Navy representatives in an attempt to reach agreement on basic principles upon which a bill could be drafted. It should be noted that since the previous winter, with the Thomas subcommittee's rejection in S.2044 of JCS control of the military budget and with the President's decision against the single chief of staff and the curtailment of the Marine Corps' combatant functions, a number of lines of cleavage between the War and Navy Department coalitions had become resolved. Since the concept of some kind of Secretary was now also accepted by all the parties including the Navy, the remaining scope of disagreement was relatively small. It included the exact definition of the Secretary's scope of authority over the military services, the question of a separate air force and of the control of the Navy's land-based air, and the question of whether whatever functions were agreed upon for each service were to be written into the legislation or remain a matter for executive branch determination.

The first point was obviously still the crux of the matter. The previous spring, while Patterson and Forrestal were defining their points of agreement and disagreement for their letter to the President, Ferdinand Eberstadt had suggested to them that there might be still another form that unification could take in addition to either a single department completely under the control of a single Secretary or a Presidential deputy merely to preside over the Council of Common Defense.[80] Eberstadt was thinking of "something of the nature . . . where the Secretary would be not in the departments, but let us say over the departments for specific purposes." Forrestal and the Navy had appeared favorably inclined toward a concept of this sort, but after careful consideration Patterson and Eisenhower felt that "it would not suit their needs."

Some time during the summer, Eberstadt found the opportunity to talk to Admiral Leahy and Clark Clifford about his idea, and both of them "thought in principle it was worthy of consideration." Eberstadt decided to seek "allies" within the War Department coalition and in late September approached John McCloy, who had resigned as Assistant Secretary of War the previous year, and Robert Lovett, who had more recently resigned as Assistant Secretary of War for Air. At a meeting in Lovett's New York business office, Eberstadt pointed out that while he saw no substantive reason to change the recommendations he had originally made, it seemed to him "there was such obvious advantages in the services getting together that some adjustment was necessary." After Eberstadt outlined his plan, McCloy and Lovett agreed to talk to people in the War Department and see "whether the War Department views could not be brought in line with the Navy Department's, with a view to a compromise." Eberstadt later wrote to McCloy:

I do not think there can be any misunderstanding between us, but to guard against even the most remote possibility, I take the liberty of stating below the kind of set-up that I understood us to have discussed.

1. That there are to be three autonomous departments: Army, Navy, Air, each to be headed by a Secretary with its conventional staff of assistant secretaries, etc., nothing to be said whether the departmental secretaries should or should not be members of the Cabinet. . . .

2. There shall be . . . a secretary of national security . . . to coordinate various matters of common or conflicting interest between the three military departments. . . . Subject to the President . . . the Secretary of National Security . . . shall, for example, have authority to integrate the budget, to coordinate and integrate logistic and procurement matters, research programs, military intelligence, education and training, personnel policies, etc., and the general power to determine conflict between the services. . . . This . . . Secretary, however, shall have no general nor specific responsibility with respect to

the administration of the three military departments nor any general control over them other than the authority specifically conferred upon [him] nor any right to interfere therein. . . .

The above is a brief statement in principle of what I had in mind.[81]

McCloy went down to Washington from his law practice in New York and reportedly "talked to this one and that one in the War Department" and finally there was a disposition to discuss Eberstadt's idea. A conference was therefore held on November 7 in Forrestal's Georgetown home including the Secretary, Admiral Sherman, now Deputy Chief of Naval Operations (Operations), Admiral Radford, General Norstad, and Assistant Secretary of War for Air Symington, who since the previous spring had increasingly come to concern himself with unification on behalf of the War Department. After considerable discussion [82] all appeared to accept the compromise concept of three administrative departments (including one for a separate air force) under a Secretary of Defense with "full authority to take such action as he considered required" for their effective coordination but with his staff "sharply limited in number" to fifteen to twenty-five "$10,000-a-year men" and military officers in order to make certain "that he could not undertake any detailed administration."

Both Symington and Norstad agreed to the Navy's definition of the Marine Corps functions and for the first time "agreed unmistakably to the continuance of naval patrol land-plane squadrons for antisubmarine warfare," while the Navy representatives "agreed to Army preparation and training to augment naval antisubmarine squadrons when needed." On this question of land-based air, the War Department representatives were agreeing specifically "that for a period of three years, without prejudice to the ultimate allocation by competent authority of the roles and missions involved, the Navy would be authorized to maintain their 160 land-based aircraft plus 100% reserve for anti-submarine patrol and shipping reconnaissance."

Symington and Norstad offered to provide an "agreed statement" on the Marine and naval air functions from the responsible civilian and military heads of the War Department but would not agree to those functions being incorporated into legislation. Forrestal appeared to accept this proposed arrangement, and Sherman and Norstad were then directed "to work up an agreement" on this and the other points discussed. Sherman would later recount that this November 7 meeting marked the time "when we agreed to make concessions, and make a compromise, and to get an organization in which we realized that each side would have to make important concessions." [83]

For the next two months, Sherman and Norstad met two or three times a week, sometimes with Forrestal, Symington, and others, on various aspects of the unification problem and also spoke to one another by telephone a number of times a day in connection with their regular duties.[84] In the course of these meetings seeking to reach final agreement, many old grievances came up to sour relations between the two sides. The Army still contended, for example, that "Nimitz, Halsey and other naval commanders had been in thorough agreement on the merger but had been dissuaded from that view [only] by the influence of King," that "the Marine Corps was an unnecessary duplication of Army units," and that "the Navy was ambitious to be the *sole* instrument of national defense."

The Navy, on the other hand, complained that "the Army's approach to this whole thing had been most unfortunate—that it had been unilateral and non-consultative" and contended that if the Collins Plan were looked at "today in the light of what had occurred since, it was clear what a monstrosity that . . . was," and how unjustified were the accusations of "stodginess, lack of cooperation and almost disloyalty" that had been directed against the Navy "because we expressed that view." The Navy leaders also continued to charge that the granting of separate status to the Army Air Forces was only a "first step in much larger and more ambitious plans of the Air Forces to take over the whole business of national defense." [85] * Furthermore, somewhere in the process the Navy

* Additional support for this impression came to the Navy just at this time in the form of certain remarks made by Army Air Forces Brigadier General Frank A. Armstrong, Jr., at a goodwill dinner given on Dec. 11 by Norfolk businessmen for about seventy high military officers. After dinner the chairman had made a short speech of welcome, which was followed by other short, innocuous talks by a number of naval officers and by the senior Army ground-force general present. General Armstrong then was called upon to speak and chose to respond as follows:

"You gentlemen had better understand that the Army Air Force is tired of being a subordinate outfit. It was a predominant force during the war, and it is going to be a predominant force during the peace, and you might as well make up your minds whether you like it or not, and we do not care whether you like it or not. The Army Air Force is going to run the show. You, the Navy, are not going to have anything but a couple of carriers which are ineffective anyway, and they will probably be sunk in the first battle.

"Now as for the Marines, you know what the Marines are, a small bitched-up army talking Navy lingo. We are going to put those Marines in the Regular Army and make efficient soldiers out of them.

"The Navy is going to end up only by supplying the requirement of the Army Air and the Ground Forces, too. The Army is going to take over Norfolk. We are here now, and we are going to stay. We know this is a Navy town, and a Navy hang-out, but Army Air is still going to stay, and we are going to take over, too." [86]

had changed its mind about the acceptability of a statement from the War Department heads on the Marine and naval air functions and first asked that the statement be signed by the President and, when that was agreed to, proceeded to insist that the legislation itself deny the over-all Secretary any authority over the functions of the services.[87]

So disturbed had Norstad become over this turn of events, that about the middle of November he reported to Army Chief of Staff Eisenhower that he was considering withdrawing from the negotiations and conveying "the idea that the reason I no longer feel I can be a party to further discussions . . . is that I no longer have confidence in the good faith of the Navy on this particular subject." [88] The Navy made the required concession and the negotiations continued, but at a luncheon on December 4 with Symington, Norstad, Sherman, and Admiral Radford, the discussion became so heated that this time Forrestal left the meeting with the feeling that "we were farther away than ever from reaching an agreement." [89]

Nevertheless, about a month later there was a sudden and sharp change of atmosphere. Riding back with Forrestal from a Cabinet meeting on January 3, 1947, Secretary of War Patterson spoke of being "much disturbed in the growing evidence of bitterness between the Services." Patterson said that "if the Army and Navy officers went down to testify [on unification] in a mood of bitterness and hatred, they would do serious damage to the Services and to the national defense." The Secretary of War told Forrestal that he was "not rigidly or stubbornly committed to any one plan, that he was willing to be flexible on the question of [the Marines and naval air] roles and missions, and that anything done heavy-handedly or without the freely given support of the officers of all Services would not be successful." Patterson thought that the different services "must have the attitude that they're truly brothers in arms." "The whole conversation," Forrestal recorded in his diary, "was in an entirely different key and tenor than any talk I've ever had before with Patterson." [90] Just two weeks later, the intra-executive branch bargaining finally paid off. On January 16, Sherman, Norstad, and Symington finished working on the final draft of a joint letter from Patterson and Forrestal to the President telling him that since their previous letter of May 31 they had managed to reach agreement on all aspects of the unification problem.[91]

6

Congress Enacts the Agreement

As in their letter of the previous May, Patterson and Forrestal agreed in their new communication to the President to support legislation establishing a Council of Common Defense, a National Security Resources Board, a Central Intelligence Agency,[1] and a statutory JCS to head the military command and planning structure and to advise on the "integration of the military budget." It should be noted that the JCS were to perform their duties "subject to the authority and direction of the Secretary of National Defense" and that no mention was made of any right of direct access to the President. Provision was, however, included for a full-time "Joint Staff" of not more than 100 officers drawn from the three services and operating under a "director" to "carry out the policies and directives of the Joint Chiefs of Staff."

The crucial point of the new Patterson-Forrestal agreement was the acceptance of there being no single military department but instead three departments of the Army, the Navy, and a separate Air Force, over which a Secretary of National Defense would preside as "head" of the "armed forces establishment." Each of the military departments was to have its own Secretary and "under the over-all direction of the Secretary of National Defense" was to be administered "as an individual unit." The Secretary of National Defense would, however, have the authority "to establish common policies and common programs" for the three departments and to "exercise control over and direct their common efforts to discharge their responsibility for national security." The January 16 agreement was silent on the question of the Cabinet status of any of the secretaries, but each of the service secretaries was guaranteed the right to present to the President, after first informing the Secretary of National Defense, "any report or recommendation" relating to his department that he deemed necessary or desirable.

With respect to the functions of the different services, the Secretaries of War and the Navy agreed that "the proper method" of setting them forth was by issuance of an executive order signed by the President instead of by legislation. They provided a draft of such an order which they proposed that the President issue concurrently with his approval of a unification bill. The most significant aspect of the draft executive order was that naval reconnaissance, antisubmarine warfare, and the protection of shipping were finally assigned as "specific functions" of the Navy with the sole requirement that the air aspects of those operations be coordinated with the Air Force and full use made of Air Force personnel and facilities "in all cases where economy and effectiveness will thereby be increased." Subject to that proviso, the order held that "the Navy will not be restricted as to types of aircraft maintained and operated for these purposes." The agreed-upon executive order also assigned to the Marine Corps the right "to provide Marine Forces together with supporting air components, for service with the Fleet in the seizure or defense of advanced naval bases and for the conduct of limited land operations in connection therewith" [2] and "to develop in coordination with the Army and the Air Force those phases of amphibious operations which pertain to the tactics, technique, and equipment employed by landing forces." [3]

President Truman released the Patterson-Forrestal letter to the public the same day he received it and wrote to the Secretaries that he was "exceedingly pleased" over the compromise and that he "heartily approved" it.[4] The following day, January 17, the President sent identical letters to the President Pro Tempore of the Senate, Arthur Vandenberg, and to the Speaker of the House of Representatives, Joseph W. Martin, officially advising them of the agreement that had been reached, forwarding copies of the relevant documents, and telling them that representatives of his office and of the armed services were engaged in drafting a bill "to be submitted to Congress for its consideration." [5]

The congressional reaction to the compromise agreement ranged from reserved to moderately encouraging. Speaker Martin, for example, wanted "to see the details before I comment. We are still an independent legislative body." Senator Robertson thought that the agreement was "loosely drawn" and that it was going to be "very difficult to put into legislation." He added, "There may still be a number of controversial questions left for Congress to decide." Senate Majority Leader Wallace White, Jr., felt, however, "that if the three branches of the armed services have reached an agreement on unification, that creates a substantial presumption in favor of the plan." [6]

Between January 20 and the end of February, Admiral Sherman, General Norstad, Presidential Assistant Charles Murphy, and, at various critical stages of the proceedings, Clark Clifford met periodically to incorporate the January 16 agreement into legislative form acceptable to the War Department, the Navy Department, and the President.[7] The State Department and the Budget Bureau were also consulted occasionally. Early in the process, Forrestal noted in his diary that it was "most important that this drafting work be watched very carefully." The Secretary thought that the Navy still had "to face continued efforts on the part of the Army to enforce their conception of a single Department and a single Chief of Staff." [8]

As it turned out, the Army and Navy representatives, Norstad and Sherman, remained in complete agreement throughout,[9] even joining at one point to reject a draft bill submitted by the President's assistants that would have set up a single "executive department to be known as the Department of National Defense" [10] along the lines of the earlier War Department proposals. At the insistence of the President's representatives, Norstad and Sherman did make changes in their own original language defining the authority of the National Security Council and the National Security Resources Board to make clear that these would be advisory bodies only and "would not divest the President of his responsibilities under the Constitution." [11] Norstad and Sherman also had to strengthen the language specifying the authority of the Secretary in order to vest him "with the residual power that he must have if he is, in effect, going to coordinate and supervise and bring together the efforts of the various agencies in the National Defense Establishment." [12]

After eight drafts complete agreement was finally reached among all the interested parties. On February 26, President Truman sent this agreed-upon draft unification bill to Congress and "heartily recommended" its enactment.[13] The bill followed the Patterson-Forrestal agreement closely. Its key clauses gave the Secretary of National Defense "authority, direction, and control" over the departments and agencies in the "National Defense Establishment" as well as the specific right to "supervise and coordinate the preparation of the budget estimates" within the Establishment and to "formulate and finally determine [them] for submittal to the Bureau of the Budget." It also allowed the Secretary to appoint "from civilian life not to exceed four special assistants" to advise and assist him. The JCS were given no budgetary responsibilities at all, being confined primarily to strategic planning and direction of the military forces and acting as "the principal military advisers" to the President and the Secretary of National Defense. A Munitions Board and a Research and Development Board were also established to coordinate activities in procurement matters and in scientific research and development for military purposes.[14] (See Chart 5.)

Committee Reorganization in the Eightieth Congress

With the convening of the Eightieth Congress in January, 1947, an important structural change had taken place relevant to the unification conflict. As a result of the Legislative Reorganization Act of 1946, the Military Affairs and Naval Affairs Committees in each house were merged into new Armed Services Committees. Although the Act had been passed in 1946, no changes had been made in congressional organization that session. The Reorganization Act was considered a mandate to organize on its principles with the beginning of the Eightieth Congress, and both party leaderships were committed to it.

Early in December, 1946, Representative Sterling Cole, who had been the senior Republican on the House Naval Affairs Committee, wrote letters to all of the Republican representatives elected to the Eightieth Congress asking them to support his efforts to block the impending merger of the House Military Affairs and Naval Affairs Committees. Cole was one of the most vocal naval supporters in the House and felt that merger of the committees should come only if a consolidation of the military departments were first decided upon. He did not want the War Department coalition to be able to use the existence of a single military committee in Congress as an argument in favor of a single military department in the executive branch. So as not to be accused of personal self-seeking, Cole said that if the committees did remain separate, he would not take the chairmanship of the Naval Affairs Committee, to which he would be otherwise entitled in the Republican-controlled Eightieth Congress.[15]

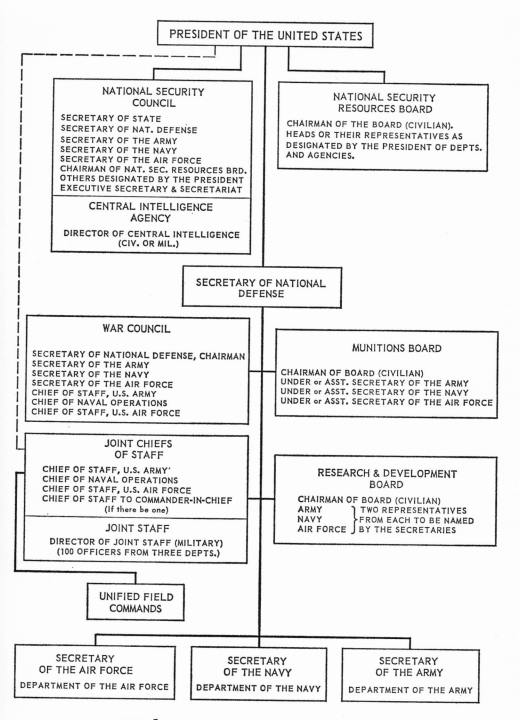

CHART 5. THE UNIFICATION PLAN FINALLY ADOPTED.

Cole's efforts ran into difficulty. The House Republican Steering Committee had voted overwhelmingly just a month before to go along with the provisions of the Reorganization Act. After receiving Cole's letter, the Republican floor leader, Joseph Martin, who was about to succeed to the Speakership when the Republicans organized the new Congress, announced that the reorganization should "go ahead." A few weeks later, Representative James W. Wadsworth, the long-time military affairs specialist and probably the leading advocate of unification in the House, took up the fight and wrote to all his Republican colleagues in support of the committee merger. Cole did manage, however, to obtain the public support of substantially all the members of the House Naval Affairs Committee and a few from the Military Affairs Committee.[16]

In the event, Cole was not even able to gain recognition during the organization of the Eightieth Congress to make his motion to block the merger of the two military committees. On January 2, immediately following the election of Martin as Speaker, Representative Leo E. Allen, the chairman of the Rules Committee, moved on behalf of the Republican conference that the rules of the old House plus the provisions of the Legislative Reorganization Act of 1946 be adopted. Cole asked Allen to yield the floor, but Allen refused and moved the previous question, thus cutting off all debate on his motion. According to the New York *Times* correspondent, Allen's motion carried with a thunder of ayes and only a small scattering of noes.[17]

As it turned out, the Republican leadership in the House decided not to refer the compromise unification bill to the merged Armed Services Committee. On February 28 the bill was introduced as H.R.2319 by Representative Clare E. Hoffman and sent to the Committee on Expenditures in the Executive Departments, of which Hoffman was chairman. On March 3 the same bill was introduced in the Senate as S.758 by Chan Gurney, the chairman of the new Armed Services Committee, and referred to Gurney's committee after a short floor fight.

Senate Referral Floor Fight

On January 27, 1947, the President Pro Tempore of the Senate, Arthur Vandenberg, announced that he had received a letter from Senator George D. Aiken, the chairman of the Senate Committee on Expenditures in the Executive Departments. The letter noted that while Truman's

January 17 communication concerning the Patterson-Forrestal unification agreement had been sent to the Expenditures Committee in the House, Vandenberg had referred it in the Senate to the Committee on Armed Services. Aiken told Vandenberg that it was the unanimous opinion of a quorum of Aiken's committee that when the promised draft unification bill arrived from the White House, it should be given to them.[18]

Although the Legislative Reorganization Act of 1946 had been calculated, among other things, to reduce overlapping jurisdictions among committees, it had failed miserably to separate the respective cognizance of the Senate Armed Services and Expenditures Committees. The Act assigned to the former committee "all proposed legislation, messages, petitions, memorials, and other matters" affecting "the common defense generally," "the War Department and the Military Establishment generally," and the "Navy Department and the Naval Establishment generally," and to the latter, "all proposed legislation, etc.," relating to "Reorganizations in the Executive Branch of the Government." [19]

When Truman's letter with the draft bill arrived in the Senate on February 26, Vandenberg announced that in his opinion the bill could go to either committee under the language of the Reorganization Act and that consequently the "decision of the chair" unavoidably became a "policy decision." Vandenberg claimed that his initial referral in January had not been influenced by the personnel on the respective committees but that he had simply followed the advice of the parliamentarian, since it had never seriously occurred to him not to send to the Armed Services Committee a bill having to do with the "entire fundamental structure of the Army and the Navy." This was particularly true in light of the fact that this committee was the successor to the two committees that had previously considered the unification problem (having been constituted of six former members of each of the Military and the Naval Affairs Committees and one member newly elected to the Senate). At Aiken's request, unanimous consent was given to have the President's new communication lie on the table a few days before referral to give Aiken and his committee a chance to examine it carefully.[20]

When the question of referral came up again on March 3, Vandenberg ruled that the President's message should go to the Armed Services Committee. Aiken challenged the ruling, arguing that a "reorganization of government" bill of such great importance clearly belonged to the Expenditures Committee. Aiken proposed, however, that since the unification bill also concerned the "common defense," it might first be referred to the Armed Services Committee if that committee would agree to permit a subcommittee of Aiken's group to sit in on its hearings and agree further to a second referral to Aiken's committee if the subcommittee found that additional committee consideration was necessary. Aiken and a number of his committee colleagues, including Senator Joseph R. McCarthy, a World War II Marine Corps veteran, made it clear that in addition to trying to protect their committee's jurisdiction in this precedent-setting referral, they also did not favor the unification bill as written and felt that opponents of the compromise would have a better chance to testify if the bill were sent to the Expenditures Committee.[21]

Chairman Gurney of the Armed Services Committee opposed Aiken's proposal. Gurney interpreted the Reorganization Act as "clearly" assigning the unification bill to his own committee. Gurney told Aiken that he would not object to having "visitors" sit with his committee during the hearings. He pointed out to Aiken that any senator could move a second referral after a bill was once reported, but Gurney would not agree to having the second referral be at Aiken's or the Expenditure Committee's option. The chairman of the Armed Services Committee did not feel that after his committee had taken the time and responsibility to hear testimony and make recommendations, it should then be asked to let "another committee take over" and, in effect, second-guess it. The issue was never much in doubt: Vandenberg put the question, "Shall the decision of the Chair stand as the judgment of the Senate?" The majority floor leader, Wallace White, supported the Chair, and the Senate upheld Vandenberg by voice vote. Immediately thereafter Gurney introduced the draft bill as S.758, and Vandenberg referred it to the Armed Services Committee.[22]

1947 Senate Armed Services Committee Hearings

Since S.758 and H.R.2319 were purportedly based on the solid agreement of all the parties to the unification conflict, little controversy was expected during the consideration of the bills in Congress. The Senate Armed Services Committee hearings started smoothly enough on March 18 with Secretary of the Navy Forrestal as the first witness. The Secretary supported all aspects of the pending bill even in the face of hostile questioning by Senators Bridges and Byrd, who did not think the Navy was being sufficiently protected. Forrestal admitted that he had originally opposed certain of the bill's features, but he pointed out that the War Department had also made concessions, so that, overall, the bill was a "fair compromise" and represented a "sound and workable solution." For this reason the Navy Secretary specifically urged that the bill be considered in its entirety because "if any single item were withdrawn or modified to the advantage of any one service the mutual accommodation would be thrown out of balance."

Forrestal denied, in response to a question by Senator Bridges, that the bill was written in such a manner as to "destroy the autonomy or independence of the Navy or its component parts." When Bridges continued to press the point by asking whether the "top man, the Secretary of Defense, would not . . . have sufficient power in the transfer of money and funds to put out of business one of the strategic arms of the Navy; for example, like the Naval Air Force, or the Marine Corps," the Secretary of the Navy replied,

I think the checks and balances still exist in the Congress and in the right of the Secretary of this particular Department to appeal to the President, a fact which I think would not be unknown to the Congress, even assuming that he was a man who did not indulge in the habit or practice of letting it leak out that he had certain reservations. . . .

There is no guarantee, Senator Bridges, that a man who would determine, for example, to extinguish the Navy or the Air Forces—who did not believe in either one or the other—might not be able to hamper them. But I think that we have enough safeguards here, again making due allowance for the form of our government, and the access to the President, which in my mind carries a connotation of wider appeal.[23]

Forrestal made it clear that he considered the most important part of the bill to be the National Security Council, which would provide for "the formal coordination between the formulators of foreign policy and the formulators of military policy [and] prevent us from coming face to face with war for which we are unwarned or militarily unprepared." [24] The Secretary of the Navy also indicated that while he did not look to the bill "for any great economies in peacetime, or certainly in any short or immediate space of time," he was confident "that there should be great savings in times of large and rapidly increasing expenditures, or in other words, in time of war." [25]

Secretary of War Patterson was the second witness to testify before the Armed Services Committee. When he appeared on March 20, Patterson, too, supported the bill under consideration "wholeheartedly" and without qualification or reservation. Patterson stressed as advantages of the bill the familiar War Department points that a single Secretary was necessary to prevent duplications and to end piecemeal consideration of the activities and budgetary requests of the different services, both in the executive branch and before Congress. Patterson disagreed with Forrestal only in that the Secretary of War believed that "very substantial" economies would result from the bill both in peacetime as well as in war, although even he could not say how great they might be and guessed that they would not begin to appear for at least two years.

Patterson agreed completely with Forrestal that the Secretary of National Defense would not get into the "details of operation" of the service departments, both because of his very small staff and because of the statutory provision that the Departments of the Army, Navy, and Air Force "under the direction of the Secretary of National Defense" were to be "administered as individual units by their respective Secretaries." Patterson explained that he read that provision "as if the words 'general' or 'overall' appeared before the word 'direction.' " [26]

The seeds for the reactivation of the interservice conflict over unification were sown when the Army Chief of Staff, General Eisenhower, appeared before the Committee on March 25 and said, as the Navy interpreted it, that "in effect . . . he was sorry that there wasn't a single Chief of Staff but he hoped that that development would come in the future." [27] Eisenhower also made it clear that he was not personally committed to the details of the compromise agreement over service functions incorporated in the proposed executive order. In response to questioning by Senator Byrd, Eisenhower indicated that although he regarded some sort of Marine Corps and naval air force as basic and integral parts of the Navy and would consequently not oppose the addition of statutory language by Congress calculated to protect them, he would object

if the same thing were proposed as to every single type of formation within naval aviation that they have ever had. I agree that naval aviation belongs to the Navy. I agree that the Navy needs a Marine Corps. Of course they do. But there can be many questions as to size, composition, method of training, method of equipment, that are not basic. They are what I would call operational and organizational details.[28]

The old Navy fears that were reawakened by Eisenhower's testimony were further stimulated when Under Secretary of War Kenneth C. Royall testified on April 15.[29] Under Senator Robertson's prodding, Royall voiced his objections to any of the service functions being written into the bill and expressed his belief that the authority of the new Secretary of National Defense would be unlimited, providing only that "the three departments are to be kept separate, administered separately, and their integrity, in a general way preserved." [30] Royall very specifically insisted that the elimination of "overlapping or duplicating functions" was the chief goal of unification and that "for the bill to have any real value—for it to accomplish what is expected of it—the Secretary of National Defense must exercise as well as possess broad authority as to functions, services, procurement and the like." In response to a question by Senator Leverett Saltonstall, Royall admitted that if the bill were amended to restrict the Secretary to a "supervisory coordinator," he would "rather have no bill at all." [31]

Actually, Royall's testimony only pointed up the difference in opinion that had been developing all during the hearings about the role of the Secretary of National Defense. Although all the witnesses agreed that the language giving the Secretary "direction, authority, and control" over all parts of the National Defense Establishment created a potentially very powerful official, there was considerable disagreement about the extent to which the Secretary should or actually would exercise his authority. Royall and the other War Department witnesses (with the exception of Secretary Patterson) stressed the absolute quality of the authority granted and indicated no qualms about the Secretary's interfering in the detailed operations of any of the military departments. The Navy Department witnesses, on the other hand, emphasized the role of the Secretary as a "top-management" person who would coordinate and referee in a limited number of matters of common interest and hence act more as an umpire and general policy-maker than as a day-to-day administrator.

Disagreement between the services had also been developing in the hearings over the method of defining the service functions. The January 16 compromise agreement had called for their being allocated by the proposed executive order, which the President could change at any time. Indeed, Royall had testified that the Secretary of National Defense himself could change the service functions "subject . . . to the President's right to direct a different course." [32] Throughout the hearings, either Senator Bridges, Senator Byrd, or Senator Robertson—all of whom had announced that they would oppose any unification bill that did not contain statutory protections for naval aviation and the Marine Corps—

would ask each of the witnesses whether he had objections to the functions of the services being written into the bill. The War Department representatives generally did have such objections, claiming that "flexibility" would be impaired by the "freezing" into the law of functions that might become obsolete and which Congress presumably could not be depended upon to change quickly enough in case of emergency. The Navy Department witnesses did not object to the functions being spelled out in the law and some strongly urged that this be done.

The Chief of Naval Operations, Admiral Nimitz, was one of the Navy "non-objectors." Nimitz testified on March 26, the day after Eisenhower, that he was "perfectly satisfied" with the unification bill as written. The Admiral managed, however, himself to bring up the "question propounded to General Eisenhower, as to whether he had objections to these functions [in the draft executive order] being incorporated into the law" and proceeded to answer it: "I certainly can see no objection to it, but I can see some difficulties in trying to write into legal language these military functions."

Nimitz also refused to admit, in response to a direct question from Senator Bridges, that "naval aviation and the Marine Corps are absolutely and fully protected" under the bill, although the Admiral submitted that they were "adequately protected." Bridges asked Nimitz what he would think of a provision written into the bill requiring that the original appropriations requests submitted by each service be included in the final budget presented by the President to Congress, to which Nimitz replied,

> Senator, it is my impression that the Constitution of the United States charges the Congress with the furnishing of armed forces. It charges the President with their use.
> The Congress, in the furnishing of the armed forces, is entitled to every bit of information that it needs, and I perceive no objection whatever in the writing into this bill of the kind of safeguards you have in mind; because it is the Congress that makes provision for the armed forces and they should certainly have the right to every bit of information that they think they need in making appropriations.[33]

When General Vandegrift, still the Commandant of the Marine Corps, appeared before the Armed Services Committee on April 22, he told the senators that, given Eisenhower's and Royall's testimony, the failure of the bill itself to assign specific functions to the Marine Corps was a "source of grave concern" to him, for it allowed "the corps to be stripped of everything but name—to reduce it to a role of military impotence." Vandegrift also complained that Marines were not made explicitly eligible for membership on the Joint Staff and the various other joint agencies being created (being eligible only implicitly as "officers of . . . the United States Navy). General Vandegrift offered draft amendments to the Committee consisting of a statement of Marine Corps functions substantially equivalent to that approved by the President in his June, 1946, letter to Patterson and Forrestal and a provision curing the purported Marine ineligibility on the joint bodies.[34] The General indicated that if those or similar amendments were adopted, his objections would be withdrawn. In the course of testimony that took two days to complete, Vandegrift also quoted from Eisenhower's and Royall's remarks to show how different their conception of the Secretary of National Defense was from his own and Admiral Nimitz' and expressed his concern over what might ensue unless the Secretary's authority were "more sharply defined." While Vandegrift was in the witness chair, Senator Robertson read to the Committee a portion of the General's 1946 testimony that referred to the still secret Series 1478 JCS papers and then proceeded to ask Chairman Gurney to try to get the papers from the Secretaries of War and the Navy. Robertson did not direct any questions about the papers to Vandegrift, and the General did not allude to them on his own.

Vandegrift's was the only serious opposition to S.758 expressed during the Senate hearings by any of the official civilian and military heads of the Navy Department, and even it was restricted primarily to the peripheral issue of how best to protect the Marine functions. More general objections were, however, voiced by Admiral Thomas A. Hart, a retired naval officer who had been Commander in Chief of the Asiatic Fleet at the outbreak of World War II and a senator from Connecticut in the previous session of Congress, by Admirals King and Halsey, both in effect retired,[35] by Brigadier General Merritt A. Edson of the Marine Corps, a Congressional Medal of Honor and Navy Cross winner who had served forty-four months in the Pacific in World War II, by the heads of the Marine Corps Reserve Officers Association and the Reserve Officers of the Naval Service, and by Ferdinand Eberstadt. All but Eberstadt wanted specific guarantees for naval aviation and the Marine Corps to be written into the bill, but the direction of their further opposition varied.

Admiral Hart, for example, objected chiefly to the establishment of a separate Air Force. Admiral King still did not even accept the concept of a single Secretary of Defense. He proposed instead that the authority granted by the bill to the Secretary be transferred to the National Security Council and that the President be given the right to appoint a full-time Deputy Chairman for the Council to preside over its meetings and coordinate not only military affairs but the whole range of overall national security policy along the lines of the Navy's earlier recommendations. The Marine Corps general, Edson, concentrated on trying to prove essentially that the unification bill was setting up a military dictatorship. The burden of Edson's argument, elicited by leading questions from Senators Robertson and McCarthy,[36] was that the various councils and boards established by the bill were dominated by representatives of the military services, and that they, and particularly the 100-officer Joint Staff and its director, created an organization "getting over on the German model" and dedicated to the theory "that the military should, in time of war, take control of the Nation and run it." [37]

Melvin J. Maas, the president of the Marine Reserve Officers Association,[38] put his organization on record as "overwhelmingly opposed" to the whole bill and in favor of further study of the unification problem. Maas particularly opposed the separate Air Force, insisted, of course, that the Marine functions should be written into any bill,[39] and went further than General Vandegrift by urging that the law not only make Marines specifically eligible for membership on the Joint Staff and the other interservice bodies, but that the Commandant be made a member of the JCS.[40] John P. Bracken, the head of the Reserve Officers of the Naval Service, also opposed the bill generally on the grounds that it was too vague, that it would probably increase rather than decrease overhead costs, and that it would concentrate too much power in the hands of the Secretary of National Defense.[41]

On the last day of the Senate hearings, May 9, Ferdinand Eberstadt came before the Armed Services Committee and gave what was probably the most reasoned and carefully prepared presentation of all of the bill's opponents. Eberstadt had four specific recommendations, all of which he considered of equal importance, but the underlying theme of his presentation was that the authority of the Secretary of National Defense was "disturbingly general and indefinite" and could therefore be given "too broad or too limited" a construction in operation. To protect the theory of Secretarial powers embodied in the compromise and against any curtailment of the Marines or naval aviation, Eberstadt urged that the specific issues over which it was contemplated that the Secretary was to exercise his authority—Eberstadt suggested "integration of the budget"; "coordination of logistics and procurement matters, . . . research programs, military intelligence, and education and training"; and "the general authority to resolve disputes among the services"—be spelled out in the bill, with a proviso added that "all powers not conferred upon the new Secretary are reserved to, and remain with, the several departments." [42]

Report of S.758 and Senate Passage

The Senate Armed Services Committee began meeting in executive session on May 20 to review the testimony it had gathered and to consider action on the pending bill. It also consulted with representatives of the War and Navy Departments and of the President and solicited their views on various proposed changes.[43] On June 5 the Committee favorably reported an amended version of S.758 by a vote of 12 to 0, with certain of its members reserving the right to propose further amendments on the floor. The Committee's changes were chiefly calculated to limit the Secretary of National Defense to the Navy's conception of his role and to protect naval aviation and the Marine Corps.

To accomplish the first objective, the Committee added a declaration of policy as a preamble to the bill, expressly denying any intent to "merge" the three military departments; it inserted the word "general" before the various clauses specifying the overall Secretary's authority, so that the right to "exercise direction, authority, and control," for example, became the right to "exercise general direction," etc. It completely eliminated the phrase that required the administration of the military departments as individual units to be "under the direction of the Secretary of National Defense," and it extended the statutory right of access on the part of the service secretaries to the President to include access to the Budget Bureau. Although the Committee retained the Secretary of National Defense's authority over the military budget, it added the requirement that the annual budget submitted to Congress show the amounts originally requested by each of the services and the changes made by the Secretary of National Defense in addition to the final recommendations of the President and the Budget Bureau. Finally, the Committee added a clause to the bill stipulating that "all powers and duties not specifically conferred upon the Secretary of National Defense by this act are retained by each of the respective Secretaries." [44]

With respect to the second objective, the Armed Services Committee reported to the Senate that

During the course of the hearings, it developed that many witnesses had apprehensions with respect to the future of naval aviation and of the Marine Corps. These apprehensions caused your committee to incorporate additional safeguards for these components. These safeguards have the concurrence of the War and Navy Departments and the Commandant of the Marine Corps.[45]

The "safeguards" consisted of the following clause: "The provisions of this act shall not authorize the alteration or diminution of the existing relative status of the Marine Corps (including the fleet marine forces) or of naval aviation." The report explained that "after long and serious deliberation" the Committee decided against incorporating a detailed specification of service functions into the bill because such a step would "seriously impair the required flexibility of the military forces" and "violate the principle of separation of executive and legislative authority traditional in American government." [46]

S.758, which had been placed on the "must legislation" agenda by Senator Robert A. Taft and the Republican Policy Committee,[47] was called off the Senate calendar for floor consideration on July 7. The "debate" was not very exciting. Senator Gurney was in charge of the bill and spoke at some length in its favor, presenting the standard pro-unification arguments about preventing future Pearl Harbors, lifting "air power," which had come of age, from its "position of inferiority," and eliminating "duplication and overlapping between the services." On this last point, Gurney told the senators that although he could not spell out "how much in dollars and cents will be saved each year by unification," he personally thought "the savings will be astonishingly large." [48] Senator Hill too argued in favor of the bill as "our big chance to really do something about economy, instead of just talking about it." [49]

Of the anti-unification die-hards, only Senator Robertson refused to accept the inevitable. He took the floor for two days to argue that the language of the bill provided for a "complete merger" in which the individual services would be "swallowed up" and lose their identities, that the savings estimated to result from the passage of the bill would not be forthcoming but on the contrary that the setup under S.758 would "vastly increase costs of operation," [50] that desirable lines of coordination between the Army and the Navy had already been informally institutionalized and so the bill was unnecessary, and that the bill fostered "militarism" and set up in the Joint Staff the "germ" from which the "great National General Staff is expected to emerge in time." [51] Robertson ended his tirade by denying that the Marines were adequately protected, reminded the senators of the past proposals to reduce the Corps to boat crews in amphibious assaults and to restrict them to a size no larger than a regiment, and concluded with this peroration:

What a fate, Mr. President, for the intrepid corps which stormed the beaches of Guadalcanal, Bougainville, Tarawa, Saipan, Tinian, Guam, Peleliu, Iwo Jima, and Okinawa! What bitter irony that the Commanding General of the Army Air Forces should propose such a fate for the gallant corps which fought the bitterest battle of its illustrious history at Iwo Jima in order that the B-29's of the Air Force might find a welcome haven when they returned crippled from the bombardment of Japan, in order that the same B-29's might have fighter protection on their hazardous trip to Japan! What a mockery if that glorious symbol of American bravery and self-sacrifice—the raising of the flag on Mount Suribachi—is to become a symbol of the passing of the Marines as a combatant corps! I ask my colleagues if they are prepared to become a party to such a desecration? [52]

It will be recalled that the Armed Services Committee, of which Robertson was a member, had voted unanimously to report S.758. Robertson had, however, reserved the right to propose amendments on the floor, and by the time the bill was opened for amendment on July 9, he had filed some twenty-five of them. After the first three of Robertson's amendments were defeated by voice vote upon the recommendation of Senator Gurney and other members of his committee, Robertson gave up the fight.[53] An amendment by Senator Taft effecting a minor change in wording was accepted without debate.[54] The only other amendment offered was Senator McCarthy's, which proposed to change the language of the single protective clause added to S.758 by the Armed Services Committee to the following:

Notwithstanding the provisions of this *or any other* act, the existing relative status of the Marine Corps (including the Fleet Marine Forces) or of Naval Aviation shall not be altered or diminished; *nor shall their existing functions be transferred to other services.**

* The italics indicate the extra margin of protection offered by McCarthy's amendment.

Senator Gurney and other members of the Armed Services Committee opposed McCarthy's amendment, assuring the Senate that the existing provision was completely satisfactory to the official head of the Marine Corps, General Vandegrift, and to Admiral Sherman. Senator Baldwin indicated that the question of how to protect the Marines had received more time, attention, and discussion in the Committee than any other, with the Committee finally hitting on a formula which they expected would offer some measure of protection without infringing on the President's authority as Commander in Chief to assign functions to the services. In every exchange between Senator McCarthy and his opponents, however, the clincher was that General Vandegrift had approved the clause as reported. To this, McCarthy finally blurted out an essential truth about the process by which the reported version of the bill had come to be written:

> Mr. President, I think that is the whole trouble with the drafting of the bill. We have called in generals from the various branches of the service, and if a certain amendment or section met with their approval, it was given no further study. . . .
> I was not a member of the Committee on Armed Services, but I did attend many of its meetings, and watched much of the deliberation. . . . As the Senator says, General Vandegrift said that this language met with his approval, and the committee concluded that it was all right. . . .
> I suggest to the Senator that the mere fact that the committee may have sold General Vandegrift a bill of goods does not make the provision right.[55]

McCarthy's amendment was defeated on a 19-to-52 roll-call vote, and immediately thereafter the Senate passed S.758 by voice vote and sent it on to the House.[56]

1947 House Expenditures Committee Hearings

The compromise unification bill was to have even tougher going in the House. The Committee on Expenditures in the Executive Departments began its hearings on April 2, and by May 15 all the official leaders of the War and Navy Departments had been heard. Their positions were the same as in the Senate: the Army and Army Air Forces representatives—Patterson, Eisenhower, Spaatz, and Norstad—supported H.R.2319 and generally objected to any changes being made in it, Norstad testifying that he "personally would not change a word, period, or comma." [57] The Navy Department representatives—Forrestal,

Nimitz, Vandegrift, and Sherman—with one exception also strongly supported the bill but did not object to the functions of the services being incorporated in the bill in general terms.[58] The exception, General Vandegrift, testified that he could not endorse the pending bill unless the Marine Corps functions were written into it and its language was changed to make explicit that Marine officers were eligible for membership in the various joint bodies other than the JCS.

Two things became clear about the Committee's attitudes during this part of the hearings. There was strong sentiment in favor of "doing something" for the Marine Corps. As Representative John W. McCormack, the former Democratic majority floor leader of the House who at the moment was the minority whip, told Secretary Patterson,

Mr. Secretary, Mr. Manasco asked you some questions about the amendments in connection with the Marine Corps, and I might suggest from what I have observed, . . . [a] very strong feeling on the part of the members of the committee in favor of something being done that will assure the organizational set-up of the Marine Corps. . . . I just make that observation knowing that you will understand the probabilities and try to resolve any differences. . . . I do not mind stating that I have that same feeling myself. . . .

I have just made an observation, and having been here a few years, I think that I have been able to draw some deductions through my experiences that there is a very strong sentiment in favor of something being put into the bill that will preserve, beyond doubt, the Marine Corps. . . .

The question resolves itself as to what you or others might do in collaboration to try and present something to the committee that might be of a satisfactory nature.[59]

In this connection Chairman Hoffman made a concerted effort to get hold of the Series 1478 JCS papers in order to demonstrate that the Marine Corps' fears were justified. He asked Secretary Patterson for the papers during the first day of the hearings, but Patterson explained that they were JCS papers and therefore not in his possession. Hoffman then wrote to Admiral Leahy, but the Admiral did not immediately reply, probably trying to stall Hoffman as the JCS had successfully stalled Robertson in the Senate. Hoffman finally announced on April 29 that "until I get a look at those papers, . . . I will never be able to make up my mind" about the bill. A few days later Hoffman announced that the papers were available for the members to look at in the Committee's office.[60]

Hoffman and a few of the other members of the Committee proceeded to use the JCS papers by questioning Nimitz, Sherman, and Vandegrift about Eisenhower's proposals with respect to the Marines. The questions were obviously calculated to elicit controversial statements about the Army having wanted "to destroy" the Corps. The Navy leaders were uncooperative, however, with not only the two admirals but even General Vandegrift playing down the significance of the 1946 controversy over the Marine functions.

The JCS papers were used to better effect during Eisenhower's own testimony. Eisenhower announced in his opening statement to the Committee that he found "around this town in the last year that I have been accused of being an enemy of the Marine Corps." The General claimed that he was "nonplussed to find out why." [61] On the third day of Eisenhower's appearance, Chairman Hoffman tried to help the General dispel his professed confusion. Hoffman began the hearing on May 13 by asking Eisenhower a series of specific questions about whether it had not been his opinion the previous March that "the emergency development of the Marine forces" in World War II was not "normal," that "bridging the gap between the sailor on the ship and the soldier on land" was the proper function of the Marine Corps, and that the Marines should be restricted to "small, readily available and lightly armed units" and be denied "the heavier weapons of war." It became obvious that Hoffman was reading from Eisenhower's own JCS proposal, and the General, therefore, agreed that he had felt that way. Hoffman then asked the General, "Do you not believe that was the source of the fear that the Marine advocates had," to which Eisenhower replied,

I do not know, sir. . . . They said that was the reason they were fearful? I suppose they said that, but I cannot see how any sane man can read those statements and think that I have any thought of eliminating the Marines; therefore, I do not see why they should be fearful about me [!].[62]

Hoffman continued to press Eisenhower, asking him whether he did not know for a fact that his views had created the belief among "high-ranking officers in the service . . . that there was a proposal on the part of the Army to eliminate the Marine Corps as an effective combat element." Eisenhower gave a half-dozen evasive answers but finally admitted that he did after Hoffman showed him that the statement had been a verbatim quote from Nimitz' reply as CNO to Eisenhower's JCS proposal.[63]

In addition to "doing something" for the Marines, Chairman Hoffman and some of the other committee members indicated a strong desire to be able to hear from persons within the Army or the Navy who might still be opposed to the compromise bill on other grounds. Both Forrestal and Sherman were questioned about purported gags on dissident members of their service, but both men denied that such gags were in effect and indicated that all officers were free to come to the Committee to express their opinions. Sherman admitted, in response to a direct (and obviously planted) question, that Vice Admiral Radford, who had represented the Navy before the Thomas-Hill-Austin subcommittee in 1946, opposed the January 16 Patterson-Forrestal compromise agreement.[64]

No hearings were held by Hoffman's committee between May 16 and June 9. On June 10 the Committee met again and, at the request of some of its members, had Secretary of the Navy Forrestal come before it for a second time. Hoffman opened the hearing by announcing with some irritation that the

statement quoting your chairman as to the fact that if the Army and the Navy did not quit shoving around [they] would not get any bill was not an accurate statement as to what the chairman said. He said something to the effect that if they did . . . quit their shoving and pushing around they might get further sooner.[65]

Representative Porter Hardy, whose district included the naval base at Norfolk, Virginia, told Forrestal that he had "been trying to dig up some opposition to this bill [H.R.2319] in order that we might try to improve it in some way" but that it had been "virtually impossible to get anyone to express any opposition to it." Hardy insisted that he knew that widespread opposition did exist within the Navy and that a "high-ranking Navy officer" had told him that if a poll were taken of all naval officers, "there would be at least 80 percent voting against the bill." Hardy claimed that when he suggested to the officer that he testify before the Committee, the officer replied, "If I did, I would be sent to the Antarctic." [66]

Forrestal implicitly conceded that opposition still existed within the Navy as a result of the fears engendered by the original War Department unification proposals. "The thought of [Army-style] 'merger,' " the Secretary explained, had "become stuck in the minds of many people. . . . This town is rather a miasma. It is a brooding thing. People can nurture their sense of injustice, and the conception of an idea which gets planted in the minds of the men is apt to stay there." [67]

Forrestal did not believe, however, that the opposition was as extensive as claimed by Hardy and denied vehemently that there was basis for any naval officer fearing retaliation for expressing his views to a congressional committee so long as he, Forrestal, was Secretary of the Navy. When Hardy mentioned the existence of Articles 94 and 95 of Navy Regulations, which prohibited communications between Navy or Marine officers and members or committees of Congress without being forwarded through the Secretary of the Navy and receiving his consent, Forrestal alleged that the regulations had to be read in connection "with the context of my communications on this subject which have clearly and specifically removed any inhibition, restraint, penalty, or fear of any kind whatsoever upon any naval officer who is called here to express an opinion upon this legislation." [68] While Forrestal was before the Expenditures Committee this second time, he continued to recommend passage of the legislation but did indicate that he thought the Senate amendments should be incorporated into the House bill.[69]

The next two witnesses to testify during the second part of the House hearings were Melvin Maas and John P. Bracken, who reiterated their opposition to H.R.2319 even with the Senate Committee amendments. Maas called the single protective clause for the Marines and naval aviation "weasel words" and insisted that if any bill were passed, detailed guarantees be provided for the Marine Corps. Both men strongly opposed the separate Air Force. Maas emphasized the degree of opposition to the bill which to his knowledge existed within the Navy and urged the Committee to look into it. Maas told the Congressmen that he had discussed the bill personally with 75 or 100 flag officers and that "all but one of them, or possibly two and I am not so sure that one of those really is not," were against it. Maas at first refused to give the Committee any names so as not to "embarrass, maybe crucify," the officers concerned, but after being pressed, declared, "All right, give me a Navy Register, and I will cross off the few names of those who are for the bill." [70]

Opposition military witnesses began to appear before the House Committee on June 17, when General Edson, who had already scored the compromise bill in the Senate, repeated his opposition for the representatives. A few days later Rear Admiral Ellis M. Zacharias, who had retired the previous November after thirty-eight years of active naval service, testified and strongly opposed H.R.2319 for two days. Admiral Zacharias' chief arguments were directed against a separate Air Force, which he feared would, among other things, retard "the progress of our scientific research on guided missiles" because "if missiles are going to eliminate aircraft, . . . there is going to be an inherent opposition, subconsciously, to the furtherance of those developments." [71] The Admiral also informed the Committee that he had recently taken a private poll of naval officers on active duty and that, out of 200 polled, only two were in favor of the House bill. [72]

On June 26 highly placed naval officers who were still on active duty began to come before the Expenditures Committee to oppose the pending unification bill. Three days before, Secretary of the Navy Forrestal had sent an official naval message to all commands advising them that officers wishing to testify on the unification bill did not need to channel their communications to Congress through the Secretary of the Navy. The message was sent after persistent urging by Hoffman and other members of the Expenditures Committee and by Representative Sterling Cole, who was carrying out an independent campaign against the compromise bill. [73] Forrestal wrote that he had "recently become aware that a feeling of restraint may exist among naval personnel in regard to their latitude of expression before committees of Congress on the proposed National Security Act of 1947." Since that feeling, "which [was] counter to the statutes and to the orderly processes of free expression, may have been engendered by a misinterpretation of Articles 94 and 95, U.S. Navy Regulations," Forrestal was explicitly waiving those provisions with respect to the unification bill. The Secretary of the Navy made it clear that this was "without in any way weakening my endorsement of the January 16, 1947, agreement between the War and Navy Departments which was promulgated by ALNAV 21." [74]

Forrestal's message opened the floodgates to a torrent of Navy opposition. During the last three days of the hearings most of the unofficial leaders of naval aviation appeared to testify against H.R.2319. By July 1, when Hoffman's committee had previously voted (22 to 3 over his objections) to end the hearings so as to be able to report and pass a bill before the end of the session, at least twenty-three more high-ranking Navy and Marine officers had asked for an opportunity to be heard. The Navy fliers who testified on June 26 and 30 and on July 1 vehemently opposed the creation of a separate department for the Army Air Forces. [75] With less intensity, they also argued for a Presidential "deputy" or "assistant" for overall national security affairs to take the place of the Secretary of National Defense and for the addition of a second naval officer to the JCS with the statutory requirement that one of the Navy members be an aviator.

These naval aviator admirals were still predicting at this last stage of the unification conflict that a separate Air Force "would gradually swallow up naval aviation" and that not "even Congress could stop them." [76] But the Navy fliers' chief contention was the more serious one that a separate Air Force department would institutionalize strategic bombing of the World War II type by means of large high-level bombers, which, they claimed, were becoming increasingly more vulnerable and ineffective because of the greatly improved weapons of air defense, particularly the jet fighter and the proximity-fused (V.T.) antiaircraft shell. As Admiral Radford put it,

I just feel that World War III is going to be different, and I would hate to see our new organization patterned after the organization of World War II. I think that that is the trouble, the basic trouble with this bill. It is setting up permanently the pattern established by World War II. That is usually, historically, the way we work. We organize for the next war by following the pattern of the last one.[77]

The Navy fliers argued that strategic bombing even with atomic bombs could best be carried out by smaller, faster, more evasive aircraft launched close to the potential enemy from overseas bases and aircraft carriers. It was, of course, unnecessary to state that both would have to be supported by a powerful fleet. When Representative William Dorn, one of the Air Forces sympathizers on the Expenditures Committee,[78] challenged the Navy line of thought by remarking that "The major base of the next war might be the United States. We might launch our aircraft from here to distances as far as Moscow, Russia, or even the Urals," Admiral Ralph A. Ofstie, who had been testifying, responded, "That is where I completely disagree with you, because we have no such aircraft." [79] Ofstie had explained a few minutes earlier,

There has been a suggestion brought forward that things are going to change greatly within a very short period of time, we are going to have supersonic speeds and tremendous aircraft that can get by anything.

That simply is not the fact; we have nothing in sight today. . . . Unquestionably, I believe in due course and in years to come after we get new materials, new fuels, other new developments, we will get into the trans-sonic and supersonic range, but we have nothing in sight today, and the belief that we will [successfully] continue strategic bombing in the old manner, such as was carried out against Germany and Japan, is, I think, a mistake.[80]

But even if sufficiently long-ranged bombers could be developed technically, Ofstie still would not concede the desirability of basing them in the United States:

Surely, you could do a much better job from in close, and surely you would have to be in close if you are going to be escorted, and I think it is accepted that you have to be escorted if you are going to fly over enemy territory today because of the short range jet fighter plus the really improved antiaircraft. These are going to make it impossible to get out, and I do not think we have Kamikaze pilots in this country.[81]

In short, the admirals were beginning their longer-term campaign against the theory of strategic atomic bombardment applied by the large high-level bomber, on which the Army Air Forces were at this point staking their claim for separation and would later base their claim for the lion's share of the military budget.* In trying to prevent that separation, the naval aviators were apparently convinced that an independent Air Force, whose primary function would admittedly be strategic air warfare, would never let the Navy "muscle in" on that function and intrude its views about its most effective application, whereas an Army Air Forces within the War Department would have no better claim for a monopoly of strategic bombing and the use of the atomic bomb than the Navy. But underlying all of the admirals' specific objections was undeniably the intangible feeling that a unification bill setting up a separate "United States Air Force" with no mention of naval aviation or only a clause pertaining to it necessarily downgraded the naval air organization. As Admiral Ofstie explained in commenting on the single protective clause for the Marines and Navy air put into the bill by the Senate Armed Services Committee,

You see, Mr. Wadsworth, the feeling there is that naval air and marine air is sort of a stepchild, whereas in fact, as I said before, it is just as important, many times more so, sometimes a little less, than this separate Air Force to the security of this Nation, and in the bill the two, Navy and Marine Air Forces really are considered step-children, where the Air Force is set forth as the major important fighting force in the air, and it is not.[82]

---

* The campaign against this kind of strategic bombing, and particularly against the B-36 bomber, would come to a head in 1949 during the so-called "revolt of the admirals." See *National Defense Program—Unification and Strategy,* Hearings before the House Committee on Armed Services, 81st Cong., 1st Sess (1949); Paul Y. Hammond, "Super Carriers and B-36 Bombers," in Harold Stein, ed., *American Civil-Military Decisions: A Book of Case Studies* (University, University of Alabama Press, 1963), pp. 465–568.

Report of H.R.4214 and House Passage

As has been noted, the House hearings on H.R.2319 ended on July 1. About two weeks later, on July 16, "Mr. Hoffman, by direction of the Committee on Expenditures in the Executive Departments," reported a clean bill, H.R.4214, which Hoffman had introduced that day, with the recommendation "that the bill do pass." H.R.4214 contained almost all the Senate changes to the original compromise bill but in addition incorporated the language of the proposed executive order on the general functions of the Army, Navy, and Air Force and on the specific functions of the Marine Corps.[83] The bill eliminated the provision giving the Secretary of National Defense the right to "formulate and finally determine the budget estimates for submittal to the Budget Bureau" but added a different provision giving him authority to "take appropriate steps to eliminate unnecessary duplication or overlapping in the fields of procurement, supply, transportation, storage, health, and research." Finally, the clean bill prohibited any person who had ever held a commission in a regular component of the armed services from being appointed Secretary of National Defense and changed the requirement that the military departments be administered "as individual units" to "as individual executive departments." [84]

Immediately following the five-and-one-half-page official Committee report came nine pages of "Additional Views of Clare E. Hoffman, Chairman." Hoffman explained that early in the hearings it had become apparent to him that a majority of the Committee was determined to report a unification bill. He pointed out that he had not voted against the bill and had filed the report "because and only because legislation seems inevitable and . . . H.R.4214 is the best bill that was obtainable." Hoffman wrote that, as chairman, he had prepared a report to accompany the bill, but that the Committee had rejected it and appointed a subcommittee consisting of himself, Wadsworth, and McCormack to prepare another one. Since he could not agreed with Wadsworth and McCormack on what should be included in the report, Hoffman yielded to their views and decided to submit his separate "additional views" "because the official report does not in the opinion of the writer tell the whole story" on the testimony developed during the hearings.[85]

The remainder of Hoffman's remarks consisted of the report that he had originally prepared. Although the explanatory language on the bill was substantially the same as that of the adopted version, Hoffman's report told the House that the Committee had been handicapped during the hearings by Articles 94 and 95 of Navy Regulations because they required communications from naval personnel to the Committee to be through the Secretary of the Navy. Hoffman printed in full Forrestal's ALNAV waiving those provisions and explained that just as "a very significant degree of intelligent opposition to certain provisions of the bill within the naval service" was making itself heard, the Committee voted over his objection to cut off the hearings. Hoffman also explained why the functions of the services were written into the bill, quoting long passages from Eisenhower's and Spaatz' Series 1478 JCS proposals for the emasculation of the Marine Corps and the taking over by the Air Force of the Navy's land-based aircraft.[86]

The same day that H.R.4214 was reported, the majority floor leader, Charles A. Halleck, took the floor to ask unanimous consent that it be in order to consider the bill at any time, that all points of order be considered as waived, and that general debate be confined to five hours, whose control would be divided between the chairman and the ranking minority member of the Expenditures Committee. Halleck explained that the purpose of his request was to avoid the necessity of appearance before the Rules Committee in order to secure a special rule and, presumably, the possibility of further delays in bringing the bill to a vote. Representative Cole objected, so Halleck's request was denied.[87] Later the same day, Halleck again asked that unanimous consent be in order to consider the bill beginning two days thence, with the other provisions of his request remaining the same. There being no objection this time, the request was granted.[88]

Three days later, on July 19, Hoffman moved that the House resolve itself into the Committee of the Whole House on the State of the Union for consideration of H.R.4214. Representative Cole raised a parliamentary inquiry. Cole explained that he had originally opposed the unanimous-consent request on July 16 because prints of the clean bill were not available to members of the House. Cole had not objected to the second request because he had been assured that copies of the bill would be available at least twenty-four hours before the bill was called up. Cole explained that the printed bill had only become available at 9:30 that morning, and he wanted to know whether he could raise a point of order against its consideration. Speaker Martin ruled that under the unanimous-consent agreement all points of order against the bill had been waived, so that Cole's did not lie. Cole then asked whether he could raise a point of order on the grounds that the committee report was still not generally available and did not contain the existing provisions of law changed by the bill as required by the Legislative Reorganization Act of 1946. Martin again ruled that the point of order would not lie and advised Cole that his only recourse would be to defeat Hoffman's motion to resolve the House into the Committee of the Whole for consideration of the bill. Cole made no such attempt and Hoffman's motion carried.[89]

The House "floor debate" was a series of statements by about twenty-five persons explaining for the record why they were in favor of the bill, why they were not in favor of the bill but would vote for it none the less, or why they were still opposed to it. There were no new arguments. The proponents of the bill, led by James Wadsworth, stressed, mostly in general terms, the great benefits to national security that would accrue and continued to express hopes for future if not immediate economies. The most enthusiastic proponents were those who saw the bill primarily as granting independent status to the Army Air Forces.[90]

The opponents of the bill and the unenthusiastic supporters were still concerned mainly about sufficient protection for naval aviation and saw a separate Air Force as a "disunifying" development that was not called for, simply because of the admittedly great destructive power of aircraft.[91] Clare Hoffman, who was nominally in charge of the bill on the floor and was "not opposing it," finished off the general debate with a long speech that stated his fears about the emergence of a military dictatorship, ridiculed the claims made for economy, and questioned why Congress was abdicating its responsibility over the armed forces by allegedly giving power to the military leaders of the country.[92]

Fourteen amendments were proposed to H.R.4214. The seven that were not opposed by members of the Expenditures Committee were adopted. The most significant amendments were Representative John Taber's, which struck out the provision originally added by the Senate Armed Services Committee requiring the original service appropriations requests and the changes made by the overall Secretary to be shown in the annual military budget sent to Congress, and Representative Cole's, which added a more detailed statement of the functions of the Navy, including specific language protecting land-based naval aviation for long-range reconnaissance, antisubmarine warfare, and the protection of shipping.[93] Cole's attempt to delete the words "control" and "direction" from the Secretary of National Defense's grant of authority was defeated by a 36-to-190 division vote.[94]

After all the amendments had been offered, the Committee of the Whole rose and reported the bill and the approved amendments back to the full House, which proceeded to pass them by voice vote.[95] Immediately thereafter, Hoffman called up the Senate bill, S.758, and proceeded to have the House strike out "all after the enacting clause," substitute the provisions of H.R.4214 as passed by the House, and send the bill back to the Senate with a request for a conference. On July 21, the Senate disagreed to the House amendment to S.758 and acceded to the request for a conference.[96]

Conference Report and Final Passage of National Security Act

On July 24, after five different meetings, the conference committee reported a compromise version of S.758, which was passed on the same day by the Senate and the following day by the House.[97] The conference adopted substantially the House amendment to the Senate bill, relaxing, however, the absolute prohibition against the appointment of former regular military officers to the post of Secretary of Defense to those who had been on active duty within ten years prior to appointment, eliminating some of the Cole amendment's language with respect to the Navy functions without deleting the specific guarantees for land-based air, and reinstating the Senate-passed provision giving the Secretary of Defense authority "to formulate and finally determine" the military budget.[98] A last-minute hitch developed when Senator Henry Cabot Lodge, who strongly disapproved of the incorporation into the law of the service functions, threatened to object to the unanimous-consent request for the immediate consideration of the conference report during the end-of-session jam in the Senate. The request was withdrawn for a short time, during which Lodge was apparently persuaded to drop his objection.[99] The enrolled unification bill reached President Truman on July 26, the last day of the first session of the Eightieth Congress. Truman immediately signed it into law, issued the prepared executive order on the service functions, and nominated James Forrestal to be the first Secretary of Defense. The Senate confirmed Forrestal under suspension of the rules minutes before final adjournment.[100]

Thus in July, 1947, after nearly four years of almost continuous conflict, "unification" was enacted into law with the passage of the National Security Act. Its form deviated considerably from the original War Department coalition proposals. A Secretary of Defense and a separate Air Force were both established, but the Secretary was not even provided with a "department" and the Navy's land-based aircraft were protected by law from being incorporated into the new Air Force. The World War II JCS structure was continued by statute, but the Chiefs were denied either dominant control over the military budget or independent access to the President on matters of strategy and military policy, and no overall chief of staff was added to their membership. The Marine Corps, finally, came out of the unification conflict not only without its World War II combatant functions curtailed but also with those functions enshrined for the first time in statutory language that would presumably protect the Corps against Army campaigns for its emasculation evermore.

Determinants of
Congressional Behavior

7

Intra-Legislative Influences

The unification conflict was resolved ultimately according to the terms imposed by voting majorities of the two houses of Congress in passing the National Security Act. Part IV will analyze the major sources of influence that bore on the formation of these voting majorities during the conflict and try to explain how the different influences were able to affect congressional behavior on unification. This chapter will examine the major sources of influence that operated from within the legislative body itself: the senators' and representatives' own personal policy preferences, the committees, the "subject-matter experts," and the party leaderships; the following chapter will examine the key sources of influence from outside the legislative body and from outside the government: the President, the executive branch department heads and other official leaders, the unofficial executive branch leaders, political interest groups, and "public opinion."

Personal Policy Preferences

One crucial source of influence on the behavior of senators and representatives both in constituting voting majorities and in earlier stages of the unification conflict was their own pre-existing personal policy preferences.[1] For, obviously, members of Congress often do start out with ideas of their own about what is desirable in various areas of public concern. They are, as David Truman has put it, not "equivalent to the steel ball in a pinball game, bumping passively from post to post down an inclined plane." [2] To the extent that these personal policy preferences are very strong and that the effects upon them of the proposals being disputed in a conflict are clear, the legislators can make up their minds independently with their own preferences virtually controlling their actions. To the extent, on the other hand, that these policy preferences are weak or that the consequences of the disputed proposals are not easily ascertainable but are open to debate, the preferences will probably only set limits on the behavior of individual senators or representatives within which a variety of other influences can operate. From among those legislators in the first category will most often be drawn, incidentally, the small core who become the "ball-carriers" or active congressional supporters or opponents of the controverted proposals within the legislative body.

SERVICE-IDENTIFIED PREFERENCES

It was the possession of personal policy preferences that essentially coincided with the key organizational goals of the War and Navy Department coalitions themselves that appears to have accounted for the behavior of most of the active, hard-core congressional supporters of those coalitions in the unification conflict. These legislators had come to develop such preferences as a result of an unusually strong sense of "identification" [3] with one or another of the military services. Although the general process by which individuals acquire goals and group identifications is highly complex and still imperfectly understood,[4] the sense of identification that operated in the unification conflict seems to have been caused by the senators or representatives having enjoyed fairly long-term, gratifying relations with the service concerned, through handling its business before Congress as members of the Military Affairs or Naval Affairs Committees or the Military Appropriations or Naval Appropriations Subcommittees, through actual military duty in the service's active or reserve component, or as a result of the service maintaining key military installations such as Army camps, Navy shipyards, or Army Air Forces airfields in the legislators' constituency. Table 1 indicates that the single factor most consistently associated with an active pro-War Department or pro-Navy Department coalition position was service on the Military Affairs or Naval Affairs Committees. As Tom Connally, at the time a member of the House and later Chairman of the Senate Foreign Relations Committee, once commented,

TABLE 1
Bases for Service Identification

Member of Congress	Military Service	Substantive Committee Service	Appropriations Subcommittee	Major Installations
		Pro-War Department Coalition Position		
Gurney	WWI Army	SMA 1939–46	SMAS 1941–47	AAF
Hill	WWI Army	HMA 1923– (Ch. 1937–) 1937 SMA 1938–46		A, AAF A, AAF
Johnson (Colo.)		SMA 1937–46		A, AAF
Thomas	WWI Army	SMA 1933– (Ch. 1945–) 1946		
Wadsworth	Sp.-Am. War Army	SMA 1918– (Ch. 1920–) 1926		
		Pro-Navy Department Coalition Position		
Bridges	(son WWII USN)	SMA 1937–46	SMAS 1937–43 SNAS 1941–46	N, AAF
Byrd	(brother Reg. USN)	SNA 1933–46		A, N
Cole	Nav.Res.	HNA 1939–46		
Hoffman	. . .	. . .	. . .	. . .
May		HMA 1931– (Ch. 1939–) 1946		
Robertson	Boer War British Army	SNA 1945–46		AAF
Russell		SNA 1933–46	SMAS 1933–47	A, N, AAF
Saltonstall	WWI Army (son and daughter WWII, USN; son WWII MC killed in action)	SNA 1945–46	Ch. SNAS 1947	A, N, AAF
Tydings	WWI Army	SNA 1933–46	SNAS 1939–46	A, N, AAF
Vinson		HNA 1918– (Ch. 1931–) 1946		
Walsh		SNA 1919–26; 1928–(Ch. 1937–) 1946		A, N, AAF

Code: SMA (Senate Military Affairs Committee), SNA (Senate Naval Affairs Committee), SMAS (Senate Military Appropriations Subcommittee), SNAS (Senate Naval Appropriations Subcommittee), HMA (House Military Affairs Committee), etc.; A (Army), N (Navy), AAF (Army Air Forces), MC (Marine Corps).

Sources: *Current Biography* (1940–60), *Congressional Directory, 63d–80th Congress* (1913–47); *Congressional Quarterly Weekly Report*, March 24, 1961.

A gentleman is elected on the Committee on Naval Affairs because he has a predilection for the Navy. What is the result? The result soon is that they become "bugs" on the particular matter with which their committee deals. The naval committeeman soon grows into the belief that the Navy is the most important arm of the Government, and that we ought to have the greatest Navy in the world. The member who gets on the Committee on Military Affairs, where he associates with Chiefs of Staff and Secretaries of War, soon gets the opinion that the Army is the most outstanding branch of this Government.[5]

Among the original hard-core War Department coalition supporters, Wadsworth had been a member and then chairman of the Senate Military Affairs Committee during World War I and in the early 1920s, as well as having seen active service with the Army in the Spanish-American War. Although not a member of the House Military Affairs Committee, Wadsworth had nevertheless resumed his close and cordial relations with the War Department since his election as a representative in 1932.* Senators Thomas and Hill, who had both served with the Army in World War I, had been members of the Senate Military Affairs Committee during World War II, with Thomas reaching the chairmanship and also serving as an ex officio member of the Military (War Department) Appropriations Subcommittee and Hill having been a long-term member and eventually chairman of the House Military Affairs Committee before his election to the Senate in 1938. Both Thomas and Hill had key Army and Army Air Forces installations in their states, and Hill's original House constituency in Montgomery, Alabama, was the home of Maxwell Air Force Base, the very fountainhead of strategic air warfare doctrine.[6]

None of the pro-Navy congressional partisans had as many bases for identification as Thomas or Hill. Vinson and Walsh, for example, had no military service in their backgrounds; the influence controlling their actions clearly appears to have been the sense of identification with, if not proprietorship of, the Navy, developed through a combined total service of fifty-seven years on the House and Senate Naval Affairs Committees, twenty-six of those years as the committee chairmen. By the time of the unification conflict, Vinson was known variously as "the ad-

---

* Secretary of War Stimson's Diary is full of consultations with Wadsworth immediately before and during World War II about legislative matters of interest to the War Department. According to Stimson, Wadsworth would drop in occasionally even without having anything special to talk about: "It always is a comfort to have him come in because he is intelligent, broad-minded, and very friendly." Stimson Diary, Oct. 17, 1942, Yale University Library.

miral," "Mr. Navy," and "the father of the modern Navy." He is reported to have been in the habit of referring to Cabinet members as "the best [or worst] Secretary of the Navy I ever had." [7] In short, Vinson and, to a lesser degree, Walsh and their committees had pretty much built the World War II fleet which the War Department coalition apparently wanted in part to scuttle.[8] Committee service seems also to account for the policy preferences of, among others, Senators Tydings, Saltonstall,[9] and Robertson, the first two of whom had served with the Army in World War I, and the last with the British Army in the Boer War. It is true that Tydings and Saltonstall (and Walsh) had major naval installations in their states of Maryland and Massachusetts, but their constituencies included major Army and Army Air Forces bases as well.[10]

Substantive committee membership does not account for the actions of Congressman May or Senator Bridges. Both men opposed the position of the War Department, with whose affairs they dealt as chairman of the House and a ranking member of the Senate Military Affairs Committees, respectively. There is no evidence available to account for May's behavior,[11] but it will be noted in Table 1 that Bridges, while dealing with the Army as a Military Affairs Committee member, also maintained relations with the Navy through his service on the Naval Appropriations Subcommittee and as a senator from a state, New Hampshire, with a major naval installation—Portsmouth Naval Shipyard.

Some other explanation must, of course, be found to account for the behavior of Clare Hoffman, who became an active opponent of the War Department coalition in the 1947 House action. As Table 1 indicates, Hoffman had never had military service, had no military installations in his Michigan constituency, and had never served on a Military Affairs or Naval Affairs Committee or military appropriations subcommittee.

CONGRESSIONAL-CONTROL PREFERENCES

Another set of pre-existing personal policy preferences that appears to have significantly affected the behavior of members of Congress and led them specifically to support or be responsive to various parts of the Navy Department coalition's unification position were those based on strong "free-floating," or general, attitudes favoring maximum congressional control of executive branch agencies. Such preferences became directly relevant to the Navy's insistence on individual service autonomy and on detailed specifications of the services' combatant functions.

The two chief formal methods of exercising congressional control over the executive branch agencies are through the appropriations process and through statutory determination of their organizational structure and programs.[12] Whatever the exact method, it is obvious that the exercise of effective control requires information. A military structure with separate or relatively autonomous military departments, each with its own set of spokesmen appearing before Congress, could provide the legislators with more than a single point of view on military matters and thus give them some freedom of action in formulating policy. As Congressman May put it during the Woodrum Committee hearings with specific reference to the unification issue, but in a statement which illustrates the congressional-control position generally,

Well, for one on the committee, I haven't any fixed opinion about [unification] at this time. I would like to wait until I see how much scrapping is done between the Army and Navy representatives; the more they do of that, the better it is for the committee, I think, because we will get an issue then, and in your differences here we will find out the reasons and the whys. I think it is fortunate that you do come up her, and one take one side and the other take another side, because we might be suspicious if you had agreed on something. But lay your cards on the table, and we will decide then what we will do.[13]

Congressional control through appropriations is effected by determining the final amounts of money that can be spent by the executive branch agencies on their various programs—in the case of the military, the different kinds of weapons-systems and military forces. Such control can be exercised not only by making cuts in the amounts recommended by the President's budget but also by adding programs or increasing the requested levels of expenditure. But the latter course of action requires information about practicable additions or increases, which generally means the original budget estimates submitted by the executive branch departments and agencies to the Budget Bureau. The Budget and Accounting Act of 1921 and various Presidential directives normally restrict executive branch officials from making that kind of information available to Congress.[14]

Senator Bridges' proposal for a triple-column military budget showing the amounts originally requested by each of the military departments and by the Secretary of National Defense, in addition to those finally recommended to Congress by the Budget Bureau and the President, while obviously calculated primarily to protect the Navy by law from having its original appropriations requests cut without the Congress knowing about it, also served to increase congressional control of the military services generally by providing the additional knowledge of possible alternative lines of appropriations action. Apparently because of this second function, Bridges' Navy-favored proposal drew support not only from the Navy identifiers and the uncommitted but even from among the War Department coalition's own congressional allies. Thus, when House Armed Services Committee chairman Walter G. Andrews, a pro-War Department unifier, testified before the Senate Armed Service Committee in 1947, one of his key recommendations was that Bridges' proposal be incorporated into the law. When Andrews made this recommendation, Senator Tydings, as could be expected of a Navy friend, commented that it had

outstanding merit . . . because it is perfectly obvious there is to be some rivalry in getting money between the three departments. If the over-all Secretary indicates what alterations he has made in the budget for either one of the three departments, it puts Congress on notice that he is being partial or he is being impartial in his effort to bring the over-all expenditures into line.

I think there cannot be much debate on that.

Otherwise we will be in a position of not knowing whether he is taking partial or impartial action on it without hearing from the grapevine.

Only Senator Saltonstall, the chairman of the Subcommittee on Naval Appropriations and another of the Navy's most faithful friends, raised the question whether that "would . . . not require a whole change in the budgetary law," to which Tydings replied,

We could put a provision in there that [the Secretary of Defense] could submit the Armed Services budget to both the Appropriations Committees, the two Armed Services Committees on National Defense, who deal with this particular point, and leave the [Bureau of the] Budget completely out of it.

At this point Senator Hill, probably the most intense War Department identifier and most active unifier in the Senate, added, "Certainly give us the information we ought to have." [15]

The other major means of exercising congressional control over the subordinate parts of the executive branch is through the determination of their programs and organizational structure. Except for the Presidency, all the departments and agencies in the executive branch are statutory creatures of Congress. The question of relative influence between the President and his chief subordinates, on the one hand, and Congress, on the other, has to do with the degree to which the statute prescribes organizational detail, the organizational level at which program authority is placed, and the methods of making subsequent changes in organizational structure and functions. Although there have been instances in the last decades indicating a move away from overly detailed statutory organization by Congress and in the direction of granting authority to the President, subject to limitations and varying types of congressional vetoes, to make organizational changes and to transfer programs between agencies,[16] this pattern still runs counter to the congressional-control maximizing preferences held by many Congressmen. On any particular issue Congress may act upon those preferences and still insist on retaining detailed control. Thus, Carl Vinson was probably not speaking only for himself and other Navy Department identifiers when he told one of the Army witnesses in 1944 with respect to the War Department's proposal that the President be given statutory authority to effect unification through executive order in such a way and at such a time as he himself saw fit:

Should [not] Congress know how [any new department] is going to be operated before Congress gives its authority for the operation of it? . . . As far as I am concerned, blanket authority, as far as legislation is concerned, has ceased. . . . Otherwise, Congress will have no control . . . and will wake up some morning and read in the paper where such and such a thing is happening; and then we will say we did not intend it to happen that way.[17]

The questioning by the House Expenditures Committee in 1947 indicated that it contained a sizable number of strong, anti-executive order people. For example, Carter Manasco, its former chairman in the Seventy-ninth Congress, who had come to support unification generally in the Eightieth, still could say to Secretary Patterson about Patterson's insistence that at least the service functions be left to determination by the President through executive order,

I have seen a lot of Executive Orders that were issued that were supposed to have been authorized by legislation that Congress passed. I do not think that there was a single member of Congress who had any idea that the act they were passing would give such an authorization. One of those I recall was the Fair Employment Practices Committee. I do not think any member of Congress had any idea that was going to be issued under the War Powers Act; quite a few others. For that reason, I am a little afraid to grant this much power to the Executive Department to write laws. I think it is the duty of Congress itself.[18]

Chairman Hoffman was and continued until his retirement in 1962 to be opposed even to general reorganization acts subject to congressional veto,[19] and the rest of the active minority in the Expenditures Committee consisted largely of Republicans who were not motivated to give the Democratic President any more authority than they could help.[20]

It should be noted that among the warmest supporters of the statutory definition of the service functions were those members of Congress who doubted the effectiveness of congressional control of the executive branch through the appropriations process alone. Senator Bridges, who at the time was chairman of the Senate Appropriations Committee, made that clear in an exchange with Secretary of War Patterson, who was assuring him that no damage could befall naval aviation and the Marines as long as Congress controlled the purse and that consequently writing the draft executive order into the law was unnecessary:

Senator BRIDGES.   You know the story that has been told here for the last few years; if you come in here with a [budgetary] recommendation which the Congress modifies, immediately the hue and cry goes up that we are interfering with the defense program of the country, the security of the country. And if we have before us a recommendation of this Super-secretary who had an overall picture, and we modify it, Congress would certainly be starting under a handicap, would it not?

Secretary PATTERSON.   No; not a handicap. Their powers are as firm as they are today. You have it under the Constitution; the power of the purse.

Senator BRIDGES.   Yes, but do you not recall how, so often, if there was any major difference as to the recommendations in a period of emergency, . . . the accusation would go out that Congress was trying to interfere with the workings of the War and Navy Departments? And we are told that General So-and-so, and Secretary So-and-so, who are devoting their whole time to it, should know more than Congress. That is, very frankly, the situation.[21]

Similar thoughts were expressed to the Secretary of War in the House by Representative Clarence Brown in another discussion of the service functions issue:

Mr. BROWN.   It is my thought that we ought to retain that responsibility and authority by writing into statutory law our decisions and our directions rather than to depend upon the President to issue Executive orders. I have always questioned, in my own mind, the constitutional authority and validity of the theory that the President can legislate by Executive order, which he has done in many instances

Mr. PATTERSON.   You do it every year, Mr. Brown, when the armed forces come down here for money.

Mr. BROWN. That is the one control, the control of the purse strings, that the Congress still has, or I hope it still has, over the affairs of the Government Sometimes when I see the pressure letters and telegrams and telephone calls that too often are instigated by departments, I am not so sure that we still control the purse strings.

Mr. PATTERSON. What a power it is! What a power it is on the armed services! You make them or break them every year.

Mr. BROWN. I agree with you, but we have had a few that I have been trying to break for several years, and somehow or other they just do not break; they bend a little bit but they find some method by Executive order, to transfer the functions and activities and employees over to some other branch or division of Government, and on it goes. So, I am not as confident as you are that we have complete control of the purse strings any more, and can accomplish by that control the things we want to do as the Congress.[22]

Although their influence was admittedly great, neither the personal policy preferences of the War or Navy Department identifiers nor the preferences favoring maximum congressional control of the executive branch can be said to have accounted by themselves for the behavior of Congress in the unification conflict. For the Wadsworths and Vinsons were simply not numerous enough to form majorities in either house of Congress, and although a majority of Congressmen probably did share congressional-control preferences, these were not of overriding importance for most members,[23] nor were they directly relevant to every aspect of the unification proposals being disputed. Furthermore, the connection between the proposals and two other sets of policy preferences that were relevant and that no doubt were universally held within Congress—those favoring combat effectiveness and economy—was just not clear enough to allow most individual senators and representatives to make up their own minds on what position to take on unification. As a result, other sources of influence were also able to affect the actions of actual or potential congressional voting majorities during the conflict. But for the most part, these influences were obviously restricted by, and forced to operate through, the pre-existing policy preferences of the individual members.

The Committees

It should not be surprising to find that the committees provided the main source of influence within Congress on the substantive positions taken by its voting majorities in the unification conflict. Woodrow Wilson had argued almost three-quarters of a century earlier that it would be "no great departure from the fact," to describe our entire political system as "a government by the Standing Committees of Congress." As he had seen it, power was

> nowhere concentrated; it is rather deliberately and of set policy scattered. . . . It is divided up, as it were, into . . . seignories, in each of which a Standing Committee is the court-baron and its chairman lord-proprietor. These petty barons . . . may at will exercise an almost despotic sway within their own shires.[24]

More recently, two experienced legislators have explained the role of the committees with somewhat greater charity, as follows:

> No individual could hope to become fully informed on the hundreds of complex questions upon which Senators must vote each year. Members of the committees concerned with these questions can become thoroughly informed, and a Senator must frequently rely upon the judgment of the committees. . . .
> Congress, like most large organizations, functions through a division-of-labor method known in this case as the committee system. Members must trust their colleagues to specialize and to do the necessary research and conduct the necessary investigations in the various fields.[25]

In this division of labor, the committees are authorized by standing rules to receive proposals in the form of bills for consideration after introduction. The committees then decide whether or not to hold hearings and can conduct the hearings in a favorable, unfavorable, or mixed manner toward any particular point of view. They can change the content of the proposals by rewriting the language of the introduced bills and decide whether or not to report them to the floor. The committees, if they report a bill, prepare the case for or against its adoption (or both) in the formal report and most likely provide the leaders of the floor debate. The committees, finally, provide the members of the conference committee that in case of disagreement between the two houses will formulate the final version upon which a vote will be taken. Given the traditional atmosphere of deference to the committees that pervades the American Congress, favorable committee action becomes with very few exceptions a prerequisite for passage of a bill and is in many instances a sufficient condition.

The great influence of the committees during the unification conflict should already be clear. In the Seventy-ninth Congress, the decision of the Senate Military Affairs Committee to begin holding hearings on unification bills shortly after the end of the war with Japan, when interest in military matters was still high, gave the War Department coalition a momentum that it never lost. By providing a well-reported forum in which the famous World War II civilian and military leaders of the War Department could argue the general merits of unification and also put across their specific proposals, the hearings probably created a favorable climate of opinion toward a single military department both within Congress and among the public and "made a record" on the basis of which a pro-War Department "clean bill" could later be written.

Although the Military Affairs Committee was strongly committed to the War Department's general plan for unification,* the Navy and Marine Corps witnesses, while occasionally being subjected to sharp questioning, were not harassed. After all, the war had just ended, and it would have been considered bad form to attack any of the men who had played major roles in winning it. When, however, Secretary of the Navy Forrestal suggested to Chairman Thomas that in view of the unanimity of thought being expressed by the officers from each of the services, he require the War and Navy Departments explicitly to inform their officers that anything said before the Committee would not be made part of their service record or otherwise held against them, Thomas refused. Forrestal expressed his belief that there were "many officers throughout the Army, who, if they were not afraid of injury to their future careers, would express clear and strong opinions against the proposed step," but Thomas insisted that the Committee was getting entirely "free thought." [26]

The Senate Naval Affairs Committee showed in 1946 how hearings could be used exclusively as a propaganda vehicle without any intent to report legislation. These hearings purportedly were on S.2044, the Thomas-Hill-Austin bill, which was about to be reported by the Military Affairs Committee. It should be noted that the bill had not been formally referred to the naval group, but since its chairman, Senator Walsh, "thought that additional hearings on unification were necessary," he held them anyway.[27]

The Naval Affairs Committee called in a different naval war hero or member of the Navy Department secretariat each day so that the mass media could give the Navy case against the War Department's proposals

---

* Its chairman, Thomas, admitted on the floor of the Senate that he "did not have to be converted" to supporting unification, but "entered upon the task with zeal." *Congressional Record,* XCIII (1947), 2093.

maximum and continuous coverage in the hope, presumably, that there would be feedback on the attitudes of potential congressional voting majorities directly from the media themselves and indirectly through the congressmen's constituencies. The presentations by the Navy Department witnesses were usually carefully prepared and calculated to stress a number of specific themes. When Admiral Halsey appeared on July 2 without, surprisingly, a prepared statement, Senator Byrd was greatly disturbed. The exchange went like this:

Senator BYRD. Let me ask you this question, Admiral Halsey, do you have a prepared statement?
Admiral HALSEY. No, sir; I have not.
Senator BYRD. I think it is vitally important for the Admiral to get out to the public his views on this bill because he has a tremendous following among the people at this time.
Admiral HALSEY. The statement that I made to the Military Affairs Committee in October or November. . . . I haven't changed my opinion, and I am prepared to submit that as a statement again.
Senator BYRD. It is pretty hard to get the publicity on it again unless you prepare it. Don't you think if it was prepared—
The CHAIRMAN [Walsh] (interposing). We can take it down, and get it released.[28]

In addition to providing a forum for the promulgation of prepared statements, the Committee was at times almost too helpful with leading questions whose intent was apparently to establish a pro-Navy record for possible use in fighting the Military Affairs Committee's bill on the floor of the Senate. For example, while Forrestal was trying to justify the retention of the Secretary of the Navy in the Cabinet by explaining in his prepared statement how in the early part of the war he had returned from a trip to Guadalcanal in a state of alarm over the prospects of the United States' holding on to that island and pressed hard for additional reinforcements, which were finally sent and purportedly turned the tide of battle, Senator Tydings interrupted to ask:

What do you mean there—I appreciate what was done—but what do you mean by saying that you might have lost had you not been able to express your views, the Navy's views, with vigor at the highest levels? . . .
Secretary FORRESTAL (interposing). The immediate thing we were pressing for was long-ranged fighters, P-38's, which had a range sufficient to go up the "slot," intercept the Japs coming down, and get back to base. . . .
Senator TYDINGS. Was there a movement to deny you these?
Secretary FORRESTAL. I wouldn't say deny—

Senator TYDINGS (interposing). Rather, to reallocate.

Secretary FORRESTAL. The P-38's were freshly out, they were needed everywhere, they were the first long-range fighters of the Army Air Forces and demand was very great to get them.

Senator TYDINGS. And you feel that because you could go to the highest authority and press your point of view, that you obtained the means of making victory certain, without which you might have lost if you had not had that access and that avenue of approach?

Secretary FORRESTAL. It is always hard to be quite as definite as that, Senator, and maybe I overestimate the effect of what I said; but I do know that from the President down, we were able to generate a much greater feeling of alarm, which was completely justified.

Senator TYDINGS. Well, you have answered my question all right.

At this point, Senator Gerry took up the digression:

Senator GERRY. Mr. Secretary, may I ask you another question? Does this not also go into the question that the Navy had a separate type of plane from the Army, and that there was a good deal of controversy in regard to it, and the Navy plane was very much more successful and effective?

Secretary FORRESTAL. Well, that is a little bit too technical for me. Our planes were built for shipboard use.

Senator GERRY. The type of motor, though, as I understand it, the Navy type of motor, was the more effective one?

Secretary FORRESTAL. That goes back to 1936, when the air-cooled versus liquid-cooled engine controversy arose. We stuck to the air-cooled motor, which subsequently carried approximately 85 percent of all the combat aircraft employed in the war. It was not the type of plane so much as the type of engine, and the fact that we stuck to that.

Senator GERRY. That was the point I was trying to bring out, because it was the insistence of the Navy on the type of engine that was so very important in the planes.

Secretary FORRESTAL. Yes.

Senator GERRY. And I know from talking to men who were in the Air Force in the Mediterranean, how much that counted, how superior the Navy plane was, although they were men in the Army Air Forces.

Secretary FORRESTAL. Yes.[29]

In the Eightieth Congress, it was the Senate Armed Services and House Expenditures Committees that finally formulated the solutions to the unification conflict that the voting majorities adopted on the floor, without the House members having had more than a few hours' opportunity to see copies of the reported bill and without the committee report having been generally available to them. It will be recalled that both committees were able to prevent even a single amendment to their bills that they opposed from being adopted during floor consideration. The leaders of these two committees then proceeded to write in conference the final version of the unification bill, which their parent houses were obliged under the rules either to accept or reject *in toto,* and which, given the predominant sentiment in favor of some sort of unification that existed, they had no choice but to accept in the closing days of the session, without the senators even having had access to the conference report.[30]

Of course, the most final and irrevocable action that a committee can take on a bill is a negative one—to hold no hearings at all. It will be recalled that while the conflict was raging in the Senate committee rooms during the Seventy-ninth Congress, the House scene was quiet and peaceful. All of the House committees to which unification and other kinds of military reorganization bills had been referred simply ignored them, thus guaranteeing that the state of affairs embodied in the legislative *status quo* would continue.

To sum up, the standing committees exercised great influence within Congress on the substantive position taken by its voting majorities in resolving the unification conflict. As a result of the necessary division of labor that required all proposals to be referred to committees specializing in the subject matter involved before their consideration on the floor, potential floor majorities had little chance to pass on any alternatives not reported back by the committees and little basis for choosing between alternatives other than the facts and arguments that these same committees presented. Apart from the general deference that exists within Congress toward committee recommendations, the committees' influence rested essentially on their ability to define or "structure" the conflict situation for potential floor majorities. This the committees did by providing, through the propaganda effects of their hearings, their official reports, statements during the floor debate, and other informal means of communication, what became the dominant perceptions or views of reality [31] about the consequences of the disputed proposals for the policy preferences presumed to be widely held within the two chambers.

This whole discussion should not be interpreted, however, as signifying that the committees could have gotten voting majorities to approve automatically any legislative solutions they chose. The personal policy preferences of the individual members of potential majorities—sometimes referred to as the "temper of the house"—did set varying limits on the solutions that could have been recommended without serious risk of defeat on the floor and a consequent lowering of that particular committee's intra-chamber prestige and influence in future dealings. It is an indication of skill that in 1947 the committees anticipated those limits and stayed within them. Thus, there is some evidence that after the testimony of the naval aviators, a majority of the Expenditures Committee might have been willing to eliminate the separate-air-force provision from its reported clean bill. But this was not done, reportedly because it was decided that such action would invite the substitution by a rebellious voting majority on the House floor of the Senate-passed amended version of S.758 (without even the statutory definition of the functions of the Marines and naval aviation) in order to protect the popular Army Air Forces.[32]

Furthermore, the committees' (or any other intra-legislative influence source's) ability to impose a recommended solution on potential floor majorities also depended on the perceptions of reality on which that solution was based being supported to some extent by representations in the record from the political actors being directly affected by the matter at issue. Congressional committees and their members are recognized by their colleagues as having no first-hand knowledge of the consequences of most disputed political proposals, and the committees' definitions of the situation gain credibility largely to the extent that they are based on the views of those extra-legislative actors widely conceded as being in a definite position to know. Senator Byrd admitted this explicitly during the second part of the Walsh Committee hearings in 1946. He expressed great dissatisfaction to Assistant Secretary of the Navy Kenney because of Forrestal's June 24 letter to the President, which agreed to support the "objective" of unification. As Byrd explained,

I don't want to belabor [the point], except the only way we can make a fight, Mr. Kenney, is to show that the Secretary of the Navy did not agree with what is in this bill. We may as well be frank about it. That is the only way that those of us who are opposed to unification can make a fight on the floor of Congress. . . . There has got to be a clear, unequivocal statement from the Navy Department in order that this fight be made effective.[33]

Similar reasoning obviously lay behind the great efforts that were made in 1947 by the anti-unification diehards in the House and Senate to find and to record the testimony of military officers on active service who still remained opposed to the compromise agreement worked out between the War and Navy Departments' official leaders. Indeed, in his questioning of Admiral Sherman before the Senate Armed Services Committee, Senator Bridges tried to create the impression in the record that even Sherman was actually opposed to the bill before the committee. Through a long, drawn-out interrogation, Bridges got the Admiral to admit that the draft bill submitted to Congress by the President in February was not identical with the draft that he and General Norstad had originally agreed to on behalf of the two military departments, that the pending bill was, in fact, based on an eighth draft, and that it contained changes from the original which had been insisted upon by the President's assistants, Charles Murphy and Clark Clifford. The Senator then went on to try to mold the record:

> Well, what I want to show here is that this is not the bill at all which you, representing the Navy, and General Norstad, representing the Army, agreed upon; that the bill before us is a wholly different document. . . .
>
> We had received word, which had been flashed all over the Nation, about how the Army and Navy had agreed upon this bill. Members of this committee were called upon the telephone and told that agreement finally had been reached upon a draft. Then the draft disappears into thin air, and this bill [S.758] later reappears. . . .
>
> We want to know whose bill this is, who drafted it, who submitted it, what influences were brought to bear.[34]

As it turned out, Senators Tydings and Russell nullified the potential effects of Bridges' line of questioning by giving Admiral Sherman an opportunity to dispel "any inferences in the record as to mysterious influences which may have operated on this bill" and to explain that he had never considered the first draft agreed to by himself and Norstad as a final version and that he believed "this final draft is the most workable draft; and it is a better draft than its predecessors." [35]

It should be noted that not only the committees to which the bills had been referred were able to exercise influence on their final disposition during floor consideration. For if the leaders of any committee, and especially of a generally powerful one like Appropriations, can convince the House or Senate that the subject matter of some part of a bill under amendment rightfully "belongs" to them by being within their acknowledged jurisdiction, they may succeed in getting voting majorities to strike out parts of the reported version or prevent incorporation of other provisions which the reporting committee might like to include. Thus, during the House debate on H.R.4214, Congressman Taber, the chairman of the Appropriations Committee, rose to condemn the provision in the reported bill that called for the original budgetary requests of the military services and of the Secretary of Defense to be included in the budget submitted by the President to Congress. Taber argued that this triple-column budget provision was unnecessary, since the military services purportedly had and would continue to have no trouble getting an opportunity to express their desires to the Appropriations Committee on anything they intensely needed. He also felt that the provision could be destructive in encouraging the services to make maximum budgetary requests, since they would no longer fear Budget Bureau excision.[36] When, while the bill was open to amendment, Taber moved to strike out the whole relevant section, Hoffman and the ranking minority member of the Expenditure Committee, Manasco, arose and conceded in effect that Taber and the Appropriations Committee were the experts on budgetary matters and that consequently they would not oppose the amendment, which proceeded to carry by voice vote.[37]

An even more striking illustration of how carefully allocated are the scopes of authority of the different committees was the reaction to Congressman Mitchell's attempt during the House floor action to specify limits on the tenure of the director (eight years) and the members (four years) of the JCS's subordinate Joint Staff. Mitchell's purpose was to protect against an overly powerful military director emerging as the result of long continued service over the years and to force rotation of staff personnel between headquarters and the field to prevent them from losing first-hand contact with operational problems. The chairman of the House Armed Services, Walter C. Andrews, rose to oppose the amendment as not being within the province of the bill and a matter for the future consideration of his own committee. Congressman Chet Holifield, a member of the Expenditures Committee and a floor manager of the bill, then took the floor and explained that although a majority of the Expenditures Committee were sympathetic to the purpose of Mitchell's amendment, they agreed that it lay within the jurisdiction of the Armed Services Committee, on which they had been very careful not to trespass. Holifield hence also urged that the amendment be defeated —which it was, by a 37-to-117 teller vote.[38]

INTRA-COMMITTEE LEADERSHIP

Although the standing committees exert great influence on the actions taken by floor majorities in their parent bodies, specific individuals must provide leadership to determine the positions of the committees themselves. In the unification conflict, only a minority of any of the committees, consisting of some combination of the more senior members and those especially interested in the unification problem, attended most of any set of hearings [39] or otherwise actively participated in committee consideration of the pending bills. Usually in Congress this kind of "active minority," with the control it exercises over the development of the record and the detailed knowledge it gains of the specific issues being disputed, can dominate the committee proceedings in executive session during the crucial "marking-up" stage of the bill and thus write its own preferences into the version being reported.

Within the active minority, and most often the key committee influential, is of course Woodrow Wilson's "lord-proprietor"—the committee chairman. Depending on the committee rules, the chairman schedules committee meetings, decides on the bills to be taken up, appoints standing or *ad hoc* subcommittees to conduct hearings or "write up" bills, presides over hearings when present, and has major influence over the committee staff. Moreover, the chairman himself manages or names the floor managers for reported bills, has controlling influence over the designation of the conferees from his chamber, and, in holding a recognized status, serves generally as the committee's representative in its formal relations with other political actors. Still, the chairman's powers are not absolute. They depend on those holding formal authority within the committee—a majority of the individual members—agreeing for one reason or another to go along with the chairman's wishes. Too often the power actually wielded by a committee majority is ascribed to the chairman, with the inference that the latter can ride roughshod over the almost unanimous opposition of his committee and determine its actions.

In the Seventy-ninth Congress Chairmen Thomas and Walsh of the Senate Military Affairs and Naval Affairs Committees and Chairmen May, Vinson, and Manasco of the House Military Affairs, Naval Affairs, and Expenditures Committees all were able to get their groups to go along with their own preferred positions on unification. There is no evidence to indicate that the predominant sentiment within any of the House committees was opposed to that of their chairmen, and the evidence is very clear that large majorities within each of the Senate committees actively supported the positions of theirs. The question of the degree of control that a committee chairman could exercise over his committee did not therefore really arise, however great that control might have appeared on the surface. It was the situation in the Eightieth Congress that indicated both the weight of influence of a committee chairman and its limitations.

When it became apparent that Chan Gurney would become the chairman of the new Senate Armed Services Committee in 1947, Navy Secretary Forrestal had serious misgivings.[40] Gurney had appeared to be in favor of the Collins Plan and had voted to report the Thomas-Hill-Austin bill, S.2044. He talked of expecting great economies through unification and had not appeared bothered by either the single-chief-of-staff–military-control-of-the-budget aspect of the War Department's proposals or of their threat to the organizational integrity of the Navy and Marines. Moreover, Gurney had been a general legislative friend (and a World War I veteran) of the Army, having just led its battle in the Seventy-ninth Congress for extension of Selective Service.

Yet, despite his pro-Army leanings, Gurney did not even insist upon, let alone succeed in getting reported unamended, the compromise bill prepared by the Army, the Navy, and the White House, which was closer to his original preferences than the reported, amended version. First of all, seven, and possibly eight, of the thirteen members of the Armed Services Committee had definite pro-Navy orientations.[41] Furthermore, of the four senators—Gurney, Saltonstall, Robertson, and Tydings—who attended over half of the hearings and who, it appears from other evidence as well,[42] constituted the "active minority" and exercised the most influence on the unification bill, only one—Gurney—was not pro-Navy.

But Gurney's inability to impose his views more effectively on the committee was not entirely due to the unfavorable line-up of forces. Some chairmen can get favorable votes through their manipulation of the committee rules or the personal esteem they enjoy, even though a majority of their committee might be predisposed to oppose them on the merits of the proposal in question. Gurney, however, had never before been a committee chairman and had no experience in running a committee. Moreover, it appears that he was not a particularly strong or aggressive person. Finally, although Gurney was chairman of the committee, Bridges, and not he, was the senior majority member in terms of Senate service, and of the Democrats, Tydings, Russell, Byrd, and Hill were also senior to him, as well as being in the Senate "club," [43] which Gurney apparently was not. Given these adverse circumstances, Gurney not only did not enjoy absolute control over his committee, but he may also not have been even first among equals.

The pattern in the House was similar, although there the chairman preferred to kill the pending bill rather than get his committee to report a version in accordance with his views. Hoffman's Expenditures Committee voted by a lopsided 22 to 3 to overrule him and end the hearings in time to report a bill before the end of the session and then proceeded even to reject the formal report that Hoffman presented to accompany the bill. An effective majority was obviously prepared to send out a unification bill, and it was within those limits that Hoffman's influence could operate—which it did with great effectiveness.

Early in the hearings Hoffman threatened to "put the bill in my pocket" [44] until he got copies of the top-secret Series 1478 JCS papers and got them. Senator Robertson had also been insisting on getting hold of the papers during the Senate hearings, but since Robertson was forced to rely on his own chairman, Gurney, to press the matter with the executive branch and since Gurney dragged his feet, Robertson's efforts failed. As chairman, Hoffman was also able to suspend the House hearings for almost three weeks until he found strong opponents to the compromise bill, to whom, again as chairman, he was able to grant the opportunity to testify in order to have them make a record justifying major changes in the bill. Hoffman chose the subcommittee writing up the clean bill and automatically became a member of it himself. He exercised the predominant influence in getting it to adopt stricter guarantees for the Navy and Marine Corps than had the Senate Armed Services Committee, which was loaded with Naval Affairs Committee alumni and other Navy friends. Hoffman put himself in charge of the bill on the floor of the House and was probably instrumental in preventing opposition from within his committee to Sterling Cole's amendment further adding to the language guaranteeing the naval air and Marine functions. Finally, Hoffman, as chairman, almost automatically became a member of the conference committee, where he reportedly took a rigid stand in favor of statutory protection of the service functions and thus, with some help from Senator Byrd, forced the Senate conferees to withdraw from the position they had taken after long and serious consideration.[45]

Individual Subject-Matter Experts

In addition to the standing committees there are individual senators or representatives who, without holding any formal position of leadership within Congress, sometimes become accepted as "subject-matter experts" and then exercise disproportionately large influence over the positions taken by voting majorities on certain areas of legislative policy.

The ideal-type subject-matter expert in the unification conflict was James W. Wadsworth. From 1944 to 1947 Wadsworth was neither chairman nor ranking minority member of any of the committees considering the unification problem nor did he hold any post within the Republican party leadership. Yet Wadsworth's influence was enormous. Pretty much single-handed, he managed to get the resolution adopted in 1944 setting up the Select Committee on Post-War Military Policy. Throughout the conflict Wadsworth was widely believed to be masterminding the War Department's campaign in the House,[46] and in 1947 he provided the leadership for the pro-unification forces within the Expenditures Committee.[47] Because of Wadsworth's high personal standing, Hoffman could not help but choose him as one of the seven members of the subcommittee that wrote the clean bill, and Wadsworth provided the margin of victory within the subcommittee in saving the Administration's bill from complete emasculation.

Wadsworth's aura of expertise had started to build up some thirty years before when he had been Senator from New York. He had been a member of the Senate Military Affairs Committee during World War I, became its chairman in 1920, and remained chairman until he was defeated for reelection to the Senate in 1926. In those years Wadsworth had introduced and gotten passed the National Defense Act of 1920, which reorganized the War Department, and generally took good care of legislation requested by the Army.[48] Wadsworth was elected to the House in 1932 and became a leading preparedness advocate in the years before World War II, sponsoring and promoting what became the Burke-Wadsworth Selective Service Act before the Roosevelt Administration itself would come out for peacetime conscription.

By 1947 the measure of authority that Wadsworth had built up in military affairs is suggested by a comment made by Representative Clifford Case during the floor debate on H.R.4214. Case explained that he personally could not determine whether the bill could accomplish its stated goals and then concluded, "As to such matters, I must and do accept the judgment of the gentleman from New York . . . whose experience is far greater than mine." [49] Similarly, in 1947 Representative Cole's success in promoting the fortunes of naval aviation can be said to have been based on subject-matter expertise, built up through his fairly long prior service on the defunct Naval Affairs Committee and through his naval reserve affiliation.

The Party Leaderships

Another source of intra-legislative influence on the formation of voting majorities during the unification conflict were the "elective" party leaders of the two houses. Among the more important of these leaders are in the Senate the floor leaders—especially the majority leader—the chairmen of the Policy Committee and the Committee on Committees (the Democratic floor leader is also the chairman of these two committees), and the President Pro Tempore and in the House the Speaker and the floor leaders—again especially the majority leader.[50]

It is, of course, well known that in the Congress of the United States, unlike the British House of Commons, the party leaders cannot automatically create floor majorities behind proposals or positions they endorse. The power of even the most important American leaders—the Senate majority leader or the combination of Speaker–majority leader in the House—is limited and highly personal, with its sources hidden and hard to identify. Apart from the leaders' personal prestige, these sources include the leaders' "more than casual connection with the filling of committee vacancies," the ability to grant or withhold favors ranging "from the allocation of space in the Senate [or House] Office Building to the expeditious handling of a pet bill," the possession of maximum legislative intelligence from the leaders' key positions in the communications network, and, probably most important, control or predominant influence over the legislative schedule.[51] The party leaders acting as presiding officers—the Speaker and the President Pro Tempore—also hold the right to recognize members to speak on the floor and the right, subject to being overruled by the whole chamber, to refer bills and communications to appropriate committees and to make other parliamentary rulings.

During the Seventy-ninth Congress the influence of the party leaders on the unification conflict was minimal. Although unification was one of the high-priority bills of the Democratic President, Harry Truman, neither in the Senate nor in the House did the Democratic party leadership as such take any overt action calculated to advance the fortunes of the various bills introduced, although Senator Hill, the Senate Majority Whip, was extremely active on his own. The resources of the party leaders are limited, and they will not be squandered in a legislative campaign without a high probability of some degree of success. Thus, when the parliamentary situation in the Senate indicated in the spring and summer of 1946 that the favorably reported Thomas-Hill-Austin bill was unlikely to pass if brought up for consideration, it was the Majority Leader, Alben Barkley, who informed the President that it would be well to postpone any further action, to which the President agreed.[52]

The influence of the congressional party leadership was strongly felt in the Eightieth Congress. It will be recalled that in December, 1946, Representative Sterling Cole had tried to spark an attempt to prevent the merger of the Military and Naval Affairs Committees during the organization of the House the following month. Minority Leader (and Speaker-to-be) Martin made it clear that he was in favor of the reorganization, and this made it difficult for Cole to get more than a handful of allies from among the Republicans. Finally, when Cole tried to get the floor during the first day of the new Congress in order to make his motion, he was ignored by Speaker Martin until the question of adopting the provisions of the Legislative Reorganization Act was undebatable.[53] Whether or not Cole's motion would have carried, which is doubtful, the Speaker's power of recognition proved to be the key in preventing a representative's trying to defeat a measure from even getting an opportunity to have the whole House vote on his motion.

Another exercise of the party leaders' influence was the referral of the compromise unification bills to the standing committees. We have described how the chairman of the Senate Expenditures Committee, Aiken, challenged the President Pro Tempore's original referral to the Armed Services Committee and tried to get the legislation for his own committee. Vandenberg's referral was an important move, since the Expenditures Committee, and especially its chairman, was much more hostile to the terms of the agreement than the Armed Services Committee, and especially its chairman.[54] The authority to make the original referral constituted a source of power—it was a "policy decision" in Vandenberg's words—even though it was theoretically overrulable by a majority of the Senate.[55] A ruling on an important bill engages the presiding officer's prestige, and few members will care to vote against him unless there are compelling reasons to do so—which in this case were not apparent.[56] This is particularly true when the presiding officer is highly esteemed and, like Vandenberg in 1947, has presidential possibilities. Finally, when the majority leader, Wallace White, also supported the ruling of the chair from the floor, the combined weight of influence of the two party leaders was enough to overwhelm that of a dissident committee chairman.

The referral decision was even more complex and crucial in the House. There the party leadership decided to send the Administration's bill to Hoffman's Expenditures Committee rather than to the Armed Services Committee, as was done in the Senate. The latter committee had been constituted of fifteen former members of each of the Military Affairs and Naval Affairs Committees and three newly assigned congressmen. The chairman was Walter G. Andrews, a strong unifier, and the ranking minority member was Carl Vinson. The overall complexion of the committee is not clear, but recalling that the Military Affairs Committee had given no evidence in the previous Congress of being predominantly in favor of unification and that virtually all the members of Vinson's old committee had been hostile to it, it may be inferred that the distribution of power in the new committee was against the chairman's position. This inference is supported by two additional facts: the willingness with which Andrews surrendered jurisdiction of the unification bill, one of the session's major measures, to the Expenditures Committee and Hoffman's explicit statement during the House floor debate that "They could not shove [the unification bill] through the Committee on Armed Services so they put it over in our committee." [57]

The Expenditures Committee had, of course, also not been in favor of unification in the Seventy-ninth Congress, refusing, under its Democratic chairman, Carter Manasco, even to hold hearings on the various bills referred to it. After the organization of the Eightieth Congress, however, the Republican leadership, working through its committee on committees, assigned to the Expenditures Committee the second-, third-, fourth-, fifth-, and sixth-ranking majority members of the Rules Committee, who, the party leaders must have expected, would be responsive to party leadership while holding predominant influence within Hoffman's group.[58]

Actually, it appears that the Republican leadership counted on the possibility of an even more fortunate development through this move: Clare Hoffman was well known as an extreme isolationist who had never shown much interest in foreign or military affairs. Moreover, Hoffman was in 1947 also an important member of the Committee on Education and Labor, which was to consider a major labor-management relations bill—a subject that deeply concerned him.[59] The hope was that with one of the additions from the Rules Committee being James Wadsworth— the acknowledged "subject-matter expert" in the House on military affairs—Hoffman might choose to appoint a subcommittee headed by Wadsworth to hold hearings on the unification bill and allow him generally to handle it in the House.[60] Hoffman disappointed the party leaders and kept the bill in the full committee under his own direction; and, given the additions he managed to include, the bill might actually have fared better in the Committee on Armed Services. Nevertheless, the original referral was an exercise of influence over the course of the legislation, even if it turned out to have had unanticipated and undesired consequences.

In any event, without the "pressure" reported to have been exerted by both party leaderships on their respective followers within Hoffman's committee,[61] it is unlikely that it would have defied its chairman in the manner already described. Halleck, as majority leader, also furthered the unification bill's fortunes in the House by securing unanimous consent to have it come up for consideration without being sent to the Rules Committee, a procedure which would have consumed additional time in the last week of the session. Finally, Martin, as Speaker, overruled Cole's points of order against the consideration of the bill on the floor at a time when any delay might have prevented final passage.

The party leadership also participated in the Senate after the original referral. It became known that Senator Taft, the chairman of the Republican Policy Committee [62] and in the Eightieth Congress probably the most powerful man in the Senate, wanted some form of unification bill to be reported. Although Taft's wishes may have had only a marginal effect on the content of the amended bill, he did insure that the Policy Committee put it on its "must legislation" agenda and that the bill was called up for consideration under favorable conditions.

In sum, it should be clear that the party leaderships' influence on the substantive positions taken by voting majorities was not as determinative as the committees' and it was much more indirect: the party leaders (particularly the majority party's) through their influence over committee make-up, the referral of bills, the legislative schedule, and the parliamentary situation generally, were able to facilitate or hinder the development and adoption of different general kinds of committee recommendations on unification. Only once, apparently, did the party leaders try to affect the voting majorities' position more specifically, when they used some of the influence that could be derived from personal persuasion and from what can be called their "general facilitating-hindering capacity" to get individual members of the Expenditures Committee to vote out a bill more in line with the party leaders' desires.[63]

The Influence of the Rank-and-File Member

The preceding analysis of the disproportionately large influence exerted by the committees, subject-matter experts, and party leaderships in the unification conflict should not be interpreted as meaning that the rank-and-file senator or representative was completely powerless. All members of Congress are Constitutionally equal (even if, like George Orwell's animals, some are "more equal than others"), and the recommendations and rulings of any of the intra-legislative "influentials" can theoretically be rejected within committee or on the floor by the votes of a majority of the rank-and-file members.

The difficulty for the rank and file is that such majorities simply cannot form spontaneously; they form only in response to alternative leadership. This means that for the most part, the rank and file's ultimate formal authority can be converted into actual influence only when the various influentials that are activated in a particular conflict become divided among themselves along such lines as committee majority versus committee minority, party versus party, or committee versus party and thus proceed to offer competing recommendations about the policy preferences that should be promoted and about how these different preferences would be affected by the proposals in dispute. It was in this kind of situation that in 1947 the rank and file determined in the Senate by a vote of 52 to 19 that the Senate-passed bill should contain the Armed Services Committee version of the single clause protecting naval aviation and the Marines instead of Senator McCarthy's more protectionist language and that the rank and file determined in the House, by rejecting Representative Cole's amendment 190 to 36, that the new Secretary of Defense's grant of authority should include the words "direction" and "control" as provided for in the compromise agreement and the Expenditures Committee bill.

It should also be noted that occasionally even an individual rank-and-file senator or representative can influence the actions of floor majorities through his right to raise points of order or to object to requests for unanimous consent. These latter rights become especially important near the end of a session, when any kind of delay may well prevent final passage of a bill before adjournment. Thus, it is not unlikely that Representative Cole's price for not continuing to object to floor leader Halleck's unanimous consent request on the arrangements for calling up the Expenditure Committee's bill in the House in 1947 was that no resistance would be offered to the inclusion of his own floor amendment on the functions of land-based naval aviation. Similarly, Senator Lodge's threat to object to the consideration of the conference report in the Senate during the next-to-last day of the session also represented real potential influence, even though for various reasons he was persuaded not to exercise it.

8

Extra-Legislative and
Extra-Governmental Influences

The positions taken by voting majorities in Congress during the unification conflict were not, of course, determined exclusively by the policy preferences or activities of its own influentials and rank-and-file members. Congressional action was also affected by a whole variety of political actors who exerted influence from outside the legislative chamber and in certain cases from outside the government.

The President

One of the most important extra-legislative sources of influence on congressional majorities was the President of the United States. A President has, after all, by Constitutional right, a share of the authority to make laws. He can disapprove bills passed by Congress, and such bills subsequently become laws only through repassage by an extraordinary two-thirds majority in each house of Congress. He is also given the obligation, and hence the right, "from time to time [to] give to the Congress information of the state of the Union, and recommend . . . such measures as he shall judge necessary and expedient," to call special sessions of Congress "on extraordinary occasions," and to adjourn Congress if the two houses cannot themselves agree as to a time for adjournment.

Despite the ultimate Constitutional basis for the President's participation in the legislative process, except for the ability to use the threat of a veto or the calling of a special session as bargaining counters, his most important resources in seeking to influence Congress affirmatively are extra-Constitutional and informal. Thus, President Truman's greatest resource in the unification conflict was essentially the existence of the widely held predisposition within Congress in the mid-twentieth century to accept as legitimate Presidential submission of detailed legislative recommendations and to give to these submissions more attention than would be given to the average legislative proposal.[1] The President is recognized by Congress as the one officer of the government elected by a nationwide constituency and the one on whom widespread public (and even congressional) sentiment focuses the major responsibility for the guidance of the Republic. Furthermore, Congress finds the Presidential recommendations useful:

> In practical effect, they represent a means whereby Congress can gain from outside what comes hard from within: a handy and official guide to the wants of its biggest customer; an advance formulation of main issues at each session; a work-load ready to hand to every legislative committee; an indication, more or less, of what may risk the veto; a borrowing of presidential prestige for most major bills—and thus a boosting of publicity-potentials in both sponsorship and opposition.[2]

Since in the unification conflict the President's recommendations affected the means by which he was to carry out his specific Constitutional office of Commander in Chief, they appear to have carried more than the normal weight.

To say that there existed a sentiment, held to a greater or lesser extent by almost all members of Congress, that it was legitimate for the President to recommend detailed positions to potential legislative majorities on unification does not mean that it was easy for him to convert these predispositions to give attention and consideration into actions to approve. "Presidential power," at least over Congress, is, as Neustadt has pointed out, only "the power to persuade," [3] and the persuasive capacities of the President can be strictly limited. Thus, when Truman called Chairmen Walsh and Vinson of the Senate and House Naval Affairs Committees to the White House in the fall of 1945 to try to convince them that his unification plan would not hurt the Navy, not only were the two legislators not persuaded, but they even tried to turn the tables on the President and talk him out of sending his special message to Congress, Vinson warning that a unification bill "would not pass either this winter, next winter, or the winter after." [4]

A prerequisite to the President's (or, for that matter, any other extra-legislative political actor's) being able to create majorities in support of a proposal he is recommending is the existence of key Senate and House influentials who themselves are actively committed to the proposal because they share its goals or for other reasons of their own. Without such intra-legislative allies to "carry the ball" within Congress by introducing the necessary bills, arranging for the holding of hearings, and "chaperoning" the legislation generally on the floor and elsewhere, any attempt to get a proposal adopted will almost certainly prove fruitless. To facilitate the efforts of this core of original congressional supporters, the President may try personally to influence other strategically placed senators or representatives by such techniques as using logical argument, drawing on friendship or personal or party loyalty, or promising favors on such matters as appointments or support of pet legislation. Finally, the President can try to affect the legislators' general willingness or reluctance to "go along" by using the various propaganda vehicles available to him —special messages, news conferences, speeches—to try to expand and to mold public opinion to his point of view in the hope, stated or implied, that the public will then exert influence on Congress.

Truman was fortunate in the unification conflict that he had Senators Thomas, Hill, and Gurney, Representative Wadsworth, and a few others in Congress firmly committed on their own both to unification generally and, with minor exceptions, to the specific plan the President preferred. It will be recalled that not until 1947 did Truman take it upon himself to send draft legislation to Congress. Before that he had simply specified his objectives, chiefly in his December, 1945, special message, leaving to his friends and former colleagues on the Senate Military Affairs Committee the task of drawing up a detailed bill. Indeed, not even after the Thomas-Hill-Austin bill was introduced in the spring of 1946, with his own private blessings, did the President ever announce that it was "his" bill, which the Congress should pass without modification. When asked to comment on the Thomas bill at his April 11 news conference, President Truman replied that it had "a lot of good points" but that it was not customary for the President to take a position on legislation before it was presented to him for signature.[5]

Actually, the immediate post-World War II period was just the beginning of the general congressional acceptance of overt Presidential urging of specific draft bills. Moreover, Truman himself, according to Neustadt, had succeeded to the Presidency with his senatorial distaste of White House interference in congressional "tactics" intact and "with his mind set on restoring 'proper' balance between the President and Congress." [6] Thus, when Senator Thomas suggested in the summer of 1946, after the Seventy-ninth Congress had adjourned, that Truman put into effect by executive order those agreed-upon aspects of unification that did not strictly require legislation, the President refused, "feeling that this assumption of executive powers might militate against the possibility of getting legislation passed at the [next] session." [7]

Nevertheless, the President's contribution to the eventual formation of congressional majorities should not be underestimated. Apart from whatever influence he may have had on individual legislators privately, Truman's special message, his press conference statements, and his letters to Congress at critical stages of the conflict all gave unification the standing of a Presidential program. This kept the issue alive and on the congressional agenda despite powerful opposition to it, strengthened the hands of its congressional proponents, and greatly increased its press coverage. The last in turn probably helped to develop and expand the sentiment in favor of some kind of single military establishment both within Congress and among the general public.[8] Truman's wishes also appear to have been decisive on such specific issues as the Senate Armed Services Committee's not incorporating in 1947 the service functions into its reported version of S.758 but adopting the single protective clause for the Marines and naval aviation.[9] Finally, because he was President, Truman was able ultimately to influence Forrestal and the other official leaders of the Navy to end their opposition to a single Secretary of Defense and to agree to some form of unification compromise. The price that the President had to pay for the agreement of his formal subordinates has already been explained, but the point is that if the main source of extra-congressional opposition to the President's legislative recommendations had not been the Navy but had come from outside the executive branch, his ability to reduce it would have been much smaller and he might have lost the fight in Congress completely.

Cabinet Secretaries and Other Official Executive Branch Leaders

Another set of extra-legislative influences on congressional majorities in the unification conflict came from the cabinet secretaries and other official leaders of the War and Navy Departments. As the President's subordinates, these executive branch officials a fortiori did not have the authority or power automatically to create voting majorities behind proposals or positions they preferred. Moreover, they had neither the facilities nor the prestige of the President for commanding nationwide audiences. Still, they did have other advantages, which allowed them to be more influential in certain respects than the President himself.

Normally, the great strength of the President's cabinet secretaries and other subordinates in the executive branch is that they are likely to be actively concerned with a much narrower range of major issues than is the President and thus can concentrate greater amounts of personal time and energy and staff resources on the particular proposal that they are trying to get adopted or defeated. Secondly, these subordinates—especially the career officials or long-term political appointees like Forrestal—have had the opportunity over the years to build up more cordial and intimate ties and more good will with the particular members of Congress who sit on the committees that deal with the affairs of their departments or agencies. Thirdly, the subordinates of the President in the line departments are almost certain to know more about the background and specifics of any proposal in dispute within the legislative body, to have played a more active and direct part in devising its details or those of an alternative, and, much of the time, to be capable of having their opinion about the effects of a proposal within their own area of special competence accepted as more valid than the President's. Finally, a few executive branch subordinates may be speaking for agencies—like the FBI, the Army Corps of Engineers, or, in the unification conflict, the Marines and the Army Air Forces—that, regardless of the issues, are simply much more popular in Congress than is the President of the United States.

Life is complex at the high levels of the executive branch (or of any other large organization), and its official leaders almost invariably have more potential problems impinging on their attention than they have the time and energy to deal with. Yet any attempt to influence successfully congressional voting majorities on the disposition of a disputed proposal requires vast amounts of human time and energy both to prepare the specific recommendations, the detailed testimony, and the background materials for presentation at hearings and to carry out the direct lobbying, public relations, and propaganda activities also commonly believed necessary in a controversial legislative campaign. A major resource of the Secretaries of War and the Navy and their chief military subordinates in the unification conflict was that they could easily provide such time and energy because they had virtually unlimited staffs to whom they could assign the promotion of the department's position on unification as a full-time primary duty. Thus, as early as 1943, the War Department set up the Special Planning Division to begin planning for postwar problems in general and for postwar military organization in particular. After the end of the war, a special board was created within the Operations and Plans Division of the General Staff to prepare the unification proposal that General Collins finally presented to the Senate Military Affairs Committee in 1945 and to coordinate a public relations campaign in the conflict was suspended in July, 1947.[15]

At the end of the hearings the board was dissolved and General Norstad, who was then Chief of the Air Staff and slated to take over as Director of the Plans and Operations Division of the War Department General Staff, was designated by Secretary of War Patterson to head the new staff group to which the unification problem was assigned.[11] During the 1946–47 stages of the conflict, Norstad had active control over the formulation of the War Department's unification position under the general direction of Patterson, the Chief of Staff of the Army, Eisenhower, and the Assistant Secretary of War for Air, Stuart Symington.

The Navy Department was no more remiss than the Army in designating special groups to handle its part of the unification campaign. The preparation for the Woodrum Committee hearings, which took place while Frank Knox was still Secretary of the Navy, was handled by the Navy General Board. The General Board, it will be recalled, had been created in 1900 as a top-level advisory group to the Secretary of the Navy. The Board had been completely bypassed by Admiral King and his CNO-COMINCH staffs during World War II on strategic or operational matters, and it appears almost as if it took over the staffing for the unification campaign for lack of anything better to do.[12] After the War Department witnesses had presented their plan to the Woodrum Committee, the General Board, on May 5, sent out a classified memorandum to "all Offices, Bureaus and Agencies of the Navy Department" outlining the Navy position on unification and indicating a long list of arguments as to why such a development would be unsound. The memorandum explained that it intended to "be helpful to officers who may be called to testify before the Woodrum Committee" and advised its addressees that "when possible it would be desirable for all officers designated to appear before the Committee to consult with the General Board (Capt. Steele) *before* preparation of any written presentations." [13]

About a week later, when Secretary Knox died, Forrestal took over the leadership of the Department and appears to have immediately prepared a memorandum setting up a special "task force" to handle "unostentatiously" a public relations campaign on the "Single Department of National Defense." The task force was to try to sell the Navy line on unification through magazines, radio, and speaking engagements and to lobby veterans' organizations, such as the American Legion, and other general patriotic groups into passing resolutions favorable to the Navy's point of view. Task force members were to take news correspondents on guided tours of impressive naval installations where promising new weapons were under development. Two of the officers were charged specifically with obtaining opportunities for high-ranking Navy combat heroes to write magazine articles and make speeches. Another officer was assigned to "prepare and circulate among all Naval District Public Relations Officers a kit of materials from which speeches can be written" and to "keep posted on all speeches made by officers and officials of the Navy Department, arranging to have the Navy doctrine inserted in them."

The memorandum explained that "the doctrine to be preached by the Navy officially would be: *This is no time to raise a controversial issue between the services,*" without, however, openly criticizing the Army for bringing up the matter. "Unofficially" the task force would be free also to "inform" the Navy and "push" generally what came to be almost all of the standard detailed Navy Department arguments against unification. The seven men on the task force were explicitly given their assignment "as one of over-riding priority which would take precedence over all other duties." [14]

It appears that before Forrestal could actually issue his memorandum, he reached the agreement with Secretary of War Stimson and Chairman Woodrum of the Select Committee that led to postponing the showdown on the unification issue, so the formally organized public relations campaign was called off. Forrestal did set up a similar group, unofficially called SCORER (Secretary's Committee on Research on Reorganization), under Rear Admirals Radford and Thomas H. Robbins, Jr., in the fall of 1945, which worked directly out of his office and with some changes of personnel handled the staff work for the unification campaign until its favor.[16]

The War Department was similarly organized to conduct public relations activities. Throughout the period of the conflict, and particularly in the fall of 1945 and the spring of 1946, hardly a week went by that a speech by Patterson, Symington, or one of the high Army and Army Air Forces generals, did not, whatever its nominal subject, also manage to promulgate the War Department "doctrine" on unification. On February 19, 1946, while the Thomas-Hill-Austin subcommittee was drafting what became S.2044, General Norstad wrote to General Collins, at that time the Army's Chief of Public Information, recommending that "an extensive press and radio program should now be organized to be touched off at the moment the text of the bill is announced." Norstad thought the "program might include releases from the President, Senators Thomas, Hill, and Austin, key members of the House, the Secretary of War, veterans organizations, etc." and that "charts and other graphic materials should be prepared." Norstad concluded that "in view of the amount of misconception as to unification proposals which we have already encountered," a careful "indoctrination" of key press and radio men was "essential," and he specified a number of "lines" that favorable editorial comment could take.[16]

The Army Air Forces, incidentally, set up characteristically its own separate "Organization for Unification" in the fall of 1945. On November 13, General Arnold sent the following instruction to his five Assistant Chiefs of the Air Staff:

To answer all of the inquiries being received from the public, the press, Congressional committees, and other organizations and individuals interested in the unification of the armed services, it is necessary to perfect an organization to insure that the work is well done and closely coordinated. To that end the following has been approved and will be put into effect as quickly and as vigorously as possible:

a. General Spaatz will serve as representative of Commanding General, Army Air Forces on the whole program. . . .

b. A group of the civil heads of the aeronautical organizations have been asked to combine to form an advisory committee. This committee will work out a program that will undoubtedly call upon the Army Air Forces to perform a part of that program.

d. . . . there will be established in this office small committees to deal with each of the avenues of public information: press, radio, motion picture, columnists and public speakers. It will be the function of each of these committees to assemble and prepare materials as called for. . . .

e. From time to time, perhaps daily at first and as often as required, General Spaatz will assemble the committees and individuals named above for conference.[17]

Even before this formal organization of a unification staff, the Army Air Forces in September, 1945, had three of its top generals pilot B-29's nonstop from Japan to Chicago,[18] obviously trying to demonstrate by propaganda of the deed the possibility of (at least one-way) intercontinental strategic bombing from bases in the United States.

In addition to its own public relations activities, each service could rely on its various "satellite" or "backstop" [19] interest groups for promulgating its propaganda. The Navy's point for example, of view was being put forth by the Navy League's *Seapower* and by the Fleet Reserve Association's *Naval Affairs*.[20] The opposite view was being presented by, among others, the Air Power League and eventually the Air Force Association.

In October, 1946, the Air Power League issued a special, illustrated thirty-two-page booklet detailing the strength in (non-Navy) aircraft and Air Force personnel needed for the defense of the country, as well as arguing the case for independence of the Army Air Forces and unification under a single Department of Defense. The booklet explained that although the League's conclusions were not official Army Air Forces policy, they were "founded on the views of the highest aviation and military authorities." The League's president at the time was F. Trubee Davison, who had been Assistant Secretary of War for Air during the Coolidge and Hoover administrations and an Army Air Forces general in World War II; the League's executive vice-president, who was described as a veteran in various press releases, was actually a regular AAF officer carried as "on duty" with the Air Power League.[21]

The League was not above other deceptions. Just a few months after stipulating to the Treasury Department that it would not "engage in propaganda or otherwise attempt to influence legislation," thus securing a ruling that contributions to it would be tax-deductible for the donors, the executive committee of the League adopted a resolution "unqualifiedly" endorsing "the establishment of a Department of National Defense with coequal status for Army, Navy, and Air Force" and resolving "that up to $50,000 would be spent in support of the campaign for a Department of National Defense." The League hired a New York advertising firm to help its campaign and spent at least part of its money sending its clip sheet—*Air Power News*—to newspaper editors all over the country with arguments in favor of unification. The League boasted at one time that it was also supplying propaganda material to over 2,000 women's clubs in the United States.[22]

Although the services and their satellites concentrated most of their "indirect lobbying" behind public relations campaigns which were obviously intended to influence congressional majorities through their prior effects on unorganized public opinion, in at least one instance the Army Air Forces organized a direct letter-writing campaign in favor of unification to members of Congress themselves. Early in 1946 all the officers assigned to Hamilton Field, an Army Air Forces installation in California, were directed to report to the station theater for a meeting. As they entered the door to the theater, they were each assessed 5 cents and handed five one-cent postcards and a collection of mimeographed material which included the following:

1. A list of the full names and states of each senator.

2. A list of the full names, states, districts, and post-office addresses of each representative.

3. A paper entitled "Facts about the President's Plan for Unification of the Armed Forces."

4. A paper entitled "Nine Reasons General Eisenhower Gave to the Senate Military Affairs Committee" in favor of unification.

5. A sample form for a letter to be sent home to friends or to hometown newspapers.

6. A sheet containing six sample forms of letters to be sent on postcards to senators or representatives.

Each officer was then requested to fill out the postcards and to mail them, signing them with his name only so as not to indicate that he was in the Army and making especially sure that the cards were mailed from outside the installation.[23]

The form letters were so unsubtle as to be ludicrous. The letter for "back home" took the form of a plea from an "old buddy . . . still here on the job," explaining the need for his friend "to take positive action for unification by writing your lawmakers in Congress." The friend was warned that failure to unify the services would invite disaster "deadlier than Pearl Harbor," was quoted Eisenhower's "Nine Reasons" in full, and had the whole political situation summed up for him as follows:

Unification in the Army, Navy, and Air Forces would do so much to strengthen and economize . . . operations, that you would think everyone would be for it automatically; and yet there are a few misguided politicians and other selfish groups who are actively opposing this legislation.

The letter closed with the admonition, "Take a positive stand, now, before it is too late." Some of the sample form letters to the Congressmen went like this:

Honorable Sir: I will vote for the man who is for unification of our armed forces, because . . . .

Honorable _____: As a taxpayer, a citizen, and one of your constituents, I charge you to vote for proposed legislation toward unification of our armed forces. . . .

Honorable _____: You can save us taxpayers a lot of needless taxes if you will promote and vote for the proposed bill for unification. . . .

I want to hear your statement as to your position regarding the plan. If you're for it, we're for you.[24]

The public relations significance of hardly any event was overlooked by the War Department. It appears that when the Strategic Bombing Survey team evaluating the effectiveness of the strategic bombardment of Japan was preparing its final report in the spring of 1946, the first polished draft prepared by its civilian members included the following statement:

These lessons [of the Pacific War] do not . . . support the view that an independent and coordinate role exists for the Air Forces. They rather support the view that both at land and at sea the prime objective is control of the air and that all forces should be geared into a coordinated team to achieve that objective.

At least two later draft versions maintained the same position, but after intense pressure was reportedly put on the Survey committee by the Army aviators, the final report, published on July 1, 1946, not only left out the statement just quoted but also explicitly called for "an equal and coordinate position for a third air establishment" within a single military department.[25] Similarly, when William Bradford Huie, a popular writer on military affairs and apparently a confidant of the War Department, published his book, *The Case Against the Admirals,*[26] in the winter of 1946, the Army sent a copy to each congressman and congressman-elect under the guise that it came directly from the author, using letterhead paper that Huie had supplied for the purpose.[27] The book was a slashing, highly distorted attack on the Navy which in effect argued that surface fleets had been obsolete since World War I and that (land-based?)

"airpower" had won World War II and was the sole necessary means of defense for the country.[28]

The War and Navy Departments obviously invested enormous effort in these public relations and propaganda activities calculated to convert public and congressional opinion to their point of view on unification. Just what their actual effects were cannot, however, be readily determined. Key has labeled maneuvers of this sort "rituals" and argued that generally

they are on the order of the dance of the rainmakers. That may be too brutal a characterization, for sometimes these [public relations and propaganda] campaigns have their effects—just as rain sometimes follows the rainmakers' dance. Yet the data make it fairly clear that most of these campaigns do not affect the opinion of many people and even clearer that they have small effect by way of punitive or approbative feedback in the vote.[29]

Whatever the net effect of these "rituals" in the unification conflict (and the evidence does not contradict Key's generalization), there can be no doubt that the greatest influence exerted by the official leaders of the two military departments on congressional voting majorities was the result of more direct forms of lobbying. By means of the various plans presented during the hearings in 1944 and 1945, the letters incorporating the points of agreement and disagreement in June, 1946, the draft compromise bills in 1947, the various private recommendations, and the direct staff assistance provided by military officers to the committees at different times throughout the conflict, the War and Navy Departments supplied the verbal formulas on which (with varying degrees of revision) were based all the different solutions ever seriously considered within the legislative body. Congress itself had neither the staff resources, the store of relevant information, nor the time to be capable independently of developing unification solutions of its own. Even the much considered single protective clause added to S.758 in 1947 by the Senate Armed Services Committee was actually written by General Norstad. Given the predominant sentiment within the Committee just after the close of the hearings, Chairman Gurney had asked both Norstad and Admiral Sherman to submit appropriate general langauge to protect the Marines and naval aviation. Norstad's language was incorporated into the bill without change, while Sherman's language was substantially that offered unsuccessfully by Senator McCarthy as an amendment during the Senate floor consideration.[30]

The other vital part of the War and Navy Department leaders' direct lobbying campaign consisted of developing or maintaining cordial, sympathetic relations and a consequent store of generalized goodwill for themselves or their organizations with their congressional identifiers and other influential senators and representatives. The objective was obviously to make the legislators maximally responsive to the different proposals embodying their departmental point of view.

Such cordial relations could not be built overnight, but, as Fenno has written in a similar vein, had to be "the cumulative product of many small efforts and courtesies—mostly unrecorded." [31] Although the "efforts and courtesies" remained largely unrecorded in the unification conflict, too, Forrestal appears to have been a master at them. Through the deliberate use of such devices as luncheon, dinner, and breakfast invitations, personal telephone calls, "tailor-made" correspondence, personal remembrances of birthdays and anniversaries, and "boatrides" on the Secretary's official yacht or on Navy men-of-war for a variety of legislators, Forrestal had developed an unusually wide and sympathetic acquaintanceship in Congress.[32] Early in the war, for example, while Forrestal was still Under Secretary of the Navy, Secretary Knox had asked him, Assistant Secretaries Bard and Gates, and Knox's own special assistant, Adlai Stevenson, to list those members of Congress whom they knew fairly well in order to coordinate efforts to improve the Department's legislative relations. Whereas each of the other officials listed fifteen to twenty names, Forrestal listed seventy, a number that had no doubt increased by the time of the unification conflict.[33]

Forrestal's memoirs and the appointment calendars in his private papers indicate frequent contacts with influential legislators he knew at the various crucial stages of the controversy.[34] Two other instances illustrate specifically the very great pains that Forrestal was in the habit of taking to protect the goodwill that he had already built up. It will be recalled that when the Secretary of the Navy appeared before the Senate Military Affairs Committee in the fall of 1945, he had brought along the Eberstadt Report's proposed organizational chart and described its recommendations in general terms. At the conclusion of Forrestal's testimony, Senator Hill asked the Secretary if the Committee could not be given a copy of the complete report, to which Forrestal carefully replied, "I should think it should be, Senator Hill. Out of courtesy, if I may say so, to the committees which we report to in the House and Senate, I should like to ask their permission to do so." [35]

Similarly, in January, 1947, after Admiral Sherman, General Norstad, and Assistant Secretary Symington had reached agreement on the draft letter to be sent to the President by the Secretaries of War and the Navy announcing the compromise they had negotiated, Forrestal wrote in his diary that Presidential assistant Clark Clifford wanted the letter released to the press immediately. Forrestal, however,

> insisted that that not be done until I had an opportunity to inform the principal Navy friends in the House and Senate—Senators Robertson, Byrd, Tydings, Brooks, Russell . . . , ex-Chairman Vinson of the Naval Affairs Committee, Cole, etc., in the House. I said this was desirable not merely from the standpoint of the Navy's obligation to these men, but also by way of enlisting their sympathetic cooperation in the future.[36]

Unofficial Executive Branch Leaders

The influence exerted on congressional majorities from within the executive branch need not be from the latter's official leaders. In the spring of 1947, while Secretary of the Navy Forrestal and Admirals Nimitz and Sherman were steadfastly supporting the compromise agreement of the previous January, General Vandegrift, General Edson, and a group of leading naval aviator admirals testified against its enactment. The Marines did not, however, rely merely on presenting testimony in public hearings in order to gain adherents to their point of view. Their "supplementary" activities constitute a classic example of effective, unofficial, covert executive branch lobbying.[37]

High officers in the Marine Corps had never been satisfied with the January 16 agreement worked out by Norstad and Sherman and accepted by Patterson and Forrestal for the War and Navy Departments. The Marines had not been directly represented in negotiating the compromise, and it appears that the Commandant of the Marine Corps had not even been advised in advance that it had been reached and was about to be released.

The chief Marine complaint was over the Navy Department's concession on the method of specifying the functions of the different services. After Eisenhower's and Spaatz' Series 1478 JCS proposals, most Marines felt that they could not be safe unless their key role in amphibious warfare were spelled out and guaranteed by statute. The Marines were also dissatisfied with the wording of the proposed executive order, which restricted the Fleet Marine Force to service with the fleet in the seizure or defense of advanced naval bases and for the conduct of "limited land operations in connection therewith," preferring their function to include the conduct of "such limited land operations as are essential to the prosecution of a naval campaign." After the draft bills were introduced in February, the Marines also had complaints that their officers were not made explicitly eligible for appointment as military assistants to the Secretary of Defense or as members of the Joint Staff, but were only implicitly eligible as being included within the meaning of the terms "officers of the United States Navy."

Immediately after the January 16 agreement was released to the public, a group of highly placed officers at the Marine Corps headquarters in Quantico, Virginia, tacitly came to the conclusion that since their formal superiors in the Navy Department would no longer fight for the statutory specification of the Marine functions, they would do so on their own. Beginning in February, certain loosely coordinated efforts were made to make contact with members of Congress who might be sympathetic to the Marine Corps point of view and to solicit newspaper editors, radio commentators, and private organizations for stories and resolutions in support of the Corps' position. A highly important accomplishment of these early activities was to successfully interest the Veterans of Foreign Wars to take a public stand in favor of increased protection for the Marines. The VFW not only released appropriate press statements from time to time, which Marine officers helped to prepare, but, more important, it also allowed its "National Legislative Representative" and his assistant (who happened to be a lieutenant in the Marine Corps Reserve) to take part in the direct lobbying campaign of individual members of Congress.*

Around the middle of March the opposition of the Marine Corps to the pending bills was given some degree of official sanction when the Commandant, General Vandegrift, appointed a special board of eleven

---

* One of the Marine officers at Quantico had contacted high officials of the VFW in his home state of Michigan and persuaded them to support the Marine campaign. These officials in turn stimulated a meeting of the National Legislative Committee of the VFW in Washington to consider organization policy toward the pending bills. The Committee consisted of representatives of the various geographical sections of the country and had authority to recommend policies to the VFW Commander in Chief, who in turn could commit the organization to any policy not conflicting with the resolutions of the previous VFW national convention. After listening to explanations of the reasons for the Marines' fears of the War Department, the Committee passed a resolution which led to making increased protection for the Marine Corps official organizational policy.

officers under General Edson "to conduct research and prepare material" in connection with the pending unification legislation. The board defined its mission as being solely "to protect the Marine Corps interest in the proposed unification bill" and organized itself accordingly. Some of the board's members concentrated on preparing statements and supporting data for the Commandant to present when he appeared before the Senate and House committees. Others continued their lobbying of newspaper correspondents and editors in Washington and wherever else they happened to have contacts. Still others concentrated on trying to influence key congressmen directly.

The campaign to get the Senate Armed Services Committee to include full statutory specifications of the functions of the Corps ended in failure. The Marines were able to "reach" Senators Robertson and Bridges, but these two Senators could not get the rest of the Committee to go along with them. One of the difficulties, from the point of view of the members of the special board, was that General Vandegrift decided at some point against using before the Armed Services Committee the statement prepared by the members of the board. This statement had attacked the compromise unification bill as a step toward excessive concentration of power in military hands and explained the need for statutory protection of the Corps by explicitly bringing up the Series 1478 JCS papers and ascribing to the War Department General Staff the wish "to destroy" the Marines. The statement that the Commandant eventually used, on the other hand, was silent on the Series 1478 JCS papers and did not impugn anyone's motives. Furthermore, in the course of the questioning, Vandegrift did not even rigidly insist on the adoption of the submitted amendments with their detailed specification of the Marine functions but agreed to consider alternative methods for effectively protecting the Corps.[38]

Vandegrift's relatively mild attack on the compromise bill had two sets of consequences: it purportedly did not convey to the Committee the impression that the Marine Corps was intensely opposed to the bill, and it did not provide the mass media with sufficiently controversial material to give the Marine Corps extensive coverage. On this last point, for example, one of the board members had gotten in touch, before Vandegrift's appearance, with a leading CBS radio commentator who had a fifteen-minute program over a 132-station network. The reporter was sympathetic and in fact devoted five minutes of one of his broadcasts to the Marine Corps campaign, at the same time promising to follow it up, provided the Commandant made a controversial enough statement. Various newspaper correspondents had indicated similar attitudes, and the members of the board were consequently distressed when Vandegrift did not provide the basis needed for their planned publicity campaign.[39]

In a desperate effort to save the situation in the Senate, General Edson decided that he should testify on the unification issue. Senator Robertson invited him, and the General made the broadside attack on the unification bill already described. So that he would bear sole responsibility for the views advanced, Edson had the special board formally dissolved just before his Senate appearance. The activities of the board members continued, however, substantially unchanged. After General Vandegrift's appearance before the Senate Armed Services Committee, the board decided that its cause was very likely lost in the Senate and decided to shift its major efforts to the House. It also decided that it must plan its future campaign without counting on the official support of the Commandant. The situation in the House looked promising. One of the members of the special board, Lieutenant Colonel James D. Hittle, was acquainted with Chairman Hoffman of the Expenditures Committee, and the VFW representatives also had good contacts on the Committee. This "privileged access"[40] allowed Hittle and the VFW to plant numerous questions with sympathetic members of the Committee throughout the hearings, which developed the Marine Corps' case for the record. Indeed, so many questions about the Marines were asked of the first witness, Secretary of War Patterson, that at one point in the questioning he complained with considerable irritation about all the "talk of the Marine Corps and the Marines," contending that the Marines were "not treated any differently here or discriminated against in any way."[41]

Of course, the underlying basis for the entire unofficial Marine campaign was the great popularity that the Corps enjoyed both within Congress and among the general public.[42] This was based largely on the belief, valid or not, that the Marines were "the greatest fighting force in the world."[43] As Raymond F. Brandt of the St. Louis *Post-Dispatch* once expressed the popular stereotype,

There can be no question that the Marines are our best trained and fiercest fighting force, that they have the highest morale and unexcelled esprit de corps. Army officers will concede that a Marine sergeant is equal in training and experience to any Army lieutenant and that a Marine private could take over an Army sergeant's job.[44]

Thus, when in a meeting of the unification participants on April 18 Clark Clifford was stressing the "great importance" from the President's point of view of the bill not containing detailed language on the service functions, Senator Tydings declared that the whole question was "not a matter of logic but of emotion" and predicted that in a showdown

all that would be necessary, particularly in the House, would be for someone to get up on his feet when the bill was under debate and say that logical arguments about the bill were all very well but that, after all, "these young men, thanks to their traditions and their fighting history, were the troops that we needed to take Mount Suribachi." [45] *

The pro-Marine sentiments of the House Expenditures Committee had become so clear during Patterson's appearance through the planted questions and the volunteered statements, such as Representative McCormack's clear warning to Patterson that some sort of additional protections had to be provided for the Marines,[46] that Clark Clifford is said to have called General Norstad and Admiral Sherman and finally conceded that "the issue of the Marine Corps was becoming a focal point of all opposition to the bill and unless some concession was given to the Marine Corps, the whole thing was liable to blow up in their faces in the House." It was apparently at this point that Norstad and Sherman began working on proposed language for the single protective clause that the Senate Armed Services Committee later adopted.

By the beginning of June the adoption of the single protective clause by the Senate Committee and General Vandegrift's satisfaction with it had become matters of common knowledge, thus seriously undercutting the efforts of the special board members and their allies in the VFW, who were continuing to press for full specification of the service functions. We have seen that General Edson testified on June 17 before the Expenditures Committee and reiterated his opposition to the compromise unification bill. Edson publicly took issue with his superior, General Vandegrift, during the questioning, giving his view that the single clause did not provide adequate protection for the Marines. Before his House testimony Edson had applied for retirement from the Marine Corps, announcing to the press that "he did not agree with the continued encroachment of the military upon the civil functions of the Government and did not want to be a party to such militaristic events," [47] presumably

---

* Forrestal, who was at Iwo Jima when the famous flag-raising took place, reportedly observed to his companion, General Smith, "Holland, the raising of that flag on Suribachi means a Marine Corps for the next 500 years." Holland M. Smith and Percy Finch, *Coral and Brass* (New York, Scribner, 1948), p. 261.

by following official Corps policy and supporting the Senate Committee version of the compromise unification bill.

At Chairman Hoffman's request, Edson submitted a draft bill incorporating his views on unification a few days after his testimony. After checking with Colonel Hittle and Colonel Merrill B. Twining, another of the leaders of the now formally defunct special board, Hoffman introduced the bill on June 25 as H.R.3979. Edson's draft bill provided for a Secretary of National Security restricted to establishing "general policies and programs of common concern to departments and agencies comprising the National Military Establishment" and to "supervising" the military budget. Two other key points were that the Commandant of the Marine Corps was to be included in the membership of the JCS and the service functions completely spelled out, with the Marines being treated generously, to say the least, and the separate Air Force being limited to "strategic air operations and the air defense of the United States and its possessions." [48]

Toward the end of the second part of the House hearings, Hoffman asked Colonel Hittle to help prepare a comparative analysis of the various pending House and Senate unification bills, which Hoffman later had printed for Committee use during executive session. The analysis, as Hittle has put it, "did not misstate any facts but needless to say the phrasing of the analytic notes was not detrimental to the Marine Corps or the Naval Service and national security." [49] Hoffman also asked Hittle to "assist" the Committee in writing up a clean bill, but Hittle felt obliged to decline unless Hoffman first secured official permission for him from the Commandant of the Marine Corps. This Hoffman did, and Hittle served consequently during the key stages of the House consideration of the unification bill as "Special Adviser to the Chairman [of the House Expenditures Committee] in Relation to the National Security Act." [50]

Soon after the end of the House hearings on July 1, Hoffman appointed a seven-man subcommittee to draw up a clean bill. Its members consisted of Hoffman himself and of Representatives George H. Bender, Henry J. Latham, and Wadsworth, from the majority side, and Representatives McCormack, Manasco, and Holifield from the minority. There were two broad issues before the subcommittee: the question of the general concept of the compromise bill with an overall Secretary whose grant of authority included the words "direction" and "control" and the right to formulate the military budget, as opposed to the strictly supervisory powers granted to the Secretary in H.R.3979, the bill drafted by

Edson and introduced by Hoffman; and the question of the adoption of the Senate's single protective clause or the incorporation of the full service functions. Hoffman, Bender, and Latham were at this point definitely sympathetic to the Marine Corps point of view on both issues. Wadsworth was opposed. The three Democrats, who were generally committed to their President to bring out a unification bill, held the balance of power.

The unofficial Marine lobbyists concentrated their efforts accordingly on the three Democrats, and especially on McCormack, who was already leaning toward the Marine position. Throughout the House hearings McCormack was being "visited" by a senior Marine Corps officer who originally came from McCormack's district in Boston. The officer had also been "visiting" the Boston newspaper editors, and, perhaps not by coincidence, two important ones had come out editorially in the spring of 1947 in favor of increased protections for the Marines. During the latter part of June and in early July the effort with McCormack was stepped up, with another Marine officer from Boston commuting back home from Quantico each weekend, stimulating letters and telegrams from individuals, veterans' organizations, and other interest groups. At the same time, the VFW representatives were lobbying Manasco and Holifield on an almost day-to-day basis, both of these representatives having worked closely with that organization in the past.

In the event, the lobbying was successful and the subcommittee voted 5 to 1 in favor of specifying the service functions in the bill with the language the Marines preferred, Wadsworth being the lone opponent.[51] The Democrats refused, however, to go along with the attempt to substitute completely the concept behind H.R.3979 for the compromise bill generally and, with Wadsworth's vote, reportedly carried that point of view very narrowly.[52] The full Expenditures Committee adopted the bill prepared by the subcommittee without significant change. At this point, Representative Wadsworth submitted a draft committee report to Hoffman, which Hoffman, believing that the report had actually been written by General Norstad, asked Hittle to edit. Hoffman's idea was that it was better strategy to revise the Wadsworth report than to present a completely new alternative.[53] The Committee rejected the version finally offered by Hoffman and adopted a draft later prepared by Wadsworth and McCormack.

The Marine Corps campaign to insure the statutory definition of the Marine functions was still not finished even with the approval by the whole House of substantially the Committee's bill.[54] The Senate committee had after long consideration rejected the incorporation of the service functions in the bill and settled on the single protective clause, and General Vandegrift was still on record as being personally satisfied with that arrangement. Just before the first meeting of the Senate-House conference, one of the members of the Marine special board approached Vandegrift and informed him that Senator Byrd, a conferee, was willing to send a letter asking the Commandant whether he preferred the Senate or House version with respect to the protection of the Marines. Vandegrift's response must have been encouraging, for the latter was sent, and Vandegrift answered it by pointing out the advantages of the House version.[55] It is reported that Senator Byrd read Vandegrift's letter to the conference committee at a critical stage of the proceedings and that this broke the resistance of the majority of the Senate conferees to inclusion of the service functions in the compromise version.[56]

At the same time that these letter-writing maneuvers were going on, both the members of the Marine special board and of the VFW continued their lobbying of selected conference committee members. The lobbying at this or, indeed, at any other point was not, of course, one-sided: the specific details of the War Department's efforts at this point are not available, but it is known that the Army and Army Air Forces leaders made an all-out attempt to get the conference committee to adopt the Senate version of the bill, to the extent of having high officers wait outside the door of the conference room in order to try to sway individual conferees.

The Marines were, however, represented inside the door, and this made the difference. Hoffman had asked Colonel Hittle to prepare a three-stage compromise bill in case concessions had to be made to the Senate. Hittle proceeded to mark up the House bill in three different colors: red indicating the absolutely essential language (from the Marine and Navy point of view), blue the desirable but not essential, and brown the language that had been included largely for bargaining purposes. Hoffman took the marked-up bill into the conference room, and when the conference version finally emerged, only the minimal concessions had been made on the issue of the service functions.[57]

Although the exact details are not available, there is evidence that at the same time that the Marines were conducting this unofficial campaign for the inclusion of their own service functions in the unification bill, retired Admiral Zacharias was leading a similar unofficial Navy effort in favor of additional protections for naval aviation and against a separate air force.

Political Interest Groups

Another extra-legislative, and in this case also extra-governmental, source of influence on congressional majorities in the unification conflict was organized political interest groups. Interest groups consist of individuals holding common goals, preferences, or interests on the basis of which they combine to seek political action enhancing those goals, interests, or preferences or warding off any threatened damage to them.[58] Political interest groups engage in a wide variety of activities in their efforts to influence governmental policy, including propaganda, electioneering, and lobbying of individual members of Congress, of other interest groups, and of representatives of the mass media.[59]

Except for the activities of the VFW already described, interest group activity did not play a major role either in the creation or the resolution of the unification conflict.[60] Most of the groups which the evidence shows were involved restricted themselves to passing resolutions and sending telegrams and did not even bother to send representatives to testify before Congress. An inspection of the names of the organizations (Table 2) will suggest why this was so.

TABLE 2

Group for and against Pending War Department Proposals

For Proposals	Against Proposals
Air Force Association	Marine Corps League
Air Power League	Marine Corps Reserve Officers
Air Reserve Association	Association
American Legion	Navy Club, U.S.A
Army Ordnance Association	Navy League
Catholic War Veterans	Niagara Frontier Detachment,
Daughters of the American	Marine Corps League
Revolution	Reserve Officers of the
Disabled American Veterans	Naval Service
National Aviation Clinic	Veterans of Foreign Wars
National Cooperative Milk	
Producers Federation	
Reserve Officers Association	
South Carolina Department,	
Reserve Officers Association	

Note: These organizations all took some action which was either reported in the New York *Times* or sent messages or passed resolutions which were inserted in the body or appendix of the *Congressional Record* or the record of the various hearings.

With the exception of the incongruous "Milk Producers Federation," the groups break down into two categories: narrow, service-identified associations and general patriotic and veterans' organizations. As far as the first category is concerned, the testimony of its leaders was not likely to have as much effect within Congress as that of the official leaders of the "parent" service, who almost certainly had much higher prestige and who were more directly affected by the matters at issue. Moreover, the membership of these groups was not extensive enough plausibly to suggest retaliation at the polls, although the Niagara Frontier Detachment of the Marine Corps League did remind its local congressman in 1946 that it was sure it bespoke the "sentiments" of its "7000 to 8000"-man membership from "western New York." [61]

The chief function of the service-identified or "satellite" associations was to express the widespread feeling that existed within a military service when, for one reason or another, the service's official leaders could not or would not do so themselves. As President John P. Bracken of the Reserve Officers of the Naval Service (RONS) told the House Expenditures Committee in 1947, his organization was "to a certain extent the conscience of the Navy . . . we can come up here and speak up the way we feel our brother officers in the Regular service would like to speak if they could." [62] Thus, of all the service-identified groups, only RONS and the Marine Corps Reserve Officers Association sent representatives to testify before congressional committees, and this was in 1947, when many of the rank-and-file officers of the Navy and the Marines still distrusted the compromise agreed to and being supported by Forrestal and the other official Navy leaders but felt obliged to remain silent. The other satellite associations, such as the Air Force Association and the Navy League, participated in the conflict almost exclusively through public relations and propaganda activities among the general public. [63]

The more broadly based organizations, such as the American Legion, which had substantial memberships that could conceivably exert influence at the polls, could not afford to take a very active role, since their memberships included veterans of all the services and the service identification of the members was likely to be stronger than their associational identification. So it was that when the American Legion took its major unification stand during its 1946 national convention, it merely endorsed very generally "the principle of a unified command of our armed forces with the Army, Navy, and Air Force on an equal level" and requested Congress "to enact appropriate legislation to establish a single department for national security." [64] Similarly, when the American Legion representative testified before the House Expenditures Committee in June of 1947, he would not take a position as between the House bill or the amended Senate version but only urged generally the enactment of some form of unification legislation that session.[65]

Unorganized Public Opinion

"Public opinion" is an elusive concept in many ways. There is great difficulty in discovering its dimensions on various issues and even more difficulty in identifying its effects on the actions of congressional majorities. Strictly speaking, the "public" on the unification issue included the active participants in the conflict—the President, various senators and representatives, cabinet secretaries, military chiefs, interest groups—as well as the individual members of the general public who were aware that a unification conflict was raging.[66] Since the opinions and influence of all but the last have been discussed, the following account will be confined to an examination of what can be called "general," or "unorganized," public opinion.

It is impossible to establish the dimensions of public opinion on the unification conflict with any degree of certainty or precision. If we judge, however, by the amount of space and the favorable and unfavorable comment given to the unification conflict by a representative sample of the nation's newspapers in general and the New York *Times* in particular, by the results of the one available Gallup poll, and by the recollections of various members of Congress, we can infer that the public was large and almost unanimous in the opinion that "unification" was desirable but very small and divided on the preferred form of putting it into effect. Throughout the unification controversy, the attack on Pearl Harbor was seen to have proven the need for unification from the point of view of combat effectiveness, and the existence of "overlapping," "duplication," and "enormous waste" to have proven it from the point of view of economy. Unification was also seen as inextricably tied up with giving the Army Air Forces the "independence" that it "deserved." "Unification," however, had no clear empirical referent for more than the handful of people directly involved in the conflict and was generally identified by the public with the most current proposal of the War Department coalition.[67]

PEARL HARBOR

The Pearl Harbor belief appears to have crystallized almost overnight [68] when the official reports of the War and Navy Department investigations of the surprise attack were finally released to the public on August 30, 1945, just two weeks after the end of the fighting in the Pacific.[69] The reports cannot be summarized in brief compass and, indeed, did not agree completely between themselves on the cause of the disaster, but neither the Army nor the Navy report appears on its face to provide very strong support for unification.

The War Department report placed the major blame for the overwhelming success of the Japanese attack on the commanding general of its Hawaii garrison, Lieutenant General Walter C. Short. It alleged that Short had failed to alert his command adequately for war after receiving on November 27, 1941, the warning, "Japanese . . . hostile action possible at any moment," with directions to report the measures taken to meet the situation. The report also directed substantial criticism toward the War Department General Staff in Washington (particularly the Chief of Staff, General Marshall, and the Chief of the War Plans Division, Major General Leonard T. Gerow) for failing to notice the inadequate state of alert instituted and reported to the War Department by General Short and for failing to pass on to the Hawaii commander fuller information on the critical turn taken by the Japanese-American diplomatic negotiations in late November, 1941, and on intercepted Japanese messages to Tokyo reporting ship movements and harbor berthings at Pearl Harbor. In this connection Secretary of State Cordell Hull was also criticised for allegedly failing to pass on to the military departments information which they in turn could pass on to their commanders in the field. The War Department report, finally, criticized Short for not taking steps to reach agreement with the naval commanders in Hawaii for the implementation of existing joint Army-Navy war plans or to inform himself of the extent of the long-range air search and reconnaissance conducted by the Navy and for failing to remove inefficient staff officers.

The report of the Navy Department's investigation of the Pearl Harbor attack directed its major criticism against its own top commander in Hawaii, Admiral Husband Kimmel, the Commander in Chief of the Pacific Fleet, for failure to conduct a more continuous long-range air search. The report also criticized the Chief of Naval Operations, Admiral

Harold Stark, for allegedly failing to pass on sufficient information to Kimmel warning him of the possible danger of war with Japan, despite the fact that Stark had sent Kimmel a much sharper message than the War Department alert on November 27, beginning with the words, "This dispatch is to be considered a war warning" and containing the statement that "an aggressive move by Japan is expected within the next few days." The message also directed the Navy fleet commander to "execute an appropriate defensive deployment" and to inform the Army commanders of its contents.

These War and Navy Department reports, the essence of which probably could be condensed into Secretary of War Stimson's phrase that the "sentinels on post" were not alert to their own peril,[70] were very far from attributing the success of the surprise attack to faulty Army-Navy coordination, though such a factor did play a role. The findings that concerned failure of interservice coordination were: (1) Operating under the principle of "mutual cooperation," General Short assumed that the Navy was conducting a 360-degree long-range reconnaissance such as required by the joint Army-Navy war plan and did not inquire if one was in fact being carried out. (Actually Kimmel did not have the aircraft required for a full search, but Short did not know that.) (2) Admiral Kimmel assumed that Short had put his command on a full, rather than a sabotage alert and hence that the search radar under Army control was operating around the clock instead of stopping at 7 A.M. Both these findings indicated the need for a single commander in the field controlling both Army and Navy activities to insure that some single individual received all the relevant facts and had final command responsibility.

Such a development—unified command in the field—had been put into effect, as we have seen, in January, 1942, during the ARCADIA conference and in 1945 was not opposed by anyone. The other significant findings at all relevant to organizational structure—that Hull purportedly did not pass sufficient information to the military on the state of foreign affairs and that no single agency ever had possession of all the key intelligence information available in the total governmental system—were defects that could be cured more readily by bodies such as Eberstadt's National Security Council and Central Intelligence Agency than by unification as proposed by the War Department.[71]

A majority of the newspapers reporting and commenting on the Pearl Harbor reports decided, however, to advocate unification as a rational response to the catastrophe of four years earlier. The position of the New York *Times* in an editorial entitled "Failure of a System" was probably typical of the kind of thinking that converted the results of almost gross personal inefficiency into arguments for the "creation of a single Department of Defense with a straight line of both command and responsibility from the very top to the very bottom." As the *Times* editors saw it,

the most important element in the reports is the plain evidence that Pearl Harbor was not so much the fault of men as the fault of a system. . . . Such a conclusion is inescapable even without further evidence. For the men now blamed for America's greatest defeat are surely among the best and most distinguished leaders America has produced, men who have proved their mettle before and during this war. It might be possible to blame one or two of them for errors and derelictions, it is impossible to blame all of them without indicting the whole system that did not insure itself against the inevitable shortcomings of the human factor.[72]

Except for the Army Pearl Harbor Board's report, General Marshall had not been publicly criticized during the entire war and it appears as if a scapegoat, even if it were an organizational form, had to be found on which to focus the blame and protect his and other generals' and admirals' reputations.* In any event, from the fall of 1945 on—and probably until the present day—the idea that lack of unification "caused" the Pearl Harbor disaster has been accepted by a large part of the general public as an article of faith to be challenged only by Navy obstructionists.[73]

ECONOMY

The second widespread belief—that unification would save money and would have saved millions (or billions) if it had been in effect in World War II—cannot be ascribed to any single concrete event. Certainly money had been wasted, in the sense that certain items were procured in greater quantities than could possibly have been used and some facilities were built that did not, and should have been seen as unlikely to, contribute in any way to the successful prosecution of the war. This much even the Eberstadt Report admitted. Also there had obviously been

* Similarly, America's failure to match the Soviet achievements in space and missile efforts in 1957 was widely attributed not to incorrect policy decisions at the highest level but to inadequate defense organization and led to proposals for change in the Department of Defense to "eliminate interservice rivalries."

some competitive bidding by the Army and the Navy for scarce items early in the war which sent up the price that the government eventually paid, but steps had been taken to sharply reduce, if not to eliminate, that type of inefficiency by the middle of the war, both through better inter-service cooperation in procurement and through renegotiation provisions in munitions contracts and excess profits taxes.

But that large amounts of money had been wasted "made sense." A major part of the public is always ready to believe that nothing that the government does can be efficient and unwasteful. Moreover, the spending of the war years had, in fact, been utterly fantastic by previous standards —a total of over $250 billion. Finally, some 12 million men who had been in the armed forces had seen instances of "waste." Given the great desire to reduce expenditures in the postwar period, the connection be-tween unification and economy was simply asserted forcibly by the unification protagonists, including such high-prestige figures as the Presi-dent and the famous World War II generals, and it was accepted at face value.

When, for example, General Eisenhower was reported to have testi-fied before the Senate Military Affairs Committee in November, 1945, that the war could have been fought by a unified military department with a 25 percent saving in money—a sum of some $66 billion—the New York *Times* simply accepted the figure as established truth and proceeded to castigate the Navy editorially for continuing to oppose unification in the light of the savings to be effected.[74] The total absurdity of this position is highlighted by the fact that even Eisenhower had not actually made such a claim. When the General returned to Washington to relieve Marshall as Chief of Staff, he wrote to Chairman Thomas of the Military Affairs Committee that the record of his testimony in the transcript of the hearings was in error on this point and that what he had said was that the war could have been won under a single depart-ment with a 25 percent saving in manpower rather than in money.[75]

AIR FORCES INDEPENDENCE

The third widely held belief was that the performance of "air power" in World War II had proved that the Army Air Forces should have their own independent organization and that such an organization was in-extricably tied up with unification. The connections for these *non sequi-turs* were never spelled out even by the Air Forces generals and so did not form any part of public opinion. The Navy arguments that "air power" included naval air power and that the latter had performed brilliantly while being fully integrated with the surface forces was never apparently perceived either by the press or by the general public. The disturbing paradox that if the Army Air Forces had performed as efficaciously as claimed under the existing machinery, there was no need for new institutional arrangements, was also ignored. What the public was aware of was that it had seen news films and read press reports throughout the war of the dropping of enormous tonnages of high explosives by Army Air Forces bombers. When the Air Forces leaders, who by the end of World War II had achieved a glamor surpassing the Navy and not even approached by the ground Army, claimed that independence was their due, there was a consequent widespread disposition to accept the claim at face value and almost no disinclination to such a development. Finally, with the development of the atomic bomb it became "unthinkable" that the organization which controlled "the ultimate weapon" should remain subject to the Army or the Navy.

CONFUSION AS TO DETAILED FORM

That the size of the public knowledgeable about the preferred form for putting unification into effect was extremely small can be established only by indirection. Even the editorial page of the New York *Times,* however, did not appear able to distinguish clearly between the various plans presented over the years. It commented favorably on the McNarney Plan in 1944, on the Collins Plan in 1945, on S.2044 unamended and amended in 1946, and on the compromise agreement of 1947, the draft bill, the Senate and House amended versions, and the enacted National Security Act, each time using roughly the same arguments for the need of the particular plan discussed and prophesying substantially the same beneficial consequences from its enactment.[76] The sample of nationwide newspaper opinion previously cited showed the same pattern of support. The *Times* recognized the situation itself, commenting on President Truman's 1946 Army Day speech, which called for Universal Military Training, extension of the draft, and unification in order to maintain strong defenses in the face of the worsening relations with the Soviet Union in the Middle East:

The President did not repeat his arguments of last December in favor of unification. That is a complex and detailed subject. Aside from a general acceptance of the principle, most persons probably feel themselves unqualified to pass on the details.[77]

The hypothesis that great confusion existed with respect to what "unification" entailed is supported by two other events: the newspaper response to a press statement issued by General MacArthur in October, 1945, and the report of a Gallup poll released on November 8, 1945. The day before the Senate Military Affairs Committee began its hearings in the fall of 1945, General MacArthur released a statement in Tokyo declaring, "The victory [in World War II] was a triumph for the concept of the complete integration of the three dimensions of war—ground, sea, and air" and that "the great lesson for the future is that success in war depends on a complete integration of the services." While questioning Secretary of War Patterson the next day, Senator Hill, with some degree of fanfare, had the MacArthur statement inserted into the record of the hearings and then proceeded to lead Patterson to agree that the War Department was merely asking that the integrated team described by MacArthur as indispensable, be set up through unification.[78]

Five days later, when Secretary of the Navy Forrestal appeared before the Committee, the Secretary digressed a moment from his prepared statement and with some degree of sarcasm remarked,

> It seems to me that there is a good deal of confusion on the issue of unification. This is indicated by the general editorial interpretation of the recent statement of General MacArthur when he said, "The victory was a triumph for the concept of the complete integration of the three dimensions of war—ground, sea, and air."
>
> General MacArthur obviously was referring to the victory which had just been achieved by the system which now exists. It cannot mean anything else. Certainly it does not mean that a glorious victory was achieved by a system which doesn't yet exist.[79]

The Gallup Poll pointed up the same kind of confusion. On November 9, 1945, Senator Hill inserted into the record of the Military Affairs Committee hearings an article from the Washington *Post* reporting that the American Institute of Public Opinion had found in a recent poll that 52 percent of a sample of the population "had a reasonably correct idea" of the term "unified command" and that, of that 52 percent, 64 percent approved "of unified command for the armed forces of this country." [80] The point is that the term "unified command" connoted to the well-informed observer "unified command in the field under a single commander," something which was never in dispute. Throughout the Gallup release the terms "unification," "merger," and "unity of command" were used interchangeably, which casts some doubt on the Institute's finding of the percentage of the population having a correct notion of what they were approving when apparently its own pollsters were themselves confused.

EFFECTS OF PUBLIC OPINION

The effects of public opinion on congressional majorities are even more difficult to determine than its composition. In so far as individual members of Congress court the good opinion of the mass media—and especially the "prestige papers" and "prestige commentators"—they might be motivated to support a measure that the media were strongly endorsing.[81] Likewise, the President and the congressional party leadership—each of whom feels himself to be a trustee to some extent of the party record and looks to a nationwide constituency—might be interested in the increment of prestige to accrue to them from the passage of a popular measure in a vital field.

The original unification conflict activists in Congress do not appear, however, to have been influenced more than marginally by the opinion of either the general public or their constituencies. Except possibly for a small group of hard-core Marine identifiers among the general public, the unification issue was not close enough to daily experience to permit individual constituents to perceive the specific positions of their congressmen on the various plans being considered and then to connect that position to some marginal increment of combat effectiveness, economy, or some other widely held interest and have this calculation justify retaliation at the polls. It is simply inconceivable that Senators Byrd, Hill, Tydings, or Saltonstall, for example, or Representatives Vinson, Wadsworth, or Hoffman (each of whom had won his last election by over a 60 percent plurality [82]) gave a second's thought to the reaction of their constituency electorates to their own positions on unification.

The firmest connection between public opinion and congressional behavior in the unification conflict was that most members of Congress probably did not like to oppose continuously a policy apparently desired by a preponderant majority of the public. As befits public officials in democratic polity, our national legislators generally act as if they believe that at least with respect to broad purpose and over the long run, public opinion should prevail. This outlook insured that eventually some measure called "unification" would be passed but had almost no effect on the specific form of the enacted legislation—which was, of course, the crux of the conflict among the President, the military services, and the activists in Congress.[83]

Part V

Conclusions

9

The Outcome of the
Unification Conflict

Analysis of the unification conflict suggests that the development of political conflict in general requires three conditions:

1. The existence of a set of actors with incentive to propose the adoption of some particular course of governmental action and the existence of a second set of actors with incentive to obstruct it.

2. The possession by both sets of actors of the capacity to influence the actions of the appropriate unit of government.

3. The determination by neither set of actors that participation in the conflict is "uneconomical."

Analysis of the unification conflict suggests also that a political conflict will become resolved as soon as at least one of those conditions ceases to operate and that the outcome of the conflict will represent the status of the disputed proposals at the time of the conflict's resolution.

Conflict and Incentive

Since political conflict has been defined as a kind of interactivity in which one actor promotes and another actor obstructs or interferes with the adoption of some proposed course of governmental action, its development requires the existence of two actors with incentives for mutual opposition. As was pointed out in Part II, these incentives can be based on any combination of "pure goal conflict," "goal incompatibility," and "means-end disagreement." Pure goal conflict consists of the goal or goals directly sought to be furthered by the first actor and one or more goals of the second actor being mutually exclusive. Goal incompatibility consists of the goals of the first and second actors not being mutually exclusive by definition but of the second actor's perceptions of reality being such that he expects the proposal in question to bring about a particular empirical situation where, in fact, the advancement of the first actor's goals would be at the expense of his own. Means-end disagreement consists, finally, of the two actors' possessing different perceptions of reality and thus disagreeing over the effectiveness of a proposal for furthering goals that they both share.

One way for a political conflict to become resolved is obviously by the disappearance of the actors' incentives toward mutual opposition as a result of changes in their goals or in their perceptions of reality. Such an incentive-vanishing process played only a very minor role in resolving the unification conflict. There is no evidence that any of the goals originally held by either of the coalitions—combat effectiveness, economy, civilian control of the military, a separate air force, separate air force control of all land-based planes, restriction of the Marine Corps, military control of the budget, adequate ground troops, a strong Navy, Navy Department organizational integrity, special Presidential stakes—was ever given up in the sense of the states of affairs implicit in these goals ceasing to be favored. Nor is there any evidence that either coalition's perceptions of reality about the consequences of the original War Department proposals ever changed radically even after nearly four years of exchange of views.

Conflict and Influence

Political proposals become adopted or rejected when the officials constituting the appropriate unit of government (or some specified number or proportion of them) perform certain requisite acts as defined by various standing rules, statutes, or constitutions.[1] Normally, the acts amounting to formal adoption or rejection will be preceded by a multiplicity of other acts tending to bring about that adoption or rejection. Political conflict in these terms consists essentially of both sets of acts being performed within the governmental unit at the same time. Political influence is the ability to affect any of these acts in an intended way.

Both actors must possess political influence in order to convert any goal conflicts, goal incompatibilities, or means-end disagreements into active and prolonged conflict over the adoption of some concrete proposal: To the extent that neither actor has such influence, the governmental unit will simply not become involved, and to the extent that only one actor has influence, the relevant proposal will be quickly accepted or rejected without conflict. To the extent, on the other hand, that both actors have influence over the actions of the governmental unit, a conflict can develop that will continue until such time as either one of them aggregates sufficiently great influence to control that unit's actions and thus get the proposal in dispute accepted or rejected despite the other actor's countervailing efforts.

PATTERNS OF INFLUENCE: 1943–44

The unification conflict began when General Marshall, with General Arnold's support, proposed in November, 1943, that the JCS adopt his proposal for unifying the War and Navy Departments into a single "Department of War" in the postwar period. Adoption of the proposal in the JCS was presumed to be instrumental to its eventual approval by Congress, whose action would be Constitutionally necessary to establish a new government department. Marshall was unable to persuade his naval colleagues on the JCS, Admirals King and Leahy, to agree to the concept of a single department even in principle; and continued conflict within the JCS at that time was precluded only by farming the conflict out to a subordinate staff group.

Although the staff group reported a unanimous recommendation in March, 1944, in favor of immediate agreement by the JCS on a single military department to guide the detailed study of the problem by the special JCS committee, which the staff group also recommended, King and Leahy continued to hold out against such an agreement, purportedly to allow the special committee full latitude in its investigations. Since, according to their rules of operation, adoption of a proposal in the JCS required unanimous concurrence by its four members and since the Navy coalition directly or indirectly controlled two of the concurrences in the persons of the admirals, the Navy was able to prevent the adoption of the single-department principle and to force the referral of the problem to the Richardson Committee without a preliminary decision on the central issue.

While the final instructions were being drafted to transfer the unification conflict once again out of the JCS and into another subordinate staff group, one of the War Department's congressional allies managed to divert it directly into Congress. James Wadsworth, who was close to the War Department and apparently knew of its recent conversion to support of unification, introduced the resolution setting up the Select Committee on Post-War Military Policy. Given his widely acknowledged subject-matter expertise and the lack of any opposition to develop, Wadsworth quickly got his resolution adopted with the general congressional understanding that the Committee would consider the question of a single military department.[2]

There was little congressional interest in or awareness of the unification issue in the spring of 1944. The War Department coalition's strategy apparently was to have the Select Committee serve as a forum within which, at the least, the Department could air its views and increase public and congressional awareness of the issue and, at the most, the War Department could successfully sell its argument that "unification will increase combat effectiveness and economy" and secure a recommendation in favor of a single department either immediately or at the end of the war. The Navy coalition began mobilizing its own resources after the Woodrum hearings started, principally by presenting testimony in opposition to any immediate decision in favor either of unification in general or of the War Department's specific plan and thus demonstrating that any attempt by Congress to deal with the merits of unification during the war would create great acrimony between the services and thus injure the Committee's and the services' common goal of combat effectiveness in wartime. This Navy delaying strategy succeeded, with Secretary of War Stimson and the active minority of the Woodrum Committee agreeing with Forrestal that the emergent conflict within Congress should be cut off.

The Navy coalition was unable to prevent the War Department from achieving its minimal objective, and the Woodrum hearings no doubt did increase the number of persons aware of the unification issue and developed newspaper opinion that was predominantly in favor of a single military department.[3] The hearings also hardened the Navy's opposition, however, by demonstrating to its highest officials and congressional friends that the War Department's plans constituted a real danger to the Navy's existence and one that they would have to make an all-out and determined effort to defeat.

PATTERNS OF INFLUENCE: 1945–46

After the Navy coalition had succeeded during the spring of 1944 in reconfining the unification conflict to the top-secret spaces of the JCS structure, the highest echelons of both coalitions abstained from any further direct clashes, preferring to wait for the Richardson Committee's conclusions, which the evidence suggests each coalition expected to be in its own favor. The Richardson Committee reported in April, 1945, what was in effect a compromise unification plan somewhere between the War and Navy Department coalition positions as developed before the Woodrum Committee, but, as in 1944, the naval members of the JCS refused to accept the recommendations of the staff group, apparently believing that the Navy coalition could prevent the adoption of still more aspects of the War Department's original proposals.

While King and Leahy were obstructing the adoption of the Richardson Committee recommendations in the JCS, Forrestal and some of the Navy's congressional allies began to think of developing and recommending an alternative pattern of unification which would provide formal means of coordination between the military and the State Department and which could also possibly satisfy the evolving, but undifferentiating, public and congressional consensus in favor of "unification" without the establishment of a single military department. The Eberstadt Report provided such a pattern, recommending essentially the retention of an improved World War II command structure with a National Security Council to institutionalize coordination between the formulators of military and of foreign policy and with a separate air force but without any single individual short of the President with authority to give orders to the highest officials of the Navy. The Eberstadt Report solution was never formally presented by the Navy for adoption within the JCS but was held in reserve, presumably for the congressional hearings on unification that all of the parties realized were certain to come. It was obvious that, once the war was over, the War Department coalition would again seek to extend the unification conflict into Congress, where, unlike in the JCS, it could hope with its congressional allies to aggregate enough influence by activating voting majorities in its support to impose its preferred solution on the Navy regardless of the latter's continued opposition.

The unification conflict did spread into Congress in the fall of 1945, when the Senate Military Affairs Committee began to hold hearings, purportedly on two unification bills introduced by its own members but quite obviously for the real purpose of giving the War Department coalition an opportunity to gain additional attention for unification and to present specific proposals on the basis of which a new bill could later be written. Actually, it appears that even before the hearings began in the Seventy-ninth Congress, as a result of previous informal communications between the leaders of the War and Navy Department coalitions and interested legislators, two small cores of senators and representatives had already formed, one supporting and the other opposing a single military department along War Department lines. These cores consisted generally of those members of Congress who because of their past experiences identified with one or another of the military services, shared its organizational goals, and thus came to support generally the parent department's unification position. For the remainder of the conflict these "identifiers" pretty much spontaneously "carried the ball" within Congress for their executive branch allies.

The War Department and Navy coalitions' direct influence upon them consisted merely of reinforcing their sense of identification through favorable personal relations, of "interpreting" wherever necessary the various plans and proposals advanced by the opposition with respect to the consequences for "their" service, and of providing the concrete recommendations, the detailed background data, and the staff assistance that were necessary for the legislators to support effectively the different services' positions in the legislative in-fighting. But since neither set of hard-core identifiers was numerous enough to constitute potential voting majorities in either house of Congress, each of the two coalitions was forced to be also concerned with the as yet uncommitted.

The War Department's congressional identifiers, who dominated the Senate Military Affairs Committee, moved actively toward converting the uncommitted into voting majorities in support of the Army's unification proposals. By favorably reporting the Thomas-Hill-Austin bill (S.2044), which was essentially the original Collins Plan as modified slightly by General Eisenhower and Assistant Secretary of War McCloy and with the addition of some of the uncontroversial superdepartmental coordinating bodies proposed by the Navy. Ordinarily, this support of a proposal by an overwhelming majority (including the chairman, the second- and third-ranking majority member, and the ranking minority member) of the committee which considered it would virtually have assured its adoption on the floor. Not only is there operating the general congressional predisposition to accept a committee recommendation but the Military Affairs Committee, through the testimony developed in its hearings by such high-prestige figures as Stimson, Patterson, Marshall, and Eisenhower, through various informal means of communication with other Senate members, by means of its favorable report on S.2044, and with the aid of the President's special message, had apparently also been able to create the widespread opinion within the Senate by the spring of 1946 that "unification" was desirable because it would further combat effectiveness ("prevent," among other things, "future Pearl Harbors") and economy ("eliminate wasteful duplication") and give the Army Air Forces its "deserved" independent status. Moreover, this opinion was buttressed by the further widespread feeling that the President's strong wish for assistance in the performance of his role as Commander in Chief by the establishment of some sort of sub-Presidential coordinator in military matters should not be completely denied.

The structural situation in the Seventy-ninth Congress caused, however, the advantages of the Military Affairs Committee's favorable recommendation and the additional support accruing from the President's personal endorsement to be much less than decisive. Unification affected the Navy Department as well as the War Department, and on matters dealing with the former, the members of Congress were predisposed to listen to the advice of the separate Committee on Naval Affairs. This Committee was dominated by the Navy identifiers—Walsh, Tydings, Byrd, Robertson, and Saltonstall. It was largely the Naval Affairs Committee's opposition to the Thomas-Hill-Austin bill that prevented the War Department's congressional allies from being able to activate a floor majority of the Senate in support of their position or even from explicitly making that attempt by a formal vote on their reported bill.

It is not, of course, literally true to say that the Naval Affairs Committee *prevented* the backers of S.2044 from calling it off the Senate calendar. The rules of the Senate in effect provide that any member can move to bring a reported bill up for consideration on the floor at almost any time.[4] What would have happened if the bill had been called up is impossible to say with certainty, but the existence and activities of the Naval Affairs Committee were certainly a key factor in not making the attempt. First of all, the informal "rules of the game" of the Senate (internalized by individual senators as attitudes about what "is done" or "is not done") condemn the short-cutting of any senator or group of senators from considerating of a bill in which they are deemed to have a legitimate interest. The Naval Affairs Committee was considered to have such an interest in the unification bill, and any attempt to pass the bill while that Committee was still holding its hearings could very likely have been perceived as a violation of Senate norms and defeated on that account alone. Senator Thomas made it clear that he, himself, shared this norm when he appeared before the Naval Affairs Committee hearings and told Senator Walsh that the "one thing I have never done and one thing I hope never will do is try to short-cut any consideration of any bill." [5]

Secondly, in addition to this norm-conforming disincentive to taking the bill off the calendar, the possible outcomes of such a move were not encouraging: a filibuster by Walsh, Tydings, Byrd, and company would have been next to impossible to defeat, but such a desperate effort might not even have been necessary, since it was not at all clear that a majority was ready to support a bill that had aroused the suspicions of those sympathetically interested in, even if not identified with, the Navy and particularly its widely popular Marine Corps. The testimony before the hearings, the public speeches, and the inspired articles, as perceived by the rank and file in Congress through the press or otherwise, had not only created the opinion that "unification will further combat effectiveness and economy." The Navy Department coalition had at first tried to destroy this belief simply by arguing that the case for unification had never been affirmatively proved, but this strategy was abandoned when it found that conversion of an existing opinion was extremely difficult. The Navy resorted consciously or unconsciously, therefore, to what students of mass communications call "side attack," [6] an attempt to redefine the situation by building an additional opinion about the effects of unification that would dominate the average Congressman's calculations in favor of the Navy's point of view without necessarily destroying the beliefs he had already assimilated. Thus, the Navy's high-prestige persuaders—Forrestal, King, Nimitz, Vandergrift—in the friendly forum provided by the Walsh Committee hearings, gave its congressional friends ammunition to build up the additional opinion that the Army's unification plan (even if it would "save money" and increase "combat effectiveness," which the Navy denied) would hurt or destroy the Navy and the Marines and diminish the traditional pattern of civilian control of the military establishment on the secretarial level.

The civilian-control argument does not appear to have been very effective within Congress among the rank and file. The most extreme parts of the War Department's provisions for maximizing military control were given up during the Military Affairs Committee hearings, largely, it appears, because of the personal objections of Senator Edwin Johnson, the temporary acting chairman, while the single-chief-of-staff provision was later abandoned during bargaining within the executive branch as a concession to have the Navy go along with the rest of the unification plan and not because of any groundswell of opposition to it either in Congress, the public, or the press.[7]

The "unification will hurt the Navy and Marines" argument was successfully sold, however, and the widespread good will felt toward the Navy and particularly the Marines, coupled with the apparent general reluctance in Congress to injure unnecessarily any legitimate actor on the American political scene, would, in a showdown, probably have stimulated a voting majority in the Senate to defeat the Thomas-Hill-Austin bill, a belief shared at the time by the majority party leadership.[8] One important indication of the strong pro-Marine sentiment existing in the spring of 1946 was the House Appropriation Committee's action just after Nimitz and Vandegrift had made public their paraphrases of the Series 1478 JCS papers. The Committee gave the Marines money for the full strength they had requested (while cutting all the other services) and went out of its way to praise the Marine Corps highly in its formal report to the House.[9]

Finally, apart from the possibility of a filibuster or defeat, the pay-off value of even the best possible outcome—passage of the bill in the Senate —was not sufficiently great to risk a formal defeat on the floor and the probably freezing of any further action for years. Whatever happened in the Senate, the activation of a pro-War Department majority in the House was extremely unlikely. The House Expenditures Committee, to which most of the unification bills had been referred, had not even held hearings on any of them, and its chairman was against unification.[10] Furthermore, the chairmen of the two other House committees to which bills on military organization had been sent—those on Military and Naval Affairs—had both publicly announced their opposition to unification and had also refused to hold hearings.

In short, during the 1945–46 period the influence pattern within the JCS remained essentially unchanged with the War Department coalition once again able to raise consideration of unification in the form of the

Richardson Committee report and the Navy coalition again able to prevent the adoption of any unification proposal by continuing to withhold its concurrence. But with the war over and interservice harmony during joint combat operations no longer an immediate and overriding concern, the Navy coalition lost its ability to keep the War Department coalition and its allies on the Senate Military Affairs Committee from forcing the issue into Congress for disposition this time on the merits. The two coalitions then proceeded to mobilize extensive staff resources to conduct major direct lobbying and public relations campaigns and, each working through standing congressional allies who in the Senate controlled established "structures of influence" in the Military Affairs and Naval Affairs Committees, managed to instill the following key beliefs in the members of potential voting majorities: "unification" would save money, promote combat effectiveness, give the Army Air Forces its "deserved" independence, and provide the President with necessary assistance in coordinating military matters; the particular unification plans proposed by the War Department coalition would seriously hurt the Navy and the Marines. The result in the Seventy-ninth Congress was therefore a stalemate. The Navy Department coalition and its allies, by drawing on its store of generalized goodwill and popularity among the legislators, could mobilize enough influence to prevent the adoption of any unification proposals that it claimed seriously threatened any of its components. The War Department coalition and its allies, on the other hand, by drawing on the widespread preferences for improved economy and combat effectiveness and on the popularity of its own Air Forces component, and enjoying the support of its Presidential member, could itself mobilize sufficient influence to keep the unification issue alive and prevent the Navy from defeating all aspects of its proposals once and for all.

PATTERNS OF INFLUENCE: 1947

The different outcome of the unification conflict in 1947 was essentially the result of three changes in the previous influence pattern: Forrestal's withdrawal from his active anti-unification position and the consequent creation of a new *ad hoc* coalition between the War Department and the official leaders of the Navy Department in favor of the compromise unification proposals; the merger of the two sets of military committtes in the Eightieth Congress, coupled with transfer of party control to the

Republicans; and the activation of both the majority and minority party leaderships in support of the adoption of some form of unification.

The key change was, of course, Forrestal's withdrawal, which was primarily the result of his determination that continued participation in the conflict was no longer "economical" for the Navy. This withdrawal meant that the "unification will hurt the Navy and Marines" definition of the situation could not easily be maintained in the Eightieth Congress. The most authoritative past purveyors of that definition—Forrestal, Nimitz, and Sherman—now represented that the particular unification plan embodied in the compromise bill "adequately safeguards the morale and autonomy of the Navy and its components, including particularly the Fleet Marine Force and naval aviation." [11] It thus became enormously difficult for any remaining congressional opponents of unification plausibly to claim on their own authority that a grave threat was posed by a proposal that the highly respected official leaders of the Navy testified was innocuous, and the basis for continued widespread opposition to unification was effectively removed.

A second effect of Forrestal's and the official Navy leaders' abandonment of their anti-unification position and support of the compromise bill was that it almost automatically convinced a number of the Navy Department identifiers within Congress to stop opposing unification except for matters of detail, thus thinning the ranks of the intra-legislative anti-unification influentials themselves and decreasing their overall power. As Senator Tydings, who had been one of the leaders of the Senate anti-unifiers in the Seventy-ninth Congress, explained to Admiral Hart when the Admiral appeared and objected to the compromise bill,

We had a bill up here [in the 79th Congress], you will recall, which you and I were not in favor of. And I happen to feel that many of the high officers of the Navy were not in favor of it, and certainly the Secretary of the Navy was not in favor of it. Because it scrambled the departments together and was a very radical step and nobody could assay what its ultimate effects would be.

But after that bill was allowed to die, of its own weight, this unification bill came up, which was an attempt to keep the integrity of the branches and to unify them in fields which they had pretty well explored and unified themselves. That was the burden of Admiral Sherman's testimony: That this was simply writing into the law what experience had pretty well proved was desirable; and that assuming that Naval Aviation was protected and the Marine Corps was protected, the bill represents a step forward.

I believe I almost quote him verbatim: "A step forward." . . . I sat here and thought: "Well, if Admiral Sherman testified to this effect, from his long association with many high-ranking officers, such as yourself and Admiral King and Admiral Nimitz, and many others, the Navy must be reasonably satisfied that with the safeguards thrown in here, the bill is a step forward." [12]

The third major effect of Forrestal's shift was that it deterred the many senior naval officers on active duty who did continue to oppose unification from expressing their views publicly and thus strengthening the position of the remaining die-hard anti-unifiers in Congress. Although opposition at a lower level than the top of the Navy hierarchy would undoubtedly have been discounted at some rate by potential voting majorities, such opposition still would have come from an actor being directly affected by the proposals at issue and thus lent plausibility to an intra-legislative attack on the compromise. Apparently recognizing this, two days after the January 16 compromise agreement was reached, Forrestal sent an official message to all commands telling them that support of the agreement was the official position of the Navy Department and expressing his opinion that the agreement was "deserving of the loyal and wholehearted support of all within the naval service." Forrestal's message concluded with the hope that "study and consideration" would lead all persons to conclude that they too should support the agreement.[13]

Although Forrestal indicated in a number of forums that naval officers were still free to express their personal beliefs before committees of Congress, except with respect to the Marines, the message had the intended effect.* Only after the "clarifying" ALNAV sent out on June 23, explicitly waiving the restrictive provisions of Navy Regulations, did naval officers on active duty feel generally free to express disagreement, and by then the conflict was virtually over and its outcome largely determined. Admiral Bogan explained the situation to the House Expenditures Committee. After telling Representative J. Edgar Chenoweth that high naval officers had opposed the compromise bill all along and now wanted to be heard, the Congressman asked:

Do you know why individuals have not asked to appear?
Admiral BOGAN. Because we were given to understand that this legislation was favored by the high command and it was hoped that we would all support

---

* Forrestal admitted that a policy set down by the Secretary of the Navy "both out of courtesy to Congress and out of a sense of discipline, is generally followed, and I think it is fair to say that most naval officers would endeavor not to be engaged in a controversy on that ground. On the other hand, remember that what I have said may be the general rule, but it is not always true in the Navy, nor is it always true in other departments." 1947 House Hearings, pp. 366–67.

it. Being unable to support it, we had nothing else to do but keep our mouths shut

Mr. CHENOWETH.   Do you feel free now to oppose it?

Admiral BOGAN.   I do now.

Mr. CHENOWETH.   Since when and why?

Admiral BOGAN.   Because we have complete freedom of speech and testimony before any Congressional committee.

Mr. CHENOWETH.   You have always had that; have you not?

Admiral BOGAN.   Yes, sir; but we have not had the opportunity to offer to testify.

Mr. CHENOWETH.   I just do not get that. Do you mean because you have not been asked to appear before a Congressional committee?

Admiral BOGAN.   No, sir; because we were told that it was expected that all members in the service would support the bill. It would be disloyal, under those circumstances, to oppose and I think that is why most of us did not feel justified, to come to members of this committee and request the opportunity. That restriction has been recently waived.[14]

The chief effect of the second change in 1947 from the previous influence pattern—the merger of the military committees and the transfer of party control in the Eightieth Congress to the Republicans—was that the continued opposition to unification by the small group of congressional die-hards was no longer critical. The die-hard opponents, who under the old system and Democratic control could probably have dominated an established "structure of influence" in the Senate Naval Affairs Committee,[15] now spoke only for themselves as individuals, and their ability to define the situation for the other members of the Senate was consequently much less than it would otherwise have been. Both the merger of the committees and the transfer of party control, it should be noted, were the results of events completely external to the unification conflict and might be said to illustrate the continued influence of what Machiavelli long ago called *fortuna* on political affairs.

Finally, the third change in 1947—the activation of the party leaderships in support of unification in the Eightieth Congress—resulted in the bills embodying the compromise proposals being referred to the committee in each house expected to be least hostile to them and also assured other favorable parliamentary rulings on the floor. In anticipation of the referral decision in the House, the Republican leadership acted in a fairly unprecedented move to "pack" the Expenditures Committee with a dominant group likely to be responsive to itself and then later interceded to strengthen the hand of the pro-unification members of the

Committee, who might otherwise not have been able to overcome the remaining unification opponents and report a bill favorably. The Republicans had taken control of Congress for the first time in sixteen years and apparently looked forward to the presidential election the following year, when they could claim credit for having passed a popular measure in an important policy area. As Neustadt has written about the 1947 Republican congressional leadership, "With confidence in the advent of a Republican administration two years hence, most of the gentlemen were in a mood to be responsive and responsible. The war was over . . . , Truman a caretaker, theirs the trust." [16] Under the circumstances, the Democratic leadership could do no less than also support the measure in the interests of building a record for the president of their own party.

Given these three developments in 1947, the influence that could be mobilized by the now truncated Navy coalition to prevent the adoption by Congress of unification legislation generally was drastically reduced, and the outcomes that could still be affected concerned primarily the specific statutory definition of the Secretary of Defense's authority and the kind of protections for naval aviation and the Marines. On the first point, the pro-Navy majority that effectively controlled the Senate Armed Services Committee wrote into the bill language that would more clearly restrict the overall Secretary to the role of general coordinator and dispute-settler envisioned by the Navy and that would, by protecting individual service autonomy, also tend to maximize congressional control over military affairs. Eisenhower's and Royall's unguarded testimony, plus various extreme public and private statements by other members of the War Department coalition coming to its attention, such as General Armstrong's remarks to the Norfolk businessmen, convinced the Armed Services Committee that more explicit statutory specification of the compromise agreement was necessary than Forrestal had been able to obtain in the intra-executive bargaining of the previous fall and winter. Forrestal, it should be pointed out, although "somewhat shaken by the recurring evidence of the Army's intransigence" demonstrated by the Eisenhower-Royall testimony,[17] does not appear to have requested changes in the bill's language, even privately. The active minority of the Senate committee was sufficiently displeased with the Eisenhower-Royall testimony [18] to take the initiative on the matter, although it must be conceded that Eberstadt's recommended changes on the last day of the Senate hearings could be interpreted as representing some of Forrestal's own unexpressed misgivings.

On the question of statutory protections for the Marines and naval aviation, the pleas of General Vandegrift, of the retired naval officers like King and Hart, and of the Marine and Navy satellite interest groups plus the "non-objections" of Nimitz and Sherman were enough, in the context of the Eisenhower-Royall testimony, to get the Senate Committee to give some protection in the form of the single clause. The Committee appears to have been ready to write in the basic parts of the draft executive order—as was later done in the House—but the President's intense feeling that such a move would trespass on his Constitutional authority, together with Forrestal's refusal [19] to claim that such guarantees were necessary, led to a compromise on the single clause, which was at least minimally acceptable to Admiral Nimitz and General Vandegrift, on the one hand, and to the President, on the other. The Senate as a whole then dutifully accepted the Committee version, rejecting attempts by Senators Robertson and McCarthy to amend it on the floor even more to the Navy's advantage.

In the House the active minority of the Expenditures Committee, although having no past record of pro-Navy sympathies, behaved as an *ad hoc* Navy coalition ally, seemingly impelled most of all to maximize congressional control and keep at a minimum the discretionary authority over the military establishment of a President of the opposite party and of a Secretary of Defense who was expected to be the President's man. Since action in this latter direction coincided with the pleas of the Marines for maximum statutory definition of their combat functions, the Committee was glad to oblige and put itself on record as the defender of the popular but beleaguered Corps, the threats to whose existence the Committee was able to expose in part by making public Eisenhower's and Spaatz' 1946 JCS papers and thus use as a justification for its actions. The naval aviators, incidentally, did not have nearly as strong an independent appeal as the Marines. Admiral Sherman, for example, felt forced to remind the Expenditures Committee during the hearings that

There has been a good deal of discussion about the security of the Marine Corps and the future of the Marine Corps under this bill. . . . I think the future of naval aviation and the security of naval aviation under the bill deserve equal attention and equal emphasis. . . .

When you approach that problem [of statutory safeguards], as far as the naval service is concerned, there are those two aspects to it.[20]

But once the precedent was established of writing in some functions, the Committee found little disincentive to be generous to the naval aviators too. The Expenditures Committee then did not oppose the still more detailed protections that were proposed on the floor of the House by Representative Cole and adopted. The War Department coalition was in an extremely weak tactical position at this stage, since the session was running out and any attempts to restore the terms of the original compromise would have to overcome standing committee opposition and probably would have resulted in no action being taken at all. The War Department coalition, finally, was at its weakest in the conference committee, which was dominated by the House congressional control-maximizers and the pro-Navy senators,[21] with the senators after some initial resistance finally agreeing to yield and go along almost completely with the House maximum-protection version in order to save the overall objective of some sort of unification that session. As Senator Saltonstall explained about the incorporation of the service function during the consideration of the conference report on the floor of the Senate, "I do not like this language, not one of the Senate conferees liked it, but it was the best we could get. . . . The necessity of getting unification this year is far ahead, in value, in comparison with the broad general language that is inserted." [22]

Political conflict, as has been pointed out, requires that both potential actors have the capacity to influence the appropriate units of government. In the unification conflict both the War and Navy Department coalitions were able to influence the JCS through their own military leaders' formal membership on that body, but their influence on voting majorities in Congress operated more indirectly. Except for the President's almost inherent ability to keep the unification issue on the legislative agenda, the coalitions had to rely essentially on whatever intra-legislative influence could be developed by standing or *ad hoc* senatorial and House allies whose policy preferences happened to coincide or run parallel to the unification goals of the coalitions. The development of that influence necessitated and was, of course, buttressed by such resources as the coalitions' acknowledged expertness in the subject matter in dispute, the personal and organizational good will and popularity they enjoyed within the legislative body, and their virtually unlimited staffs for preparing detailed alternative proposals and for conducting public relations campaigns calculated to develop at least the illusion of massive public support for each coalition's respective position. One additional important

resource enjoyed only by the Navy coalition was the organizational structure of Congress, which facilitates resistance to changes in the *status quo*.

The total amount of influence that political actors can exert does not
depend only on the quality and size of their own resources, but also on
the suitability of the strategies employed for their use. The unification
conflict is probably atypical in that both coalitions mobilized their extensive resources almost completely and, with one possible exception,
employed the most effective strategies realistically open to them. The
exception concerns the ground-Army component of the War Department
coalition. Whoever else can be said to have won at least a partial
victory in the unification conflict, the ground Army clearly suffered
defeat in that substantially none of its original objectives were achieved.
It is interesting to speculate about what might have been the outcome
if the ground-Army generals had chosen to limit their objectives early
in the conflict, given up then the single-chief-of-staff concept and their
claims for the restriction of the Marine Corps (and possibly persuaded
their Air Forces colleagues to surrender their own claims to the Navy's
land-based aircraft), and formed a coalition with the Navy admirals to
concentrate all their resources on promoting a JCS-dominated overall
military establishment to further their shared goal of maximum military
appropriations. As it was, by attempting to restrict the Navy at the same
time they were trying to change the traditional pattern of civilian control
of the military, the Army generals overextended themselves and forced
a split within the professional military hierarchy on this first major issue
of general military policy in the postwar period. This internal division
among the military men both presaged and set the pattern for future
civil-military relations, in which civilian actors would take advantage of
disagreements among the military and, by picking and choosing which of
the different service positions to ally with, remain free to determine themselves the content of major military policies.[23]

Conflict and Economy

In addition to the existence of two actors with incentives for mutual
opposition and with the capacity to influence the prospective adopting
unit of government, political conflict requires that neither actor have an
overriding disincentive to participating in conflict—a disincentive that
might restrain actual opposing activity even though the incentive and the

capacity both exist. The operation of such a disincentive gives rise to what might be called the "economizing" problem in political conflict.

Engaging in political conflict obviously involves costs. The costs may be stated in terms of the resources—time, money, energy, goodwill—immediately consumed in the process or in terms of the value of the foregone alternative uses to which the resources might have been put at the time of the conflict or at some later date.[24] A rational [25] political actor will consequently engage in a political conflict only so long as the value of the anticipated gains of participation discounted by their improbability exceeds the value of the expected costs discounted by theirs. It should be noted that only in the most unusual cases can the expected gains be equated with the value of an actor's most preferred outcome, for the consequences of political participation are risky, and there are almost always a variety of possible outcomes ranging from complete success—the actor's most preferred alternative being realized—to complete failure—the least preferred outcome being realized. In consciously or unconsciously calculating the "economy" of participation, the actor must in effect discount the value of each outcome by the improbability of its occurrence and then assign some rough average value to the whole complex, or "lottery," of probable outcomes, with similar calculations being made to determine expected costs.[26]

In the 1943–44 period the War Department coalition was not adverse to becoming involved in a conflict over unification within the JCS structure (where it could presumably be kept under control), and the coalition's military leaders just below the highest level were even willing to allow the conflict to spread to Congress for the chance that they might secure a quick decision there in favor of their preferred plan. Similarly, the Navy leaders were prepared to engage in conflict both in the JCS and in Congress in order to frustrate what appeared to them as a tremendously costly outcome in the Army plan's adoption.

The highest political officials—Stimson, Forrestal, and Woodrum—thought, however, that the costs of a public conflict in terms of loss of morale and decrease of interservice cooperation outweighed the gains of any possible quick decision, whatever its content might turn out to be. Since these men effectively controlled all the other potential participants, the overt political conflict was cut off and the dispute reconfined to the executive branch. So convinced had Chairman Woodrum, who himself was in favor of a single department, become of the "dis-economy" of conflict over unification at the time, that when Senators Allan J. Ellender and Lister Hill introduced a unification bill in the Senate on May 29, 1944,[27] Woodrum gave out a press statement expressing the opinion that even consideration of the bill would "deter" the effective prosecution of the war.[28]

In the 1945–46 period the stakes involved in the adoption of the War Department's unification plan remained roughly the same, highly profitable to the Army and extremely costly to the Navy. The costs of engaging in the conflict were, however, much lower than the year before. Once the war was over, combat effectiveness could no longer be directly threatened, and the attention of the high military and their staffs was free for other involvement. The net costs to the War Department of engaging in the conflict were, indeed, almost nonexistent. During the Senate Military Affairs Committee hearings, the Army witnesses testified, they were praised by the press and by the Committee members, and they were conscious of promoting a program desired by their Commander in Chief, the President of the United States.

The costs to the Navy, on the other hand, were considerable. The Navy leaders were branded as obstructionists by much of the public press and by their Army colleagues, but as opposed to the gains of defeating the War Department's proposal, the Navy found it was quite economical to oppose unification completely, at least until the President's special message. The President's message imposed additional costs on the Navy for continued opposition—the displeasure of the Commander in Chief and the violation of any internal predispositions to comply with his wishes. Still, even the consequences of the President's displeasure were not unacceptably costly: the ultimate penalty—dismissal—was not very likely to be applied to the civilian or military leaders of the Navy less than a year after its illustrious victories in the war, particularly if they made some tactical concessions and ceased opposing unification "in principle." Furthermore, many of the high officers were close to or had already reached retirement age, so that to them the threat of dismissal was not particularly impressive.

The considerations that led the President to withdraw his support from parts of the original War Department unification proposals and thus gain concessions in return from the Navy have already been discussed in Part III. However much the President might have preferred the original Army plan, when discounted by the improbability of its adoption, the plan's overall value to him was low. On the other hand, the costs of protracted conflict were high both in terms of the less controversial parts of the proposals also being obstructed and in terms of the expenditure of inherently scarce Presidential time and energy that could be devoted to a wide range of other programs and goals. Consequently, of all the active participants, the President found the conflict uneconomical first, and he took steps to end it in the spring of 1946 by trying to impose a solution intended to be accepted by both the Army and the Navy as a satisfactory compromise. It should be pointed out that throughout the conflict the non-Presidential members of the War Department coalition had little choice but to go along with the President's concessions, since what the President could not get Congress to adopt, the generals by themselves certainly could not. The President's concessions were not sufficient to satisfy the Navy's calculations of economy, and at the adjournment of the Seventy-ninth Congress, the conflict still remained unresolved.

By the beginning of 1947 Forrestal and the leaders of the War Department coalition had agreed to end the unification conflict on the basis of the compromise plan. In the intra-executive bargaining during the fall of 1946, the War Department made substantial concessions in order to prevent continued Navy opposition. Forrestal, on the other hand, conceded very little from his June, 1946, position, which had already accepted a Secretary of Defense with limited authority: The organization set up by the compromise bill was almost exactly the original Eberstadt Plan with the addition of an overall Secretary who did not even have a "department" and who had only a very small staff. The Navy as an entity was to continue "as is," presumably subject only to the coordination of the overall Secretary on matters of key policy—matters which Forrestal had always been in favor of coordinating on the sub-Presidential level. The Secretary of the Navy was expected to continue to appear before Congress to defend the Navy's budget; and as for his being removed from the cabinet, Forrestal regarded it "not as of very great consequence," his view of cabinet meetings being that "not much business is done in meetings." [29] Finally, the compromise agreement guaranteed one of the valued functions of cabinet membership—direct access to the President—both by specific provision and by the inclusion of the Secretary of the Navy in the National Security Council, which Forrestal expected to become the really important policy-making body in foreign and military affairs.

Forrestal did, of course, concede that the service functions be specified only in an executive order, which the President had the authority to change at any time. But this was not a severe cost for him personally, since the concession was in line with his belief that "you can[not], by law, direct the way that organizations run." [30] As he explained it more fully to the Expenditures Committee,

This whole matter of functions . . . of the services comes down to a matter of confidence in the good faith of the Secretary of War, the Secretary of the Navy, of General Eisenhower, of Admiral Nimitz, of General Spaatz of the Air Forces, and of their respective intentions to carry out the letter and spirit of the Executive order as agreed upon between us and approved by the President. I rely greatly on the breadth and vision of these men. If I am wrong in that reliance I do not see how we can have any hope that this or any other bill can be made to work.[31]

Even while the conference committee was meeting to decide between the Senate single-clause protection and the House incorporation of parts of the executive order, Forrestal could say to the acting chairman, Senator Saltonstall, that he regarded the question of statutory definitions "as of little consequence," since his business experience had taught him that "there were few occasions that I could recall where the language of the mortgage had made the bonds good." [32] In short, Forrestal did not think that the extra increment of protection to be gained through statutory guarantees for the unimpaired operation of the Navy and the Marines above that afforded by the political, and more specifically, the appropriations process, justified the costs of reopening the whole conflict with, among other disadvantages, the renewed unpredictability of ultimate outcomes. These outcomes included both the possibility of the loss of the *Navy's* definition of the functions of the Marine Corps and naval aviation and the defeat of the unification bill completely.

There is every reason to believe that by 1947 Forrestal sincerely wanted the establishment of a Secretary of Defense and of the National Security Council and would have considered defeat of the unification bill a serious cost.[33] Relations with the Soviet Union were rapidly deteriorating, and continued conflict could very likely once again begin to have direct consequences for the goal of combat effectiveness in wartime. As Forrestal put it when he was questioned by a member of the Expenditures Committee about the "saving" to be achieved through unification,

The saving in my mind is not in terms of money, and I do not like, in a sense, the word "saving." The reasoned aim for this bill . . . I believe it will provide a medium; I believe it will make it possible for us to get all the disputes behind us; to get behind us the near bitterness of controversy, and get down to the business of what the armed services are for, namely, for the protection of this country; and that is the real saving.[34]*

The only members of the War or Navy Department coalitions who continued in 1947 actively to fight the unification proposals embodied in the compromise bill were the Marines and the naval aviators. Their calculation of the economy of continued conflict was different from Forrestal's. Whereas Forrestal felt responsible for the whole Navy Department and was willing to sacrifice the possibility of certain marginal gains in protection for some of its constituent parts to get a scheme that would leave the Navy generally autonomous in operation, the Marines and the naval aviators placed a higher relative value both on their own specific subunit goals and programs and on the necessity and effectiveness of statutory guarantees to protect them. These military men felt that they had already made substantial concessions and taken considerable risks in agreeing to a Secretary of Defense. They did not share Forrestal's faith in protection through the political process. As General Vandegrift explained to the Expenditures Committee with respect to his own organization,

What I would like to do if possible is to write into the basic law of the land a protection for the Marine Corps, so that the Marine Corps in the future could put its entire effort on trying to do its job in the defense of its country rather than putting a lot of its effort in the job of fighting for its existence.[35]

The naval aviators and the Marines had, in short, retained their distrust of the War Department coalition's intentions much more intact than Forrestal,[36] and they could gain a great deal more reassurance from, and consequently place a much higher value on, achieving symbolic guarantees in the form of statutory specifications of their functions.[37]

* It is an open question whether any prospect of being appointed Secretary of Defense affected Forrestal's 1947 calculations. Until Secretary of War Patterson announced his intention to leave government service in July, it was he and not Forrestal who was commonly regarded as the most likely candidate for the appointment. New York *Times,* July 19, 1947.

The first mention of the appointment in Forrestal's diary is under the date, July 26. Forrestal was at the White House, waiting with the President for the engrossed copy of the unification bill to arrive from Congress: "The President told me he proposed to send my name up as Secretary of Defense, Bob Patterson wouldn't take it. He said he had talked to him about it, but Patterson was so hard put to it for money that he was unable to stay longer in government. I told the President I would have been very happy to serve under Patterson for as long as I could be useful to both of them. The President repeated that Patterson could not be considered for the reason stated." Forrestal Diaries, p. 295.

It should be pointed out that participation in political conflict has pay-offs aside from legal enactments. Any realistic appraisal of the situation in June, 1947, should have convinced the naval aviators that stopping the establishment of a separate air force at that late date was impossible.[38] Yet the naval aviators so advocated, and in the expression of their griev-ances before a congressional committee probably found sufficient emo-tional benefit to justify the costs incurred.*

The President, it should finally be noted, if he had been willing to keep the conflict alive, could obviously have nullified whatever gains were scored by the naval aviators and the Marines by vetoing the final bill, in the hope that a new version could be passed in the next session more to his and to the rest of the War Department coalition's liking. But so weary had everyone concerned with the unification question become by the summer of 1947 that even Secretary of War Patterson and his key mili-tary advisers, despite their intense dissatisfaction with the final outcome, recommended that the President sign the bill anyway and bring the con-flict to a close.[39]

---

* Although the advocacy of so extreme a position made it easier to achieve the more limited goal of statutory definitions of the functions of naval aviation, this does not appear to have been the chief objective of the flying admirals. As it turned out, however, the combined activities of the component elements of the Navy Department coalition constituted the best possible strategy in 1947: while Forrestal's whole-hearted support of the compromise agreement deterred the War Department coalition from reopening the conflict and thus protected the gains that the Navy had already won, the unsanctioned opposition of his subordinates managed to improve the deal even further.

10

Conflict, Unification, and the Policy Process

Whether acting as individuals or in groups, human beings are essentially goal-seeing animals. Their objectives include an almost infinite variety of material, nonmaterial, tangible, ideological, and other types of desired satisfactions. At times the goal-directed activity of human beings goes on unimpeded, but at other times it becomes blocked because of their own limited resources or capacities, because of the interfering actions of other human beings, or because of some combination of both. Under the second set of conditions, the individual or group actors concerned can decide to accept not being able to achieve their goals, or they can try to overcome the obstacles by augmenting their capacities with the services and resources of other actors or by restraining the other actors' interference. The techniques for securing assistance or attempting to impose restraints can be exercised directly against the actors whose resources or activities are relevant, or indirectly through some intermediary person, group, or institution. One extremely valuable intermediary for the purposes of securing the resources of others and of regulating their behavior is government—that complex of positions and interactions that carries in any society the widest and highest degree of authority and that can dispose of the most effective powers of coercion.

Not all actors whose goals are being blocked turn to government for assistance. Unfortunately, the systematic exploration of the general factors that tend to promote or inhibit resort to governmental action for the furtherance of human goals has not advanced very far.[1] In the case of the unification conflict, the War Department coalition's goals could be furthered only by some form of governmental action, and thus there was no choice. Under other circumstances it might be speculated that an actor will not turn to government if he considers political action to be either inexpedient, illegitimate, or inefficacious. That is, despite the government's great financial and other kinds of resources and despite its extensive coercive powers for regulating human behavior, an actor may still find it less difficult to overcome his obstacles through private means, or he may think that despite the expediency of governmental action it is simply not "right" or "proper" for the government to become involved in certain kinds of matters (such as economic regulation sixty years ago and perhaps higher education or free speech today), or he may just not perceive the relevance of any kind of governmental action for the furtherance of his goals. To turn around a statement of Lasswell's on this last point, "Although under some conditions a community which is visited by the plague will demand the resignation of the health commissioner, under other circumstances the community will only pray." [2]

If an actor does decide to propose some course of governmental action in order to advance his goals, that proposal, despite the impression conveyed by the reportorial practices of the mass media and even by the writings of political scientists, will not always generate intense and prolonged conflict over its adoption. The vast majority of bills introduced in each session of Congress, for example—all of which are in form, even if not in intent, proposals for government action—lead to no controversy whatever, and it is only a handful of measures that incite major legislative campaigns with full mobilization of opposing forces and extended debate. Similarly, most proposals for purely executive branch action are disposed of in routine fashion, and only very few provoke extensive conflict before their eventual adoption or rejection. As we have seen in the last chapter, for a political conflict to develop, there must be a second actor who perceives and has incentive to oppose the proposal in question because of conflicting or incompatible goals or differences in perceptions of reality, both the proponent and the opponent of the proposal must have the capacity to influence the relevant unit of government, and neither must find participation in the conflict uneconomical.

General Strategies for Conflict Resolution

Once a political conflict does develop, the overall objective for each actor becomes to resolve it with an outcome as favorable as possible to his own point of view.* Either actor can try to achieve such a favorable resolution by eliminating his opponent's incentive for opposition through changing his goals or perceptions, by rendering his opponent's continued opposition uneconomical through the offer of some benefit in exchange for its cessation or by overcoming that opposition through the threat of inflicting some harm. The general strategies of influence that are implicit in these activities can be called, respectively, "persuasion," "bargaining," and "coercion." [3]

A strategy of persuasion consists of one actor's simply trying to talk the other actor out of the goals or perceptions of reality that give him the incentive to promote or obstruct the proposal that is being disputed. This is the process usually referred to by such terms as conversation, argument, discussion, or debate. The underlying assumption for this strategy is that (1) if the goals affected by a proposal are shared and the conflict is based on differences in perceptions of reality, the exchanges of information between the actors during the course of the discussion will bring about changes in these perceptions and lead to a convergence of expectations about the consequences of the proposal, and (2) if the goals are not shared and the conflict is based on goal conflict or goal incompatibility, the goals of the actors need not be taken as permanently fixed but can be modified in the discussion process. Thus, in the earliest stages of the unification conflict, the War Department coalition concentrated primarily on trying to persuade the Navy leaders in the JCS and elsewhere that they should support the Army plan for unification in the interests of their shared goals of combat effectiveness and economy, asking them implicitly to change their expectations about the unfavorable consequences of a single department for the Navy's budgetary fortunes and to give up the goal of preserving all the World War II functions of the Marines and naval aviation unimpaired.

Probably to the extent (1) that in a conflict based on means-end disagreement the potentially available fund of knowledge about the consequences of a proposal for the shared goals is complete and the goals are themselves concrete or "operational," [4] (2) that in a conflict based on

---

* This discussion applies, of course, only to what Lewis A. Coser has defined as "realistic conflict," which arises "from frustration of specific demands . . . and from estimates of gains of the participants and . . . is a means toward a specific result," and not to "unrealistic conflict," which is "not occasioned by the rival ends of the antagonists, but by the need for tension release by at least one of them . . . and is not oriented toward the attainment of spesific results." *The Functions of Social Conflict* (New York, Free Press, 1956), p. 49.

goal conflict or incompatibility the goals involved are not intensely held by at least one of the actors, and (3) that in either case the personalities of the actors are accommodating and flexible rather than authoritarian and rigid, simple persuasion as a strategy may prove effective and a reconciliation be effected.[5] But in the unification conflict such was not the case with respect to at least the first two conditions.

This analysis should cast some doubt, incidentally, on the unbounded faith frequently placed in discussions and maximum exchanges of information as means of resolving conflict in a wide variety of matters ranging from international politics to marital discord and race relations. The implicit assumption in this outlook is obviously that "better understanding" will always reduce or eliminate incentives for mutual opposition. Although this may be the result when the incentives are in fact based on one or both actors' misunderstanding the nature or the consequences of their opponent's proposals or goals, there are also situations where increasing information and the sharing of expectations not only may not lead to a reconciliation but may actually exacerbate a conflict.[6]

In a political conflict based on intensely held and accurately perceived conflicting or incompatible goals, for example, no amount of additional information can reconcile the logical or empirical incompatibility of those goals, while it can intensify the conflict by demonstrating even further how well founded the original opposition was. Thus, the additional information about the War Department proposals that became available between the time of the Richardson Committee interviews in the summer of 1944 and the Senate Military Affairs Committee hearings in the fall of 1945 to the Navy admirals who had been fighting in the Pacific, made clearer the potential threat of Army-style unification to the Navy's goals and stimulated rather than removed the admirals' opposition. Conversely, the lack of complete information available about the effects of all aspects of the War Department proposals accounts at least in part for the viability of the "antagonistic partnership" between the ground Army and the Army Air Forces, since each remained capable of believing that the single chief of staff could be used ultimately at the expense of the other, whereas fuller data and shared expectations as to who would exploit whom might have driven the partners apart.

When the Navy coalition was found nonpersuasible in the early negotiations, the War Department coalition, to the extent that it supported the Richardson Committee majority's compromise plan in the spring and summer of 1945, shifted to a strategy of bargaining. Bargaining in a conflict situation takes the continued existence of the incentives for mutual opposition for granted and consists essentially of one actor trying to affect the other actor's calculations of economy by offering to confer certain benefits in consideration for modification of the obstructive behavior. In political conflict this very often takes the form of one actor's offering to make concessions in changing or withdrawing from some parts of his original proposals in exchange for the other actor's ceasing to oppose the remainder. The possibility of such exchanges is enhanced, incidentally, when, as in the unification conflict, more than a single proposal is involved in the conflict or when the proposal in effect has various "detachable" or "separable" provisions. The motivation for either actor to enter into the bargain lies presumably in the value of the certainty of the outcome embodied in the bargained compromise exceeding the value of the possibility of achieving a more preferred outcome through continued conflict when discounted both by the possibility of achieving an even less preferred outcome and by the additional costs to be incurred by the conflict's continuation.[7]

After the War Department coalition's attempts at bargaining within the JCS on the basis of the Richardson Committee plan proved ineffectual, the coalition returned in the fall of 1945 to its original unification proposals and changed its strategy primarily to coercion, attempting to aggregate enough influence in Congress to activate voting majorities behind its proposals and thus get them imposed on the Navy regardless of its continued opposition. Even then, however, the War Department coalition could not abandon its attempts at persuasion and bargaining completely, for in political conflict, persuasion, bargaining, and coercion are mutually interdependent strategies.

Normally, the amount of influence necessary to get a proposal adopted or rejected by a high-level unit of government such as Congress will vary in part with the amount of influence mobilized in opposition to it. If an actor held such enormously large influence resources as to be virtually certain that he could dominate the actions of his opponent directly or that he could control the actions of the relevant governmental unit regardless of any opposition, that actor would have no need to persuade or to bargain at all. But in American, and particularly in congressional politics, such a degree of concentration of resources is almost nonexistent. Not even the formal authority of the President over his Secretary of the Navy, for example, was sufficient to enable the former to coerce compliance by the latter. Consequently, the more that one actor can reduce the net incentive behind the other's opposition through persuasion and bargaining, the smaller the influence resources that the latter is likely to mobilize and the smaller the resources necessary to enable the first actor to overcome whatever resistance remains.

Similarly, the greater the resources that one actor believes his opponent capable of mobilizing or the smaller the resources he believes capable of mobilizing himself, the higher becomes the relative value of the certainty of a bargained compromise because of the increasing improbability of his being able to achieve a more preferable outcome through continued conflict. It should be noted in this connection that with the exact amount of influence that any actor can aggregate with his resources being impossible to establish except in the rare case of an actual showdown, the operative factor is each actor's beliefs and expectations about such influence. Consequently, an essential part of bargaining tactics consists of "bluffing," in the sense of overrepresenting one's own influence position while minimizing that of one's opponent.

Thus, in the spring of 1946, when it became clear that with full mobilization of the War Department coalition's resources, the total influence that it could aggregate fell short of that necessary to create congressional voting majorities in support of its original proposals (even as modified in S.2044), the War Department leaders had no choice but to begin to sacrifice important parts of their overall plan in periodic bargains in order to reduce the Navy opposition to still other parts. Forrestal, incidentally, had been predicting to the War Department coalition all along that S.2044 would not pass, the obvious implication being that concessions were in order,[8] but the non-Presidential members of the War Department coalition were insisting until just before the President's intervention in May, 1946, that "the weight of good political opinion" was contrary to Forrestal's view and that "with the proper support" the bill could actually be passed.[9] When, on the other hand, the results of the 1946 congressional elections plus the expected merger of the separate military committees in the Eightieth Congress appeared to be improving the War Department's influence position,[10] the highest echelons of the Navy coalition became more willing to agree to a compromise solution that left out statutory definition of the combatant functions of naval aviation and of the Marines as had previously been insisted upon. In any event, concurrently with the bargaining and the attempts at coercion in the 1946–47 period, the War Department coalition also continued its attempts to reduce Navy coalition resistance by persuasion, eventually convincing Forrestal that the single-Secretary-of-Defense–single-military-budget aspect of unification without the additional features of the earlier proposals would have only a marginal effect on the Navy's existing budgetary relations with Congress.

To sum up, in terms of general strategies, each actor in a political conflict will be seeking through persuasion and bargaining to reduce the other actor's opposition to an amount that can be overcome by the influence resources at his own disposal. The substantive content of the outcome will represent one from among an indeterminable range of possible bargained or persuaded modifications of the disputed proposals on the basis of which such a development can take place. It should be noted that to the extent that the actual bases of cleavage or disagreement in a conflict do not actually become eliminated through persuasion and a total reconciliation is not truly effected, changes in the influence position or other bargaining advantages of either actor can be expected to lead to the conflict's reactivation. Thus, the issue of "unification," or more accurately of "defense reorganization," was not permanently settled in 1947 but has been reopened whenever from time to time new alliances or external events made it appear economical for at least one actor with influence to do so.

The Unification Conflict and the Public Interest

The outcome of a conflict over some proposed governmental course of action does not only affect the goals of the actors immediately involved. It also constitutes public policy. Yet it should be clear that the outcome of the unification conflict, like that of most major policy conflicts in American politics, was not determined primarily through some analytical, problem-solving techniques that consciously discovered an optimum solution for promoting the "public interest." That outcome was determined almost exclusively through bargaining and the exertion of other kinds of influence and probably did not represent the preferred solution of even a single one of the participants. Although there have recently been a small number of studies that recognize the various positive functions of political conflict and of the techniques associated with its resolution,[11] the predominant view still appears to be that conflict essentially represents a pathology of the normal policy process.

One critical factor in any evaluation of conflict as part of the policy process is, of course, one's own conception of the "public interest." The views that are held on this point are numerous, and the discussion has been extensive,[12] so that no attempt can be made to summarize or definitively to resolve that question here. The term "public interest" will be used in the remainder of this discussion simply to refer to any predisposition that is relatively widely shared among the general public favoring some goal or state of affairs relevant to a proposal being disputed.[13] Since the question of the existence and content of any public interest or interests thus becomes an empirical one, the only authoritative way of answering it is by taking a poll of the population involved. This being generally impractical for a political scientist, particularly when trying to reconstruct a situation years after the events, the statements of the "public interest" that follow must be recognized as being to some degree tentative.

There is nevertheless little reason to doubt that in the unification conflict the most widely shared public interests involved were "combat effectiveness" and "economy." Almost anyone who might have been asked was sure to have favored a form of military organization that could provide the military forces necessary to insure national security and carry out other foreign policy objectives effectively and that could do this at the least monetary cost. Another, though somewhat less certain, public interest appears to have been "civilian control of the military," not necessarily in the specific form articulated by the Navy coalition, but more vaguely as the feeling that professional military officers should not have undue influence over national policy.

Any valid negative evaluation of the political conflict that developed over unification must rest on the assumption that there was some optimum organizational structure uniquely calculated to further these public interests, that this structure was in fact being promoted by one of the actors, and that those resisting its adoption and causing the conflict were consequently motivated by narrow selfish interests which they sought to have prevail over the admittedly morally superior interests of the public. In theory, such an optimum organizational structure is discoverable. The process would involve formulating the full range of possible alternative structures for furthering the relevant public interests, anticipating all the consequences of each alternative including the advantages and disadvantages bearing on these interests, and finally choosing the alternative calculated to produce the greatest net balance of advantages.[14]

Something approaching this ideal can occasionally be carried out in practice in certain low-level organizational matters such as assembly-line routines in factories or the flow of paperwork in offices, where the immediate objectives to be furthered are clear and the number and ramifications of alternative approaches fairly limited.[15] But in high-level, large-scale organizational changes like those involved in the unification conflict, such an optimum determination is not possible. The capacities of the human mind and human energy both being limited, all the possible alternatives could never be formulated and considered. Also, overall public interests like "economy" and "combat effectiveness" refer to objectives on a very high level of generality and represent preferences for what are really incredibly complex states of affairs. Consequently, the connection between even those alternatives that might come to mind and these public interests becomes highly problematical, with the full range of advantageous and disadvantageous consequences not susceptible to any easy or exact calculation. Given, therefore, this inherent uncertainty in the effects of the unification proposals for the various public interests, it was almost inevitable that the different actors with their different backgrounds and past experiences would make their calculations differently and become convinced that their own set of proposals was closest to the theoretically optimum one, thus laying one basis for the conflict.

Furthermore, proposals for large-scale organizational change are almost certain to affect goals besides those coinciding with one or more public interests. For one thing, the specialized tasks and other goals of the different parts or branches of a large, complex organization like the military establishment as a whole, which theoretically should have value to the members of those parts or branches only in so far as they contribute to promoting the overall or official objectives of the organization, in fact often become ends in themselves.[16] Thus, the different unification proposals were reacted to not only on the basis of how they were perceived to affect "combat effectiveness," "economy," and "civilian control," but also on the basis of their consequences for the more narrowly held, or "private," interests in "adequate ground troops," "a strong Navy," "a separate air force," "the special presidential stakes," etc. But because these private interests referred to much more highly concrete states of affairs than did the pertinent public interests, the prospective benefits or harms of the proposals upon them were more highly visible and therefore easier to calculate, making it again almost inevitable that the different actors should hinge their unification positions chiefly on the advancement or protection of these narrower objectives. Since these objectives were precisely the ones that were to a large extent mutually exclusive or incompatible, a second basis for the conflict was provided.

Ironically, the fact that none of the actors within the two coalitions did feel that he was behaving selfishly and that each sincerely did believe that his own organizational goals were vital to the advancement of one or more public interests not only did not moderate the conflict, but also probably helped to intensify it. This it did by stimulating each side to perceive its opponents not merely as annoyingly (but in any event understandably) protecting their own legitimate interests but as almost immorally and perversely frustrating objectives of unquestionable overriding value. As Simmel has written of social conflict in general,

The parties' consciousness of being mere representatives of supra-individual claims, of fighting not for themselves but only for a cause, can give the conflict . . . radicalism and mercilessness. . . . The violence of the fight . . . has become more pointed . . . owing to the consciousness of the individual that he fights not only for himself, . . . but for a great super-personal aim.[17]

It should be recalled at this point, incidentally, that not all aspects of the unification proposals did, in fact, cause conflict. For example, neither the principle of unified command in the field, the retention of at least the amount of interservice coordination represented by the JCS, nor the establishment of the National Security Council was ever seriously controverted. All these features were clearly more conducive to combat effectiveness than any proposed alternatives, while at the same time they did not affect adversely and differentially the private interests of any of the actors.

In short, the intense conflict over military unification was far from being some sort of pathological result of certain political actors squabbling selfishly to promote their own private interests at the expense of the interests of the public. It represented, instead, an almost inherent part of the normal process of policy-making on a complex, highly charged, and widely ramifying subject like organization for national security, where the different actors being affected by the unification proposals held multiple goals—some of which were shared but some of which because of their different backgrounds and responsibilities were conflicting or incompatible—where the exact consequences of the alternative proposals for many of these goals were intrinsically unknowable and therefore subject to honest disagreement but where the outcome would nevertheless crucially affect the relative ability of the different actors to influence the process through which all future military policy was to be made.

Later Conflicts over Defense Organization

Similar considerations account for the less extensive conflicts that were to occur over defense organization in 1949, 1953, and 1958. In 1949 the dispute was largely over two issues: (1) the extent to which the Secretary of Defense's formal authority and staff assistance were to be increased while still preserving the integrity and operational autonomy of the different military departments and services and (2) the scope of authority of a new chairman that was to be added to the JCS. The outcome, as represented by the passage of the National Security Act Amendments of 1949,[18] changed the National Military Establishment into a regular executive Department of Defense, removed the word "general" from the Defense Secretary's various grants of authority, thus leaving him with full "direction, authority, and control over the Department of Defense," removed the clause specifying that the "powers and duties not specifically conferred upon the Secretary of Defense" were retained by the service secretaries, removed the service secretaries from membership on the National Security Council, added a Deputy Secretary and three Assistant Secretaries of Defense (one of the latter to be Comptroller and function as the Department's chief budget officer) to the Office of the Secretary of Defense, added new protective provisions requiring that the service departments be "separately administered" by their respective secretaries and explicitly forbidding that any of the major combatant functions specified in the National Security Act of 1947 be "transferred, reassigned, abolished, or consolidated," added a Chairman to the JCS to act as presiding officer, provide the agenda, and inform the Secretary of the issues on which agreement by the JCS could not be reached (after rejecting proposals for the establishment of a single chief of staff or for the designation of the Chairman to be the "principal military adviser" to the Secretary and the President with precedence over all other military personnel), increased the size of the JCS's Joint Staff from 100 to 210, and added a new protective clause explicitly allowing any service secretary or member of the JCS to present to Congress "on his own initiative, after first informing the Secretary of Defense, any recommendation relating to the Department of Defense that he may deem proper."

The dispute in 1953 was over changes in and additions to the Office of the Secretary of Defense and over the extent of the increase in the authority of the Chairman of the JCS. The outcome, as represented by the taking effect of Reorganization Plan Number 6 of 1953,[19] abolished such joint agencies within the Office of the Secretary of Defense as the Munitions Board and the Research and Development Board with their built-in service representation and replaced them with six additional Assistant Secretaries of Defense and a General Counsel of equivalent rank, transferred from the JCS collectively to the Chairman the responsibility for the organization and management of the Joint Staff, and made the selection and tenure of the Joint Staff's Director and members subject to the Chairman's approval.

In 1958 conflict was essentially over four proposals for further change in the defense structure: (1) the extent of the elimination of any remaining statutory limitations on the Defense Secretary's formal authority or of any other statutory provisions protecting individual service autonomy, (2) the granting of formal authority over the service departments to the various Assistant Secretaries of Defense, (3) the raising of the limit on the size of the Joint Staff to permit the establishment therein of an "operational section" and the institution of a new chain of command directly from the JCS and its Joint Staff to the field commanders that would eliminate the World War II "executive agency" arrangement and thus exclude the military departments and their service staffs from direction and control of military operations, and (4) another increase in the authority of the JCS Chairman. The outcome, as represented by the passage of the Defense Reorganization Act of 1958,[20] changed the 1949 requirement that the service departments be "separately administered" by their respective secretaries to that they simply be "separately organized," allowed the Assistant Secretaries of Defense to issue orders to the service departments if the former were explicitly delegated such authority by the Secretary of Defense and the orders were issued "through the Secretary of such military department or his designee" (also reducing in the process the number of Assistant Secretaries by one), and eliminated the 1949 absolute prohibition against transfers, reassignments, abolitions, or consolidations of the services' statutory combatant functions, permitting unlimited temporary changes during hostilities or a Presidential finding of imminent threat of hostilities but restricting permanent changes to those that were not disapproved by a simple majority of either house of Congress within a limit of seventy days after their submission to the two Armed Services Committees. It also increased the limit on the size of the Joint Staff to 400 and made the other changes necessary for the institution of the new chain of command, denied the full extent of the increased authority requested for the Chairman of the JCS, even decreasing it in some respects by requiring that his selection of the Director of the Joint Staff be "in consultation" with and that his management of the Joint Staff be "on behalf" of the full JCS and by specifying that all the Chiefs retained the right to assign duties to the Staff, and retained the right of the service secretaries and members of the JCS on their own initiative to make recommendations to Congress.

As in the 1943–47 unification conflict, in each of these later disputes the connections between the controverted proposals and the public interests asserted—combat effectiveness, economy, efficiency, civilian control, etc.—were much more uncertain than the connections between the proposals and many of the same private interests that had been involved in the original conflict plus such newly developed ones as those of the Secretary of Defense (and the multiplicity of deputy secretaries, assistant secretaries, assistant deputy secretaries, and deputy assistant secretaries in his immediate office) and of the Chairman of the JCS in increasing their own formal authority and effective influence over the separate military departments, the different services, and the individual Joint Chiefs. Although the rhetoric of the proponents of change each time was phrased largely in terms of increased "economy" and "efficiency" through the "reduction of interservice rivalries" and the "elimination of unnecessary duplication," sizable costless economies as a result of the organizational changes themselves (as distinguished from certain improved management practices) proved on each occasion to be as unattainable as after the passage of the original National Secretary Act. Furthermore, the integration of the different services' policies and operations that accompanied increased unification not only failed to accomplish its purported purpose of decreasing active interservice rivalry but actually served to augment it. As Huntington has pointed out,

> Interservice competition was not so much the cause of decentralization, duplication, and increased expenditures as it was the result of the desire to eliminate these supposed evils. More harmony among the services could be

brought at the price of disunity, duplication, higher costs. . . . [T]he less unification there was, the greater was the freedom of the services to go their own way, the less fear they had of control by a central organ dominated by a hostile service, and hence the less likelihood there was of serious interservice rivalry. In comparable fashion, duplicating ambitions were a cause of interservice rivalry; duplicating programs and functions were a means of reducing that rivalry. . . .

What people identified as the consequences of interservice competition were really the alternatives to it. Interservice competition became a ubiquitous, inherent, and permanent feature of the defense establishment simply because it would cost too much to eliminate it.[21]

Similarly, under a single military budget and in the face of the unrealistically low ceilings imposed on total military appropriations (except for the Korean War period) during the years between 1947 and 1960, each service was virtually forced to attack the validity of its sister services' shares of the budget in order to have a chance of increasing its own and still remain within Presidential and Defense Department policy.

In short, with a few possible exceptions, such as the streamlining of the military chain of command in 1958 through the elimination of extra administrative layers and echelons, the real, continuing, and underlying differences over defense organization have not predominantly concerned technical proposals for advancing in any clear and direct way consensual goals like "combat effectiveness," "economy," "efficiency," or "interservice harmony." They have instead involved the critical issue of how influence over the various types of key strategic, operational, and administrative (particularly weapons development and procurement) decision-making within the military establishment is to be distributed among its various officials and echelons. Although the actual distribution of such influence undoubtedly affects the quality of the decision-making process and ultimately the ability to achieve all these consensual goals, the optimal pattern is no more subject to exact determination (even with the Pentagon's latest high-speed computers) than was the solution to the original unification conflict. It depends essentially on the relative value to be placed on such objectives as, on the one hand, centralized direction and uniformity of practice [22] throughout the military establishment, the restriction of disagreements to relatively low administrative levels, and the exercise of predominant control over key decisions by individuals with the kinds of backgrounds and perspectives likely to be recruited into the Office of the Secretary of Defense, the JCS chairmanship, or some proposed single Chief of Staff and such different objectives as, on the other hand, diversity of practice, the preservation of important disagreements for consideration at higher levels, and a greater dispersion of influence and decision-making among those with the kinds of backgrounds and perspectives found in the civilian and military leaders of the individual military departments and services and the individual members of the Joint Chiefs. Individual stands on how these questions should be resolved will also generally be colored by anticipations of what specific substantive views the particular officials who will hold the different positions are likely to take on such major matters as the kinds of military contingencies to plan for and the kinds of military capabilities and weapons-systems to maintain; they will also be colored by various kinds of past experience that cause different actors almost automatically to perceive certain threats as inherent in some recurrent proposals like, for example, the single chief of staff.

Whatever the actual merits of these organizational issues, the trend in defense structure has been steady and unmistakable: The "National Military Establishment" set up in 1947 consisted of three almost completely autonomous military departments and services, whose military chiefs constituted the top planning and command body and used their individual service staffs to direct the various field commands, and all of which were under the loose control of a Secretary of Defense conceived of as a top policy-maker with only "general" authority and with a staff not to exceed four "special assistants" and a few dozen other top administrative personnel in his immediate office. From this pattern there has evolved a full executive Department of Defense in which the military departments and their service staffs have lost substantially all their strategic planning and operational functions and exist almost exclusively to recruit and train personnel and to develop and supply equipment for the various field commands into which have been organized virtually all of the country's combat forces and which are directly subordinate in operational matters to the JCS and its "trans-service" Joint Staff. Furthermore, units like the Defense Supply Agency, the Defense Intelligence Agency, and the Defense Communications Agency have been established as part of the Office of the Secretary of Defense to perform even certain support functions previously in the hands of the individual military departments and services. Finally, the Secretary of Defense has managed to accumulate virtually unlimited formal authority over all parts of his department and increasingly tries to exercise detailed administrative control with an office of some fifteen persons with the rank of Assistant Secretary or higher, close to 4,000 other administrative personnel, and with a Chairman of the JCS, who even if not yet clothed with the formal authority of a single Chief of Staff, has turned into "a sort of party whip, charged with conveying the official line to the [other] chiefs in the hope and expectation that they will be guided thereby in their actions." [23]

Hopefully, the key civilian and military positions in the Defense Department will hereafter always be filled by persons who recognize the indeterminate and "multiple contingency" nature of the future and who will therefore, on their own, seek alternative advice and maintain multiple and varied military capabilities, despite the increasing inability of the different services (or other subordinate components within the defense structure) successfully to provide such advice or to fight for particular capabilities against opposition at the highest level. Hopefully, also, the top civilian position will always be filled by individuals with the extraordinary high intellectual capacity and level of energy necessary to coordinate personally the vast array of service secretaries, assistant defense secretaries, defense-wide support agencies, military chiefs, and unified commands now directly responsible to the Secretary of Defense. Apart from the damper that its excessive layering and its requirements for multiple clearances, reviewing, and re-reviewing probably already impose on the innovation of new weapons and ideas, were a structure with the present degree of concentration of power to be captured by persons like some of the more extreme World War II Army Air Forces generals, who were certain that they could predict the future and could therefore scrap the regular Army and the Navy and maintain only a single military capability in the form of the large manned bomber for strategic warfare to meet the single-contingency future they incorrectly anticipated, or were the position of Secretary of Defense again to be filled by individuals as passive and as uninterested in politico-strategic matters as some of its past occupants, the consequences for the nation might be catastrophic and this time irreversible.[24]

The Functions of Political Conflict

Even if one accepts the argument about the near-inevitability of disagreements over unification, defense organization, or indeed any other kind of high-level policy proposals with widespread ramifications, can anything be said in conclusion about an overall political system such as our own, whose decentralization of authority and dispersion of political resources facilitates or even encourages the conversion of those disagreements into active conflict? If the unification conflict is at all typical, policy-making in this kind of system does appear, first of all, to discriminate against what might be called the "anti-public interest" proposal, for, however difficult it may be to determine the best of a number of competing proposals each of which tends to promote one or more public interests, some proposals can be seen as quite clearly working against all such interests.[25]

A policy formulated and adopted without the opposition associated with conflict depends exclusively on the personal values of the individuals that constitute the adopting unit of government for not promoting the private interests of the few at the expense of the many. But when a proposed policy consisting of some complex set of proposals like those included in the unification package becomes a basis for active conflict, it attracts wider attention, thus increasing the number of actors involved, and provides all of them with incentive to look for and to make visible any "anti-public" features involved in order to generally discredit their opponents. This is so even when as a matter of personal preference, any particular actor might actually favor those features himself. Thus, with the exception of Forrestal and the few other civilian members in the Navy Department secretariat, none of the executive branch participants in the unification conflict seemed to be inherently opposed to changing the traditional pre-World War II practice by institutionalizing a military group like the JCS with predominant influence over the military budget and strategic policy and subordinated to no civilian in the executive branch but the already overburdened President. As has been explained in Part II, however, the tactical advantage presented by taking the "civilian control" position in the overall conflict led at least in part to even the admirals opposing that aspect of the proposals, raising its visibility, and thus insuring its eventual defeat.

Still, high-level policy-making does not normally involve conflict over proposals that seek simply to injure a public interest. Most major policy conflicts in American politics appear to involve alternative proposals, all of which have some plausible, even if vague, tendency to promote one or more public interests but at the same time also affect a variety of private interests and affect these latter interests differentially. The public interests affected may incidentally themselves be incompatible, as, for example, in determining the proper level of defense spending, where adding incremental gains to the public interest in combat effectiveness will be at the expense of incremental costs to the presumed public interest in lower taxes. The overwhelming majority of conflicts really involve, in short, disputes over which one of a number of marginally different proposals tending to promote and to injure some particular combinations or "mixes" of public and private interests should be adopted as public policy.[26] On this question there is almost never an overall public interest in the sense of there being some widespread predisposition among the general public in exactly how the balance should be formulated.

The chief benefit of having these "mixes" determined through bargaining and the other kinds of play of influence associated with our pluralistic political system is, as the authors of the *Federalist Papers* correctly predicted, its built-in tendency to produce nonoppressive policies. Given the relatively large number of officials whose concurrence is necessary for the formal adoption of most kinds of major policy, it is highly probable that any actor being adversely affected will be able to exert some degree of influence on at least one of them, thus giving him the capacity to obstruct the rapid adoption of the proposed policy and providing an incentive to its proponents to devise a compromise in which the public interests will be furthered at the least cost to any legitimate private interests also involved.

Thus, whatever their other merits or demerits, the total War Department unification package was clearly oppressive to the Navy in so far as it impinged on naval aviation and on the Marines and upset the Navy's favorable budgetary relations with Congress. As a result of the system allowing the Navy to resist and cause conflict, a solution was finally formulated which was not obviously less efficacious in promoting the public interests of economy and combat effectiveness but which was however much less oppressive to the Navy's private interests.* This is an example of what appears to be the general tendency of the American political system, particularly in the congressional arena, to discriminate

* The British Navy, too, had opposed the divestment of its naval aviation and its incorporation into the Royal Air Force after World War I. But the concentration of influence in the Cabinet and the lack of autonomous centers of countervailing power in the legislature to which they could appeal precluded the Navy leaders from being able to block that oppressive and, as it turned out, costly policy.

against any highly certain sacrifice of a legitimate private interest for some postulated, but uncertain and incremental advantage to a general public interest.

This tendency may be especially useful when the private interests involved are themselves related to the public interests in an instrumental fashion. As a result only in part of hindsight, the value of the unimpaired capabiilties of the Navy (as well as of a sizable ground Army) for dealing in the post-1947 period with limited war and other military exigencies, such as in Korea, Lebanon, the Taiwan Straits, and Viet Nam, that could not be handled by the big manned-bombers or even the land-based missiles of the separate Air Force has now been widely recognized. But there is great doubt whether a Navy with its existing capabilities in carrier operations and missile-launching submarines and Marine strength (or of a sizable ground Army) could have survived had not the unification conflict prevented the original War Department proposals from being adopted.[27]

This does not mean, unfortunately, that the development of public policy through conflict, even if it does tend to discriminate against "anti-public" and oppressive proposals, necessarily produces the most correct solutions as judged by later events.[28] As in any kind of policy-making process, events may occur that none of the participants correctly anticipated, or the most nearly correct solution may have been held by someone without even the minimal influence necessary to affect the relevant unit of government. Furthermore, in policies developed as a result of conflict, so many concessions may have to be made in order to protect private interests and reduce opposition, that it can become questionable in the end whether the policy actually adopted makes any advance at all toward the promotion or protection of the public interests postulated.[29] Later events in Korea and elsewhere, for example, were strongly to suggest that retention of the tactical air force within the ground Army would have been the best means of providing ground troops with the amount of close air support and air transport needed for effective combat operations. But those in the Army that preferred that solution were largely without influence, and the recommendations of the admirals to this effect were dismissed as devious, self-serving pleading, with the admirals choosing to reserve the exertion of the bulk of their influence for the protection of interests closer to home. Similarly, the insertion of the word "general" before the Secretary of Defense's various grants of authority in order to furnish additional protection for service autonomy, instead of clearly delimiting the kinds of matters over which the Secretary's authority was to lie and within this scope making it complete,[30] should have been seen as making the Secretary's position untenable, was found in practice to do so, and had to be eliminated in 1949.

A number of points can, however, be made in extenuation. There is no good reason to believe that any particular single actor who might be given dominant control over either the general policy-making process or the policy-making process within the military establishment could anticipate the future better than the larger number who become involved in a more pluralistic, conflict-producing system, nor is there any guarantee that the same actor would conceive of the most correct solution in every respect. Given the ability to affect the formulation of public policy that the present system gives to a variety of actors, strong incentives are provided for a larger number of possible solutions to become devised and presented to the relevant governmental officials than would otherwise be the case. This increases the range available for consideration and makes at least theoretically possible the adoption of the best features of each. As Aristotle put it some 2500 years ago in one of the earliest defenses of pluralistic policy-making, "This is the reason why the Many are also better judges . . .; some appreciate one part, some another, and all together appreciate all." [31] The more basic answer is that despite the dispersion of influence resources in the American political system, by far the greatest concentration is still held by the various elected public officials who constitute the governmental institutions with the highest authority. In the last analysis the formulation and adoption of governmental policies with the proper combination of responsiveness to public interests, non-oppressiveness to private interests, and correctness as judged by later events will depend not nearly so much on the form of the policy-making process as on the wisdom, the courage, and the good judgment of the individual officials whom the American public chooses to operate it.

Notes

Short Forms for Works Frequently Cited

Clifford Files—Personal papers on unification of Clark Clifford.

Eberstadt Report—*Unification of the War and Navy Departments and Post-war Organization for National Security, Report to Hon. James Forrestal, Secretary of the Navy,* Senate Committee on Naval Affairs, 79th Cong., 1st Sess. (1945).

Forrestal Diaries—James Forrestal, *Diaries,* ed. by Walter Millis with the collaboration of E. S. Duffield (New York, Viking, 1951).

1944 Hearings—U.S. House of Representatives, *Proposal to Establish a Single Department of Armed Forces,* Hearings before the Select Committee on Post-war Military Policy, 78th Cong., 2d Sess. (1944).

1945 Hearings—*Department of Armed Forces, Department of Military Security,* Hearings on S.84 and S.1482 before the Senate Committee on Military Affairs, 79th Cong., 1st Sess. (1945).

1946 Hearings—*Unification of the Armed Forces,* Hearings before the Senate Committee on Naval Affairs on S.2044, 79th Cong., 2d Sess. (1946).

1947 House Hearings—*National Security Act,* Hearings before the House Committee on Expenditures in the Executive Departments on H.R. 2319, 80th Cong., 1st Sess. (1947).

1947 Senate Hearings—*National Defense Establishment,* Hearings before the Senate Armed Services Committee on S.758, 80th Cong., 1st Sess. (1947).

Norstad Files—Personal papers on unification of General Lauris Norstad.

Chapter 1. The Origins of Unification

1. 1 Stat. 49.

2. Harold H. Sprout and Margaret T. Sprout, *The Rise of American Naval Power, 1776–1918* (Princeton, Princeton University Press, 1942), p. 15.

3. 1 Stat. 350.

4. Martin Smelser, *The Congress Founds the Navy, 1787–1798* (Notre Dame, Ind., University of Notre Dame Press, 1959), pp. 150–58.

5. 1 Stat. 553; Smelser, *Congress Founds the Navy,* pp. 150–58.

6. *Ibid.;* Sprout and Sprout, *American Naval Power,* p. 39.

7. For a complete account, see Lawrence J. Legere, Jr., *Unification of the Armed Forces* (Washington, D.C., Office of the Chief of Military History, n.d.), Chap. 1 (mimeographed)

8. Recounted by Daniels in 1944 Hearings, p. 246.

9. Howard K. Beale, ed., *Diary of Gideon Welles* (New York, Norton, 1960), 1, 69.

10. Legere, *Unification,* Chap. 1.

11. Quoted in R. A. Alger, *The Spanish-American War* (New York, Harper, 1901), p. 234.

12. *Ibid.,* pp. 241–44.

13. Quoted in Legere, *Unification,* p. 20.

14. See Louis Morton, "Interservice Co-operation and Political-Military Collaboration," in Harry L. Coles, ed., *Total War and Cold War: Problems in Civilian Control of the Military* (Columbus, Ohio State University Press, 1962), pp. 132–37.

15. *Ibid.*   16. Legere, *Unification,* p. 21.

17. One important question that it dealt with at length was the kind of naval base to build in the Philippines. See William R. Braisted, "The Philippine Naval Base Problem, 1898–1909," *Mississippi Valley Historical Review,* XLI (June, 1954), pp. 21–40.

18. Legere, *Unification,* pp. 21–22.

19. S. J. Res. 191, 66th Cong., 2d Sess. (1920); this resolution as well as many other documents concerning administrative reorganization are reprinted in W. Brooke Graves, *Basic Information on the Reorganization of the Executive Branch, 1912–1948* (Washington, D.C., 1949).

20. S. J. Res. 30, 67th Cong., 1st Sess. (1921).

21. S. Doc. No. 302, 67th Cong., 4th Sess. (1922).

22. See Hearings before the Joint Committee on the Reorganization of the Executive Branch on S. J. Res. 282, 68th Cong., 1st Sess. (1924).

23. S. Doc. No. 128 and H. Doc. No. 356, 68th Cong., 1st Sess. (1924).

24. U.S. Dept. of the Air Force, Office of Air Force History, *The Army Air Forces in World War II.* Vol. I: *Plans and Early Operations, January 1939 to August 1942,* ed. by Wesley Frank Craven and James Lea Cate (Chicago, University of Chicago Press, 1948), Chap. I.

25. See *Department of Aeronautics,* Hearings before a Subcommittee of the Senate Committee on Military Affairs on S.80, 65th Cong., 1st Sess. (1917).

26. See *Reorganization of the Army,* Hearings before the Subcommittee of the Senate Committee on Military Affairs on S.2691, S.2693, and S.2715, 66th Cong., 1st and 2d Sess. (1919).

27. *United Air Service,* Hearings before a Subcommittee of the House Military Affairs Committee, 66th Cong., 2d Sess. (1919–20), p. 422.

28. H. Res. 192, 68th Cong., 1st Sess. (1925).

29. See *Inquiry into Operations of the U.S. Air Services,* Hearings before

the Select Committee of Inquiry into Operations of the U.S. Air Services on Matters Relating to the Operations of the U.S. Air Services, House of Representatives, 68th Cong., 1st Sess., (1925).

30. H. Rept. No. 1653, 68th Cong., 2d Sess. (1924).

31. Quoted in Isaac Don Levine, *Mitchell: Pioneer of Air Power* (New York, Duell, Sloan and Pearce, 1943), p. 327.

32. *Ibid.*

33. See *Aircraft,* Hearings before the President's Aircraft Board (Washington, D.C., 1925).

34. *Aircraft in National Defense,* S. Doc. No. 18, 69th Cong., 1st Sess. (1925).

35. See Legere, *Unification,* p. 127.

36. See *Department of Defense and Unification of Air Service,* Hearings before the House Committee on Military Affairs, 69th Cong., 1st Sess. (1926).

37. *Ibid.,* p. 840.   38. *Congressional Record,* LXVII (1926), 8762.

39. 44 Stat. 780 (1926). For a fuller account of the post-World War I unification movement, see Legere, *Unification,* Chaps. II and III.

40. MacArthur's letter is printed in *Department of National Defense,* Hearings on H.R.4742 and H.R.7012 before the House Committee on Expenditures in the Executive Departments, 72d Cong., 1st Sess. (1932), pp. 248–50.

41. *Ibid.*

42. H.R.11597; H. Rept. No. 1126, 72nd Cong., 1st Sess. (1932).

43. H.R.11267.   44. *Congressional Record,* LXXV (1932), 9339.

45. R. Earl McClendon, *The Question of Autonomy for the United States Air Arm, 1907–1945* (Maxwell Air Force Base, Ala., 1950), pp. 139, 172, 194–97; U.S. Air Force, *Army Air Forces in World War II,* I, 30, 67.

46. McClendon, *Question of Autonomy,* p. 139.   47. *Ibid.,* p. 169.

48. *Ibid.,* p. 191.   49. Morton, in Coles, ed., *Total War,* pp. 137–38.

50. Ray S. Cline, *Washington Command Post: The Operations Division* (Washington, D.C., U.S. Dept. of the Army, Office of the Chief of Military History, 1951), pp. 44–45.

51. See Louis Morton, "Germany First: The Basic Concept of Allied Strategy in World War II," in U.S. Dept. of the Army, Office of the Chief of Military History, *Command Decisions,* ed. by Kent Roberts Greenfield (New York, Harcourt, Brace, 1959), Chap. 1.

52. For a fuller account of the activities of the Joint Board, see Legere, *Unification,* pp. 71–86, 142–62, 206–22.

53. *Federal Register,* IV (July 7, 1939), 2786.

54. Legere, *Unification,* pp. 207–09.

55. See Robert E. Sherwood, *Roosevelt and Hopkins: An Intimate History* (New York, Harper, 1948), Chap. XX.

56. Hastings Lionel Ismay, *Memoirs of General Lord Ismay* (New York, Viking, 1960), pp. 51–52. Ismay was Churchill's personal representative on the Chiefs of Staff Committee throughout World War II and gives a good account of its origins and operation.

57. William D. Leahy, *I Was There: The Personal Story of the Chief of*

Staff to Presidents Roosevelt and Truman (New York, McGraw-Hill, 1950), pp. 125–26.

58. *Ibid.*, p. 120. Leahy had been Chief of Naval Operations from 1937 until he retired in 1939 and more recently had been ambassador to the Vichy government of France.

59. See Cline, *Washington Command Post,* pp. 166–69.

60. Eberstadt Report, pp. 60–62.

61. William Frye, *Marshall, Citizen Soldier* (New York, Bobbs-Merrill, 1947), p. 325; see also King's testimony in 1945 Hearings, p. 140.

62. 1945 Hearings, p. 142.

63. Eberstadt Report, p. 60; Leahy, *I Was There,* p. 126.

64. Eberstadt Report, p. 78.

65. *Ibid.,* pp. 65, 68; Cline, *Washington Command Post,* p. 235.

66. Eberstadt Report, p. 61; see also Maurice Matloff, "Franklin Delano Roosevelt as War Leader," in Coles, ed., *Total War,* pp. 42–45.

67. See Sherwood, *Roosevelt and Hopkins,* pp. 446, 580–614, 758–808.

68. Captain T. B. Kittredge of the Historical Section of the JCS, quoted in *ibid.,* p. 948. See also the account of the relations between Roosevelt and his Joint Chiefs by William R. Emerson, "F.D.R.," in May, ed., *Ultimate Decision,* pp. 133–78. Emerson stresses the degree to which Roosevelt did act against the advice of his military chiefs before Pearl Harbor and in the first year of the war and argues that only the appointment of Leahy, who brought the thinking of the military in closer harmony with the President's, averted a "crisis" between the President and his military advisers.

69. Eberstadt Report, p. 75.   70. 1945 Hearings, p. 521.

Chapter 2. The Proposals Are Presented

1. Lawrence J. Legere, Jr., *Unification of the Armed Forces* (Washington, D.C., Office of the Chief of Military History, n.d.), p. 275 (mimeographed).

2. *Ibid.,* pp. 221–26.   3. *Ibid.,* pp. 276–77.

4. Appendix to JCS 560; quoted in *ibid.,* p. 276.   5. *Ibid.,* p. 277.

6. The report of the Joint Strategic Survey Committee is reprinted in 1945 Hearings, pp. 465–70.

7. *Ibid.*

8. Legere, *Unification,* pp. 279–82; the JCS directive to the Richardson Committee is reprinted in 1944 Hearings, pp. 142–44.

9. Wadsworth had headed the 1919 Senate Military Affairs Committee hearings on War Department reorganization, universal military training, and a separate air force. Wadsworth was defeated for reelection to the Senate in 1926 but was returned to Congress in 1933 as a member of the House.

10. H. Res. 465, 78th Cong., 2d Sess. (1944).

11. New York *Times,* March 16, 1944.

12. H. Rept. No. 1286; *Congressional Record,* XC (1944), 3207; New York *Times,* March 16, 1944.

13. 1944 Hearings, p. 2. 14. *Ibid.,* pp. 2–3. 15. *Ibid.,* p. 30.

16. Stimson, *ibid.,* p. 31; see also the statements of Under Secretary of War Robert P. Patterson, *ibid.,* pp. 78 ff.; and General Brehon B. Somervell, *ibid.,* pp. 96 ff.

17. Henry L. Stimson and McGeorge Bundy, *On Active Service in Peace and War* (New York, Harper, 1947), p. 507; Stimson Diary, April 17, 18, Yale University Library.

18. *Ibid.*

19. 1944 Hearings, p. 35; McNarney's statement begins on p. 33.

20. *Ibid.,* p. 36. 21. *Ibid.,* pp. 33–37. 22. *Ibid.,* p. 37.

23. *Ibid.,* p. 42. 24. *Ibid.,* p. 43. 25. *Ibid.,* pp. 65, 67–68.

26. *Ibid.,* p. 68.

27. *Ibid.,* p. 124. Knox had had a heart attack a few days earlier and died hours after Forrestal's testimony before the Committee. It should be noted that however favorable Knox might have been toward unification "in principle," that would not necessarily have determined his position on a specific plan like General McNarney's. Representative Woodrum explained during the hearings that Knox had told him he was in favor of the "overall idea of consolidation," providing it would not "in any way impair the [naval] service." *Ibid.,* p. 227.

28. *Ibid.*

29. Though it was not known publicly at the time, the Normandy invasion was but six weeks away.

30. *Ibid.* 31. *Ibid.,* p. 225.

32. See the statements of Rear Admirals George F. Hussey, Jr., Chief of Bureaus of Ordnance, and E. W. Mills, Assistant Chief of Bureau of Ships, in *ibid.,* pp. 273 ff. and 278 ff.

33. *Ibid.,* p. 133. 34. *Ibid.,* p. 223. 35. *Ibid.,* p. 136.

36. Daniels' statement begins on p. 241 and Yarnell's on p. 265.

37. LXIX (August, 1943), 1099–101. 38. 1944 Hearings, pp. 295 ff

39. *Ibid.,* p. 300. 40. May 20, 1944. 41. May 15, 1944.

42. Letter to the Chief of Military History, quoted in Legere, *Unification,* p. 338. As late as the summer of 1943, Roosevelt did explicitly oppose the creation of a separate air force. Letter to Senator Patrick McCarran, cited in R. Earl McClendon, *The Question of Autonomy for the United States Air Arm, 1907–1945* (Maxwell Air Force Base, Ala., 1950), pp. 233–34.

43. Stimson Diary, May 12, 1944. 44. 1944 Hearings, p. 318.

45. *Ibid.,* pp. 124–25 46. *Ibid.,* pp. 75, 95. 47. *Ibid.,* p. 75.

48. Stimson Diary, May 2, 3, 1944.

49. Stimson and Bundy, *On Active Service,* p. 519.

50. Stimson Diary, May 4, 5, 1944.

51. *Ibid.,* May 5, 1944; New York *Times,* May 12, 1944; Memorandum from H. Struve Hensel to John J. McCloy, May 6, 1944, Forrestal Papers, Firestone Library, Princeton University.

52. H. Rept. No. 1645, 78th Cong., 2d Sess. (1944), p. 4.

53. *Ibid.,* p. 3.   54. Forrestal Diaries, p. 9.

55. This report is printed in 1945 Hearings, pp. 411–39.

56. Legere, *Unification,* pp. 315–21.

57. Forrestal had been appointed Secretary of the Navy on May 19, 1944, to fill the vacancy created by Knox' death.

58. Letter to Palmer Hoyt, Sept. 2, 1944, quoted in Forrestal Diaries, p. 60. Forrestal had been advised just after the close of the Woodrum Committee hearings by the Navy General Board that

"The press has been almost overwhelmingly in favor of a merger of the armed forces into a single department. Great stress is laid on 'economy,' 'duplication,' and 'friction' between the services. Walter Lippman, David Lawrence and Ernest Lindley, however, are opposed to the merger on the grounds that nothing should be done to upset the fine balance which now exists; and that the test of the military services is winning the war, not how much money they spend." Memo of May 29, 1944, in Forrestal Papers.

59. "Our Armed Forces Must Be Unified," *Collier's,* Aug. 26, 1944.

60. Forrestal Diaries, pp. 46–47.   61. *Ibid.,* p. 60.

62. Walsh's letter is reprinted in the Eberstadt Report, pp. iii–iv.

63. *Ibid.,* p. v.

64. Forrestal's letter is reprinted in Eberstadt Report, p. 1.

65. The staff included a number of present academicians—Pendleton Herring, Milton Katz, Myron P. Gilmore, Elting Morison, and Louis Hartz— and two men who reached high posts in the Eisenhower administration— C. Douglas Dillon and Maxwell Rabb.

66. Eberstadt Report, pp. 3–14.   67. *Ibid.,* p. 14.

68. Forrestal Diaries, p. 117

69. S.84 and S.1482 are reprinted in 1945 Hearings, pp. 2–4.

70. It should be noted that this was Marshall's first public statement on unification, since neither he nor any of the other Joint Chiefs had testified before the Woodrum Committee in 1944.

71. 1945 Hearings, p. 15   72. *Ibid.,* p. 14.   73. *Ibid.,* p. 50.

74. *Ibid.*   75. *Ibid.,* p. 63.   76. *Ibid.,* pp. 51–52.

77. Secretary Patterson, *ibid.,* p. 22.

78. 1945 Hearings, p. 174; Collins' statement begins on p. 155.

79. *Ibid.,* pp. 157–58.   80. *Ibid.*

81. *Ibid.,* p. 161; during a personal interview in 1961, General Collins recollected that the chart showed the preferred relationship.

82. *Ibid.,* p. 162.   83. *Ibid.,* p. 161.   84. *Ibid.,* p. 179.

85. *Ibid.,* p. 74.

86. "I believe in the future of the U.S. Air Forces. I believe that air power is this Nation's first line of defense and only in air power can we find a weapon formidable enough to maintain the peace." General George C. Kenney, *ibid.,* p. 233.

87. 1945 Hearings, pp. 290, 308.   88. Oct. 20, 1945.

89. 1945 Hearings, p. 97.   90. *Ibid.,* pp. 97–98.

91. Admiral King, *ibid., pp.* 119–20.

92. "We have an organization which we know will protect us, and we should not be misled into discarding it because there are details in need of correction." Admiral King, *ibid.,* p. 126.

93. 1945 Hearings, p. 144.   94. *Ibid.,* p. 103.

95. Admiral King, *ibid.,* p. 122.

96. 1945 Hearings, pp. 120–21. The best statements of the Navy position are by Secretary Forrestal, Admiral King, General Vandegrift, and Admiral Nimitz. *Ibid.,* pp. 97 ff., 119 ff., 143 ff., and 383 ff.

97. 1945 Hearings, p. 391.   98. *Ibid.*

99. *Ibid.,* pp. 383–84. Admiral Halsey also rescinded his endorsement of unification when he testified on Dec. 6. See *ibid.,* pp. 537 ff.

100. Armed with multicolored charts depicting "Subordinated Civilian Control in the Submission of the Budget Under Proposal of the War Department" and "Predominant Civilian Control in the Submission of the Present Naval Budget." See *ibid.,* pp. 248–49

101. *Ibid.,* p. 245.   102. *Ibid.,* 246–48, 250.

103. *Ibid.,* pp. 365–66.   104. *Ibid.,* p. 377.

105. *Ibid.,* pp. 452–53.   106. *Ibid.,* p. 462.   107. *Ibid.*

108. See *ibid.,* pp. 575 ff.

109. H. Doc. No. 392, 79th Cong., 1st Sess. (1945).

110. Forrestal Diaries, p. 118.   111. H. Doc. No. 392.

112. New York *Times,* Dec. 20, 1945

Chapter 3. War Department Coalition Goals

1. Mark Skinner Watson, *Chief of Staff: Prewar Plans and Preparations* (Washington, D.C., Historical Division, Department of the Army, 1950), p. 14.

2. *Ibid.,* p. 127; Richard M. Leighton and Robert W. Coakley, *Global Logistics and Strategy, 1940–1943* (Washington, D.C., Office of the Chief of Military History, Department of the Army, 1955), pp. 21–22.

3. 1945 Hearings, p. 49.

4. *Ibid.,* pp. 54–55. Marshall also believed, somewhat inconsistently given his prediction of the vulnerability of our mobilization base, in universal military training as the "principal feature" of our "military posture." *Ibid.*

In this he represented the dominant thinking within the War Department, which implicitly recognized the need for powerful forces-in-being to deter war but still could not by the winter of 1945–46 articulate anything better than an improved pre-World War II mobilization strategy to meet the exigencies of the developing cold war in the atomic age. See, for example, Secretary of War Patterson's statement on universal military training, which was based on "assumptions" on which there was "unanimous agreement among the men who led our troops to victory in World War II." *Universal Military Training,* Hearings before the House Committee on Military Affairs on H.R.515, 79th

Cong., 1st Sess. (1945), pp. 2 ff. See also Samuel P. Huntington, *The Common Defense: Strategic Programs in National Politics* (New York, Columbia University Press, 1961), pp. 33–47.

5. 1945 Hearings, p. 49.

6. *National Defense Program: Unification and Strategy*, Hearings before the House Committee on Armed Services, 81st Cong., 1st Sess. (1949), p. 598.

7. See Forrestal Diaries, p. 60.   8. 1945 Hearings, p. 453.

9. *National Defense Program*, p. 604.

10. From General MacArthur's "Annual Report of the Chief of Staff for 1933,"; quoted in Watson, *Chief of Staff*, p. 25.

11. 1944 Hearings, pp. 33–37.

12. 1945 Hearings, pp. 57, 158. The basis of Marshall's strong desire for a method of making the estimates of the professional military officers public without resort to "leaks" is illustrated by the following comment made to the House Armed Services Committee in 1949:

"Speaking very intimately, I saw General Pershing in the position where his views didn't count at all. He never could get them up for consideration. And yet he was a man of great prestige in this country. But the cuts, and cuts and cuts came despite what he felt. The main reason for this was that he had no opportunity to give public expression without being in the position of disloyalty. Of course, he never would have done that." *National Defense Program*, p. 604.

13. 1944 Hearings, p. 34.   14. 1945 Hearings, pp. 59–60.

15. Samuel P. Huntington, "Interservice Competition and the Political Roles of the Armed Services," *American Political Science Review*, LV (March, 1961), 40–52.

16. See Forrestal Diaries, p. 60. Marshall had explained to the Military Affairs Committee, "Our people pretty well understand naval power with ships sailing the seas, and having easily arrangeable bases . . . but they do not comprehend how much is required immediately to support such action. . . . There you become involved in land forces . . . to a much larger degree than can be maintained purely on a carrier-deck basis [i.e., Marines]." 1945 Hearings, p. 55.

Marshall's criticism of the two-budget system was probably also an indirect way of expressing his more basic dissatisfaction with the interwar strategy that accorded preference to a relatively strong Navy as the country's primary military force-in-being and made provision for only a very small (though expansible) Army.

17. Watson, *Chief of Staff*, pp. 24, 32.

18. Secretary Patterson, Generals Marshall and Collins, 1945 Hearings, pp. 14, 51–52, 158.

19. It is not clear whether the military leaders actually expected a return, in terms of absolute numbers of dollars and personnel, to the abject poverty of the interwar period or whether they only expected, at some substantially higher level of expenditures, the same relative gap to recur between the forces

maintained and the now (greatly expanded) foreign policy commitments of the nation. Although it appears astonishing in view of the changing world power structure into a bipolar system with the United States as one of the two leading participants, the military men talked and acted almost as if they expected the former. In any event, during this stage of the unification conflict they were certainly not thinking of an inability to maintain forces-in-being large enough to implement what has been called a "deterrence" strategy, but in terms of maintaining the base for an improved World War II kind of "mobilization" strategy. See Huntington, *Common Defense*, pp. 33–47.

20. 1944 Hearings, p. 36.   21. 1945 Hearings, p. 58.

22. In fairness it should be pointed out that early in the war Marshall strongly urged President Roosevelt to appoint Admiral Leahy as a single chief of staff with authority over both the Army and Navy. Stimson Diary, Feb. 25, 1942, Yale University Library. Roosevelt appointed Leahy some months later but only as personal chief of staff to himself without power of command.

23. One main difference was that the Commanding General had been independent of the Secretary of War and responsible only to the President on military matters, whereas the Chief of Staff was not. Samuel P. Huntington, *The Soldier and the State: The Theory and Politics of Civil-Military Relations* (Cambridge, Mass., Harvard University Press, 1957), pp. 208–11.

24. *Ibid.*, pp. 208–11, 251–53; Paul Y. Hammond, *Organizing for Defense: The American Military Establishment in the Twentieth Century* (Princeton, N.J., Princeton University Press, 1961), pp. 30–31, 47.

25. 1947 Senate Hearings, pp. 113–15.

26. Eberstadt Report, pp. 84–132; Robert H. Connery, *The Navy and Industrial Mobilization in World War II* (Princeton, N.J., Princeton University Press, 1951).

27. The complaints are scattered throughout the hearings, but some good catalogs will be found in Robert P. Patterson, "Patterson Urges Unity of Command Now," *New York Times Magazine*, Oct. 13, 1946, and in a speech by Senator Elbert Thomas, *Congressional Record*, XCII (1946), 2056–69.

28. 1945 Hearings, p. 632.

29. Philip N. Pierce and Frank O. Hough, *The Compact History of the United States Marine Corps* (New York, Hawthorn, 1960), Chaps. I–XIII.

30. *Ibid.*

31. *Ibid.;* William Frye, *Marshall, Citizen Soldier* (New York, Bobbs-Merrill, 1947), pp. 348–50.

32. *Ibid.;* Holland M. Smith and Percy Finch, *Coral and Brass* (New York, Scribner, 1948), pp. 170–80; for the Army's side of the Smith vs. Smith controversy, see Philip A. Crowl, *Campaign in the Marianas* (Washington, D.C., Office of the Chief of Military History, Department of the Army, 1959), pp. 191–202.

33. Frye, *Marshall*, p. 350.

34. 1945 Hearings, p. 507. Marshall's semiofficial biographer disputes this account, stating that Marshall said merely that he would not have Army troops

serving again under Holland Smith. Frye, *Marshall*, p. 350. I have what I consider unimpeachable authority that Sherman's version is the correct one.

35. Lawrence J. Legere, Jr., *Unification of the Armed Forces*, (Washington, D.C., Office of the Chief of Military History, n.d.), pp. 339–42 (mimeographed).

36. The quoted extracts from the then highly classified Series 1478 JCS proposals of the Chief of Staff of the Army, General Eisenhower, and the Commanding General of the Army Air Forces, General Spaatz, were later printed in H. Rept. No. 961, 80th Cong., 1st Sess. (1947), pp. 12–14. These same JCS proposals also argued for the restriction of naval aviation to carrier-based aircraft only.

37. Series 1478 JCS papers, quoted in H. Rept. No. 961, p. 14. Admiral Nimitz relieved King as Chief of Naval Operations and as the Navy member of the JCS in December, 1945.

38. 1945 Hearings, pp. 13–14.   39. *Ibid.*, pp. 363, 371, 373.

40. Elias Huzar, *The Purse and the Sword: Control of the Army by Congress through Military Appropriations, 1933–1950* (Ithaca, N.Y., Cornell University Press, 1950), pp. 58, 156, 159.

41. 1945 Senate Hearings, p. 431.   42. 1944 Hearings, p. 34.

43. Ray S. Cline, *Washington Command Post: The Operations Division* (Washington, D.C., U.S. Dept. of the Army, Office of the Chief of Military History, 1951), p. 91; Frye, *Marshall*, pp. 302–4.

44. Quoted in Harry Rowe Ransom, "The Politics of Air Power—A Comparative Analysis," in Carl J. Friedrich and Seymour Harris, eds., *Public Policy* (Cambridge, Mass., Harvard University Press, 1958), V, 111.

45. *Ibid.*, p. 112.

46. U.S. Dept. of the Air Force, Office of Air Force History, *The Army Air Forces in World War II*. Vol. I: *Plans and Early Operations, January 1939 to August 1942*, ed. by Wesley Frank Craven and James Lea Cate (Chicago, University of Chicago Press, 1948), pp. 5, 10.

47. *Ibid.*, pp. 18–22.

48. "The Air Service at St. Mihiel," *World's Work*, XXXVIII (August, 1919), 365, cited in *ibid.*, p. 36.

49. U.S. Air Force, *Army Air Forces in World War II*, I, 36–37.

50. Quoted in Bernard Brodie, *Strategy in the Missile Age* (Princeton, N.J., Princeton University Press, 1959), p. 93. For an excellent analysis of Douhet's strategic doctrine, see *ibid.*, pp. 71–106; see also, Edward Warner, "Douhet, Mitchell, Seversky," in Edward Mead Earle, ed., *Makers of Modern Strategy: Military Thought from Machiavelli to Hitler* (Princeton, N.J., Princeton University Press, 1943), pp. 485–503.

51. Quoted in Edward Arpee, *From Frigates to Flat-tops: The Story of the Life and Achievements of Rear Admiral William Adger Moffett, U.S.N., the Father of Naval Aviation* (Lake Forest, Ill., The Author, 1953), p. 104.

52. For the evolution of the long-range bomber, see U.S. Air Force, *Army Air Forces in World War II*, I, 54–72.

53. U.S. Strategic Bombing Survey, *Over-all Report (European War)*, Sept. 30, 1945, p. 107.

54. U.S. Strategic Bombing Survey, *Summary Report (Pacific War)*, July 1, 1946, p. 26.

55. Brodie, *Strategy in the Missile Age*, p. 107.

56. *Over-all Report; Summary Report;* see also Brodie, *Strategy in the Missile Age*, pp. 109–43.

57. In the immediate postwar era, the "nominal" atomic bomb had a yield of 20 kilotons, or the equivalent of 20,000 tons of TNT. *Ibid.*, p. 151.

58. *The War Reports of George C. Marshall, H. H. Arnold, and Ernest J. King*, ed. by Walter Millis (Philadelphia, Lippincott, 1947), pp. 462, 464.

59. Cline, *Washington Command Post*, pp. 249–57.

60. 1947 House Hearings, p. 213.   61. 1945 Hearings, pp. 511–12.

62. *Ibid.*

63. Sociologists term this kind of phenomenon "displacement of goals." See Robert K. Merton, "Bureaucratic Structure and Personality," in *Social Theory and Social Structure* (New York, Free Press, 1957), rev. ed., pp. 195–206.

64. Watson, *Chief of Staff*, pp. 40–41.

65. U.S. Air Force, *Army Air Forces in World War II*, I, 57.

66. For the bitterness in these recollections by one who explicitly denied that such bitterness persisted, see General Doolittle's testimony, 1945 Hearings, pp. 283 ff., especially at p. 286. For the reasoning behind the General Staff's decisions, see Watson, *Chief of Staff*, pp. 36, 44–45.

67. General Doolittle, 1945 Hearings, p. 295.

68. For the War Department side of this controversy over control of land-based planes, which was also aggravated by the different conceptions held by the Navy and Army Air Forces of how best to fight submarines, see U.S. Air Force, *Army Air Forces in World War II*, I, 514–53, and Henry L. Stimson and McGeorge Bundy, *On Active Service in Peace and War* (New York, Harper, 1947), pp. 508–18; for the Navy Department side, see Ernest J. King and Walter Muir Whitehill, *Fleet Admiral King, a Naval Record* (New York, Norton, 1952), pp. 451–71.

69. U.S. Air Force, *Army Air Forces in World War II*, I, 519. In a meeting of the key unification participants in November, 1946, "Mr. Symington [Assistant Secretary of War for Air] explained that the Army Air Forces actually feared that the Navy might set up a strategic air force of its own and threaten their existence." From Admiral Sherman's notes on the meeting, quoted in Forrestal Diaries, p. 222.

70. See, for example, Admiral Sherman's suggestion that the atomic bomb might have made obsolescent "the very large strategic air forces which were so effective in the war just concluded. . . . Atomic bombs may permit a reduction in the size of land based bomber forces." 1945 Hearings, p. 505.

71. *Ibid.*, p. 296.

72. *Ibid.*, pp. 295–96. Not that this deterred the Air Force from develop-

ing in later years new arguments to gain exclusive control of the ballistic missiles too! See the statement made by Representative F. Edward Hébert, one of the Navy's warmest congressional friends, during a radio debate on June 25, 1946:

"The Army must have a separate air force now because pretty soon there won't be any heavy bombers. The guided missiles are supplanting them. What will the Army aviators do unless they control that program, too, even if the program is one of ballistics and physics rather than one of aeronautics? There won't be anything left for them to do, will there? They have to get it while the getting is good"; reprinted in *Congressional Record*, XCII (1946), A14190.

73. Speech before the Wings Club as reported in the New York *Times*, March 20, 1946.

74. U.S. Air Force, *Army Air Forces in World War II*, I, 32.

75. Harry S. Truman, *Memoirs*. Vol. II: *Years of Trial and Hope* (New York, Doubleday, 1956), p. 46.

76. "Our Armed Forces Must Be Unified," *Collier's*, Aug. 26, 1944; reprinted in *1945 Hearings*, pp. 192–97.

77. Truman, *Memoirs*, II, 46.

78. *Collier's*, Aug. 26, 1944. In his special message Truman had conceded that JCS "cordination was better than no coordination at all" but denied that is was in any "sense a unified command." H. Doc. No. 392, 79th Cong., 1st Sess. (1945).

79. Truman had told his colleagues on the floor of the Senate in 1943 that the armed services knew "how to waste money better than any other organization I ever had anything to do with. They do an excellent job on the waste side. . . .

"I could stand here all afternoon and give example after example showing that tremendous sums of money are simply being thrown away with a scoop shovel." *Congressional Record*, LXXXIX (1943), 6709; quoted in Huzar, *Purse and Sword*, p. 163.

80. *Collier's*, Aug. 26, 1944; reprinted in *1945 Hearings*, p. 191.

81. *Ibid.*, p. 192.

82. Watson, *Chief of Staff*, p. 512; Roberta Wohlstetter, *Pearl Harbor: Warning and Decision* (Stanford, Calif., Stanford University Press, 1962), p. 28.

83. *Memoirs*, II, 47.   84. H. Doc. No. 392, p. 7.

85. *Memoirs*, II, 47.

Chapter 4. Navy Department Coalition Goals

1. *1945 Hearings*, p. 108.

2. See Ernest R. May, "The Development of Political-Military Consultation in the United States," *Political Science Quarterly*, LXX (June, 1955), 161–180.

3. General Somervell commented acidly, while alluding to the Eberstadt

proposals, that the War Department was "not put here trying to reorganize the [entire] United States Government; the Navy has a plan for that." 1945 Hearings, p. 704.

4. "Third Official Report to the Secretary of the Navy," Dec. 8, 1945, in *The War Reports of George C. Marshall, H. H. Arnold, and Ernest J. King,* ed. by Walter Millis (Philadelphia, Lippincott, 1947), p. 654.

5. 1945 Hearings, p. 386.   6. *Ibid.,* p. 392.

7. While testifying before the House Military Affairs Committee in November of 1945, Admiral King met the point on vulnerability by questioning that a fleet properly dispersed at sea could be seriously hurt by atomic bombs. *Universal Military Training,* Hearings before the House Committee on Military Affairs on H.R.515, 79th Cong., 1st Sess. (1945), p. 90. To examine this hypothesis, the Navy proposed the test of the effect of atomic bombs on naval vessels, eventually carried out at Bikini in June, 1946. *Ibid.,* p .97.

According to one careful student of naval policy, the Bikini tests proved inconclusive:

"The Air Force, pointing to the fact that only 9 of the 92 ships used in the project had escaped sinking, extensive damage or unacceptable radioactive contamination, said that the experiments proved what it had argued all along: ships were intolerably vulnerable in the atomic age. The Navy countered by pointing out that the target ships were of obsolete design, were anchored and unmanned, and were closely grouped in confined waters. The admirals argued that ships of modern design, properly dispersed, executing evasive maneuvers and utilizing their air defenses, would be far less vulnerable to atomic attack than, for instance, fixed air bases." B. Vincent Davis, Jr., "Admirals, Politics and Postwar Defense Policy: The Origins of the Postwar U.S. Navy, 1943–1946 and After" (unpublished Ph.D. thesis, Princeton University, 1962).

During still other hearings before the House Naval Affairs Committee in September, 1945, Secretary Forrestal explicitly denied that the atomic bomb had destroyed the usefulness of navies and suggested that the bomb might actually have increased the potential effectiveness of the fleet, testifying that the Navy intended "to adapt the atomic bomb to carrier-based planes." Hearings on H. Con. Res. 80, 79th Cong., 1st Sess. (1945), p. 1165.

Surprisingly, neither line of testimony was developed during the unification hearings.

8. 1945 Hearings, p. 276.   9. *Ibid.,* p. 505.

10. Ernest J. King and Walter Muir Whitehill, *Fleet Admiral King, a Naval Record* (New York, Norton, 1952), p. 299.

11. Julius Augustus Furer, *Administration of the Navy Department in World War II* (Washington, D.C., 1959), pp. 56–57.

12. Ibid., pp. 94–95.

13. See Harry Rowe Ransom, "The Politics of Air Power—A Comparative Analysis," in Carl J. Friedrich and Seymour Harris, eds., *Public Policy* (Cambridge, Mass., Harvard University Press, 1958), V, 116.

14. Admiral Raymond A. Spruance, 1946 Hearings, pp. 299–300.

15. Eberstadt Report, p. 8.

16. H. E. Yarnell, *U.S. Naval Institute Proceedings,* LXIX (August, 1943), 1099–101.

17. Henry L. Stimson and McGeorge Bundy, *On Active Service in Peace and War* (New York, Harper, 1947), pp. 518–19; 1944 Hearings, p. 227.

18. 1947 Senate Hearings, pp. 229–30. Forrestal himself noted in his diary that he had agreed with the remarks of the Secretary of the Interior at a Cabinet meeting in December of 1946 that "people down the line in the Budget not much above the status of clerks make allocations within Departments between various bureaus and offices of that Department" and later complained to the President "about the fact that a young man recently a seaman second class in the Navy, who had been a student of administration at the University of Colorado, . . . had been making up our figures." Forrestal Diaries, p. 237.

19. 1947 Senate Hearings, pp. 229–30.

20. 1945 Hearings, pp. 497, 507.   21. *Ibid.*

22. *Ibid.,* p. 14; quoted by Admiral Halsey, *ibid.,* p. 543.

23. 1945 Hearings, p. 272.

24. See, for example, Forrestal's and Nimitz' criticism of a pending unification bill because it might cause an "unbalanced military budget" and hinder the development of "balanced military forces." 1946 Hearings, pp. 44, 95.

25. 1945 Hearings, p. 124.

26. *Ibid.,* p. 133.   27. *Ibid.,* p. 587.   28. *Ibid.,* p. 101.

29. King and Whitehill, *Fleet Admiral King,* p. 465.

30. For a detailed analysis of the Royal Navy–Royal Air Force experience from the point of view of the American Navy, see the study by Captain J. P. W. Vest, inserted in 1946 Hearings, pp. 337–42.

31. See Ernest J. King, "First Official Report to the Secretary of the Navy," March 1, 1944, in *War Reports,* p. 476.

32. Edward Arpee, *From Frigates to Flat-tops: The Story of the Life and Achievements of Rear Admiral William Adger Moffett, U.S.N., the Father of Naval Aviation* (Lake Forest, Ill., The Author, 1953), p. 114.

33. 1945 Hearings, p. 106.

34. See Maurice Matloff and Edwin M. Snell, *Strategic Planning for Coalition Warfare, 1941–1942* (Washington, D.C., 1953); Maurice Matloff, *Strategic Planning for Coalition Warfare, 1943–1944* (Washington, D.C., 1959); and King and Whitehill, *Fleet Admiral King.*

Admiral R. S. Edwards, King's second in command as Deputy Commander-in-Chief U.S. Fleet and Deputy Chief of Naval Operations, had explained to Forrestal just as the war with Japan was ending what must have been the prevailing view at the top echelon of the Navy military hierarchy:

"Had there been a single decider [instead of the JCS] we would probably still be about a year away from the end of the war, because: 1. General MacArthur's concept was to remain on the continent of Australia or in the adjacent islands until he had mustered greatly additional strength. . . . [MacArthur] was most unwilling to move in 1943, that it was the Navy's insistence on the prosecution of a vigorous war in the East that finally 'pushed him off the cliff.' Once he got off he found he could go all right. . . . 3. [The Army] was against . . . the concept of the invasion and capture of the Marianas, the taking of which was essential to the reduction of Iwo Jima and Okinawa, and was essential for the securing of the flank of MacArthur's move north to the Philippines. 4. The taking of Guadalcanal was the result of the vigorous pressing of this decisive action by Admiral King. The Army did not like it." Conversely, Edwards pointed out to Forrestal "that if any admiral had been directing the campaign in Europe, it was most unlikely that his conception of strategy would have been sound." Forrestal Diaries, pp. 91–92.

35. 1945 Hearings, p. 125.

36. *Ibid.*, p. 491. Forrestal recalled in his diary that

"The theory of the swift and lightning-like instinctive, intuitive decision we had found had admirers during the early successes of Hitler but the great intuitive brain laid a good many eggs later on in the war. . . . It is a pretty good thing for anyone to have to maintain his point of view before an earnest and intelligent opposition." Entry for Aug. 25, 1945, Forrestal Diaries, p. 92.

37. Mitchell had testified before the House Military Affairs Committee that if he and his associates were "allowed to develop essential air weapons," they could "carry the war to such an extent . . . as almost to make navies useless on the surface of the water." Quoted in Archibald D. Turnbull and Clifford L. Lord, *History of United States Naval Aviation* (New Haven, Yale University Press, 1949), p. 178.

Mitchell's own biographer admits that "almost from the beginning, Mitchell's struggle for air power took on the character of a challenge to sea power." Isaac Don Levine, *Mitchell: Pioneer of Air Power* (New York, Duell, Sloan and Pearce, 1943), p. 201.

38. New York *Times*, Sept. 16, 1945.

39. Quoted in 1947 House Hearings, p. 506.

40. Samuel P. Huntington, *The Soldier and the State: The Theory and Politics of Civil-Military Relations* (Cambridge, Mass., Harvard University Press, 1957), pp. 208–11.

41. 1945 Hearings, p. 586.   42. *Ibid.*, p. 449.

43. In 1900 they consisted of the Bureaus of Yards and Docks, Construction and Repair, Steam Engineering, Ordnance, Equipment, Supplies and Accounts, Medicine and Surgery, and Navigation.

44. Furer, *Navy in World War II*, pp. 102–03; Huntington, *Soldier and State*, pp. 200–03; Paul Y. Hammond, *Organizing for Defense: The American Military Establishment in the Twentieth Century* (Princeton, N.J., Princeton University Press, 1961), pp. 49–53.

45. Huntington, *Soldier and State*, p. 202. Beginning in 1884, the Naval War College at Newport did engage in the preparation of some war plans. Hammond, *Organizing for Defense*, p. 52.

46. Furer, *Navy in World War II*, pp. 107–08.

47. *The New American Navy* (New York, 1903), II, 183–84.

48. Change No. 6 to U.S. Navy Regulations (1909); quoted in Furer, *Navy in World War II*, p. 108.

49. *Annual Report of the Secretary of the Navy, 1920* (Washington, D.C., 1921), p. 207.

50. This bill, as well as other key documents in the intra-Navy Department organization conflicts, are reprinted in Navy Department, *Naval Administration: Selected Documents on Navy Department Organization, 1915–1940*, Part ii, p. 8.

51. *Ibid.*, ii, 33. In 1915, the Naval Affairs Committees were still reporting the naval appropriations bills.

52. *Ibid.*, ii, 3–13.

53. Quoted in *Annual Report of the Secretary of the Navy, 1920*, p. 360.

54. The bureaus' activities with respect to what the Navy called "consumer logistics"—"the planning, timing, and distribution of the materiel and personnel needed by the operating forces"—came largely under King's control as CNO, while with respect to "producer logistics"—"procuring and producing the materiel and . . . recruiting, educating, and training the personnel necessary to meet the needs of the operating forces"—the bureaus remained directly responsible to the Secretary through his civilian assistants. Furer, *Navy in World War II*, pp. 10–11.

55. *Ibid.*, pp. 111–15.

56. Elting E. Morison, "Organizational Trends within the Navy Department," in Eberstadt Report, p. 217.

57. 1945 Hearings, pp. 101, 251.

58. In the course of the war, for example, the Army purchased approximately 90 percent of the food required by both services and the Navy purchased virtually all of the petroleum. 1946 Hearings, pp. 190–91.

59. See, for example, the detailed statement on the subject by Assistant Secretary of the Navy W. John Kenney, *ibid.*, pp. 188–93.

60. Eberstadt Report, pp. 101–18, 129–30.

61. 1945 Hearings, pp. 577–80, 589 ff.

62. *Ibid.*, pp. 101–2.   63. *Ibid.*, p. 604.   64. *Ibid.*, p. 141.

65. 1944 Hearings, p. 125.   66. 1945 Hearings, p. 27.

67. 1947 House Hearings, p. 118.   68. 1944 Hearings, p. 223.

69. 1945 Hearings, p. 225.

70. Furer, *Navy in World War II*, pp. 70–72.

71. For a similar distinction between "mutually exclusive" and "mutually incompatible" phenomena as different bases of conflict, see Jesse Bernard, "Parties and Issues in Conflict," *Journal of Conflict Resolution*, I (June, 1957), 111–21.

72. See on this point the distinction drawn between "difference in goals" and "difference in perceptions of reality" as bases of conflict in James G. March and Herbert A. Simon, *Organizations* (New York, Wiley, 1958), pp. 121–29.

73. Mark Skinner Watson, *Chief of Staff: Prewar Plans and Preparations* (Washington, D.C., Historical Division, Department of the Army, 1950), pp. 279–80.

74. A number of separate-air-force bills had been referred to these two committees during the Seventy-seventh Congress.

75. Quoted in Watson, *Chief of Staff*, p. 294.

76. Memo, DCoS for CofS, Oct. 9, 1940, quoted *ibid.*, p. 289.

77. *Ibid.*, p. 296.

78. Ray S. Cline, *Washington Command Post: The Operations Division* (Washington, D.C., 1951), pp. 249–57.

79. Richard M. Leighton and Robert W. Coakley, *Global Logistics and Strategy, 1940–1943* (Washington, D.C., Office of the Chief of Military History, Department of the Army, 1955), p. 245, and see pp. 244–46.

80. According to Assistant Secretary of War for Air Lovett, Stimson's had been the "determining influence" in 1942 in creating the largely autonomous Army Air Forces. Cited in Elting E. Morison, *Turmoil and Tradition: A Study of the Life and Times of Henry L. Stimson* (Boston, Houghton Mifflin, 1960), p. 542.

81. In 1949 General Collins would admit explicitly that the ground Army's "acquiescence in relinquishing tactical air was not arrived at idly or without doubts and misgivings in some quarters." *The National Defense Program: Unification and Strategy,* Hearings before the House Committee on the Armed Services, 81st Cong., 1st Sess. 1949), p. 544.

82. The quotation is from a press statement released by General Doolittle upon being elected president of the newly formed Air Force Association. New York *Times,* July 24, 1946.

83. "Third Official Report to the Secretary of War," in *War Reports of Arnold, Marshall, and King,* pp. 453, 469.

84. *Universal Military Training,* pp. 4–5. 85. 1945 Hearings, p. 457.

86. *Ibid.* McCloy, a World War I artillery man, had had his own difficulties with the Army Air Forces in World War II trying to get small observation planes ("puddle-jumpers") assigned to ground-force-controlled artillery units for spotting gunfire. (Interview.)

87. 1947 Senate Hearings, p. 114. Eisenhower also volunteered his opinion during the 1947 House Hearings that in war time the frontline infantry men and not the aviators should get any extra pay (p. 307).

88. 1945 Hearings, p. 354.

89. General Marshall, for example, did not include a single statement justifying separation of the Air Forces in his presentation before the Senate Military Affairs Committee in 1945.

90. 1945 Hearings, pp. 60–61. Indeed, some evidence indicates that in recognition of the political strength of the Air Forces the ground-force generals had early in the war at least implicitly promised support for a separate air force in the postwar period in exchange for the Army aviators' not pressing the issue while the war was on.

91. General Spaatz, 1947 House Hearings, p. 344. This is probably a chief reason why Marshall did not oppose the increasing degree of AAF autonomy in the immediate prewar and war years. As he remarked in 1941 with respect

to a pending AAF proposal for greater autonomy that he was about to approve, "If I have to spend my time battling others, I am lost." Watson, *Chief of Staff*, p. 292.

92. 1944 Hearings, p. 62. As late as 1947, General Spaatz, then Commanding General of the Army Air Forces, testified that he "would be against" the pending unification bill if the Air Force were not made a separate service, since "from the point of view of the Air Force [that] is the most important part of the legislation." 1947 House Hearings, pp. 342–43.

93. Watson, *Chief of Staff*, pp. 139, 144. Marshall, who was Deputy Chief of Staff at the time, had argued so vehemently with President Roosevelt on this matter that he thought he had jeopardized his chances to succeed as Chief of Staff. *Ibid.*, pp. 249–51.

94. *National Defense Program: Unification and Strategy*, p. 600.

95. Thirteen years after the separate Air Force was finally established, an outgoing Chief of Staff of the Army would review the failure of the Air Force to discharge "its obligations undertaken at the time of unification" and argue for the Army being returned "its own organic tactical air support and tactical air lift." Maxwell D. Taylor, *The Uncertain Trumpet* (New York, Harper, 1959), pp. 168–69.

The ground-force leaders' expectation of a TAC-dominated Air Force appears to have been highly unrealistic in view of the predominant status accorded to strategic bombing within Army aviation from as early as the 1920's. The ground-force leaders could not even claim that they were not warned. Aside from the Navy's predictions of lack of adequate air support for the Army from a separate Air Force, Senator Millard E. Tydings, himself a World War I Army combat veteran, was to comment:

"I think the fellows who are taking a real chance in this bill and who have the least to say about it are the ground troops, who, after all, cannot move very fast. . . . Without some air force in modern warfare to give them a lift that is more or less under the command of a ground commander, I feel sorry for them. I feel they are the fellows who are giving up more in this bill than any other single branch." 1947 Senate Hearings, p. 454.

Moreover, the ground leaders should have known that the one RAF component worse off with respect to equipment and personnel even than the Fleet Air Arm was the Army Cooperation Command—the British equivalent of TAC. See 1946 Hearings, p. 341.

96. Acting Secretary of War Kenneth Royall would write to Chairman Carter Manasco of the House Committee on Expeditures in the Executive Departments with respect to separate-air-force bills that had been referred to his committee, that the War Department was opposed to a separate air force without unification. New York *Times*, Feb. 10, 1946.

97. It might be significant that when General Arnold visited Europe in March, 1945, and "sounded Ike out on [postwar] organization for national security," Eisenhower then held that "support aviation must be part of the ground forces." H. H. Arnold, *Global Mission* (New York, Harper, 1949), p. 544. Somewhere in the process "Ike" obviously changed his mind.

98. Italics in the original. William D. Leahy, *I Was There: The Personal Story of the Chief of Staff to Presidents Roosevelt and Truman* (New York, McGraw-Hill, 1950), p. 282.

99. King and Whitehill, *Fleet Admiral King*, p. 103; Connery, *Navy and Industrial Mobilization*, Chap. XIX; Robert A. Albion and Robert H. Connery, *Forrestal and the Navy* (New York, Columbia University Press, 1962), Chap. V.

100. Executive Order 9096.

101. King and Whitehill, *Fleet Admiral King*, p. 631; Furer, *Navy in World War II*, pp. 132–33, 168.

102. 1945 Hearings, pp. 587, 589.

103. King had even been against Roosevelt's appointment of a personal military advisor in 1942 to provide liaison with the JCS because he feared that it would be detrimental to the Navy's interests and withdrew his objections only when Marshall proposed Admiral Leahy for the job. Leahy, *I Was There*, p. 119.

104. Stimson Diary, Feb. 7, 10, 1942.

105. Executive Order 9082 (March 9, 1942).

106. See Morison, *Turmoil and Tradition*, pp. 597–602. Stimson was almost seventy-three years old when he was appointed in 1940, and he retired in 1945 on his seventy-eighth birthday. Stimson had been Secretary of War for the first time during the last two years of William Howard Taft's administration, some thirty years earlier, and in addition had served as Secretary of State in the Hoover Cabinet.

107. Stimson and Bundy, *On Active Service*, p. 449.

108. Stimson Diary, April 24, 1944.

109. *Ibid.* Marshall would recall in 1949 having had "long discussions" with Stimson on the question of the relationship of the JCS to the overall Secretary:

"There was quite a lot of difference between Mr. Stimson and myself. He was such a wise chap that I was very hesitant about opposing his views." *National Defense Program: Unification and Strategy*, p. 604.

110. Forrestal Diaries, p. 164.   111. *Ibid.*

112. 1945 Hearings, p. 451. See also Stimson and Bundy, *On Active Service*, p. 45.

113. Watson, *Chief of Staff*, p. 287.

Chapter 5. Intra-Executive Branch Bargaining

1. H.R.4949, H.R.4950, 79th Cong., 1st Sess. (1945).

2. See New York *Times*, Dec. 23, 1945.

3. In Norstad Files.   4. *Ibid.*

5. Copy in Norstad Files. Some four months later, during a critical stage in the negotiations, Army Air Forces officers would again develop suspicions that the top War Department leaders might be considering withdrawing their endorsement of a separate air force, presumably to secure agreement from the

Navy on the single-department question. Eventually Secretary of War Patterson had to release a statement to the press, in which he commented on "stories appearing in the press to [that] effect," dismissed them as "absolutely without foundation," and reiterated his conviction that "the Air Forces should be given a position of full equality with the Army and the Navy in any reorganization of our national defense structure." Patterson added that General Eisenhower was "firmly of the same opinion." Copy in *ibid*.

Within the Army Air Forces itself, the question was being raised at that point, "whether it would not be wise to abandon unification and try for a separate Air Force." As one senior officer put it, "It seems wise that this problem should be frankly discussed among key officers of the Air Staff from time to time as the occasion arises. Memo in *ibid*.

6. Senator Thomas' testimony in 1946 Hearings, pp. 11–12.

7. The original letter to the Secretary of War is in Norstad Files.

8. This account of the drafting process is based on Senator Thomas' testimony, 1946 Hearings, interview with General Norstad, and Norstad Files.

9. Copies of "Confidential Committee Prints," Numbers 1–9, are in Norstad Files.

10. "Memorandum for the Record," April 5, 1946, in Norstad Files.

11. S.2044, 79th Cong., 2d Sess., reprinted in 1946 Hearings, pp. 1–9.

12. *Ibid.*   13. *Ibid.*

14. See *Twohey Analysis of Newspaper Opinion*, weekly reports Dec. 29, 1945, to April 6, 1946, inclusive.

15. New York *Times*, Dec. 20, 1945.   16. *Ibid.*, Dec. 21, 1945.

17. Forrestal Diaries, pp. 148–49.

18. New York *Times*, April 12, 1946.   19. *Ibid.*, April 18, 1946.

20. *Ibid.*   21. S. Rept. No. 1328, 79th Cong., 2d Sess. (1946).

22. Forrestal Diaries, p. 118.   23. *Ibid.*, p. 121.

24. 1946 Hearings, pp. 31, 54.

25. *Ibid.*, p. 37. Forrestal's testimony begins on p. 31.

26. New York *Times*, May 3, 1946.

27. Byrnes and Vinson had been successive heads of the Office of War Mobilization and Reconversion and Nelson had been chairman of the War Production Board.

28. 1946 Hearings, pp. 49–50.

29. *Ibid.*, p. 50. A bill that apparently incorporated these ideas of Forrestal's had been introduced on April 22 by Senator Bridges. It was based on an early draft (Confidential Committee Print No. 4) worked up by the Thomas-Hill-Austin subcommittee with Eberstadt's help and set up a "Coordinator of Common Defense," who was to be Deputy Chairman of the Common Defense Council (the President would be Chairman) and charged with the coordination of the common defense policies of the United States to the extent of bringing "into common action the executive departments, independent agencies, boards, commissions, Government corporations, and other agencies . . . as may be necessary to provide for the common defense." S.2102, 79th Cong., 2d Sess., Sec. 101b; 1946 Hearings, pp. 60–63, 184–86.

When Forrestal suggested to Senator Thomas in March that agreement might be reached if his subcommittee would adopt that early and, by the time, abandoned draft, Thomas said "he could not recede from what he called progress," and Forrestal gained the impression from him that he was "trying to convey to me the thought that he was acting under orders from the President." Forrestal Diaries, p. 147.

Other evidence indicates that the early committee prints had been drafted without consultation with any War Department representative and that Thomas had abandoned them as soon as General Norstad was called into the discussions and expressed his Department's intense opposition to the "Coordinator of Common Defense" concept.

30. 1946 Hearings, pp. 100–1.　　31. *Ibid.*　　32. *Ibid.*, pp. 83, 99.
33. *Ibid.*, p. 143.

34. *Ibid.* As early as February, 1946, Forrestal was proposing that the United States permanently maintain a task force in the Mediterranean, chiefly to buttress Italian, Greek, and Turkish resistance to Russian pressure. Forrestal Diaries, pp. 141, 144–45.

35. 1946 Hearings, p. 106.　　36. *Ibid.*, pp. 114–15.
37. *Ibid.*, pp. 118–19.

38. This account of the meeting is based on a "Memorandum for the Record," May 8, 1946, in Norstad Files.

39. This account of the meeting is based on Forrestal Diaries, pp. 160–61, and "Record of Meeting with the President," May 13, 1946, in Norstad Files.

40. Forrestal Diaries, p. 161.

41. The letter is reprinted in 1946 Hearings, pp. 348–51.

42. The letter to the President is reprinted in *ibid.*, pp. 203–7.

43. Forrestal Diaries, p. 166. Forrestal also noted that during this meeting he had been "considerably entertained by Patterson's saying . . . that he greatly regretted the impression that this merger was something the Army was trying to 'put over' " but refrained from observing that "it could be quite difficult to have any other impression inasmuch as it had been the Army's promotion from the outset." *Ibid.*

44. *Ibid.;* "Notes on Conference at White House," June 4, 1946, Norstad Files.

45. Truman's letter to Patterson and Forrestal and letter to Chairman Walsh are reprinted in 1946 Hearings, pp. 207–10.

46. *Ibid.*, p. 209.　　47. *Ibid.*, p. 211.

48. Sidney Shalett in the New York *Times*, June 18, 1946.　　49. *Ibid.*
50. Forrestal Diaries, pp. 168–69.　　51. *Ibid.*, pp. 169–70.
52. Forrestal's letter is reprinted in 1946 Hearings, p. 211.　　53. *Ibid.*
54. *Ibid.*, pp. 213, 214, 216.　　55. *Ibid.*, p. 215.　　56. *Ibid.*, p. 220.
57. *Ibid.*　　58. *Ibid.*, p. 226.　　59. *Ibid.*, pp. 217–18.
60. *Ibid.*, p. 269.　　61. *Ibid.*, p. 348.

62. New York *Times*, July 20, 1946.

63. For discussions of the general pattern, see David B. Truman, *The Governmental Process: Political Interests and Public Opinion* (New York,

Knopf, 1951), pp. 404–10; and Richard F. Fenno, Jr., *The President's Cabinet: An Analysis in the Period from Wilson to Eisenhower* (Cambridge, Mass., Harvard University Press, 1959).

64. Forrestal Diaries, p. 164.

65. These priorities appear implicit in Truman's special messages to Congress on universal military training and unification, his 1946 State of the Union message, and his 1946 Army Day speech. See New York *Times,* Oct. 24 and Dec. 20, 1945, Jan. 22 and April 7, 1946.

66. The significance of the President's formal sanctions should not, however, be completely discounted: Franklin Roosevelt is supposed to have terminated agitation within the Navy Department for a chief-of-staff type of CNO in the early years of his administration simply "by announcing that any naval officer raising his voice in support of such a plan would be instantly assigned to Guam, which in those days was a lonely limbo in which a naval career could languish and die." Louis Smith, *American Democracy and Military Power: A Study of Civil Control of Military Power in the United States* (Chicago, University of Chicago Press, 1951).

67. See *Congressional Record,* LXXV (1933), 9318–39.

68. Forrestal Diaries, p. 149.

69. *Twohey Analysis of Newspaper Opinion,* April 13, 1946.

70. Hanson Baldwin in the New York *Times,* April 14, 1946.

71. *Ibid.,* April 12, 1946.

72. See Fenno, *President's Cabinet,* p. 177; and Richard E. Neustadt, *Presidential Power: The Politics of Leadership* (New York, Wiley, 1960), pp. 86 ff.

73. Forrestal Diaries, p. 19   74. *Ibid.,* p. 152.

75. *Ibid.,* p. 167. Forrestal's full statement was: "My own conduct in this matter has been governed by three considerations: (1) to try to keep the Navy intact as a Service as distinct from a merely subordinate branch of a vast Department; (2) to obtain the improvements in our national defense organization which the war has indicated should be made *but without sacrificing the autonomy of the Navy;* (3) to discharge my responsibilities to the President as a member of his Cabinet, which means that I must go as far as I can in accepting and promulgating his views, always having the alternative, when I can no longer do so honestly, of resigning." *Ibid.*

76. According to Fenno, Jones "did not consider his relationship with Roosevelt in terms of subordination or hierarchy. He saw it, instead, as a marriage of convenience between coequal potentates." Fenno quotes Jones as having said, "I never considered that I was working *for* [Roosevelt], but *with* him for the country." *President's Cabinet,* p. 244.

77. See on this point Arnold A. Rogow, *James Forrestal: A Study of Personality, Politics, and Policy* (New York, Macmillan, 1963).

78. Forrestal *Diaries,* pp. 203–4.   79. *Ibid.,* pp. 204–5.

80. This account is based on interviews with Ferdinand Eberstadt and John J. McCloy and on Eberstadt's testimony in 1947 Senate Hearings, pp. 687–88.

81. The letter is reprinted in *ibid.*

82. This account of the conference is based on an interview with General Norstad; Forrestal Diaries, pp. 221–23; "Memorandum for the Record," Nov. 20, 1946, in Norstad Files; and Admiral Sherman's testimony in 1947 Senate Hearings, pp. 164, 170.

83. 1947 Senate Hearings, p. 170.

84. Admiral Sherman, *ibid.*, p. 164; interview with Norstad.

85. Forrestal Diaries, pp. 202, 223, 225.

86. The version of Armstrong's remarks in the footnote on p. 151 was published the following spring by Drew Pearson in the March 20 edition of the Washington *Post.* Forrestal had, of course, received full reports within days after the dinner from a number of naval and marine officers who had been present. According to the report of then Commodore Arleigh A. Burke (Chief of Naval Operations during the Eisenhower administration), before he spoke Armstrong had been drinking, "but he was by no means under the influence of intoxicating liquor. His method of delivery was excellent and effortless. His speech, while unprepared and given impromptu, was given with so much force and fervor and he made his point so clearly that it would have been a most detrimental speech to an uninformed audience." Report in Forrestal Papers.

87. "Memorandum for the Record," Nov. 16 and 18, 1946, Norstad Files.

88. *Ibid.*   89. Forrestal Diaries, p. 226.   90. *Ibid.*, pp. 228–29.

91. *Ibid.*, p. 229.

Chapter 6. Congress Enacts the Agreement

1. Such an agency was already operating under executive order.

2. Note that this was somewhat more restrictive than Truman's 1946 decision allowing "conduct of such limited land operations as are essential to the prosecution of a naval campaign."

3. The joint letter to Truman and the draft executive order are reprinted in 1947 Senate Hearings, pp. 2–5.

4. Truman's reply to the Secretaries of War and the Navy is also reprinted in *ibid.*

5. Truman's letter to Vandenberg is reprinted in *Congressional Record* XCIII (1947), 433–43.

6. New York *Times,* Jan. 17, 1947.

7. This account of the drafting process is based on interviews with Norstad and Clifford; Admiral Sherman's testimony in 1947 Senate Hearings, pp. 159–69; and Norstad and Clifford Files.

8. Forrestal Diaries, pp. 230–31.

9. Sherman and Norstad had explicitly decided at the outset not to allow themselves to be separated. Interview with Norstad.

10. Sec. 101(a), "Fifth Draft," in Clifford Files.

11. Admiral Sherman, 1947 Senate Hearings, p. 161. The relevant sections of the first four drafts had read, "There is hereby established a . . . National

Security Council [consisting of the Secretaries of State, Army, Navy, and Air Force, and the Chairman of the National Security Resources Board]. . . . The function of the Council shall be *to integrate our foreign and military policies.* . . . Subject to the authority of the President, decisions of the Council shall establish the approved policy of the departments and agencies represented in the Council." Clifford Files.

When one of these early drafts was sent to the State Department for comment, Secretary of State (and former Chief of Staff of the Army) Marshall wrote to the President that "the powers and functions which the bill would vest in this Council . . . would evidently by statute dissipate the constitutional responsibility of the President for the conduct of foreign affairs . . . and at the same time markedly . . . diminish the responsibility of the Secretary of State." Marshall recommended that the National Security Council be eliminated from the bill altogether and, if desired, be set up by executive order. "Memorandum for the President," Feb. 7, 1947, original in Clifford Files.

The Council was kept in the bill, but the language of the fifth and succeeding drafts was changed to, "The function of the Council shall be *to advise the President with respect to the integration of foreign and military policies, etc.*" *Ibid.*

12. Admiral Sherman, 1947 Senate Hearings, p. 161.

13. *Congressional Record,* XCIII (1947), 1413.

14. S.758, 80th Cong., 1st Sess., reprinted in 1947 Senate Hearings, pp. 12–21.

15. New York *Times,* Dec. 12, 1946.   16. *Ibid.,* Dec. 12, 20, 23, 1946.

17. *Ibid.,* Jan. 3, 1947; *Congressional Record,* XCIII (1947), 38.

18. *Congressional Record,* XCIII (1947), 594.

19. Quoted, *ibid.,* p. 1413.   20. *Ibid.*   21. *Ibid.,* pp. 1599–607.

22. *Ibid.*   23. 1947 Senate Hearings, pp. 22, 29–30

24. Eberstadt's original designation for the foreign policy–military policy coordinating body had replaced Thomas' "Council of Common Defense" in the introduced bills.

25. 1947 Senate Hearings, pp. 26, 29   26. *Ibid.,* pp. 62, 73–74, 78, 80.

27. Forrestal Diaries, p. 269. Eisenhower's recorded testimony was:

"Now, distinguishing my personal conviction as opposed to what I now believe we should recommend, I did recommend and I believed in the single professional Chief of Staff. . . .

"But I have come to the conclusion that it is one of those argumentative points that should be eliminated from the bill, as not being of great importance. Time may bring it about, and it may show that this is the better system." 1947 Senate Hearings, p. 99.

It was during this appearance that Eisenhower advanced his interesting theory about the preferability of a speedy though incorrect decision over a delay in reaching one. *Ibid.,* pp. 113–15.

28. *Ibid.,* pp. 97–98.   29. Forrestal Diaries, pp. 269, 271.

30. 1947 Senate Hearings, p. 358.   31. *Ibid.,* pp. 365–66.

32. *Ibid.*, p. 349.   33. *Ibid.*, pp. 136, 142, 148–49, 150–51.

34. *Ibid.*, pp. 412, 418.

35. Five-star admirals and generals are, technically, never retired.

36. McCarthy, a member of the Senate Expenditures Committee, sat in on the Armed Services Committee hearings occasionally.

37. 1947 Senate Hearings, pp. 600, 619.

38. Maas was a former Congressman and had been a Naval Affairs Committee member of the Woodrum Committee in 1944.

39. Maas' statement of Marine functions was even more generous than Vandegrift's, chiefly by eliminating the word "limited" in the Marine's responsibility for "the conduct of such limited land operations as are essential to the prosecution of a naval campaign." *Ibid.*, p. 450.

40. *Ibid.*, pp. 448–57.

41. *Ibid.*, pp. 518–24. It should be noted that the prediction of increased overhead costs was not at this point merely Navy propaganda. None of the witnesses in 1947 claimed immediate savings, and almost all admitted the possibility of an immediate increase in expenditures as a result of unification. On April 3, Senator Robertson had asked Norstad for an estimate of the net "costs of this new set-up." On April 30, Norstad and Sherman sent a joint letter to Chairman Gurney estimating that the additional cost per year for the new offices of the Secretaries of National Defense and the Air Force and the staff for the National Security Council and the National Security Resources Board would amount to $982,000. Norstad and Sherman claimed that the savings to be realized were "intangible" in nature and that they would begin to outweigh the additional costs in about a year. On May 2, Senator Robertson repeated his request for a statement of the costs of the new Establishment because he found Norstad and Sherman's April 30 accounting "almost an insult to our intelligence." Robertson pointed out that the appropriations for the office of the Secretary of War were $7,542,000 and for the office of the Secretary of the Navy, $4,785,000. "To tell us that all that the Secretary of the Air Force's office is going to be is $107,000," Robertson continued, "is on the—

"The CHAIRMAN [Gurney]. It is obviously incorrect.

"Senator ROBERTSON of Wyoming. Obviously incorrect, as you say, Mr. Chairman." *Ibid.*, pp. 244, 501–2, 531–32.

Perhaps the great emphasis now put by both the War and Navy Department witnesses on the delay in realizing savings under unification was due to their reluctance to give the economy-minded Eightieth Congress any additional excuse for making cuts in the military appropriations requests for fiscal-year 1948.

42. *Ibid.*, pp. 672–76, 681

43. Copies of these exchanges are in Norstad and Clifford Files.

44. Senate Report No. 239, 80th Cong., 1st Sess.   45. *Ibid.*

46. *Ibid.*, pp. 8–9.   47. New York *Times,* May 14, 1947.

48. *Congressional Record,* XCIII (1947), 8295–300.

49. *Ibid.*, p. 8502. Some of the bill's proponents were more candid: Senator Wayne Morse explained that he did not think "the record or the bill shows that any large economy will flow from it. . . . If one wants to vote for the bill solely on the ground of economy, he will find the evidence does not support such a vote. However, it is not a wasteful bill. . . . I suppose my economic argument could be summarized in this way: Although the bill . . . does not immediately effectuate great economies, it does provide the procedure and the administrative machinery for effecting such economies if the top Secretary and the three Assistant Secretaries keep faith with the spirit and intent of the act." *Ibid.*, p. 8505.

50. Robertson brought up the cost estimate of $982,000 a year for the new overhead positions that had been prepared by Norstad and Sherman and claimed that it was so ridiculous that "even the most ardent friends of the merger on your committee could not stomach this." Robertson branded as absurd the claim that the new Secretary of the Air Force could run his office on $107,000 a year while the Secretaries of War and Navy were at the time spending $7,542,000 and $4,785,000, respectively, and had the following to say about the estimate "that the Office of the Secretary of National Defense . . . would get along with some 100 civilian clerical and administrative personnel at a total cost of $663,000 for salaries":

"Such an estimate, Mr. President, shows a clear ignorance or willful disregard of the facts of life. If anyone who is familiar with the Washington scene imagines that an office directing the destinies of several million individuals and spending one-third of the national budget is going to operate with a civilian force of 100 persons he should see his physician at once. Washington simply does not operate that way." *Ibid.*, p. 8315. As a matter of interest, there were 298 civilian and 49 military personnel in the immediate Office of the Secretary of Defense by December, 1948. The total number of personnel in the whole superstructure (Office of Secretary of Defense, Munitions Board, and Research and Development Board) rose from 278 before unification to 1,096 by December, 1948. Carroll French Miles, *The Office of the Secretary of Defense, 1947–1953: A Study in Administrative Theory* (unpublished Ph.D. thesis, Harvard University, 1956), p. 162.

51. *Congressional Record*, XCIII (1947), 8307–20, 8490–94.

52. *Ibid.*, p. 8490.   53. *Ibid.*, pp. 8520, 8522.   54. *Ibid.*, p. 8521.

55. *Congressional Record*, XCIII (1947), 8523.

56. *Ibid.*, p. 8527. Of the Armed Services Committee members, only Roberson voted for McCarthy's amendment. Bridges was absent, and the rest, including such friends of the Navy as Byrd, Saltonstall, and Tydings, either voted or were paired against the amendment.

57. 1947 House Hearings, p. 226.

58. Actually, Forrestal never did say whether he would or would not object. He explained that he "wished it might be possible to have solid guarantees in law for the continued existence of the Navy . . . with particular reference to its aviation and Marine Corps. But I have had to balance that

wish against the consequences of failure to secure a unified structure." *Ibid.,* p. 102.

59. *Ibid.,* pp. 144–45.   60. *Ibid.,* pp. 47–48, 129, 192.

61. *Ibid.,* pp. 273–74.

62. *Ibid.,* pp. 319–20. The previous day Congressman Robert H. Rich had asked Eisenhower whether he didn't know the reason for the Marines' fears, and Eisenhower had answered, "The reason, sir? I can see no ground as far as the relationship of the Marines and the Army is concerned." *Ibid.,* p. 314.

63. *Ibid.,* pp. 320–22. During a personal interview fourteen years later, the first thing that Hoffman mentioned in response to an "open-ended" question about his role in the unification conflict was Eisenhower's disingenuousness about the JCS proposals.

64. *Ibid.,* p. 181.   65. *Ibid.,* p. 363.   66. *Ibid.,* pp. 363–64.

67. *Ibid.,* p. 368.

68. *Ibid.,* pp. 365–66. The relevant articles read as follows:

"Article 94. All . . . communications from any officer . . . whether on active or retired list, addressed to Congress, or to either House thereof, or to any committee . . . on any subject of legislation relating to the Navy or Marine Corps, pending, proposed, or suggested, shall be forwarded through the Navy Department. . . .

"Article 95. . . . [N]o officer . . . shall apply to either House of Congress or to any committee . . . or to any Member . . . for legislation, or for appropriations, or for congressional action of any kind, except with the consent and knowledge of the Secretary of the Navy, nor shall any such person respond to any request for information . . . except through, or as authorized by the Department." Quoted, *ibid.*

69. *Ibid.,* p. 379.   70. *Ibid.,* p. 387.   71. *Ibid.,* p. 494.

72. *Ibid.,* p. 490.

73. Throughout the spring of 1947, Cole was writing to Forrestal about the "general feeling of reluctance" that he found among naval officers "to speak critically of the proposed plan" even in private conversation and asked the Secretary to "suitably express" the officers' freedom to air their views. Forrestal always replied that, as he had stated to the Expenditures Committee, no restrictions had been placed on the officers, who were perfectly free to express themselves either before congressional committees or when engaged in private conversation. On May 27 Cole sent letters to approximately 175 Navy captains and admirals and Marine Corps generals, citing Forrestal's statements about freedom of expression and asking them their views on the compromise bill, H.R.2319, and on a bill, H.R.3469, that Cole had introduced, which set up a "Coordinator of National Defense" along the lines recommended by Admiral King in the Senate hearings. Cole's bill would also have established a separate air force independent of the Chief of Staff of the Army but still within the War Department under the Secretary of War and would have added the Commandant of the Marine Corps to the JCS and generally spelled out the functions of the services. Cole received 118 replies, of which

only 18 expressed approval of H.R.2319. The rest, the writers of almost all of which asked that their names be withheld, objected to the compromise bill because, in the words of one naval aviator, they had "grave doubts as to whether H.R.2319 has sincerity of purpose behind it or whether it is intended as a first step in gaining control of the Navy toward the end of depriving it of its aviation and the Marine Corps and eventually reducing it to a point where it could play but a minor role in national defense." *Congressional Record,* XCIII (1947), 7944–47.

74. ALNAV 139 of June 23, 1947; reprinted in 1947 House Hearings, p. 635.

75. The more senior of these officers were Admiral John H. Towers, the Chairman of the General Board, who had been a naval aviator since 1911 (the third in the Navy), a former Chief of the Bureau of Aeronautics, a carrier task force commander in World War II, and Commander in Chief of the Pacific Fleet after the end of the war; Vice Admiral Arthur W. Radford, commander of the Second Task Fleet in the Atlantic, who had been Deputy CNO for Air in 1946 and a carrier division commander in World War II and was eventually to become chairman of the JCS in the Eisenhower administration; Vice Admiral George F. Bogan, Commander Air Force (i.e., carriers) Atlantic, who had been a carrier and carrier division commander in World War II; Rear Admiral Joseph J. Clark, Assistant CNO for Air, who had been the heavily decorated commander of the carrier *Yorktown* and a task group commander in World War II; Rear Admiral Ralph A. Ofstie, concurrently senior naval member of the Strategic Bombing Survey for Japan, a member of the JCS Evaluation Board for the Bikini atomic bomb tests, and a member of the Military Liaison Committee to the Atomic Energy Commission, who had also been a carrier and carrier division commander in World War II.

76. Admiral Clark, *ibid.,* p. 716. It is only fair to point out that the Army aviators were constantly feeding this fear: General Armstrong's remarks of the previous December had not been forgotten, and Admiral Bogan quoted from an article that had recently been published by the AAF school at Maxwell Field, Alabama, in its *U.S. Air Services Magazine,* which explained that "unification . . . means to the Air Forces the establishment of a fully autonomous Air Force, [and] is indeed the A-1 priority of the Air Forces today. They support the present bill heartily, but have not abandoned their belief in a single chief of staff of the armed services. They feel that all air power, including the Navy's, ought to be under one command, and they are still deeply concerned—though at the moment chiefly in theory—with the antisubmarine problem." *Ibid.,* p. 692.

77. 1947 House Hearings, p. 582.

78. Dorn was an Army Air Forces veteran of World War II.

79. 1947 House Hearings, p. 641.

80. *Ibid.,* p. 632. Ofstie also brought up the question of "guided missiles, . . . which have been suggested as a proper development for the Air Force." Ofstie pointed out that the "guided missile has gone a very short distance as a

matter of fact. We are still down to about the [German] V-1 and the V-2, and again, until we have new fuels and new materials, we are going to see little progress.

"In other words, it will be 15 or 20 years before we will get anywhere with that sort of thing." *Ibid.*

81. *Ibid.,* p. 641. 82. *Ibid.,* p. 637.

83. The statement of the chief Marine function generously allowed "fleet Marine forces of combined arms, together with supporting air components, for service with the fleet in the seizure or defense of advanced naval bases and for the conduct of such [presumably unlimited] land operations as may be essential to the prosecution of a naval campaign." Sec. 203(c).

84. H. Rept. No. 961, 80th Cong., 1st Sess. 85. *Ibid.* 86. *Ibid.*

87. *Congressional Record,* XCIII (1947), 9050. 88. *Ibid.,* p. 9095.

89. *Ibid.,* pp. 9396–97.

90. Typical was the statement by Representative John B. Williams, a World War II Army Air Forces veteran:

"Mr. Chairman, I would support this bill if for no other reason than that it gives long overdue recognition to the contributions of air power to the preservation of our Nation. . .

"Not all of the combined brass hats and gold braid of the old school can refute the undeniable fact that this baby of modern warfare—the airplane— has grown to manhood. . . .

"Prior to World War II, the airplane was a suporting unit for the operations of the Army and Navy. It came into its own in World War II as [an] equal. . . . In the next war, air power will be the chief weapon, and the Army and Navy will have become supporting units. This . . . is an undeniable fact." *Ibid.,* pp. 9411–12.

91. As Representative Ralph E. Church, himself a former naval reservist, put it,

"The importance of air power is no longer a debatable question. The last war surely settled that matter conclusively. It does not follow, however, that the Air Forces should be made a separate and distinct department. In essence, the Air Forces . . . must operate in conjunction with [the Army and the Navy] and must be a part of each." *Ibid.,* p. 9421

92. *Ibid.,* pp. 9432–38. 93. *Ibid.,* pp. 9450–51.

94. *Ibid.,* pp. 9448–49. 95. *Ibid.,* p. 9457.

96. *Ibid.,* pp. 9457–58, 9473. 97. *Ibid.,* pp. 9923, 10198.

98. H. Rept. No. 1051, 80th Cong., 1st Sess.

99. *Congressional Record,* XCIII (1947), 9916–19.

100. *Ibid.,* p. 10418.

Chapter 7. Intra-Legislative Influences

1. Robert A. Dahl has called a similar concept the congressman's "private preferences"—"his inner, highly subjective feelings of what he regards as

desirable." *Congress and Foreign Policy* (New York, Harper, 1950), p. 10.

2. David B. Truman, *The Governmental Process: Political Interests and Public Opinion* (New York, Knopf, 1951), p. 332.

3. By "identification" is meant a feeling of a sense of oneness with the entity being identified with. See John P. French, Jr., and Bertram Raven, "The Bases of Social Power," in Dorwin Cartwright, ed., *Studies in Social Power* (Ann Arbor, University of Michigan Institute for Social Research, 1959), pp. 161–63.

4. See Robert K. Merton, "Continuities in the Theory of Reference Groups and Social Structure," in *Social Theory and Social Structure* (rev. ed., New York, Free Press, 1957), pp. 281–386, and Theodore M. Newcomb, *Social Psychology* (New York, Dryden, 1950).

5. *Congressional Record*, LX (1920), 2271, quoted in Howard White, *Executive Influence in Determining Military Policy in the United States* (Urbana, University of Illinois Press, 1924), p. 277.

6. Hill had been one of the active supporters of the unification title in the Economy Bill of 1932 during the House floor fight, arguing that "only through a single department of national defense can the air forces with economy take their proper [i.e., separate] place in the scheme of national defense." *Congressional Record*, LXXV (1932), 9326.

7. See *Army–Navy–Air Force Journal*, Feb. 18, 1961; *Newsweek*, XXXIII (March 28, 1949), 18–19.

8. Admiral Leahy, President Roosevelt's wartime Chief of Staff and former Chief of Naval Operations, has written:

"In my opinion, the Georgia Representative [Vinson] had, in the past decade, contributed more to the national defense [read, "the Navy"] than any other single person in the country except the President himself." William D. Leahy, *I Was There: The Personal Story of the Chief of Staff to Presidents Roosevelt and Truman* (New York, McGraw-Hill, 1950), p. 260. See also Robert G. Albion, "The Naval Affairs Committees, 1916–1947," *U.S. Naval Institute Proceedings*, LXXVIII (November, 1952), 1227–37.

9. Saltonstall's pro-Navy identification was probably a partial cause of, and was in turn reinforced by, one of his sons' and his daughter's having served with the Navy in World War II and another son's having served (and being killed in action) with the Marines. When Truman's aide, Clark Clifford, was objecting to statutory guarantees of the functions of the services during a meeting of the unification participants in the spring of 1947, "Senator Saltonstall disagreed, saying that he would like to point out very closely and respectfully that the Marines occupied a unique and singular place in the hearts of the people and that, whether or not Congress did anything about it, the people would." Forrestal Diaries, pp. 271–72.

10. It should be pointed out that the congressional "identifier" did not always agree with the position of the executive branch "identifiee." We have seen that in 1945 Senator Johnson did not approve of a figurehead Secretary of Defense, and Senator Walsh made it quite clear in 1946 that he disapproved

of the concept of a "coordinator of common defense" with authority over the common defense activities of all Executive Branch departments and agencies, as embodied in Senator Bridges' S.2102 and apparently preferred by Forrestal. 1946 Hearings, p. 60.

11. It may be speculated that May anticipated that unification would lead to a merger of the House Military Affairs and Naval Affairs Committees, with the chairmanship of the combined committee going to Vinson, who was his senior in House service. May also appears to have had strong "congressional-control" preferences.

12. See Joseph P. Harris, *Congressional Control of Administration* (Washington, D.C., The Brookings Institution, 1964).

13. 1944 Hearings, p. 237.

14. The relevant passage of the Act reads: "No estimate or request for an appropriation and no request for an increase in an item of any such estimate or request, and no recommendation as to how the revenue needs of the Government should be met, shall be submitted to Congress or any committee thereof by any officer or employee of any department or establishment, unless at the request of either house of Congress." 42 Stat. 21

15. 1947 Senate Hearings, p. 596.

16. See Marver H. Bernstein, *The Job of the Federal Executive* (Washington, D.C., The Brookings Institution, 1958), pp. 67–68.

17. 1944 Hearings, p. 116.   18. 1947 House Hearings, p. 65.

19. Interview.

20. Of course, not all members of Congress seek to maximize congressional control through overly detailed legislation, which accounts for general reorganization acts being enacted. Senator Johnson, who had himself spent two terms as Governor of Colorado, commented during the 1945 Hearings (p. 60) in support of his stand in favor of loose statutory specification of the new unified department that "no legislative body can streamline the government."

21. 1947 Senate Hearings, pp. 65–66.

22. 1947 House Hearings, p. 87.

23. Hoffman appears to be an exception, but his congressional-control maximizing preferences were coupled with a long-term, apparently temperamental predisposition to oppose proposals of the President, almost regardless of their merits. Data available for the 81st Congress (1949–50) show that not more than five or ten representatives out of 435 had lower "administration support indexes" than Hoffman. David B. Truman, *The Congressional Party: A Case Study* (New York, Wiley, 1959), p. 284. (I am indebted to Professor Truman for Hoffman's individual score.)

In the first session of the Eighty-seventh Congress (1961), fourteen years after the unification conflict, only two out of 437 Representatives had higher "presidential opposition" scores than Hoffman. *Congressional Quarterly Weekly Report*, Nov. 10, 1961.

Both in the Eighty-first and Eighty-seventh Congresses the President and Hoffman were of different parties. The data for the Eighty-sixth Congress

(1959–60) suggest that Hoffman's opposition was not due primarily to party affiliation: only four Republican representatives supported their Republican President, Eisenhower, less than Hoffman did. *Ibid.*

24. Woodrow Wilson, *Congressional Government* (Boston, Houghton Mifflin, 1885; Cleveland, Meridian, 1956), pp. 55–56, 76.

25. Senator Thomas J. Dodd and Representative Carl Albert, quoted in *U.S. News and World Report,* Sept. 12, 1960.

26. 1945 Hearings, pp. 575–77.

27. Interview with a member of the 1946 Naval Affairs Committee.

28. 1946 Hearings, p. 203.   29. *Ibid.,* pp. 40–41.

30. See *Congressional Record,* XCIII (1947), 9919.

31. See Dahl, *Congress and Foreign Policy,* pp. 17–23.

32. Committee source.   33. 1946 Hearings, pp. 219, 227.

34. 1947 Senate Hearings, p. 160.   35. *Ibid.,* p. 160.

36. Senator Russell, a senior member of the Senate Appropriations Committee, had argued along similar lines in the Armed Services Committee against Senator Byrd's feeling that the individual service secretaries be given some sort of statutory right to bring their original requests to Congress. 1947 Senate Hearings, p. 233. It might be speculated that apart from Taber's and Russell's determination of the triple-budget provision's questionable efficacy for the purpose avowed, another factor in their thinking was the realization that a published account of each service's original requests might lead nonmembers of the Appropriations Committees to make attempts on the floor to cut or to restore cuts and thus decrease the intra-chamber influence of the Appropriations Committees, which under the existing system enjoyed an effective monopoly of that kind of information *vis-à-vis* the whole House and Senate.

37. *Congressional Record,* XCIII (1947), 9448.   38. *Ibid.,* p. 9454.

39. The figures for the Senate committee are as follows:

Hearing	Average Proportion Attending Each Hearing	Proportion Attending More than Half
1945	4/16	5/16
1946	7/18	6/18
1947	6/13	4/13

The most frequent attenders in 1945 were Thomas, Johnson, Hill, Maybank, and Austin—the chairman, second- and third-ranking, and second most junior majority, and the ranking minority members. In 1946 they were Walsh, Tydings, Byrd, Willis, Robertson, and Saltonstall—the chairman, second- and fourth-ranking majority, second-ranking minority, and second and third most junior minority members. In 1947 they were Gurney, Robertson, Saltonstall, and Tydings—the chairman, third-ranking, third most junior majority, and ranking minority members.

The House hearings do not list the committee members attending each day, but on the basis of those participating in the questioning, the pattern does not appear dissimilar.

40. Forrestal Diaries, p. 227.

41. It will be recalled that the Armed Services Committee had been constituted in 1947 of six former members from each of the Military Affairs and Naval Affairs Committees and one newly elected senator. The seven certain pro-Navy members were Robertson, Saltonstall, Tydings, Russell, and Byrd— all Naval Affairs alumni—Bridges, a former Military Affairs Committee member who had filed the minority report against S.2044 in 1946, and the new senator, Baldwin, who was a World War I Navy veteran. The position of the sixth Naval Affairs alumnus, Senator Morse, is unclear, but it was definitely not anti-Navy. The pro-Navy orientation of all except Morse was confirmed in interviews with two members of the 1947 committee.

42. Interviews; Forrestal Diaries, pp. 269, 271.

43. For the concept of the inner "club," see William S. White, *The Citadel* (New York, Harper, 1956), pp. 81–94.

44. Interview.   45. Confidential interviews.

46. Much was made by sources close to the Navy Department coalition of the fact that Wadsworth was the father-in-law of Assistant Secretary of War for Air Symington.

47. Interviews; Forrestal Diaries, p. 292.

48. *Current Biography*, IV, No. 7 (July, 1943), 54–57 (pp. 798–801 of bound volume).

49. *Congressional Record*, XCIII (1947), 9453

50. Truman, *Congressional Party*, Chaps. 4 and 6.

51. *Ibid.*, pp. 104–05, 202–05. See also Donald R. Matthews, *U.S. Senators and Their World* (Chapel Hill, University of North Carolina Press, 1960), Chap. 6; Ralph K. Huitt, "Democratic Party Leadership in the Senate," *American Political Science Review*, LV (June, 1961), 333–34; Charles L. Clapp, *The Congressman: His Work as He Sees It* (Washington, D.C., The Brookings Institution, 1963), Chap. 7.

52. New York *Times*, July 20, 1946.

53. *Ibid.*, Jan. 3, 1947; *Congressional Record*, XCIII (1947), 38.

54. On the 1947 roll-call vote rejecting Senator McCarthy's amendment, which purported to increase the protection in the Senate bill for the Marine Corps and naval aviation, for example, the Expenditures Committee members who voted split evenly, with Aiken, ranking minority member John L. McClellan, and McCarthy himself voting for the amendment; the Armed Services Committee members split ten to one against it. Admittedly, a major consideration of the latter committee's opposing the amendment might have been to protect its own intra-Senate influence.

55. Although Vandenberg was probably sincere in explaining that his first referral of the President's communication to the Armed Services Committee had been made routinely on the advice of the Parliamentarian, it may be speculated, given the collective nature of the Republican Senate leadership

(see Truman, *Congressional Party*, Chap. 4; Matthews, *U.S. Senators*, p. 125), that after Aiken's January 27 letter, Vandenberg consulted with majority leader Wallace White and chairman of the Policy Committee Robert Taft before making his subsequent referral of the draft bill.

56. In the House, for example, no ruling of a Speaker has been overturned in the last thirty years. See Neil MacNeil, *Forge of Democracy: The House of Representatives* (New York, McKay, 1963), pp. 65–66.

57. *Congressional Record*, XCIII (1947), 9417.

58. Interview. See also Hoffman's comments in *Congressional Record*, CIV (1958), 9924 (daily edition). Perhaps to keep the minority members in line in support of their President's program, the Democrats assigned their former majority leader and then minority whip, John McCormack, to the Expenditures Committee.

59. The Education and Labor Committee eventually reported what became the Taft-Hartley Act.

60. A source close to Hoffman revealed that such a suggestion was made and "stoutly rejected." See also *Veterans of Foreign Wars Legislative Newsletter*, May, 1947: "Army bigwigs in pre-80th Congress strategy meeting decided to [get] unification bill to House Expenditures Committee . . . betting that Hoffman would be too busy on labor legislation . . . [and] would refer bill to subcommittee [headed by] national defense expert and top Army pal Wadsworth."

61. See the statements by Congressmen Bender and Wilson, *Congressional Record*, XCII (1947), 9402, 9414; New York *Times*, June 26 and July 10, 1947.

62. "It became, and pretty correctly so, the custom [in the Eightieth Congress] to consider Taft *as* the policy committee. William S. White, *The Taft Story* (New York, Harper, 1954), pp. 60–61.

63. Committees, subject-matter experts, and party leaderships are not the only intra-legislative sources of influence: the significance of state delegations has already been established (Truman, *Congressional Party*, Chap. 7), and it is not unlikely that friendship cliques, office neighbors, eating companions, and various other informal but persistent patterns of group interaction such as the House "prayer breakfast" and "gym" groups (see Clapp, *The Congressman*, pp. 39–40) also play a significant role. But none of these influences are generally visible to the political scientist, and none became, in fact, visible during this study of the unification conflict.

Chapter 8. Extra-Legislative and Extra-Governmental Influences

1. See Clinton Rossiter, *The American Presidency* (New York, Harcourt, Brace, 1956), pp. 19–20, 81–84.

2. Richard E. Neustadt, "Presidency and Legislation: Planning the President's Program," *American Political Science Review*, XLIX (December, 1955), 1014.

3. Richard E. Neustadt, *Presidential Power: The Politics of Leadership* (New York, Wiley, 1960), p. 10.

4. Forrestal Diaries, pp. 115–16.   5. New York *Times,* April 12, 1946.

6. Neustadt, *Presidential Power,* p. 173.   7. Forrestal Diaries, p. 204.

8. From a moderate coverage of the unification issue during the Military Affairs Committee hearings in the fall of 1945, the subject of unification was given more space on the front and editorial pages of a representative sample of the nation's newspapers the week following the President's special message than any other subject. *Twohey Analysis of Newspaper Opinion,* weekly report for Dec. 22, 1945. Similarly, press coverage shot up after Truman's intervention in the spring of 1946.

9. See Senate Report No. 239, 80th Cong., 1st Sess.; Forrestal Diaries, p. 271.

10. Interview with General Collins; "Report of the War Department Board on Unification of the Armed Forces to Deputy Chief of Staff," Jan. 10, 1946, in Norstad Files.

11. Interview with General Norstad.

12. The highest military echelons of the Navy Department—i.e., King and company—had not by the spring of 1944 yet become overly alarmed over the possibility of unification being adopted.

13. Forrestal Papers, Firestone Library, Princeton University. Emphasis in the original.

14. *Ibid.*

15. It should be noted that both SCORER and its abortive predecessor had as one of their key functions the communication of the official Navy line to naval officers themselves. For the great importance of "internal" propaganda in maintaining the cohesion of the different participants in a political conflict, see David B. Truman, *The Governmental Process: Political Interests and Public Opinion* (New York, Knopf, 1951), Chap. 7.

16. Letter in Norstad Files.

17. "Organization for Unification," in Norstad Files.

18. See New York *Times,* Sept. 19, 20, 1945.

19. See Samuel P. Huntington, *The Common Defense: Strategic Programs in National Politics* (New York, Columbia University Press, 1961), pp. 394–98.

20. See, for example, "The Merger Issue," *Naval Affairs,* February, 1946; "One Department or Three Departments?" *Naval Affairs,* March, 1946; and "An Open Letter to the Congress of the United States by Ralph A. Bard [former Assistant Secretary of the Navy and President, Navy League]," *Seapower,* February, 1946.

21. As revealed by Senator Hart, *Congressional Record,* XCII (1946), 9940–44.

22. *Ibid.*

23. As revealed by Senator Robertson, *Congressional Record,* XCII (1946), 3672–74.

24. *Ibid.*

25. As revealed by Admiral Ofstie, 1947 House Hearings, pp. 633–34. It was pointed out to me by a member of the Survey's overall civil-military committee (which reviewed and approved all of the reports) that the Survey was badly split on the implications to be drawn from the strategic bombing of Japan; the about-face on the separate Air Force question consequently need not imply a reversal of position by all the members and might have been a concession to get agreement on other disputed points.

26. *The Case Against the Admirals: Why We Must Have a Unified Command* (New York, Dutton, 1946).

27. Forrestal Papers. This information came to Forrestal's attention in December, 1946, when Huie talked about it to an old high-school classmate of his, who happened to be, as Huie knew, the District Public Relations Officer of the Eighth Naval District. This naval officer then promptly passed on the news to Forrestal's aide, who in turn passed it on to the Secretary of the Navy.

28. A sample of Huie's specific indictments against the Navy "Old School Admirals" was that "they obstructed the development of long-range war planes—strategic air power—until Pearl Harbor was in ashes; that during the war they sought to obscure and minimize the effectiveness of our strategic air power; and that even now they are trying to dodge and minimize the implications of the atomic bomb." *Case Against the Admirals,* p. 15.

29. V. O. Key, Jr., *Public Opinion and American Democracy* (New York, Knopf, 1961), p. 528.

30. Both versions are in Memo of May 12, 1947, in Clifford Files.

31. Richard F. Fenno, Jr., *The President's Cabinet: An Analysis in the Period from Wilson to Eisenhower* (Cambridge, Mass., Harvard University Press, 1959), p. 206.

32. See Robert A. Albion and Robert H. Connery, *Forrestal and the Navy* (New York, Columbia University Press, 1962), pp. 138–56.

33. *Ibid.,* p. 139.

34. About a month after the 1946 congressional elections giving control of the Eightieth Congress to the Republicans, Forrestal managed to meet Senator Wallace White, slated to become the Majority Leader, "to get [his] advice on how the Navy should handle itself on the question of unification." Two days later, Forrestal lunched with "Mr. Republican," Senator Taft, and the question of unification came up once again. Forrestal Diaries, pp. 227–28.

Throughout the following spring and summer, Forrestal kept in almost constant touch with (among others) the active minority of the Senate Armed Services Committee. The appointment calendar for this period is reprinted in Albion and Connery, *Forrestal and the Navy,* "Appendix J," pp. 302–04.

35. 1945 Hearings, p. 104. Of course, such a statement did not build up goodwill with Senator Hill, who observed,

"What you say there, Mr. Secretary, I can well understand, under our present system, as a matter of courtesy, you would like to consult with the respective committees of the House and Senate before you agree to put that report in this record.

"That is the very thing we are trying to get away from, Mr. Secretary. . . .

"You cannot have an over-all plan [for military security policy] as long as you have these two departments absolutely separate and distinct, and with separate and distinct committees here on the hill." *Ibid.*

36. Forrestal Diaries, pp. 229–30.

37. The following account is based on information obtained from confidential Marine Corps sources unless otherwise indicated.

38. Vandegrift found himself in the typical man-in-the-middle predicament: his subordinates were critical because they did not believe he took a sufficiently strong position to protect the Corps, while his superior, the President, was critical (see Forrestal Diaries, p. 295) because Vandegrift did not completely support the Jan. 16 compromise agreement. For an acute analysis of this kind of predicament, see Burleigh B. Gardner and William F. Whyte, "The Man in the Middle: Position and Problems of the Foreman," *Applied Anthropology,* IV (Spring, 1945), 1–28.

39. For further evidence of "reportability" of news being dependent on its controversial nature, see Douglass Cater, *The Fourth Branch of Government* (Boston, Houghton Mifflin, 1959).

40. See Truman, *Governmental Process,* pp. 264–70.

41. 1947 House Hearings, p. 95

42. As Representative George H. Bender was to tell the Commandant of the Marine Corps during the House hearings:

"I might say to the General that the Marine Corps has established a place in the hearts of the American people, and our constituents will not let us get away without dotting the i's and crossing the t's as far as the Marine Corps is concerned. . . .

"And one thing that we have heard most about from out constituents in the grave apprehension on the part of the people back home that whoever wrote this bill is giving the Marine Corps the 'bum's rush.' You would not say that, but I am saying that." 1947 House Hearings, p. 264.

43. Representative Prince A. Preston, *Congressional Record,* XCIII (1947), 4458–59.

44. Quoted in Robert Lindsay, *This High Name: Public Relations and the U.S. Marine Corps* (Madison, University of Wisconsin Press, 1956), p. 4. The Marine Corps has always taken great pains to see that this stereotype of the Marine persists. *Ibid., passim.*

Forrestal noted in his diary on August 27, 1946, that in a discussion that day with Army leaders about the unification conflict, "Patterson, recognizing I think, that attacking the Marines is politically unprofitable, was careful to say what high regard he had for the Marine Corps," Forrestal Diaries, p. 202.

45. Forrestal Diaries, pp. 271–72.   46. 1947 House Hearings, p. 95.

47. A somewhat different version of Edson's statement is quoted in Robert S. Allen, "Too Much Brass," *Collier's,* Sept. 6, 1947.

48. H.R.3979, 80th Cong., 1st Sess., sec. 205(f). A similar bill, also prepared by General Edson, had been introduced in the Senate on May 14 by Senator Robertson as S.1282.

49. Interview with Hittle.   50. Interviews with Hoffman and Hittle.

51. Committee source. We have seen that the definition of the Marine functions was actually even more generous than that originally proposed by the Marines themselves with the word "limited" being left out before "land operations as are essential . . . to a naval campaign."

52. The one exception was with respect to the Secretary of Defense's budgetary authority, which was drastically reduced.

53. Interview with Hittle.

54. It is interesting that not only did Wadsworth not try to get the service functions provision stricken on the floor of the House but that also when Sterling Cole offered his own amendment further increasing the protection for land-based naval aviation and Chairman Hoffman rose to explain that it had already been submitted to the subcommittee and had been accepted "unanimously, except for the opposition of the gentleman from New York [Wadsworth]," Wadsworth took the floor and the following exchange occurred:

"Mr. WADSWORTH.   Mr. Chairman, will the gentleman yield?

"Mr. HOFFMAN.   Am I wrong?

"Mr. WADSWORTH.   This gentleman from New York agreed to it.

"Mr. HOFFMAN.   The gentleman means he did?

"Mr. WADSWORTH.   The gentleman from New York agreed to it.

"Mr. HOFFMAN.   I understood he opposed it in the subcommittee and was opposing it now.

"Mr. WADSWORTH.   I am not. I am describing what it does." *Congressional Record,* XCIII (1947), 9441

Or, as V. O. Key has severely understated it, while explaining the difficulties of public and interest group retaliation against errant members of Congress, "Often the reality of official conduct is . . . ambiguous." *Public Opinion,* p. 519.

There is some evidence that Wadsworth might have stopped opposing the enactment of service functions in exchange for the friends of the Marine Corps agreeing not to offer a contemplated amendment providing that the size of the Corps should be maintained at not less than 20 percent of the Navy. The existing law provided, and this was unchanged by the unification bill, that the Marine Corps should *not exceed* 20 percent of the Navy. It may also be the case that Wadsworth expected the Senate-House conference to agree on the Senate version.

55. There is some evidence that both Byrd's inquiry and Vandergrift's response might actually have been written by the same Marine officer.

56. Expenditures Committee source.

57. Interviews with Hoffman and Hittle.

58. Truman, *Governmental Process,* pp. 33–39.

59. See *ibid.,* especially Part 3; Lester W. Milbraith, *The Washington Lobbyists* (Chicago, Rand McNally, 1963).

60. This statement refers only to extra-governmental, associational-type interest groups. What Truman has called "constitutionalized interest groups" and what Almond and Coleman have more recently called "institutional interest groups" played, of course, the major role. See Truman, *Governmental Process*, p. 46, and Gabriel Almond and James S. Coleman, eds., *The Politics of the Developing Areas* (Princeton, N.J., Princeton University Press, 1960), pp. 33, 35.

61. Letter to Representative John C. Butler, reprinted in *Congressional Record*, XCII (1946), A.232.

62. 1947 House Hearings, p. 440.

63. The Navy League sent a telegram to the acting chairman of the Senate Military Affairs Committee, Senator Johnson, on November 2, 1945 "in protest against the Senate bill S.84 and S.1482." The League explained that it was a "nonprofit, educational organization which was founded in 1902 [under whose] auspices, ever since 1922, the observance of Navy Day, each October 27, has been conducted." 1945 Hearings, pp. 237–38.

A month later the League also sent a telegram to President Truman declaring in somewhat less moderate language that the Army's unification plan "under a single dictatorship is patently a grab for power. . . . It will prove to be not a merger but a submerging of our first line of attack and defense, namely sea-air power." New York *Times*, Dec. 2, 1945.

For an article that effectively destroys the myth of the great political influence of the Navy League, see Armin Rappaport, "The Navy League of the United States," *South Atlantic Quarterly*, LIII (April, 1954), 203–12.

64. New York *Times*, Oct. 5, 1946.

65. 1947 House Hearings, p. 625. For the problem of interest group leadership in the face of multiple and overlapping affiliations of its members, see Truman, *Governmental Process*, Chaps. 6 and 7. The Veterans of Foreign Wars did, of course, take an active role, but aside from their press statements in favor of increased protection for the widely popular Marine Corps, its activities were (and have probably remained) completely invisible to its rank-and-file members. It is also possible, given the restriction of the VFW's membership to veterans that have seen overseas service, that just after World War II the Marines and Navy were disproportionately represented in the older, more influential part of the membership.

66. Truman, *Governmental Process*, pp. 218–22.

67. This account of public opinion is based primarily on an examination of the New York *Times*, 1944, to July, 1947; The *Twohey Analysis of Newspaper Opinion* ("a weekly report based on the editorial and front pages of newspapers serving all sections of the United States and representing over 20% of total daily newspaper circulation"), 1944 to July 26, 1947; and on interviews and written communications with various senators and representatives.

68. See *Twohey Analysis of Newspaper Opinion*, weekly report for Sept. 1, 1945, which shows that within four days after the release of the reports, a majority of the newspaper comment was already advocating increased

"coordination" or "unification" as a rational response to the Pearl Harbor disaster.

69. The reports were published in full as a special section of the New York *Times,* Aug. 29, 1945.

70. "[Stimson] was satisfied that the major responsibility for the catastrophe rested on the two officers commanding on the spot—Admiral Kimmel and General Short. It was true that the War and Navy Departments were not fully efficient in evaluating the information available to them, and of course it was also true that no one in Washington had correctly assessed Japanese intentions. . . . But the basic fact remained: the officers commanding at Hawaii had been alerted like other outpost commanders; unlike other outpost commanders they proved on December 7 to be far from alert." Henry L. Stimson and McGeorge Bundy, *On Active Service in Peace and War* (New York, Harper, 1947), p. 391.

There is, however, some question whether in fact all the other commanders had been alert: about half of the total bombing force in General MacArthur's Philippine command was destroyed by air attack on the ground at Clark Field some nine hours *after* news of the initial attack on Pearl Harbor had been received. U.S. Dept. of the Air Force, Office of Air Force History, *The Army Air Forces in World War II.* Vol. I: *Plans and Early Operations, January 1939 to August 1942,* ed. by Wesley Frank Craven and James Lea Cate (Chicago, University of Chicago Press, 1948), p. 203.

71. This does not purport to be a definitive account of the "true" causes of the Pearl Harbor disaster but is limited to the information available to the general public during the unification conflict. A full account would have to take into consideration some 15,000 pages of testimony developed in the postwar congressional investigation of the subject and the nearly 10,000 pages of testimony accumulated in earlier investigation, including the ones just discussed. See Report of the Joint Committee on the Investigation of the Pearl Harbor Attack, 79th Cong., 2d Sess., and the thirty-nine volumes of testimony and documents. The present account does not conflict, however, with either Samuel Eliot Morison, *History of United States Naval Operations in World War II.* Vol. III: *The Rising Sun in the Pacific, 1931–April 1942* (Boston, Little, Brown, 1947–48), or Mark Skinner Watson, *Chief of Staff: Prewar Plans and Preparations* (Washington, D.C., Historical Division, Department of the Army, 1950), pp. 496 ff. It does differ in emphasis from Roberta Wohlstetter, *Pearl Harbor: Warning and Decision* (Stanford, Calif., Stanford University Press, 1962), which, even granted its central thesis about the ambiguity (before the event) of the intelligence "signals" against the background "noise," severely underplays the personal failure or incapacity involved in not anticipating or at least being better prepared to repel a surprise attack on the fleet in Pearl Harbor.

72. Aug. 31, 1945.

73. Note the following exchange that took place before the Walsh Committee hearings in 1946:

"Senator TYDINGS. Here is a question the answer to which you will have to guess at, I know, because there is no certain answer: Do you or do you not believe that if there had not been a Pearl Harbor that the emphasis upon this unification of command would be as great as it seems to be in certain quarters?

"Mr. EBERSTADT. Senator, there are a great many influences that are on the surface and a great many that are not on the surface and it is extremely difficult to answer your question.

"Senator TYDINGS. Well, I think in the public consciousness . . . they failed to differentiate between unity of command in the theater of operations and unity in Washington; and, because of Pearl Harbor, they are now saying that must not happen again. . . .

"Senator TOBEY. He is right, when he, Mr. Eberstadt, said about things on the surface and other forces under the surface. What we lack in this whole business is a sort of superfluoroscope with which we could look through and see those forces working under the skin. If we could do that we would be surprised, wouldn't we?" 1946 Hearings, p. 174.

74. Nov. 20, 1945.

75. Eisenhower's letter to Thomas appears in 1945 Hearings, p. 560.

76. See, for example, the New York *Times* editorials on April 27, 1944; Oct. 6, 1945; April 11 and June 29, 1946; and Jan. 18, Feb. 28, June 3, July 11, and July 27, 1947.

77. April 8, 1946.   78. 1945 Hearings, pp. 23–25.

79. *Ibid.,* p. 100.   80. *Ibid.,* p. 307–8.

81. It should be noted, however, that three leading military commentators —Hanson Baldwin, Walter Millis, and George Fielding Eliot—were generally supporting the Navy coalition position on unification.

82. *Congressional Directory* (1st ed.), 80th Cong., 1st Sess. (1947), pp. 241–51.

83. It is interesting that the three probably most active congressional participants in the unification conflict used almost identical language in interviews to explain that a bill was finally passed in the Eightieth Congress because of the extent to which "sentiment had built up" in its favor by 1947. For the best statement of the relationship between public opinion and governmental policy, see Key, *Public Opinion,* Parts V and VI.

Chapter 9. The Outcome of the Unification Conflict

1. See Edward C. Banfield, *Political Influence* (New York, Free Press, 1961), pp. 308–9.

2. See the short debate on the adoption of Wadsworth's resolution, *Congressional Record,* XC (1944), 3199–207.

3. See *Twohey Analysis of Newspaper Opinion,* weekly report for April 29, 1944.

4. Rule IX, "Standing Rules for Conducting Business in the Senate of the United States," *Senate Manual* (Washington, D.C., 1953), pp. 16–17.

5. 1946 Hearings, p. 10.

6. See Joseph T. Klapper, *The Effects of Mass Communications* (New York, Free Press, 1960), pp. 90–91.

7. As Senator Robertson was to comment in 1947 during the floor debate on S.758, "Thus far the War Department General Staff has been defeated in its efforts to establish a single military commander over the armed forces—not as a result of public recognition of the danger to the Nation inherent in such a step, but because of the recognized harm to the military services [i.e., the Navy and Marines] which would accrue." *Congressional Record*, XCIII (1947), 8318.

8. Interview.   9. See New York *Times*, May 29, 1946.

10. *Congressional Record*, XCIII (1947), 9400.

11. Letter, Forrestal to Chairman Gurney, dated May 19, 1947; reprinted in 1947 Senate Hearings, p. 51.

12. 1947 Senate Hearings, p. 397.

13. ALNAV 21, parts of which are printed in *Congressional Record*, XCIII (1947), 7944–47.

14. 1947 House Hearings, p. 691. Even the active-duty officers who explicitly asserted that they would have given their honest opinions in answer to direct committee questions before the second ALNAV did not feel that they could have legitimately taken the initiative in communicating their opposition to the committee members. See Admiral Ofstie's statement, *ibid.*, p. 645.

15. But for the Democratic losses in the 1946 congressional elections and Senator Walsh's defeat by Henry Cabot Lodge, Jr., the anti-unification senators might have controlled even the merged Armed Services Committee. The four Democratic members of the Senate Armed Services Committee with the most seniority were expected to be Walsh, Tydings, Russell, and Byrd, in that order—all former members of the Naval Affairs Committee. Even under Republican control, the die-hard's power position might have been high: Senator Bridges, who, although an alumnus of the Senate Military Affairs Committee, had filed (with Senator Thomas Hart) the bitter minority report against the Thomas-Hill-Austin bill in 1946, was the ranking Republican on the combined committee, but he preferred, as could be expected, the chairmanship of the more powerful Appropriations Committee; Senator Charles W. Tobey, who had been senior minority member of the Naval Affairs Committee and generally sympathetic to the Navy, was next in line for the Armed Services Committee chair, but he preferred taking over the Committee on Banking and Currency. See New York *Times*, Nov. 17, 1946. This combination of events brought Chan Gurney to the chair of the Armed Services Committee.

16. Richard E. Neustadt, *Presidential Power* (New York, Wiley, 1960), p. 49.

17. Forrestal Diaries, pp. 269–70.

18. Indeed, in early May there was concern that the Armed Services Committee had become so alienated that it would refuse to report any bill at all. *Ibid.*, p. 274.

19. See, for example, *ibid.*, pp. 269, 271.

20. 1947 House Hearings, p. 188. Sherman had also written to Chairman Gurney of the Senate Armed Services Committee on May 2 that he felt "strongly that if amendments are made to S.758 to safeguard the Marine Corps, some similar action is essential with regard to naval aviation. Not to take such action would have a very adverse effect on a part of the naval service which I consider as important as the Marine Corps, and which has conformed closely to the spirit of the agreement of 16 January." Copy in Norstad Files.

21. The conference committee consisted of the members of the Expenditures subcommittee that wrote up the clean bill and of Senators Gurney, Saltonstall, Morse, Baldwin, Tydings, Russell, and Byrd. Gurney, who would have been chairman, could not attend the meetings because Senator Bridges' illness had forced him to preside over important sessions of the Appropriations Committee (of which Gurney was the second-ranking majority member) and Saltonstall consequently chaired the conference group. Interview with Senator Saltonstall.

22. *Congressional Record,* XCIII (1947), 9919.

23. See Samuel P. Huntington, *The Common Defense: Strategic Programs in National Politics* (New York, Columbia University Press, 1961), pp. 378–81.

24. See James G. March and Herbert Simon, *Organizations* (New York, Wiley, 1958), p. 85; Robert A. Dahl and Charles E. Lindblom, *Politics, Economics, and Welfare: Planning and Politico-Economic Systems Resolved into Basic Social Processes* (New York, Harper, 1953), pp. 164–66.

25. By "rational political actor" is meant one who engages in calculating, value-maximizing behavior. See Thomas C. Schelling, *The Strategy of Conflict* (New York, Oxford, 1963), p. 17.

26. See Richard C. Snyder, "Game Theory and the Analysis of Political Behavior," in *Research Frontiers in Politics and Government,* Brookings Lectures (Washington, D.C., The Brookings Institution, 1955), pp. 70–103.

27. S.1956, 78th Cong., 2d Sess.   28. New York *Times,* May 30, 1944.

29. 1947 Senate Hearings, pp. 37, 40.   30. *Ibid.,* p. 45.

31. 1947 House Hearings, p. 102.

32. Forrestal Diaries, p. 294. Admiral Sherman was more positively against the statutory definition of specific service functions, as had been done in the House bill, writing to Forrestal on July 17 that "the missions of the Marine Corps are set forth in new language which has no basis of agreement, which ignores the authority of the Chief of Naval Operations over the Marine Corps, ignores the position of the Navy in amphibious operations, and limits sharply the authority of the President over the Marine Corps." Sherman

thought that the changes made by the House in the Senate bill "would lower the combat efficiency of the Navy and should therefore be vigorously opposed." "Memo for the Secretary of the Navy," copy in Norstad Files.

33. On Feb. 6 of that year, Forrestal, Under Secretary of the Navy John Sullivan, and Admiral Sherman dined with the "76–77 Club, being a club of Republican members of those Congresses." Upon finding that "the majority of the people at the dinner were inclined to be against any merger," Forrestal proceeded to tell them that the compromise agreement was "a completely nonpolitical, nonpartisan accomplishment" and deserved their support. Forrestal Diaries, pp. 246–47.

34. 1947 House Hearings, p. 115.   35. *Ibid.*, p. 253.

36. Forrestal himself admitted that he believed that the ground Army still had the desire to take over the Marines' major functions, but he did not think that in 1947 this was an "objective." *Ibid.*, p. 108.

37. See Murray Edelman, "Symbols and Political Quiescence," *American Political Science Review*, LIV (September, 1960), 695–704.

38. In December, 1946, just before the compromise agreement was reached, Forrestal had in effect himself decided that stopping a separate air force was impossible and that pursuing a strategy with that goal in mind was unacceptable. Former Assistant Secretary of the Navy for Air Ralph A. Bard wrote to Forrestal apparently in response to a letter expressing that view;

"With respect to the Navy's policy on the subject of the establishment of a third department, I think your judgment . . . is proper. I do not believe you can stop a separate Air Force set-up and that opposition to it might jeopardize other things that you want to accomplish. The public generally believes that from here on Air Power is the big thing as far as actual combat is concerned."

Bard added that the Navy should continue to work quietly behind the scenes to build support while publicly contending that Congress had ample evidence on which to decide and that the Navy trusted Congress to make the wisest decision without specifying what the decision would be. Bard thought that this deferential approach would "be particularly effective if some of the fire-eaters of the Army become somewhat obnoxious and ridiculous in fighting for their selfish proposals." Forrestal Papers, Firestone Library, Princeton University.

39. Interviews with Norstad and Clifford; Memo of July 24 in Clifford Files.

Chapter 10. *Conflict, Unification, and the Policy Process*

1. But see Joseph Cornwall Palamountain, *The Politics of Distribution* (Cambridge, Mass., Harvard University Press, 1955), for a study that gives explicit consideration to the conditions necessary for one set of economic conflicts over the distribution of groceries, drugs, and automobiles to have

turned into political conflicts; see also David B. Truman, *The Governmental Process: Political Interests and Public Opinion* (New York, Knopf, 1951), pp. 104–06, and V. O. Key, Jr., *Politics, Parties, and Pressure Groups* (4th ed., New York, Crowell, 1958), pp. 46–50.

2. From Harold D. Lasswell, "The Measurement of Public Opinion," *American Political Science Review*, XXV (1931), 312.

3. This analysis was suggested by but is not equivalent to the discussion in James G. March and Herbert Simon, *Organizations* (New York, Wiley, 1958), pp. 129–31.

4. "By operationality of goals, we mean the extent to which it is possible to observe and test how well goals are being achieved." *Ibid.*, p. 42.

5. See *ibid.*, pp. 119, 155–56. Also see Kenneth E. Boulding, *Conflict and Defense: A General Theory* (New York, Harper, 1962), pp. 311–13.

6. See Boulding, *Conflict and Defense*, pp. 316–17.

7. For a discussion of the "tactics" of bargaining, see Thomas C. Schelling, *The Strategy of Conflict* (New York, Oxford University Press, 1963), Chap. 2.

8. See Forrestal Diaries, pp. 148–49.

9. Memorandum of meeting between Clifford, Symington, and Norstad, May 8, 1946, in Norstad Files.

10. Forrestal had a report in December, 1946, about a War Department confidant revealing to a Navy friend that "the Army feels that with the Republican Congress and the new committee setup the merger in some form in a cinch to go through this time." Forrestal Papers, Firestone Library, Princeton University. See also Forrestal Diaries, p. 224.

11. See Charles E. Lindblom, "The Science of Muddling Through," *Public Administration Review*, XXIX (Spring, 1959), 79–88, and *The Intelligence of Democracy* (New York, Free Press, 1965); Wallace S. Sayre and Herbert Kaufman, *Governing New York City: Politics in the Metropolis* (New York, Russell Sage Foundation, 1960; paperback edition, New York, Norton, 1965), Chap. 19; E. E. Schattschneider, *The Semisovereign Public: A Realist's View of Democracy in America* (New York, Holt, 1960); Edward C. Banfield, *Political Influence* (New York Free Press, 1961), Chap. 12; Aaron Wildavsky, *Dixon-Yates: A Study in Power Politics* (New Haven, Yale University Press, 1962), Chap. 18.

12. See, for example, the papers in American Society for Political and Legal Philosophy, *Rational Decision*, ed. by Carl J. Friedrich (New York, Atherton, 1964), and Glendon A. Schubert, *The Public Interest: A Critique of the Theory of a Political Concept* (New York, Free Press, 1961).

13. This also appears to be the most common usage of the term. See Frank F. Sorauf, "The Public Interest Reconsidered," *Journal of Politics*, XIX (1957), 616–29.

14. See Herbert A. Simon, *Administrative Behavior: A Study of Decision-Making Processes in Administrative Organization* (New York, Macmillan, 1957), p. 67; March and Simon, *Organizations*, pp. 137–38, 190.

15. See, for example, "Production Planning in the Patent Office," in Harold

Stein, ed., *Public Administration and Policy Development: A Case Book* (New York, Harcourt, Brace, 1952), pp. 1–14.

16. March and Simon, *Organizations,* pp. 40–44, 75–78, 151–54. Sayre and Kaufman, *Governing New York City,* Chaps. 8, 11.

17. Georg Simmel, *Conflict,* tr. by Kurt H. Wolff (New York, Free Press, 1955), pp. 39, 40.

18. Public Law 216, 81st Cong., 1st Sess. See also *National Security Act Amendments of 1949,* Hearings on S.1269 and S.1843 before the Senate Committee on Armed Services, 81st Cong., 1st Sess. (1949), and *Hearings* on S.1843 before the House Committee on Armed Services, 81st Cong., 1st Sess. (1949).

19. House Doc. 136, 83d Cong., 1st Sess. See also *Reorganization Act No. 6 of 1953,* Hearings on H. J. Res. 264 before the House Committee on Governmental Operations, 83d Cong., 1st Sess. (1953).

20. Public Law 599, 85th Congress. See also *Reorganization of the Department of Defense,* Hearings on H.R.11001, H.R.11002, H.R.11003, H.R.11958, and H.R.12541 before the House Committee on Armed Services, 85th Cong., 2d Sess. (1958), and *Department of Defense Reorganization Act of 1958,* Hearings on H.R.12541 before the Senate Armed Services Committee, 85th Cong., 2d Sess. (1958).

21. Samuel P. Huntington, *The Common Defense: Strategic Programs in National Politics* (New York, Columbia University Press, 1961), pp. 416–17.

22. For example, it came to light during the hearings on the 1958 proposals that the Assistant Secretary of Defense for Properties and Installations had thought it necessary to issue instructions providing uniform Department-wide standards even for collecting garbage, washing garbage cans, mowing grass, and other matters of like import. See Department of Defense Instructions Nos. 4150.8 and 4150.6 of Oct. 20 and June 7, 1955, reprinted in *Department of Defense Reorganization Act of 1958,* Hearings before the Senate Committee on Armed Services, 85th Cong., 2d Sess. (1958), pp. 161–66.

23. Maxwell D. Taylor, *The Uncertain Trumpet* (New York, Harper, 1959), p. 110.

24. For disquieting analyses of recent organizational trends in the Defense Department, see John C. Ries, *The Management of Defense: Organization and Control of the U.S. Armed Services* (Baltimore, Johns Hopkins Press, 1964), and Hanson W. Baldwin, "Slow-down in the Pentagon," *Foreign Affairs,* XLIII (January, 1965), 262–80.

In the fall of 1965, the Chief and Deputy Chief of the Navy's Bureau of Ships resigned, reportedly in protest against the undue centralization of authority and influence in the Department of Defense. See New York *Times,* Oct. 28, 1965.

25. As Key observed in his classic study of Southern politics while explaining how Huey Long dramatized himself as the "champion of the people" against the "sinister interests," *"there are sinister interests and there are champions of the people,* even though there may always be some good about

the sinister and at least a trace of fraud in self-styled champions." [Italics added.] V. O. Key, Jr., *Southern Politics in State and Nation* (New York, Knopf, 1949), p. 157.

26. See Roger Hilsman, "The Foreign-Policy Consensus: "An Interim Research Report," *Journal of Conflict Resolution,* III (1959), 361–82.

27. At one point in 1949, the Air Force, whose point of view might have been able to dominate a defense establishment organized along original War Department lines, was arguing within the JCS that the Navy had no need to operate even a single large carrier. See Warner R. Schilling, "The Politics of National Defense: Fiscal 1950," in W. R. Schilling, P. Y. Hammond, and G. H. Snyder, *Strategy, Politics, and Defense Budgets* (New York, Columbia University Press, 1962), p. 169.

28. For an excellent demonstration of this proposition, see *ibid., passim.*

29. After the many concessions for the protection of various domestic industries that were made to insure the passage of the Trade Expansion Act of 1962, it was not clear even to some of its proponents whether the result would lead to an expansion of trade or to a restriction. See Raymond A. Bauer et al., *American Business and Public Policy: The Politics of Foreign Trade* (New York, Atherton, 1963).

30. As recommended, for example, by Ferdinand Eberstadt in 1947 Senate Hearings, pp. 672–74.

31. *Politics,* III, ix, tr. by E. Barker (New York, Oxford University Press, 1946), p. 123.

Index

DATE DUE

1-29-79			
GAYLORD			PRINTED IN U.S.A